Deepshikha gupta

PRACTICAL PATHOLOGY

(With Viva Voce Questions)

PRACTICAL
PATHOLOGY
(With Viva Voce Questions)

Dr. TEJINDAR SINGH
MD, FICP, FISHTM
Director Professor, Department of Pathology
Maulana Azad Medical College, New Delhi

Dr. K UMA CHATURVEDI
MD, FICP,
Former Dir. Prof. & Head
Department of Pathology
Maulana Azad Medical College, New Delhi

ARYA PUBLICATIONS
(AVICHAL PUBLISHING COMPANY)
INDUSTRIAL AREA, KALA AMB 173 030, DISTT. SIRMOUR (H.P.)
Delhi Office: 1002 Faiz Road (opp. Hanuman Murti), Karol Bagh, New Delhi 110 005

Published by:
ARYA PUBLICATIONS
(Avichal Publishing Company)
Industrial Area, Trilokpur Road
Kala Amb 173 030, Distt. Sirmour (HP)
Ph. : 01702-238688, 238832

Delhi Office:
1002 Faiz Road (opp. Hanuman Murti)
Karol Bagh, New Delhi 110 005 (India)
Phones : 011-28752745, 28752604, 28755383
Fax : 011-28756921
Email : medical@apcbooks.co.in
Website : apcbooks.co.in

ISBN–81–7855–697-0

First Edition : 2002
Second Edition : 2007
Reprint : 2011
Reprint : 2013
Third Edition : 2015

Price : ₹ 350.00

Typeset & Designed at :
Laser Tech Prints

Printed at :
Prince Print Process
Delhi

NOTICE

Preface to Third Edition

It gives us immense pleasure to hand over this book "Practical Pathology (With Viva Voce Questions)" to the students. Undergraduate students occupy a special place in our hearts, with their specific requirements in terms of meeting curricular guidelines, pressures on their time from other subjects and above all, the great importance of building a sound foundation of Pathology knowledge as a launch pad for the future practice of medicine.

This book has been designed keeping the MBBS Pathology course as its basis. The section of this book are:

A. Techniques in Surgical Pathology

B. General Pathology

C. Haematology

D. Systemic Pathology

E. Cytopathology

F. Clinical Pathology

G. Instruments for Viva Voce and reference values

The aim is to comprehensively cover the entire range of practical exercises which are included in the second professional examination of M.B.B.S. All illustrations are in true colours and taken from slides shown to the students in their practical classes. Each chapter begins with identifying features of organs and tissues as well as of gross lesions as commonly asked from museum specimens. General Pathology and Haematology sections emphasize on the basic cell morphology so that students form a concept to differentiate inflammatory cells from each other and from neoplastic cells.

The usual starting point of the Pathology grand viva are gross specimens illustrating systemic pathology and haematology instruments. Hence, each chapter of this book contains high-resolution photographs of such classical specimens and haematology instruments. The time-tested and favorite viva-voce questions associated with these specimens as-well-as those asked at various stages of the examination are presented in each chapter.

While career histopathologists are adept at appreciating H&E slides and their photographs, the same are often extremely challenging for medical students. Therefore, the most vital photomicrographs (over 50 of them) are presented here accompanied alongside by hand-drawn diagrams. We with to express our gratitude to Dr Neha, Dr Amita, Dr Parul and Dr Poonam for their help. Our thanks to team of Laser Tech Prints for doing wonderful typesetting and Mr. Sisodiya, the artist for drawing figures. These should help them draw the same diagrams in their practical file.

This book will hopefully play a useful role in orienting students to the practical part of Pathology that is appropriate and essential for them.

– AUTHORS

Preface to First Edition

As the subject of Pathology has grown by leaps and bounds, so has the need for simple, concise, yet comprehensive, books for the undergraduate students. In recent years several such textbooks have been brought out by Indian authors.

We felt the need for such a book to help the students in their practical work too. This book is our attempt to fill that void. It is presented in the form of several sections. The section on General Pathology covers up the basis of disease processes along with the description of the slides the students are most often exposed to for its understanding. Hematology as well as Clinical Pathology including urine examination are presented in a detailed manner to help the students deal with all aspects of the subject including the principles and methods of the tests. CSF and Semen Analysis are included to give overall coverage to all branches of the Clinical Pathology. Chapter on Cytopathology deals with basic aspects of exfoliative and fine needle aspiration cytology.

In the Systemic Pathology section, all lesions commonly taught to students are described systemwise.

The most salient highlights of the book are:

(i) Help to students in viva voce. This is in the form of most commonly asked questions and their answers at the end of each chapter in Hematology, Cytopathology and Clinical Pathology.

(ii) In the Systemic Pathology section, each chapter begins with identifying features of organs and tissues as well as of gross lesions, as commonly asked from museum specimens in viva voce.

(iii) All illustrations are in true colours and taken from slides shown to the students in their practical classes. This would facilitate understanding as well as easy identification in the examinations.

(iv) Reference range and normal values of all important parameters have been concised at the end of the book for easy reference.

We sincerely hope that this book will be of immense help to students in their practicals and viva voce in Pathology.

Any suggestions for improvement would be greatly welcomed by us.

New Delhi

—Authors

Contents

SECTION A: TECHNIQUES IN SURGICAL PATHOLOGY

SECTION B: GENERAL PATHOLOGY

SECTION C: HAEMATOLOGY

SECTION D: SYSTEMIC PATHOLOGY

SECTION E: CYTOPATHOLOGY

SECTION F: CLINICAL PATHOLOGY

SECTION G: INSTRUMENTS AND REFERENCE VALUES

SECTION A
Techniques in Surgical Pathology

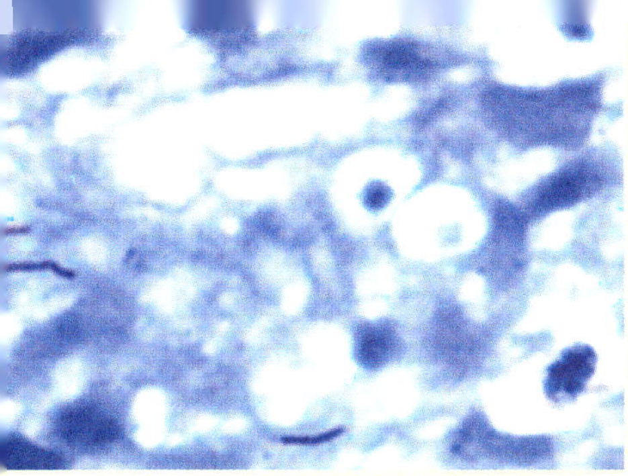

1

Techniques in Surgical Pathology

Surgical/autopsy tissue samples have to be preserved, be it for subsequent gross display in the Museum or for microscopic evaluation. This is done by **Fixation**. The aims of fixation are to:

(i) Prevent autolysis and bacterial contamination

(ii) Maintain as close a resemblance as possible to the natural structure of tissue components

(iii) Make tissue resistant to subsequent denaturation by procedures, stains, chemicals etc.

The commonest routinely used fixative for light microscopy is **Formaldehyde** – used as 10% buffered (acetate buffer) Formalin solution. Formaldehyde (in gaseous state) is dissolved in water, the saturated solution being 40% formaldehyde, known as Formalin solution. Hence 10% formalin contains 4% of formaldehyde.

Processing

Before a tissue can be cut into sections for staining and microscopy, it has to be "processed". Processing replaces water (the major tissue component) by an embedding medium which gives a firm consistency so that uniform thin sections can be cut. The most commonly used medium is Paraffin Wax. As this is immiscible with water, intermediary reagents are used.

The steps are:

(i) ***Dehydration*** – to replace the fixative and water by a dehydrating fluid, most commonly Ethyl alcohol or Acetone.

(ii) ***Clearing*** – to replace the dehydrating fluid with a medium totally miscible with the dehydrating fluid as well as with the embedding medium (Wax). Common clearing agents are Xylene and Chloroform. Xylene is used in majority of the laboratories.

(iii) ***Impregnation***— to replace the clearing agent by Paraffin wax, used in the molten state. By this, all the water in the tissue has been replaced by the wax.

(iv) ***Embedding***- the now firm tissue pieces are cast in molten wax so as to form a solid cuboidal block of wax on cooling. This can be done using "L molds" or cassettes (plastic) (Fig. 1.1).

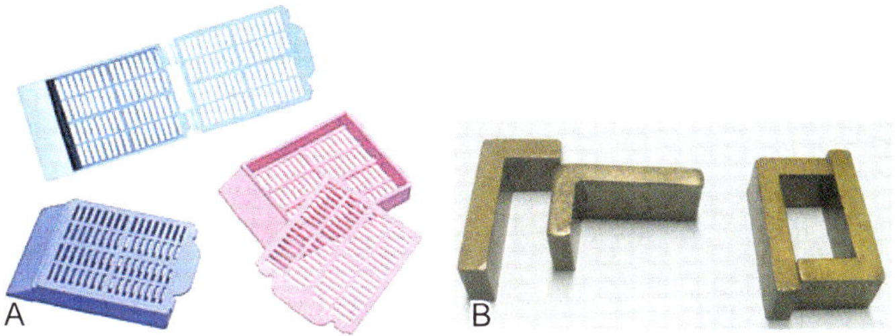

Fig. 1.1: A. Casettes (Left) and B. L molds (Right)

These steps can be done manually. However the first 3 steps are routinely carried out in a Histokinette/Tissue processor (Fig. 1.2) and embedding is facilitated by using an embedding station (Fig. 1.3).

Fig. 1.2: Tissue processor (Histokinette) with digitally programmable schedule.

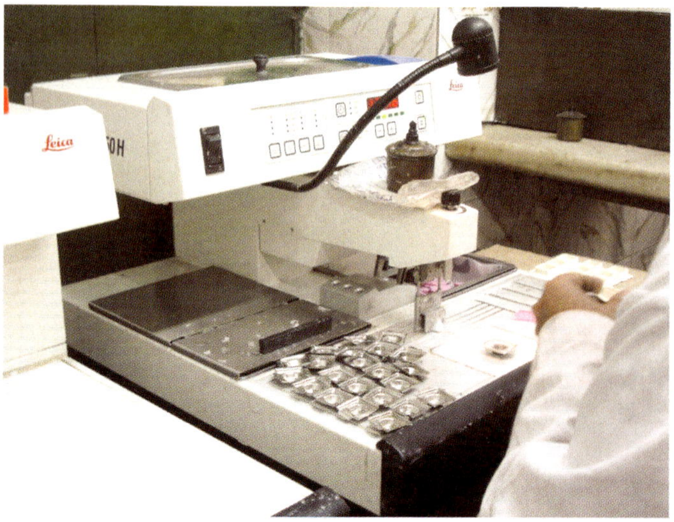

Fig. 1.3: Paraffin wax embedding station. Embedding molds are in foreground.

For proper tissue processing adequate number of changes of each solution and adequate time in each solution, preferably with fluid agitation is essential. These conditions are fulfilled using a histokinette (with a mechanical timing device) or a tissue processor (automatic timed and digitally controlled). Both these have 12 containers. A sample overnight schedule would be:

1.	10% Formalin	0 – variable. (depending on convenience/fixation status of tissues)
2.	70% Alcohol	1/2 hour
3.	95% Alcohol	1/2 hour
4.	100% Alcohol	1 hour
5.	100% Alcohol	1 hour
6.	100% Alcohol	1 hour
7.	100% Alcohol	1 hour
8.	100% Alcohol + Xylene	1 hour
9.	Xylene	1 hour
10.	Xylene	2 hours
11.	Molten Paraffin Wax	2 hours
12.	Molten Paraffin Wax	4 hours

Blocks are made using L moulds or plastic casettes. Each one of them is numbered as per the specimen number.

Microtomy (Section cutting)

This is the process of cutting thin sections of the tissue embedded in the wax block using a rotary microtome (Fig. 1.4). With disposable steel blades (Fig. 1.5), good, thin (3-4 microns), uniform sections can be obtained. These sections are floated on to a water bath (Fig. 1.4) maintained at around 5-10°C less than the melting point of wax, so that the wax softens a little and the thin section flattens out. These are then mounted on to glass slides. The slides are made to remain vertical on wooden racks to drain and dry before staining so that the section is firmly attached to the slide and does not get washed off during staining. This adherence of the section to slide is enhanced by precoating the slides with Egg albumin or Poly-L-lysine before mounting the sections on them.

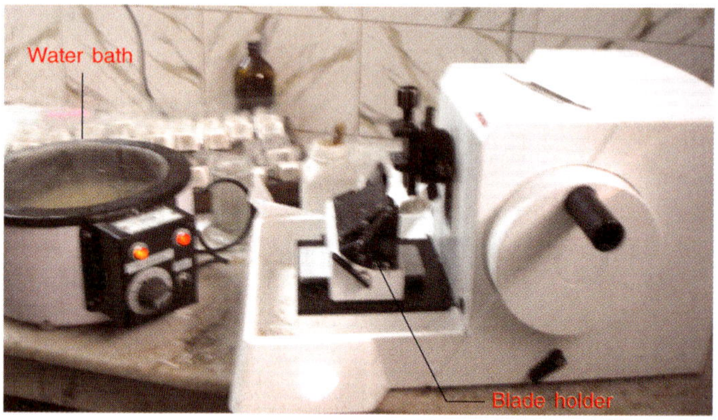

Fig.1.4: Rotary microtome. A water bath is to the left and slide rack with blocks and slides at the back. Each slide is numbered with a diamond pencil as per the specimen number

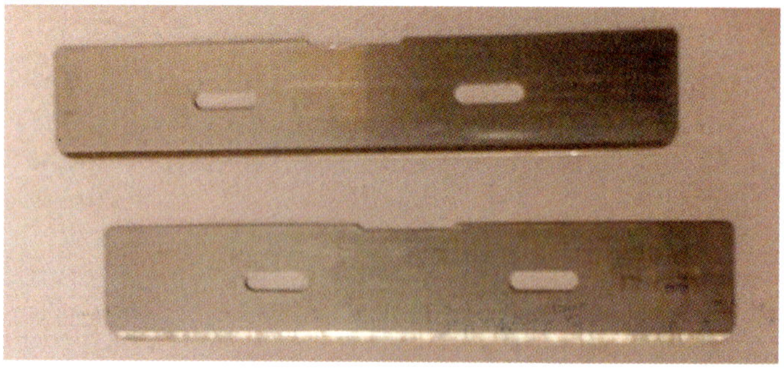

Fig. 1.5: Disposable blades are fitted to the microtome to cut the sections.

Staining

For routine microscopy all tissues are stained with **Hematoxylin and Eosin** (H & E) (Fig. 1.6).

Subsequently further sections of the block can be used for any special stains if indicated.

Hematoxylin is extracted from the logwood of a tree, and the active blue dye, Hematein, is produced by oxidation. This stains the nuclear details as bluish.

Eosin, a xanthine dye, stains the cytoplasm and most connective tissue components pink.

After H & E staining the slides are **mounted** i.e. they

are coverslipped using a mounting medium like DPX so that they can be viewed and stored without damage by dust or scratches. A good mounting medium should be:

- clear and transparent.
- have a refractive index of 1.4 to 1.5.
- should solidify rapidly, and
- should not alter the staining even after prolonged storage.

The most commonly used mounting medium is DPX.

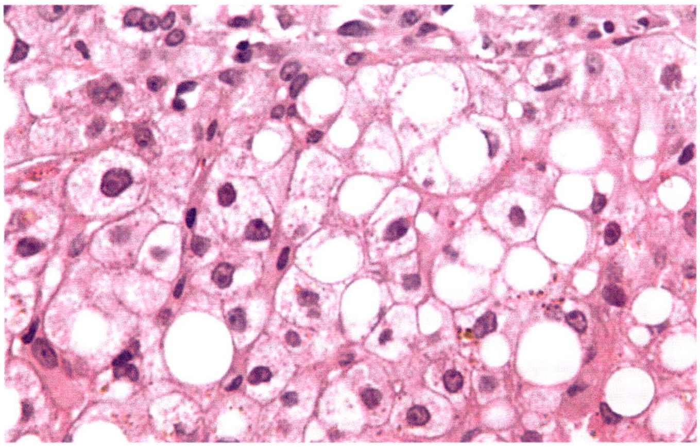

Fig. 1.6: Hematoxylin and eosin staining of liver section demonstrates blue stained nuclei, pink cytoplasm of hepatic cells.

Special stains

Special stains (histochemical stains) are used to demonstrate certain intracellular/extracellular material which may be acid fast bacilli (tuberculosis), various types of fungi *(Periodic acid schiff's stain)*, reticulin framework of the tissue *(reticulin, silver impregnation stain)*, fat *(fat stain)* and bile pigment *(Hall stain)* (Table 1.1).

Table 1.1: Special stains used in histopathology

Stain for demonstration of	Name of the stain
Fat	Sudan III, Sudan IV, Sudan Black B and Oil red O
Bile pigment	Hall stain
Acid fast bacilli (tuberculosis, leprosy)	Ziehl-Neelsen stain
Reticulin framework	Silver impregnation stain
Calcium	Von-Kossa stain, Alizarin red
Fibrous tissue	Van Gieson
Fungi	Periodic acid Schiff stain (PAS)
Amyloid	Methyl violet, Congo red
Hemosiderin-iron	Perl's stain, Prussian blue reaction

In most of the cases, H & E stain on the tissue helps in appreciating morphology of the fungi, amyloid or calcium. Specific stain and the colour produced helps in characterization of the pathology, e.g. pink staining of the acid fast bacilli in a case of tuberculosis (Fig. 1.7).

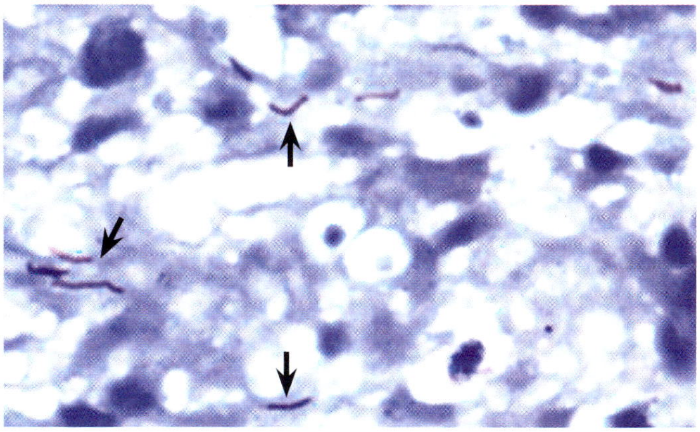

Fig. 1.7: Ziehl Neelsen stain demonstrates pink coloured long tubercle bacilli (↑)

Immunohistochemical stains: In immunohistochemistry (IHC), monoclonal antibodies directed against various specific antigens (on nucleus, cell membrane or cytoplasm) are employed and the immune complex formed is demonstrable by the peroxidase-antiperoxidase method. IHC is used to characterize the lymphomas (T cell/B cell type), histogenesis of various epithelial/mesenchymal tumours, e.g. demonstration of metastatic deposit in the bone marrow/lymphnode (Fig. 1.8). IHC is useful in differentiating carcinomas from sarcomas, carcinomas from lymphomas/round cell tumors and also to know the primary in cases where primary tumor is not known.

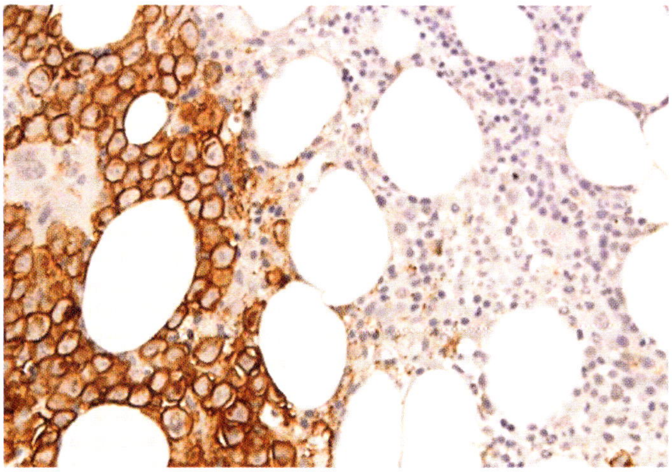

Fig. 1.8: Immunohistochemical stain. CD20 marker stains B-cell. NonHodgkin lymphoma positive-brown colour of the lymphoma cells (left half)

FROZEN SECTION

Routine processing takes a long time (overnight) and the temperature and reagents used alter/destroy some of the labile cellular constituents. Freezing the water in tissues hardens them rapidly and without the use of chemicals or heat.

Frozen section is used for:

(i) Rapid intra-operative diagnosis, especially to confirm/rule out malignancy and to determine if plane of surgical resection is free during cancer surgery.

(ii) Demonstration of enzymes (heat labile) and fats, which get dissolved by xylene.

(iii) Immunofluorescent staining and immunohistochemistry for labile antigens.

Earlier Liquid CO_2 was used for freezing but now a cooled equipment **Cryostat** is used (Fig. 1.9). The coolant used is methanol, freon or other gases. This is a refrigerated cabinet with controlled temperature, with an inbuilt rotary microtome. The tissue is frozen on a Chuck (tissue holder) and cut with a cold disposable knife. Sections are mounted on slides and stained with H&E staining.

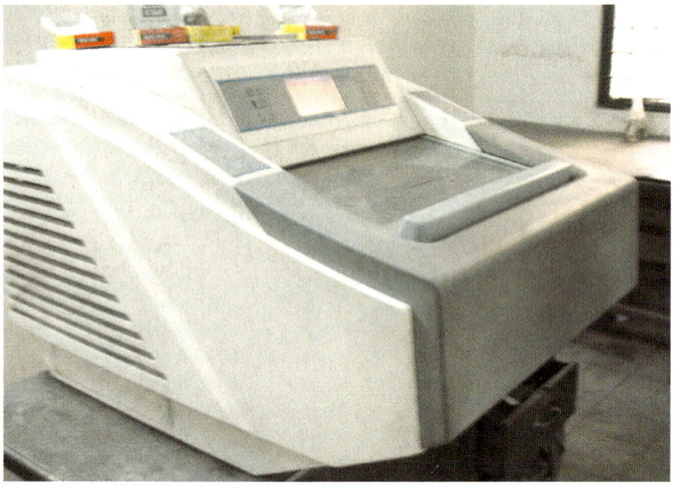

Fig. 1.9: A table top cryostat.

MICROSCOPY

The most commonly used is the light microscope, where the object is viewed using visible light and an enlarged image is produced using a set of lenses.

The essential components of a light microscope (Fig. 1.10) are:

(i) **Light source**: This may be inbuilt or external where a reflector is used to direct the light towards the object being viewed (slide).

(ii) **Condenser**: This optimally focuses the light on to the plane of the object. It is fitted with a Diaphragm whose aperture can be increased or reduced to alter the amount of light transmitted to maximize resolution with minimal glare. Usually the higher the magnification of the objective, the wider is the aperture used.

(iii) **Mechanical stage:** The slide is placed on this & secured by clips so that movement of the slide in forward-backward as well as side to side can be controlled. Vernier scales are also incorporated to facilitate easy location as well as distance measurements.

(iv) **Objectives:** These are the most important components that determine the quality of the image. These are attached at the lower end of the optical tube, just above the Stage. These have several lenses in series in order to form a real, magnified image of the object within the optical tube. The "power" of the objective is its object : image ratio (e.g., 10X means that the object has been magnified 10 times). The objectives used are: scanner, low power, high power and oil immersion.

(v) **Eye piece(s):** These are inserted into the upper end of the optical tube. There may be one (monocular), or two (binocular) eyepieces for viewing, or in a microscope with photographic attachment, a third tube (trinocular) leads to the camera. Viewing eyepiece further magnifies (usually 10X) the image formed within the optical tube and focuses it on the observer's retina.

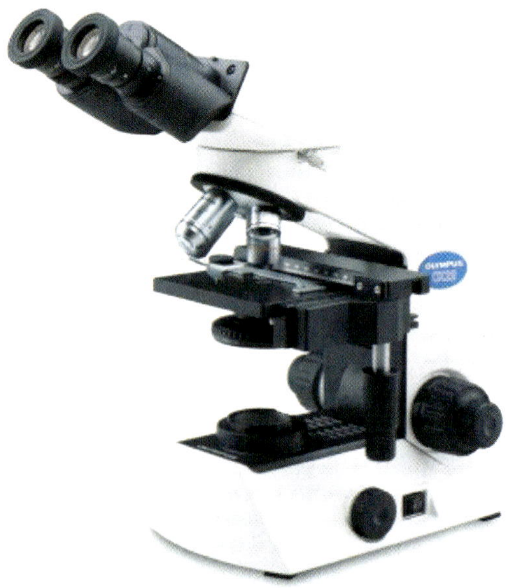

Fig. 1.10: Binocular microscope with 3 objectives.

Modifications of light microscopy

Polarisation microscopy: Polarisation is the property of certain minerals and crystals to restrict the vibration of light rays passing through them to one plane only. If 2 plates of such material are aligned one over the other and one of them rotated, visible light will pass through only in the positions where their vibration planes are parallel i.e., at 180° and at 360° and not when they are perpendicular to one another. In polarization microscopy, one plate is placed below the stage (polarizer) and the other close to the eyepiece (analyzer).

Some substances in tissues like crystals, fibres, pigments, amyloid etc. are birefringent i.e. when these are placed between these 2 plates, they alter the incident light of one plane to produce slow waves in one direction and fast waves in its perpendicular direction. This makes the crystal visible (often in a distinct colour) when the two plates are not parellel and therefore the background is dark.

Phase Contrast microscopy: This is used when it is necessary to study unstained, often live cells e.g., function and behavior of cells like mobility, phagocytosis etc. As stains are not used, we utilise the small differences in the refractive indices of various organelles. Though this can be achieved to some extent by reducing the incident light, better resolution is obtained by phase contrast microscopy. Instead of light rays of a uniform nature, rays with altered phase and amplitude are made to pass through the object. This accentuates the differences in their refractive indices so that denser organelles with higher index are much darker than others with lower index. Platelet count is best carried out under phase contrast microscope using a Neubauer chamber.

Fluorescent microscopy: Fluorescence is the property of certain substances which when exposed to low wave length rays like Ultraviolet or blue light emit higher wavelength light in the visible spectrum. Some substances like porphyrin and Vitamin A have an innate fluorescent nature (auto fluorescence, primary fluorescence), whereas others like Catacholamines can be induced to fluoresce by exposure to formalin (induced fluorescence). However fluorescent microscopy usually involves the use of fluorescent substances to label proteins and other tissue components based on chemical or immunological binding. Tetracyclin binds to calcium and this property is used in bone turnover studies. Fluorescein is widely used in immunohistochemistry where, it is tagged to specific antibodies and used for tissue localization of corresponding antigen.

The microscope utilizes a source of low wavelength light rays (mostly mercury vapour or xenon gas lamps), specific filters to allow only rays of selected wavelength to pass through the object and further filters to remove unabsorbed UV rays to prevent harm to the observer's eyes.

Depending upon the substance and the fluorescent dye, the object fluoresces, e.g. with the dye thioflavin S or T green fluorescence is produced. In Bullous pemphigoid, anti-basement membrane antibodies are visualized in the skin biopsy, using fluorescent dyes (Fig. 1.11).

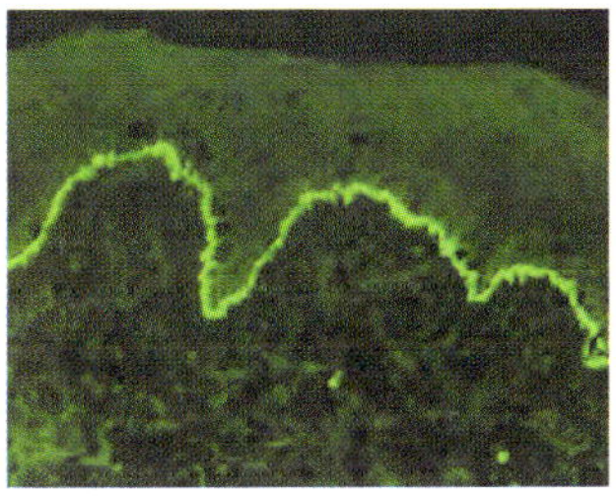

Fig. 1.11: Fluorescent microscopy: Section shows brightly stained basement membrane of the skin in a case of Bullous Pemphigoid

VIVA-VOCE

Q. What is the commonly used fixative?
Ans. Buffered formalin is the most commonly used fixative.

Q. What are the various uses of "frozen section"?
Ans. Frozen section is used for
- (a) Rapid diagnosis of malignancy
- (b) To confirm presence/absence of resected margin involvement by cancer at the time of surgery.
- (c) For demonstration of fat and enzymes
- (d) Demonstration of IgG, IgM, IgA and Complement in kidney biopsy in various glomerulonephritis by immunofluorescence.

Q. What are the fat stains?
Ans. The fat stains are
- (a) Sudan III
- (b) Sudan IV
- (c) Sudan black B
- (d) Oil red O
- (e) Osmic acid

Q. Name the special stains for demonstration of amyloid?
Ans. Amyloid is demonstrable by
(a) Methyl violet stain-Rose pink coloured
(b) Congo Red stain with polarising microscope - apple green birefrengence
(c) Fluorescent stain - Thioflavin S, Thioflavin T give greenish fluorescence
(d) Van Gieson stain - khaki colour
(e) Periodic acid Schiff stain (PAS) - magenta colour

Q. How will you demonstrate fungi?
Ans. Fungi are demonstrable by
(a) Periodic Acid Schiff stain - PAS - magenta colour
(b) Silver methenamine stain - black colour

Q. What are the special stains for calcium?
Ans. Calcium in the tissue can be demonstrated by
(a) Von Kossa stain - Black colour
(b) Alizarin Red - Red colour

Q. How is iron/hemosiderin demonstrated in tissues/bone marrow?
Ans. Iron in tissues/bone marrow is demonstrated by Perls stain (Prussian blue reaction) using acidified $K_4Fe(CN)_6$.

Q. Name the special stain for acid fast bacilli (tuberculosis)?
Ans. Ziehl Neelsen stain which stains the bacilli pink.

Q. How can you demonstrate Lepra bacilli (AFB) (Leprosy)
Ans. Lepra bacilli are acid fast bacilli (AFB) and can be demonstrated by Fite-Faraco stain and Ziehl-Neelsen stain.

Q. Which substances are positive with PAS stain?
Ans.
- Basement membrane
- Amyloid
- Fungus
- Glycolipids
- Glycoprotein
- Glycogen

SECTION B
General Pathology

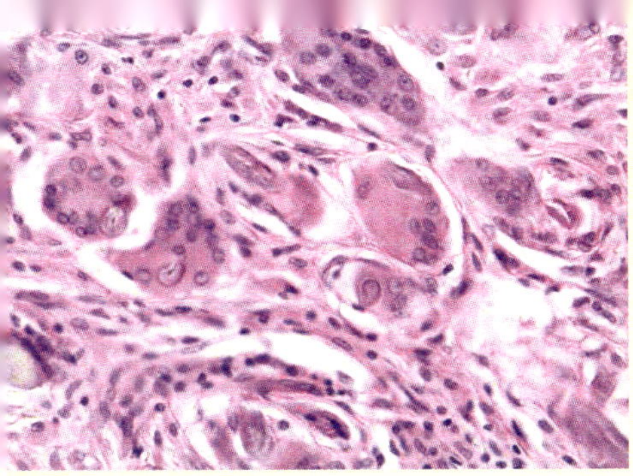

2

Inflammation and Repair

Inflammation is defined as the response of vascularised living tissue to injury. Based on the clinical course and tissue reaction it is categorized as acute or chronic.

ACUTE INFLAMMATION

Characterised by:

- vascular and cellular events
- results in a more or less stereotyped response of exudate and polymorphs
- Polymorphs are the histological hallmark of acute inflammation.

Histological features are (Fig. 2.1):

- vascular dilatation (increased calibre)
- congestion (stasis of RBC)
- margination (endothelium lined by polymorphs)
- emigration (movement of polymorphs through the capillary wall) and
- plasma exudation (accumulation of fluid in interstitial compartment).

Depending on the relative composition of its components, the exudate may be:

- serous (watery, clear)
- fibrinous (protein rich with fibrin strands)
- suppurative (pus, rich in dead polymorphs)
- haemorrhagic (vascular damage and RBC extravasation) or
- necrotising (accompanied by tissue destruction).

As the inflammation subsides or if it is due to parasitic infestation or allergic reaction, eosinophils may be seen in significant numbers along with variable numbers of plasma cells, lymphocytes and histiocytes.

Acute Appendicitis

Grossly the appendix is swollen, with congested vessels in the serosa (Fig. 2.2).

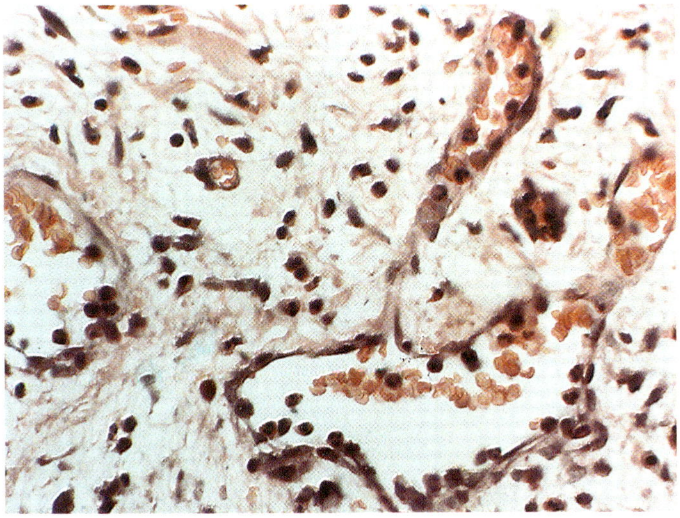

Fig. 2.1: Features of acute inflammation – dilated congested capillaries, marginated polymorphs and exudation.

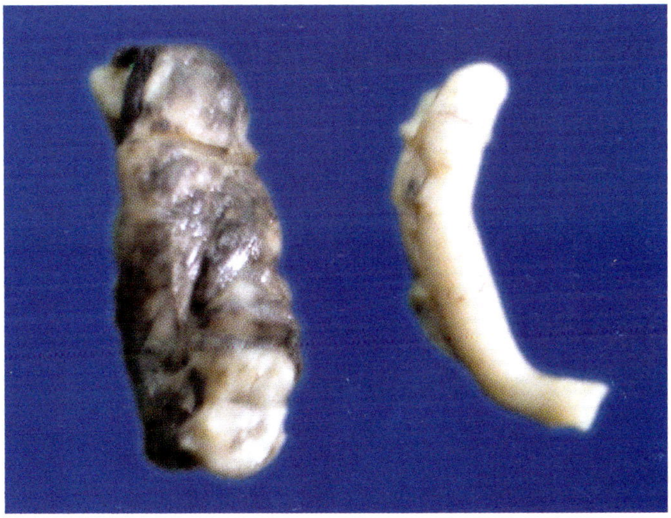

Fig. 2.2: Acute appendicitis specimen on left – swollen, dull and congested externally. Compare with normal appendix on right.

Microscopically

- Tissue is identified by the 4 layers, colonic type of mucosa, lymphoid follicles and small lumen.
- Mucosa may show focal to extensive ulceration, lined by slough and exudate (Fig. 2.3).
- Muscle coat shows separation of muscle fibres by exudate and polymorphs (Fig. 2.4).
- Congested dilated vessels are seen in the serosa
- Polymorphs are seen in the serosa as well as marginating in the dilated vessels.
- Severe cases may show haemorrhage with extravasation of R.B.C.

Acute Meningitis

- Tissue is identified by adjoining brain tissue (fibrillary background, neurons and glial cells).
- Leptomeninges show the congested dilated vessels and the exudate rich in polymorphs. Brain tissue is not inflamed but shows edema in the form of widening of the perivascular (Virchow-Robin's) space and prominent clear space around the neurons (Fig. 2.5).

Allergic Nasal Polyp

- Tissue is lined by pseudostratified columnar ciliated epithelium.
- The intense edema in the subepithelium causes the polypoidal projections grossly and is seen histologically as pale eosinophilic (plasma like) material in between the components of the interstitium (Fig. 2.6).
- Scattered in the edematous tissue, a large number of eosinophils and plasma cells are seen.

Other examples of acute inflammation are cellulitis, pneumonia, abscess etc., due to bacterial infections especially related to pyogenic cocci.

REPAIR AND HEALING

After acute inflammation the outcome may be:

(a) Resolution of the exudate by enzymatic lysis and phagocytosis. If associated tissue loss is minimal or the tissue is capable of regenerating the lost cells, total reconstitution of tissue to normal state occurs.

(b) Healing with scar formation, by granulation tissue. This occurs if:

- exudate is rich in fibrin (resulting in adhesions as in fibrinous pericarditis or peritoneal inflammation), or
- if there is significant tissue loss (as in abscess or ulcer healing), or
- if tissue is not capable of regenerating lost parenchymal cells (permanent cells like muscle), or
- if architectural framework is also lost as in submassive hepatic destruction.

(c) Progression to chronic inflammation.

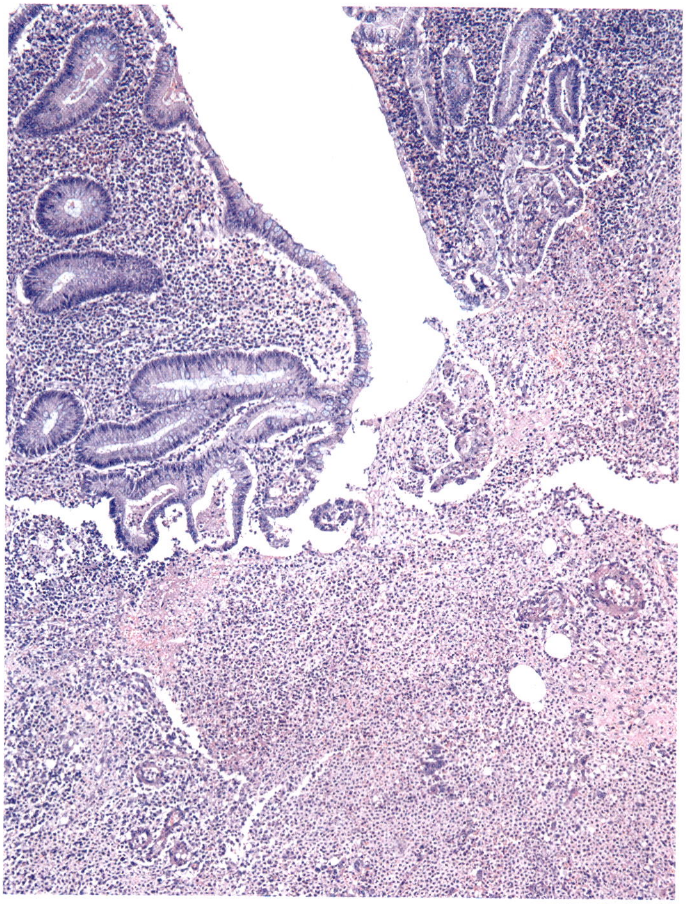

Fig. 2.3: Acute appendicitis – mucosal inflammation and ulceration with dense infiltrate of neutrophils.

Granulation Tissue

Granulation Tissue is the hallmark of healing with scar formation. It is present in a clean surgical wound also (to result in a thin linear scar ⟶ healing by first intention or primary union), but is more prominent in situations where there is significant tissue loss (e.g. ulcer) or large amounts of debris etc. have to be dealt with (e.g. organisation of a thrombus or a hematoma ⟶ healing by second intention or secondary union).

Early granulation tissue comprises of:

- proliferating fibroblasts (plump spindle cells with oval vesicular nuclei),

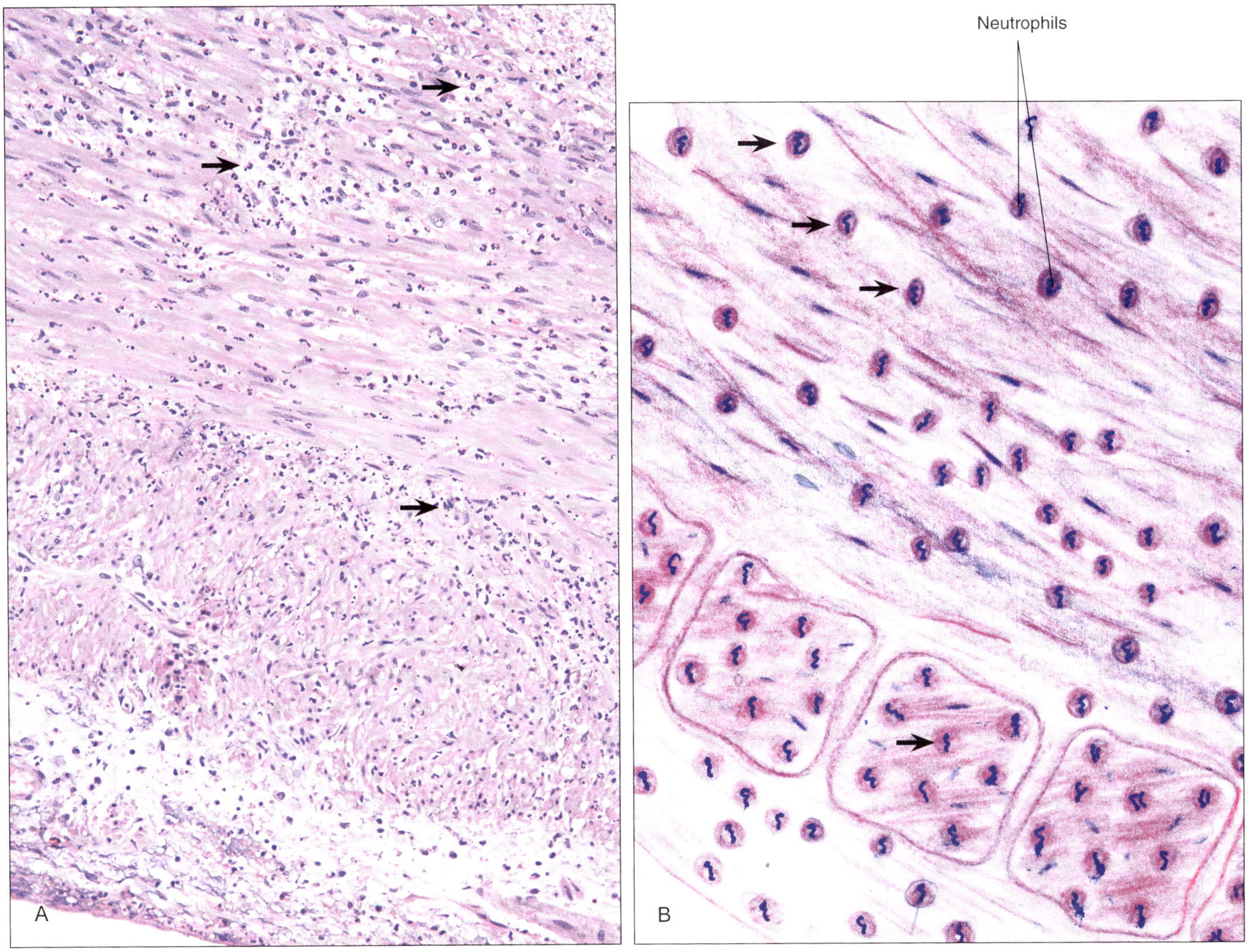

Fig. 2.4: A and B Acute appendicitis – muscle coat with fibres separated by exudates and congestion and infiltration by neutrophils (↑)

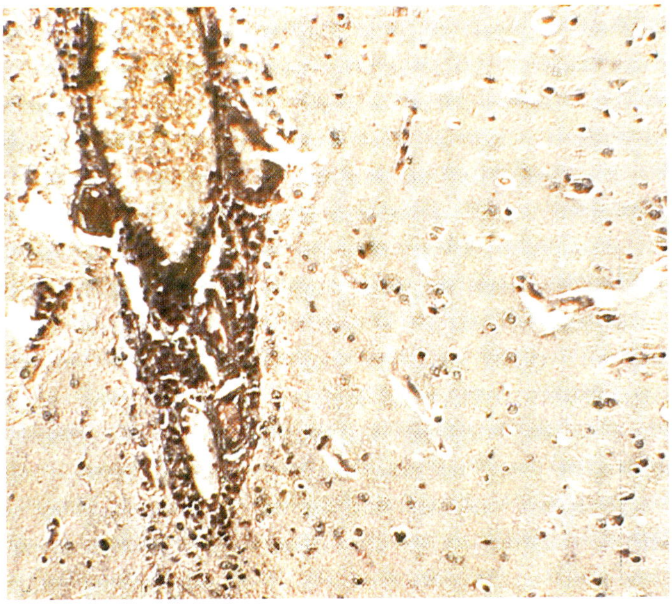

Fig. 2.5: Acute meningitis – Congestion and exudate in meninges. Brain is uninflammed.

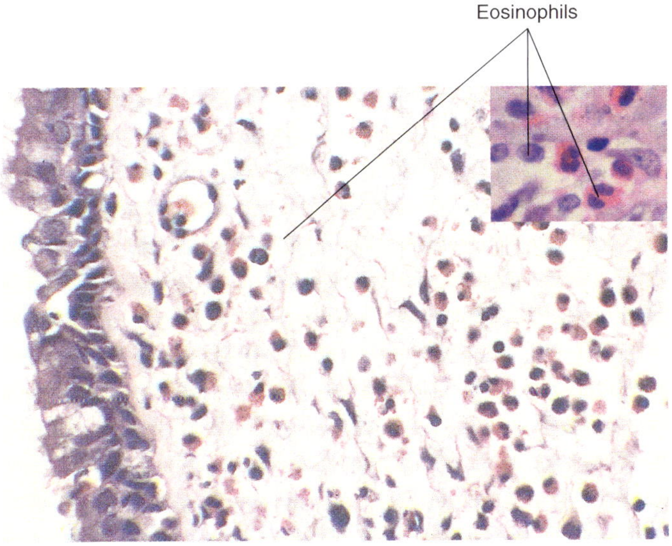

Fig. 2.6: Allergic nasal polyp – Intact respiratory epithelium with subepithelial edema and eosinophils. Inset shows eosinophils. Eosinophils are recognized by their orange-red granules and bilobed nuclei.

- newly formed capillaries (endothelial cells in rows, with or without lumina) (Fig. 2.7A),
- edematous stroma (due to the inflammation and also contributed to by the leakiness of the newly formed capillaries) (Fig. 2.7A), and
- inflammatory cells (neutrophils, soon replaced by a preponderance of macrophages).

Collagen formation is demonstrable as occasional fibrils by the 3rd day and well established by end of one week. With progressive collagenisation the scar becomes less cellular and devascularised. Inflammatory reaction subsides and over months, the tensile strength of the collagenised scar increases. If the healing is occurring on the skin or mucosal surface, re-epithelialisation of the surface occurs by regeneration and cell proliferation just beyond ulcer edge with inward migration of the cells over the proliferating granulation tissue.

CHRONIC INFLAMMATION

Inflammation may follow a chronic (protracted) course under several situations:

(a) Following acute inflammation if irritant stimulus persists or if debridement and healing are hampered (e.g. peptic ulceration, ineffective immune response or therapy in bacterial infections, enclosed tissue debris as in an abscess, splinters or shrapnel in wound, dead bone spicules in osteomyelitis);

(b) Repeated bouts of acute inflammation (as in chronic cholecystitis, chronic pyelonephritis); or

(c) Insidiously as chronic inflammation per se. This could be due to low virulent organisms or non-degradable material that resists digestion. An associated element of immune reaction may play a variable role (e.g. tuberculosis, viral and fungal infections, cholesterol rich exudates, foreign bodies like asbestos and silica in the lungs, rheumatoid arthritis and other autoimmune diseases).

Histologically chronic inflammation is characterised by inflammation and healing going on simultaneously. Inflammation is represented by predominantly mononuclear cells i.e. lymphocytes, histiocytes and plasma cells (Fig. 2.7B and C). Varying proportion of polymorphs and eosinophils may be seen in addition, especially if chronic inflammation has followed an acute stage. Healing is seen as granulation tissue and fibrosis.

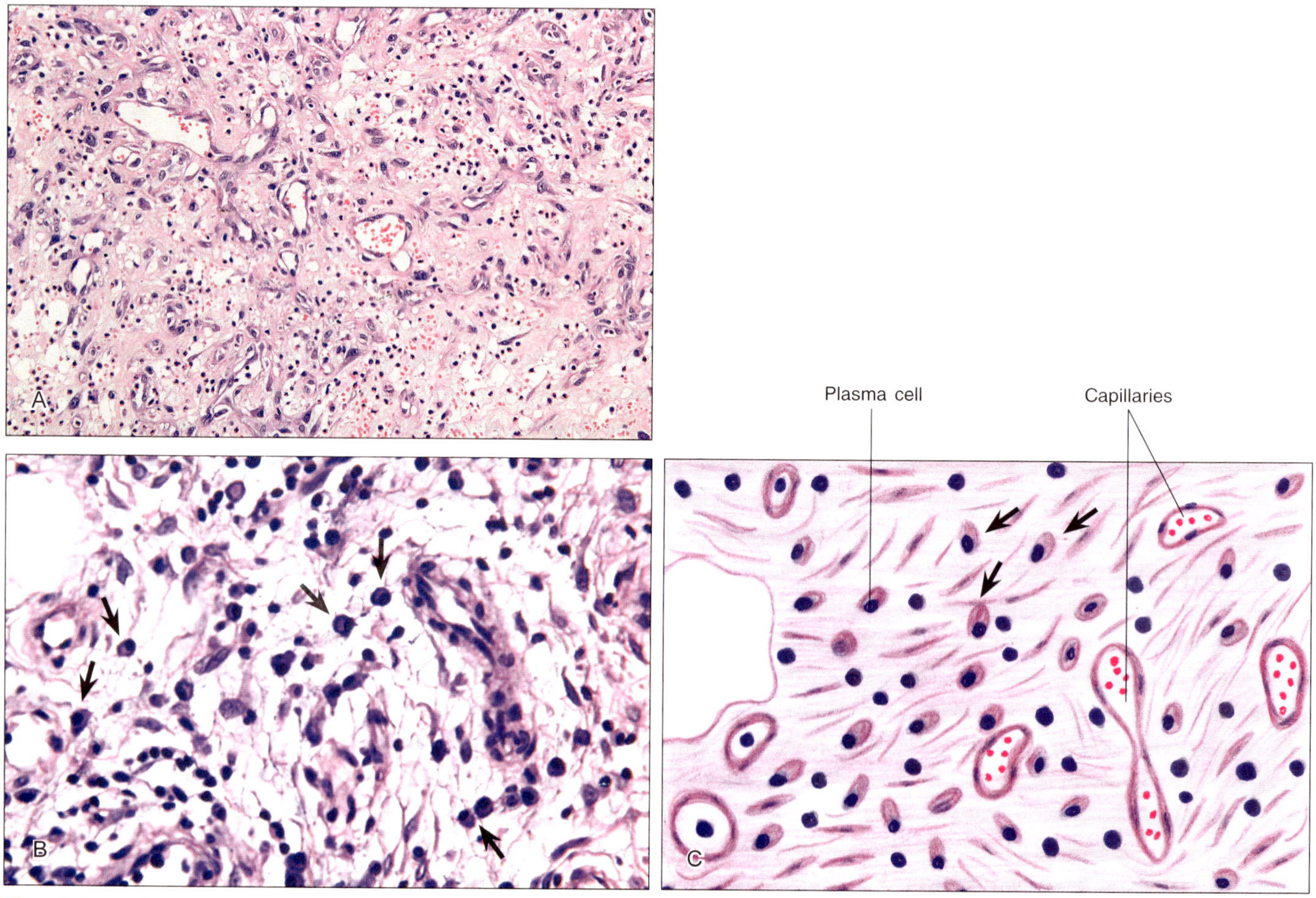

Fig. 2.7: A. Granulation tissue. Inflammatory cells, fibroblasts and proliferating capillaries in a loose stroma. **B** and **C.** Chronic inflammatory granulation tissue shows capillaries, lymphocytes, plasma cells (↑) (with eccenteric nuclei with cartwheel nuclear chromatin) and some neutrophils.

Chronic Cholecystitis

Grossly gall bladder is greyish white in colour and the wall is thickened from 2 mm to 1 cm depending upon the amount of fibrosis. Mucosa may be ulcerated. Gall bladder demonstrates single cholestrol/multiple faceted mixed stones/pigment stores (Fig. 2.8).

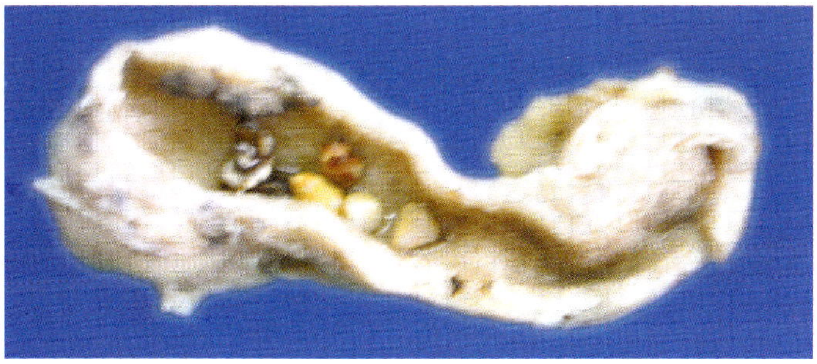

Fig. 2.8 Chronic cholecystitis with gall stones in lumen. Note thick fibrosed wall and loss of mucosal villi.

Microscopically

- Gall bladder is identified by the absence of muscularis mucosa in a hollow muscular organ with columnar mucus secreting lining.
- Normal villus processes may be distorted or ironed out.
- Muscle coat shows replacement by fibrosis.
- The mucosal lining is outpouched into the muscle coat to form Rokitansky Aschoff sinuses (Fig. 2.9).
- Mononuclear infiltrates are seen in all coats (Fig. 2.9).
- Cholesterol, if reabsorbed, is phagocytosed by macrophages in mucosa.
- Serosa shows fibrosis and the wall may be markedly thickened (Fig. 2.8 and 2.9).

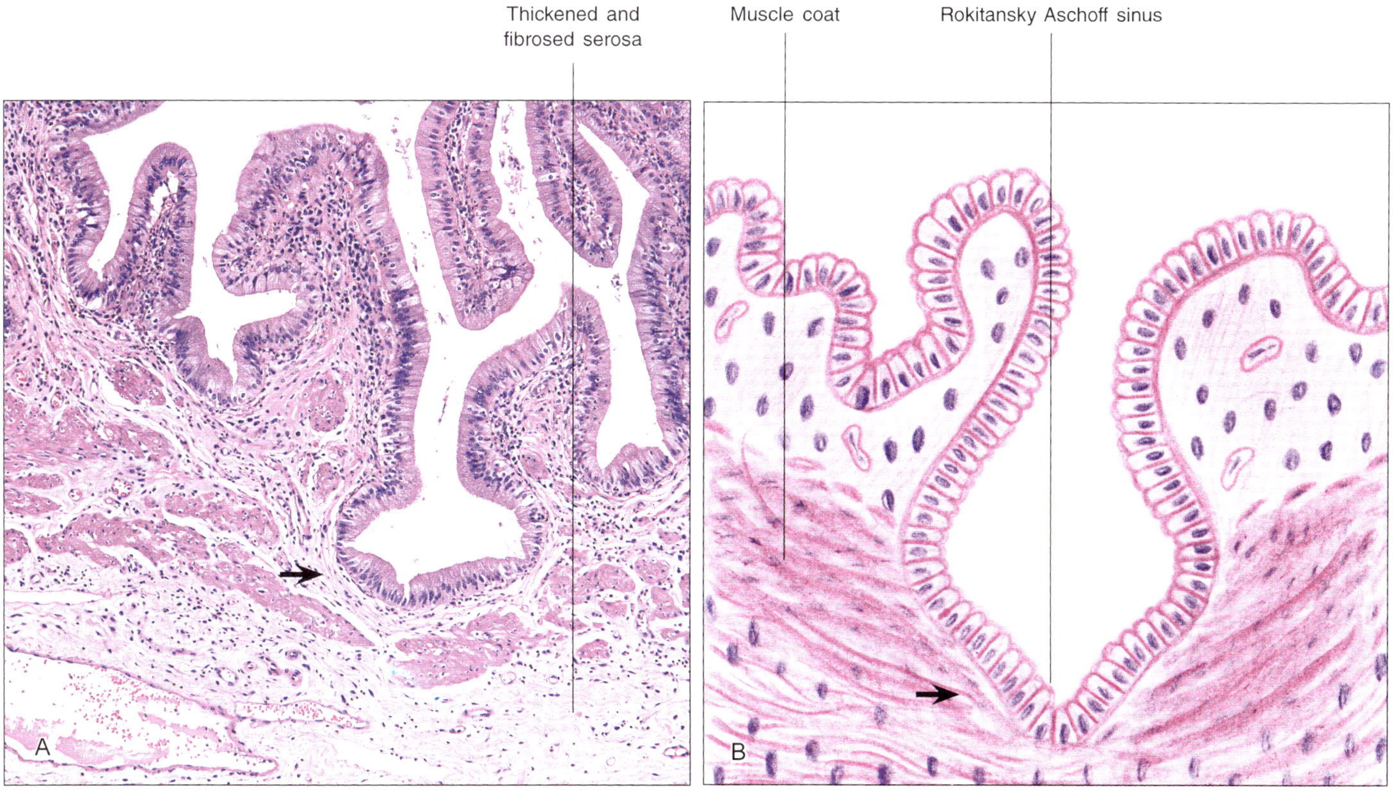

Fig. 2.9: A and B Chronic cholecystitis – Inflammation and fibrosis in muscle coat with Rokitansky Aschoff sinus (↑).

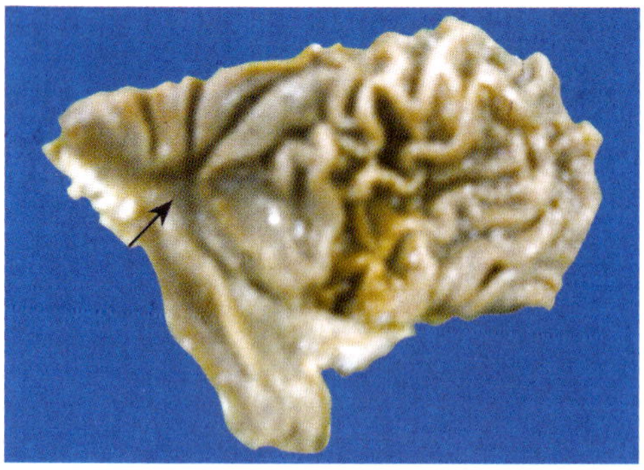

Fig. 2.10: Chronic gastric ulcer: Ulcer crater with converging rugae towards the ulcer are seen

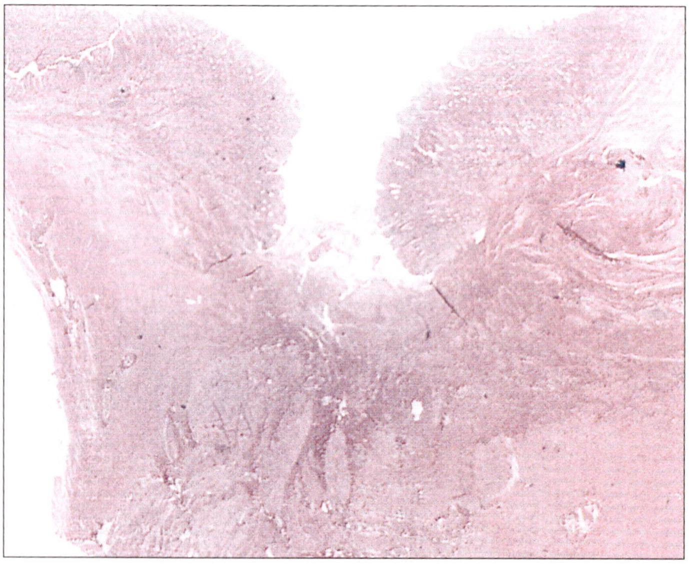

Fig. 2.11: Chronic gastric ulcer – deep ulcer with clean margins.

Chronic Gastric Ulcer

Grossly, the stomach or gastrectomy specimen is recognized by being a viscus organ (not a tubular structure). The ulcer is recognized as an ulcer crater on the mucosal aspect of gastrectomy. In chronic ulcer, radiating mucosal folds towards the ulcer are seen (Fig. 2.10).

Microscopically

- Stomach is identified by the four coats and gastric type of mucosa (thick, closely packed glands, chief and parietal cells and the surface gastric pits with mucus secreting cells) (Fig. 2.11).
- The ulcer is deep, with its floor covered by a thin zone of debris and an acute inflammatory zone (Fig. 2.11 and 2.12).
- Deep to that, are the granulation tissue and the dense fibrous scar tissue (Fig. 2.12).
- Scar tissue may extend deep enough to replace the muscle coat at the ulcer base.
- In the quiescent phase, the epithelium close to the edge of the ulcer shows regeneration.

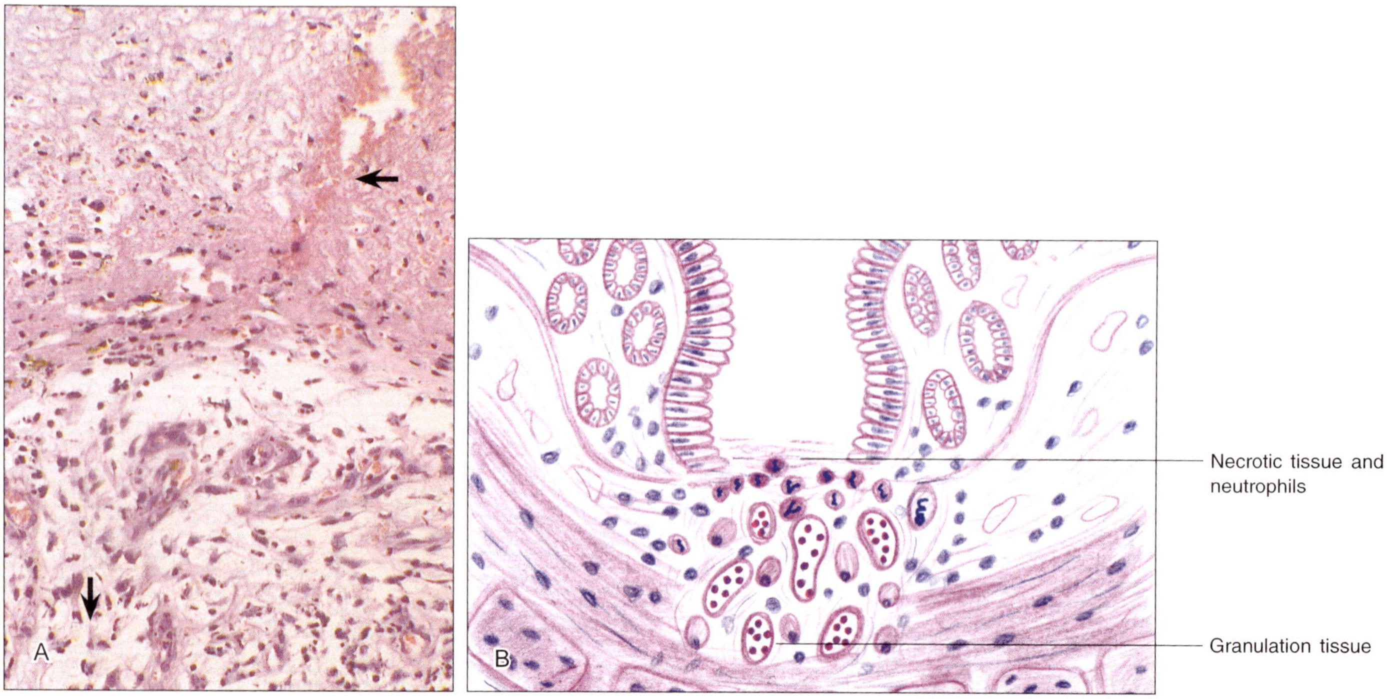

Fig. 2.12: A. and B. Chronic gastric ulcer – base with necrotic exudate (←) and granulation tissue zone (bottom) (↓).

GRANULOMATOUS INFLAMMATION

Certain agents induce a pattern of chronic inflammation in which instead of (or, in addition to) diffuse or scattered mononuclear cells, localised collections of altered or activated macrophages are seen. These collections are called granulomas. The macrophages often fuse to form giant cells.

Granulomas are induced by:

- certain chemicals (lipids, complex polysaccharides),
- indigestible materials (sutures, cholesterol crystals, foreign bodies) and
- some organisms (tubercle bacillus, fungi) along with
- an element of cell mediated immunity.

Foreign Body Granuloma

- Is usually due to particulate crystalline matter, which may be immunologically inert.
- The foreign material is seen within or enclosed by giant cells (Fig. 2.13).
- Foreign body giant cells are formed by fusion of histiocytes and have numerous uniform nuclei, scattered in a correspondingly large amount of cytoplasm (Fig. 2.13).
- Lymphocytes, plasma cells and histiocytes are seen in the background.
- The foreign body may be identifiable (e.g. suture, vegetable matter, crystals, fungus etc.) or be dissolved during tissue processing and hence be represented by cleft like spaces (e.g. cholesterol) (Fig. 2.13).
- If suspected, crystals can be confirmed by polarised microscopy and fungus by special stains like PAS etc.

Tuberculous Granuloma

- In this type, cell mediated immunity plays a major role.
- Hence macrophage activation by lymphokines is prominent, transforming them into **epithelioid cells** – larger, often polygonal cells, with abundant eosinophilic cytoplasm and vesicular nucleus (hence resembling epithelial cells) (Fig. 2.14).
- They fuse to form **Langhan's giant cells**, classically with nuclei arranged peripherally, or at the poles of the cell (Fig. 2.14).
- Tuberculoid granulomas are also seen in sarcoidosis, tuberculoid leprosy, berylliosis and some fungal infections.
- Tuberculosis can be distinguished from the above by the presence of characteristic caseous necrosis (tissue destruction) in the centre (see Fig. 3.13), yielding a granular featureless amorphous eosinophilic debris.
- However it should be confirmed by acid fast staining for the tubercle bacillus (or by culture, serological studies etc.).

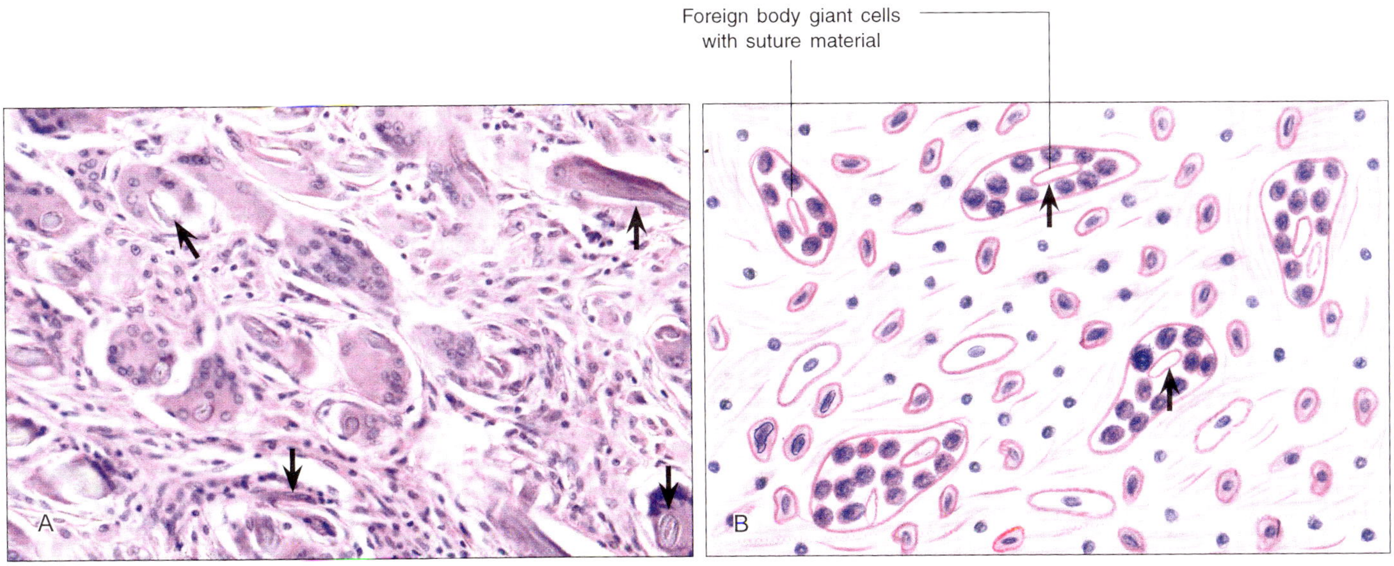

Fig. 2.13: A. and B. Foreign body granuloma – Foreign body giant cell granuloma with suture material in many foreign body giant cells (↑).

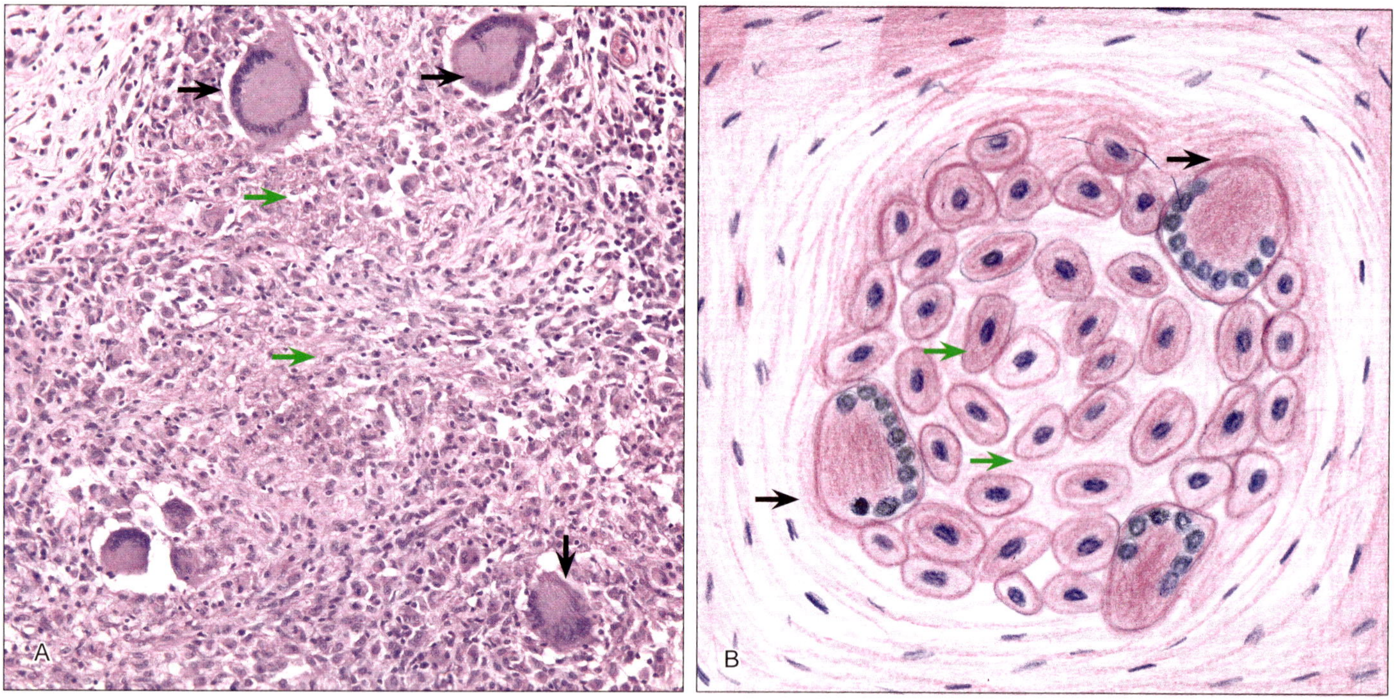

Fig. 2.14: A. and **B.** Epithelioid cells (↑) and Langhan's giant cells in a tubercular granuloma. Nuclei in the Langhan giant cell are arranged in a "horse shoe" like pattern (↑).

Xanthogranuloma

Granulomas formed in response to lipid rich material (or in hyper-lipidaemias) have collections of foamy histiocytes – large, with pale to faintly granular cytoplasm. Giant cells are fewer and may have a central dense cytoplasm surrounded by a ring of nuclei and peripheral foamy cytoplasm (Touton Giant cells) (Fig. 2.15).

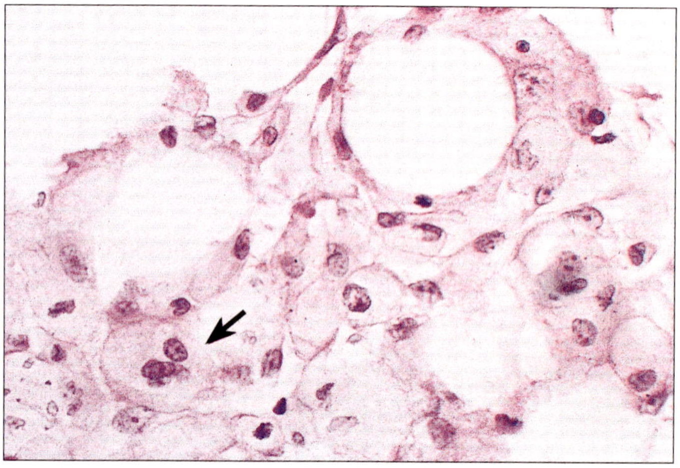

Fig. 2.15: Lipophages and Touton giant cells (arrow) in inflammed adipose tissue.

VIVA-VOCE

Q. Give some examples of acute inflammation?

Ans. Common examples of acute inflammation are acute appendicitis, acute meningitis, acute pncreatitis, acute pharyngitis, acute abscess and bronchopneumonia.

Q. Which cell in the tissues is hallmark of acute inflammation?

Ans. Neutrophil infiltration in tissues is diagnostic of acute inflammation. Acute inflammation is usually associated with neutrophilic leucocytosis in blood.

Q. What kind of gall stones are usually observed in chronic cholecystitis?

Ans. Mixed type of stones are usually associated with chronic cholecystitis.

Q. What are the types of gall stones?

Ans. **Pure stones**

Cholestrol stone - single - yellowish in colour

Pigment stones - multiple - dark in colour

Mixed stones

Cholestrol + pigment + calcium - multiple faceted - light to dark in colour

Combined stone

Nucleus of pure/mixed type with shell of mixed/pure type - multiple - dark in colour

Q. What are the complications of gastric ulcer?

Ans. The complications of gastric ulcer are: perforation, haemorrhage, fibrosis (pyloric stenosis) and malignant transformation.

Q. Name the types of giant cells.

Ans. There are two types of giant cells

A. Physiological
- Syncytiotrophoblast
- Osteoclast

B. Pathological
- Langhan type of giant cell – Tuberculosis
- Foreign body type giant cell – Foreign body granuloma
- Touton giant cell – Fat necrosis
- Aschoff giant cell – Rheumatic heart disease
- Reed-Sternberg cell – Hodgkin's disease
- Tumour giant cell – Malignancies

Q. What are the components of granulation tissue?

Ans. Proliferating capillaries, plump fibroblasts, loose stroma and inflammatory cells.

Q. What are the histological hallmarks of chronic inflammation?

Ans. The salient features are

(a) Inflammatory component of Lymphocytes, plasma cells and histiocytes

(b) Persistant tissue destruction

(c) Concurrent healing with granulation tissue resulting in fibrosis

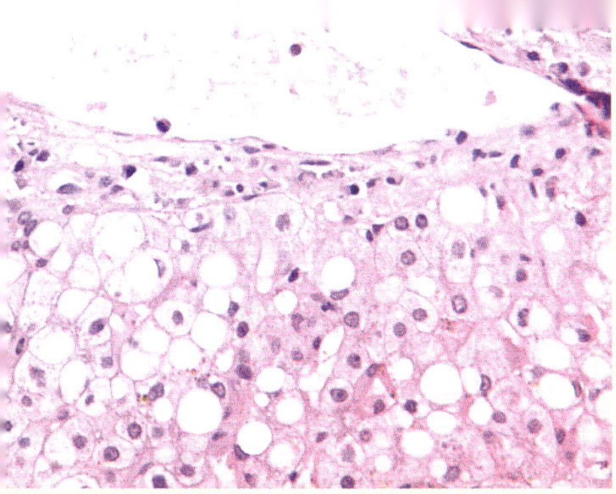

3

Degeneration and Necrosis

DEGENERATION

Degeneration is defined as the manifestation of cell response to sublethal injury. Cell may respond with alteration in its biochemical, functional or morphological state, the last of these being termed as degeneration. At light microscopic level it falls into two main categories:

(a) ***Hydropic degeneration*** (cellular swelling, vacuolar degeneration) is due to failure in maintaining water and ion homeostasis (sodium pump failure) and is reversible. This can be seen in any tissue with minor injury (especially renal tubular epithelium) as slight enlargement of the cell with paler cytoplasm. If severe, small fluid filled vacuoles are seen in the cytoplasm.

(b) ***Fatty change.*** This is classically seen in hepatocytes and in the cardiac myocytes. Though caused due to metabolic injury, there is an increase in the total lipid content of the cells (an intracellular accumulation).

Fatty Liver (Steatosis)

Grossly the liver is enlarged and pale, with smooth surface. Cut surface is yellow and greasy if steatosis is severe and diffuse (Fig. 3.1).

Microscopically:

- Liver is identified by the portal tracts, sinusoids and arrangement of hepatocytes in cords.
- If fatty change is extensive, tissue is identified by the portal tracts.
- The architecture of the hepatic lobules is normal.
- Hepatocytes contain lipid as small droplets (mild fatty change, microvesicular) or as a large vacuole pushing the nucleus to the periphery (moderate) or as fat cysts due to fusion of lipid laden cells (severe) (Fig. 3.2).
- The distribution of fat vacuoles may be diffuse, focal (patchy) or zonal (centrilobular, midzonal or periportal), depending on the severity and cause.
- Fat in tissues is removed by solvents during paraffin block making. To demonstrate fat, frozen section followed by lipid stain (Sudan IV, Oil red O etc.) has to be done.

Intracytoplasmic Accumulations which may occur without cellular injury are:

(a) ***Proteins*** (Hyaline droplets). Proximal tubules in a patient with proteinuria, reabsorb the excreted proteins. This is seen as hyaline eosinophilic material in the cytoplasm of tubular epithelial cells. Russell bodies are large cytoplasmic, hyaline globules of immunoglobulin present in plasma cells in states of active synthesis.

(b) ***Lipofuscin*** (wear and tear pigment) is seen as finely granular golden brown pigment in the cytoplasm of liver and cardiac cells due to regressive changes (old age, atrophy, chronic illness, malnutrition). It is formed due to lipid peroxidation of membranes of organelles and represents their undigestible residues.

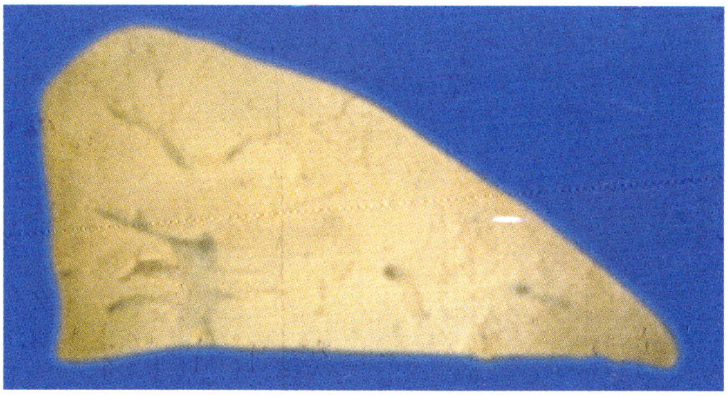

Fig. 3.1: Slice of liver showing severe diffuse fatty change – yellow, greasy cut surface.

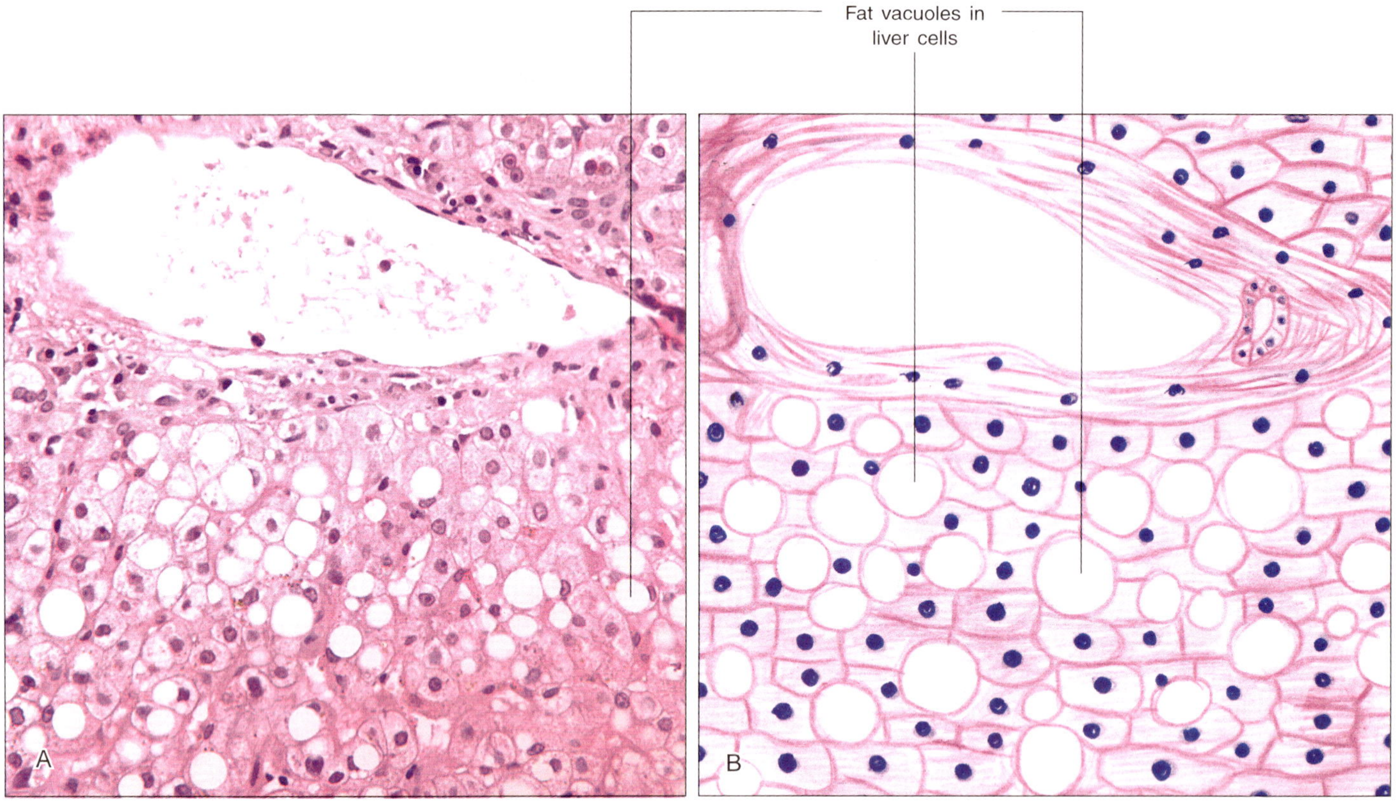

Fig. 3.2: A. and **B.** Diffuse, fatty change liver with empty round vacuoles in liver parenchyma. Tissue is identified by the portal triad (on top of figure).

(c) ***Melanin*** can accumulate in tumours of melanocytes, like naevus (benign) and melanoma (malignant). Additionally, in chronic inflammation of skin, the released melanin is taken up by melanophages in the dermis, loaded with dark brown pigment (Fig. 3.3).

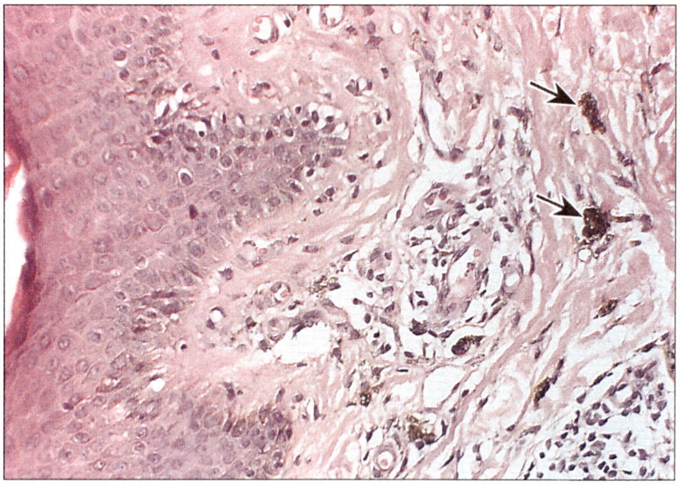

Fig. 3.3: Melanophages (arrows) in the dermis in chronic dermatitis.

(d) ***Hemosiderin.*** This represents aggregates of ferritin, the storage form of iron, and is normally seen in small amounts in bone marrow, liver and spleen. Increased amounts may occur locally (at sites of severe congestion or organising haemorrhages, where the end products of RBC breakdown are taken up by the macrophages) (Fig. 3.4) or in a systemic form known as hemosiderosis (when there is an overload in total body iron). In the latter, hemosiderin accumulates in parenchymal organs in addition to macrophages and, if severe, may cause structural and functional damage (hemochromatosis). Hemosiderin is seen as golden brown pigment, which gives a positive Prussian blue reaction (Perl's stain → bright blue colour) (Fig. 3.4).

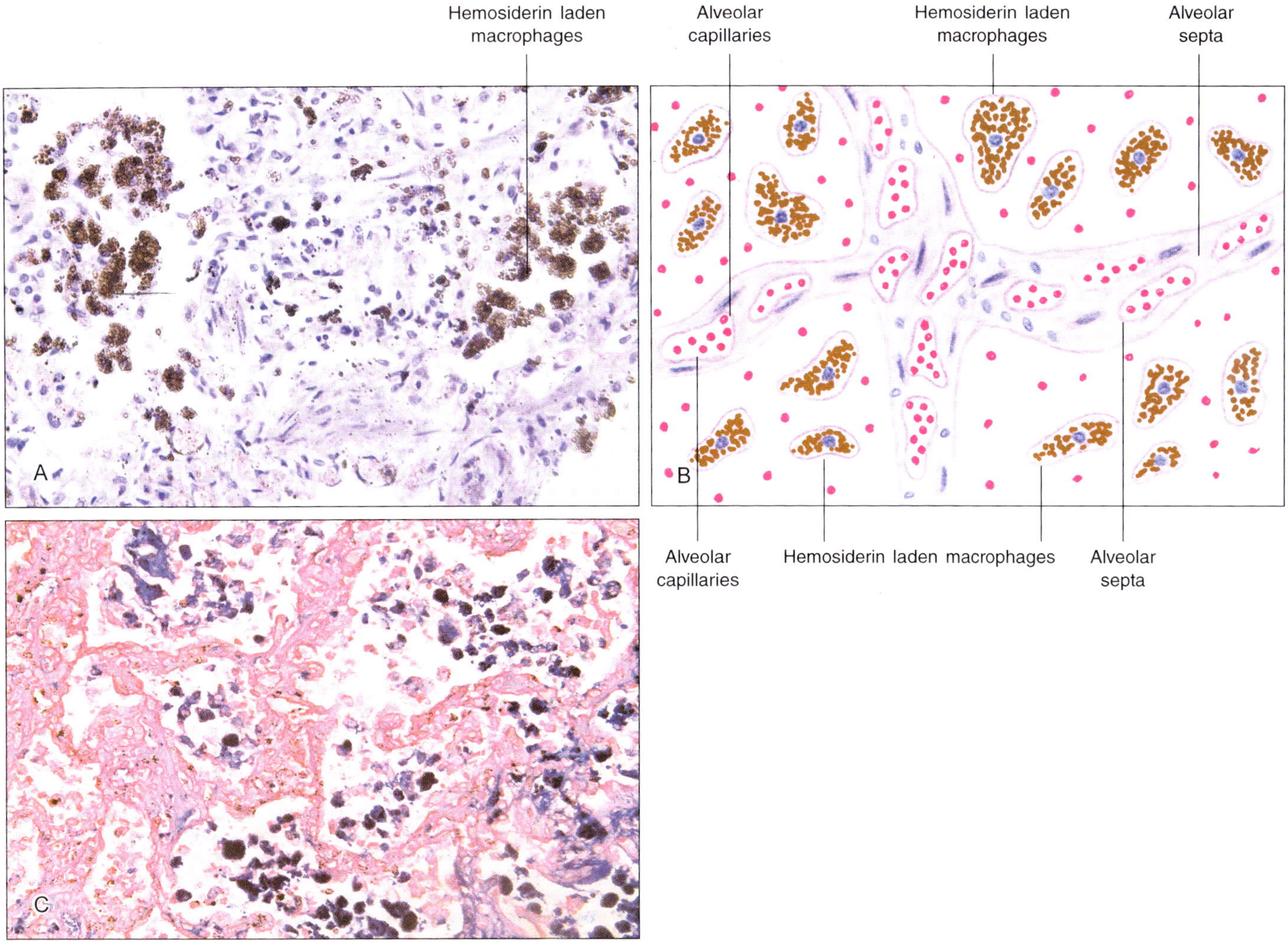

Fig. 3.4: A. and B. Haemosiderin (brown pigment) laden macrophages in lung alveoli in a case of chronic venous congestion lung. C. Brown pigment of macrophages is stained dark blue with Perls stain.

EXTRACELLULAR ACCUMULATIONS

Pathological calcification

Abnormal deposition of calcium salts may occur in two forms:

(a) ***Metastatic calcification***, where it deposits in living tissue (especially kidney, gastric mucosa and lung) due to hypercalcaemia.

(b) ***Dystrophic calcification***, which is much commoner and occurs in dead or damaged tissue, with normal serum calcium levels (Fig. 3.5).

Common sites are: atherosclerotic plaque, damaged heart valves, sites of necrosis, especially caseous and fat necrosis and media of muscular arteries in the elderly (e.g. myometrial vessels in postmenopausal women) (Fig. 3.6).

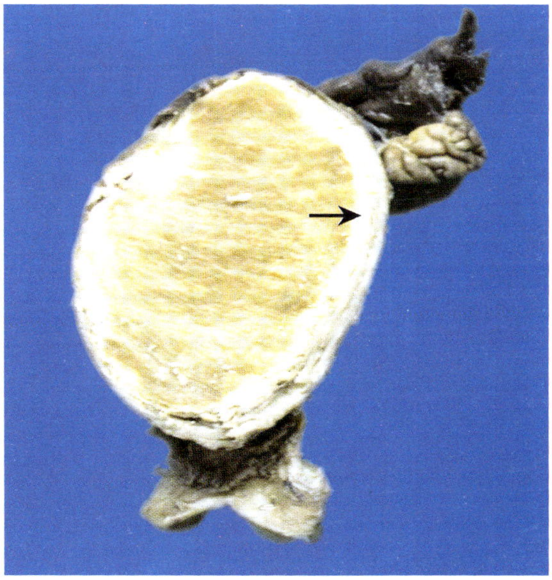

Fig. 3.5: Dystrophic calcification seen as chalky white rim (→) around a degenerated leiomyoma of uterus.

Medial calcification, uterus

- Uterus is identified by the thick muscular wall and the endometrium.
- Muscular arteries present in the outer myometrium show hyalinisation (eosionophilic, acellular deposits) in the wall with deposits of calcium (Fig. 3.6).
- The calcium salts are seen as densely basophilic granular material, which stains black with Von Kossa stain (Fig. 3.6).

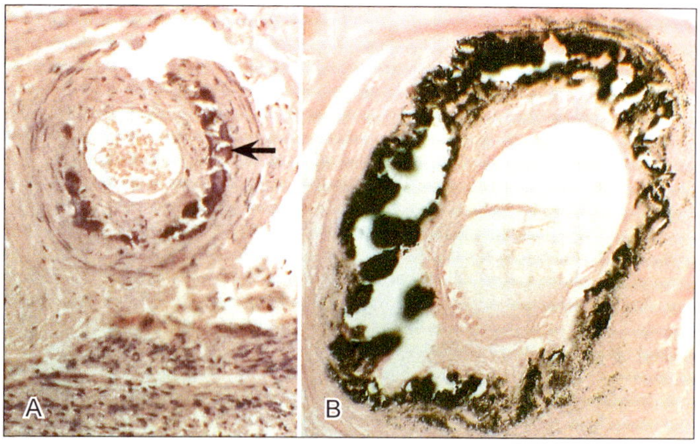

Fig. 3.6: A. Medial calcification in myometrial vessels (←). **B.** Von Kossa stain for the calcification shows that calcium is stained black.

Amyloidosis

Deposit of homogenous eosinophilic material in the interstitium, with specific physico-chemical and electron microscopic features. It may have a genetic, immunological or chronic reactive basis. Common sites of involvement are kidney, liver, spleen and blood vesels.

Amyloidosis Kidney

Grossly, the kidney is large and pale having a smooth surface (Fig. 3.7). On cutting, the kidney feels wax like.

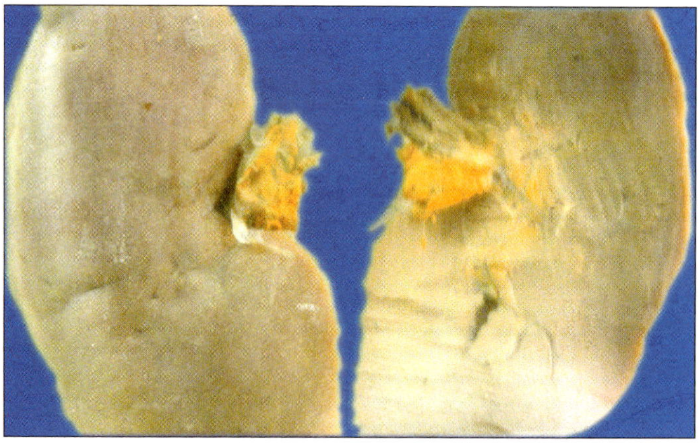

Fig. 3.7: Large pale kidney – External surface on left (smooth & pale) & cut surface on right (corticomedullary distinction lost).

Microscopically

- Kidney is identified by the presence of glomeruli and tubules.
- Homogenous eosinophilic material is seen in the mesangium and along basement membrane of glomerular tuft (Fig. 3.8 A and B).
- If extensive, the whole tuft may be converted into an acellular mass of amyloid (Fig. 3.8 C).
- Deposition also occurs along the basement membrane of blood vessels and tubules and in the interstitium.

The amyloid nature of the deposit can be confirmed by:

- *Methyl violet stain* – Magenta pink staining (Fig. 3.9) due to metachromasia.
- *Congo Red stain* – Pink staining, and green *birefringence* on polarised microscopy.
- *Electron microscopy* – Characteristic fibrils.

Amyloid tumour larynx. There is deposition of amyloid in the subepithelial tissue forming a nodule. Amyloid is positive with methyl violet stain (Fig. 3.9).

NECROSIS

Necrosis is defined as the morphological changes following and indicative of cell death in a living body. When cells die in a living body, certain substances (especially enzymes) released from the dead cells, as well as from the inflammatory reaction of the surrounding living tissue, contribute to these changes. In autolysis (i.e. in death of the organism or the decay of an organ removed from the body), the reactive inflammatory component is absent.

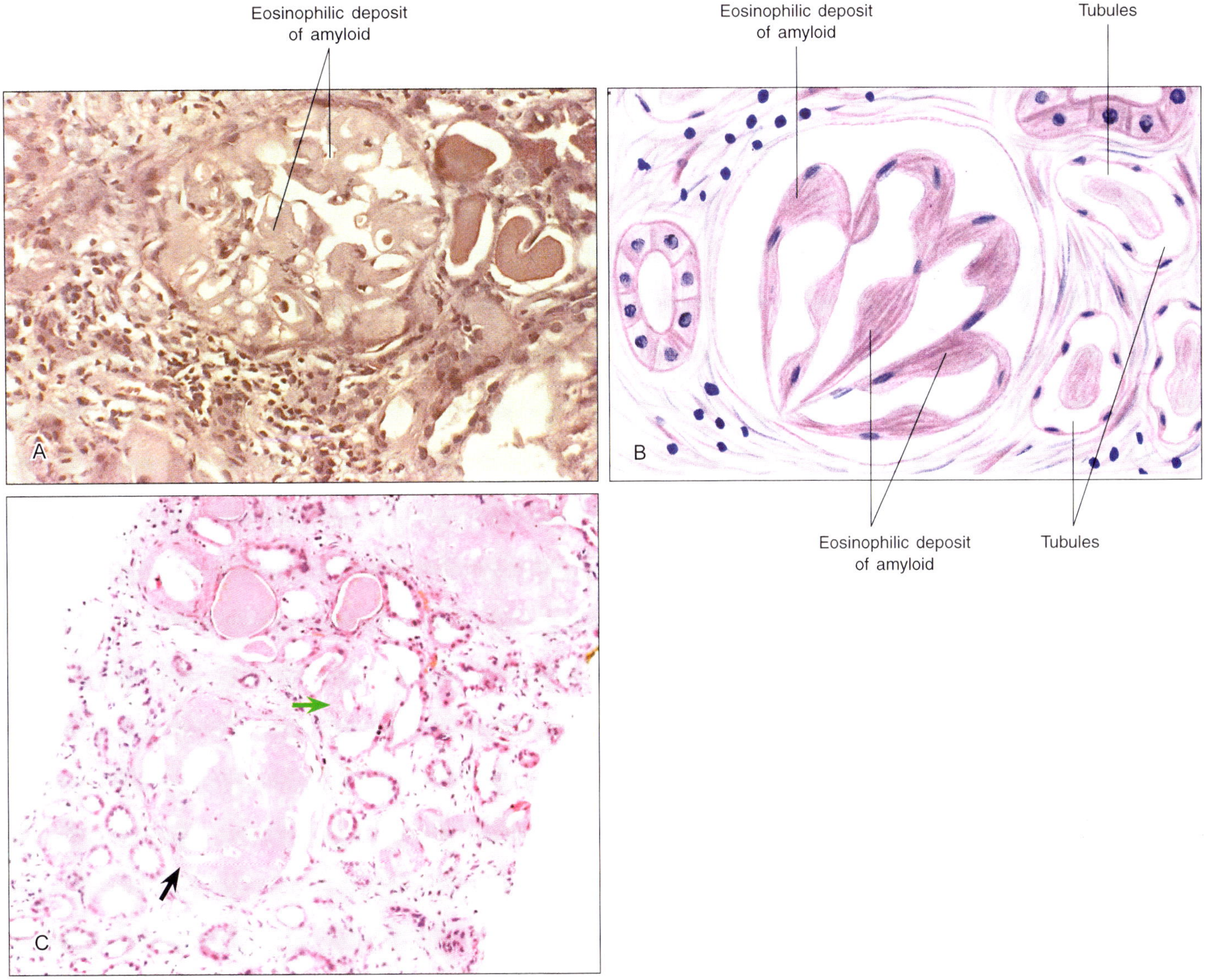

Fig. 3.8: A. and B. Eosinophilic deposits of amyloid in glomerular tuft. C. Glomeruli are hyalinised (↑) and arteriolar wall is thickened and hyalinised due to amyloid deposition (↑).

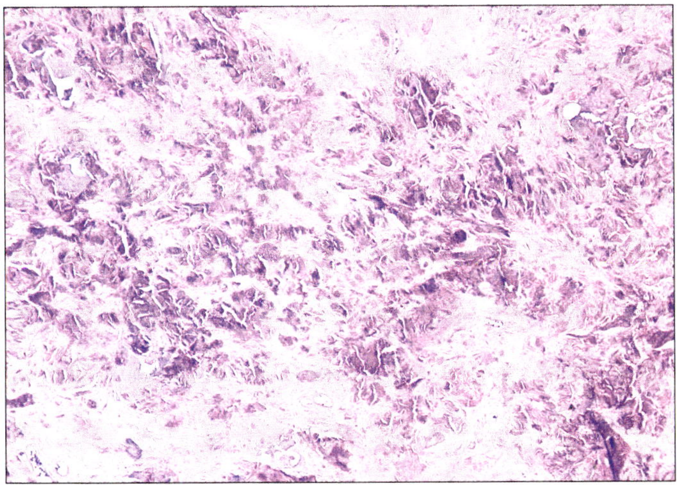

Fig. 3.9: Methyl violet stain shows amyloid deposit pink coloured in a case of amyloid tumour larynx.

Morphological Types of Necrosis:

(i) **Coagulative necrosis:**

- Seen in infarcts (death due to sudden, total occlusion of blood supply).
- Common in kidney, heart and spleen, though it can occur in any organ. It is seen as a triangular (wedge shaped) area surrounded by a hyperemic zone (Fig. 3.10).

Microscopy - Renal infarct

- Infarcted area shows maintained tissue architecture (i.e. in renal infarct, glomerular and tubular outlines are recognised) with loss of cellular details (Fig. 3.11).
- The cytoplasm is eosinophilic, granular and featureless.
- Nuclei show pyknosis (condensed, intensely basophilic and dot like), karyorrhexis (fragmentation into tiny bits) and karyolysis (total dissolution and disappearance).
- Surrounding tissue shows inflammatory reaction.

(ii) **Liquefactive necrosis:**

- Seen in necrosis due to bacterial infections (e.g. abscess).
- There is intense neutrophilic infiltration.
- The large amounts of lytic enzymes released from dead and dying polymorphs lyse the bacteria as well as the dead tissue into liquid pus.
- This is seen as granular and fibrinous material with cellular and nuclear debris.

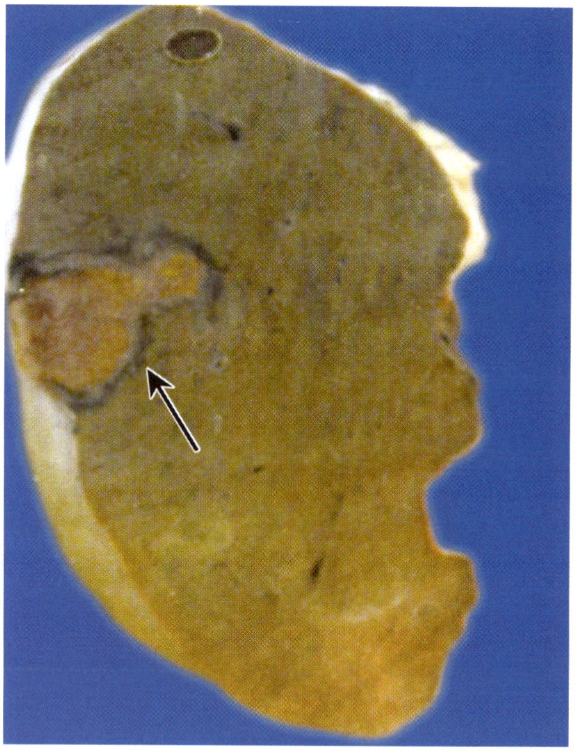

Fig. 3.10: A wedge shaped splenic infarct surrounded by a zone of hyperemia. Infarcted area, on microscopy demonstrates coagulative necrosis.

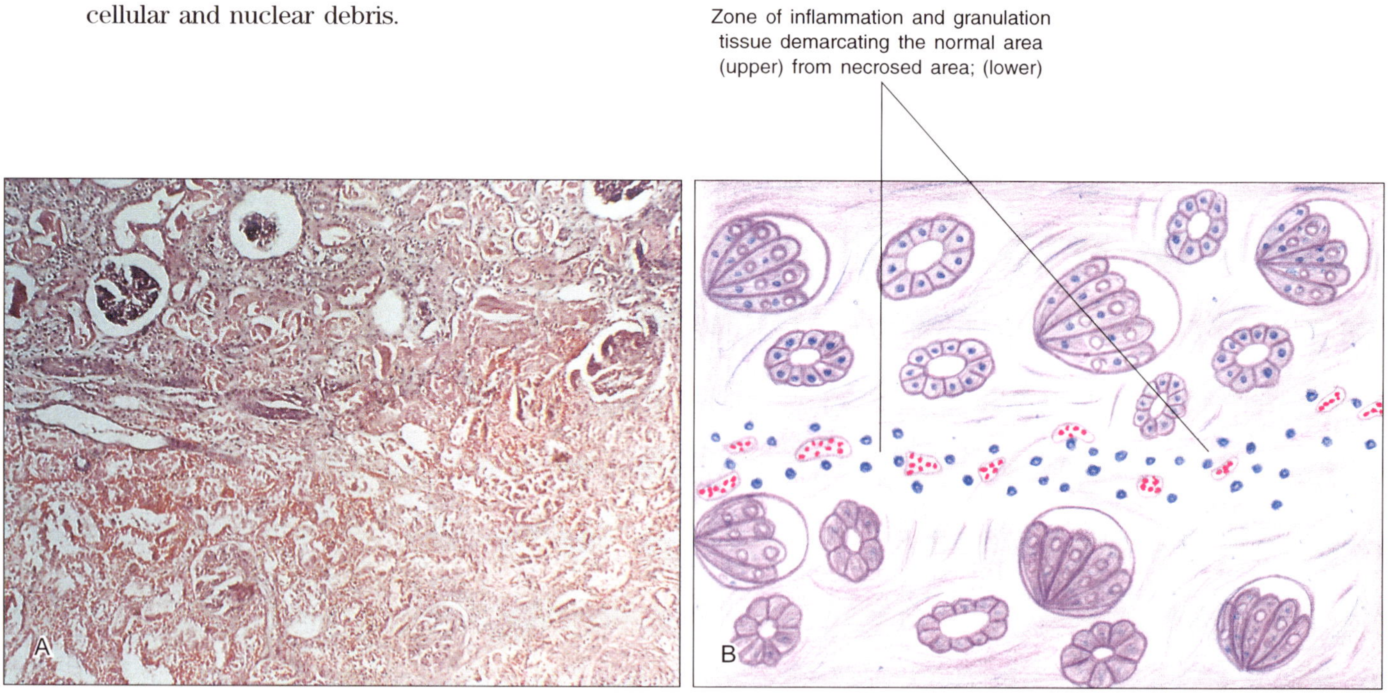

Fig. 3.11: A. and B. Renal infarct showing coagulative necrosis in lower part of figure. Architecture of the tissue is maintained but nuclei are not seen in the necrosed (lower) tissue. Ghost outline of the tissue is made out. Zone of inflammation demarcates viable from necrosed tissue (lower).

- No tissue details can be made out (Fig. 3.12).
- This may be surrounded by granulation tissue (Fig. 3.12).

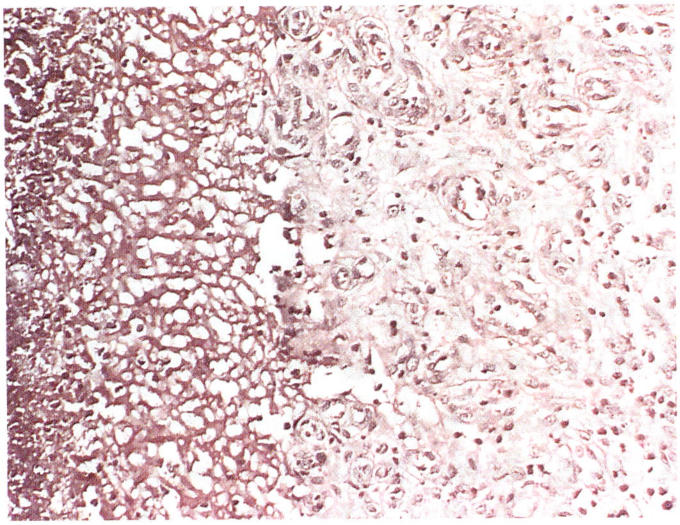

Fig. 3.12: Fibrin and suppurative necrosis (left of figure) in wall of chronic abscess. Granulation tissue is seen on the right.

(iii) **Caseous necrosis:**

- Characteristic of tuberculosis
- Seen as granular eosinophilic material without any architectural details or nuclear debris (Fig. 3.13).
- Surrounding tissue shows granulomatous reaction. Consisting of epithelioid cell granulomas with Langhan type of giant cells (Fig. 3.13).
- Acid fast bacilli are demonstrable on Ziehl Nielson stain (Fig. 3.14).

(iv) **Fat necrosis:**

- Can be seen in adipose tissue following injury and subsequent inflammation but is classically seen in omentum in patients of acute pancreatitis.

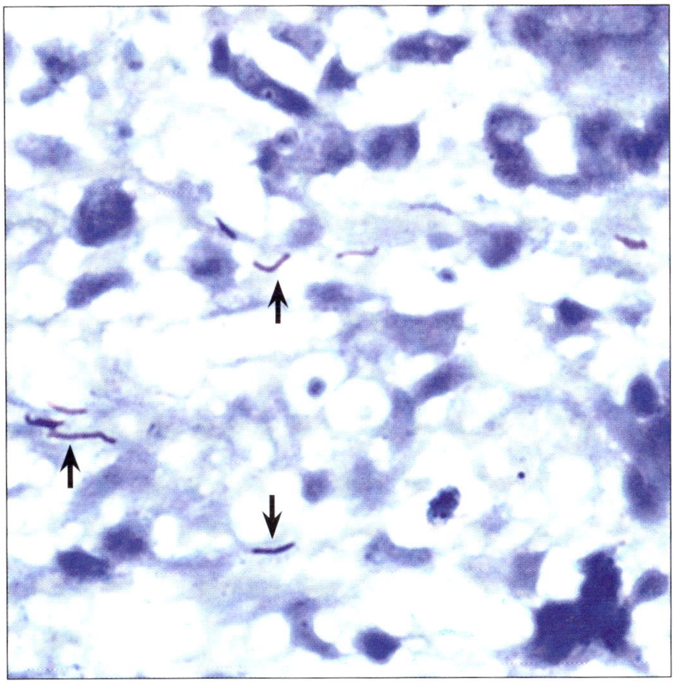

Fig. 3.14: Ziehl Neelsen stain (AFB stain) demonstrates thin pink coloured bacilli (↑) (Mycobacterium tuberculosis) in a blue background.

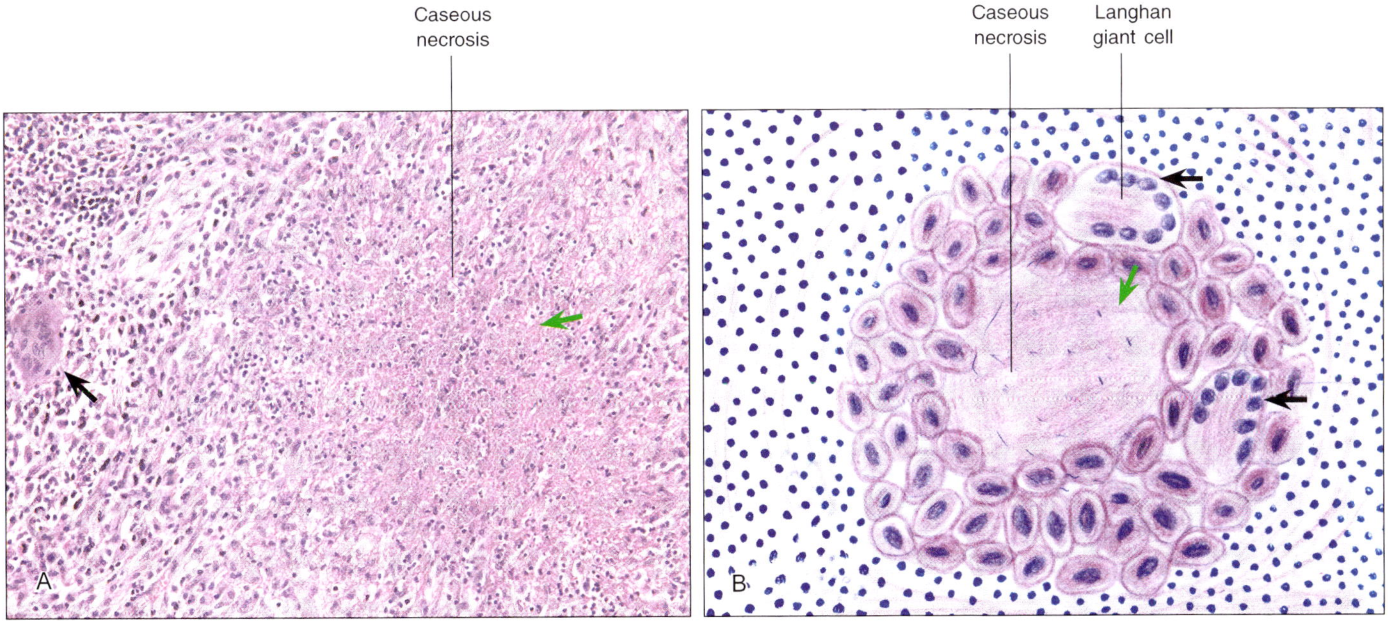

Fig. 3.13: A. and B. Tubercular granuloma with caseation in the central part of granuloma (↑). Langhan type of giant cells are seen (↑).

- The pancreatic enzymes released by the damaged acini break up the inert neutral fats into reactive fatty acids, which:
  (a) elicit inflammation,
  (b) are less soluble in the lipid solvents used in tissue processing and hence seen as shadowy fat cells, and
  (c) saponify, binding with calcium which can be visible grossly (chalky white) as well as microscopically (basophilic deposits) (Fig. 3.15).

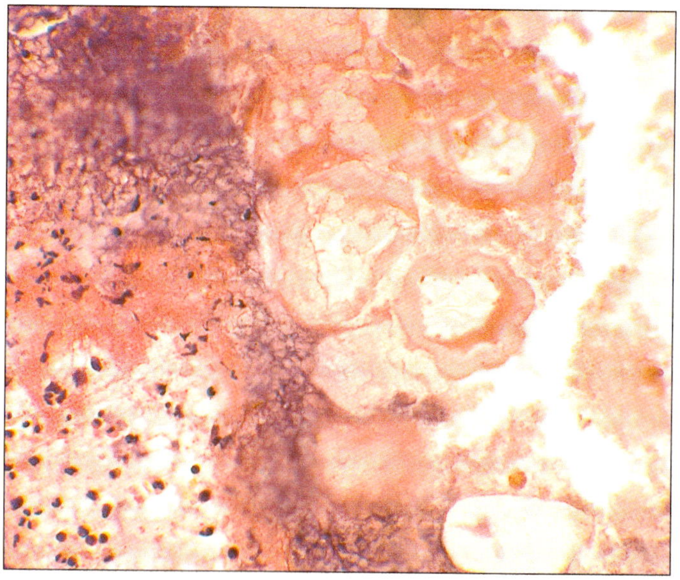

Fig. 3.15: Fat necrosis showing shadowy fat cells and surrounding inflammation.

VIVA-VOCE

Q. What are fat stains?
Ans. Fat stains demonstrate intracellular fat. Fat stains are carried out following section cutting in a freezing microtome (frozen section) using Sudan III, Sudan IV, Sudan black B, Oil red O and Osmic acid stains.

Q. Special stain for various pigments?
Ans. Melanin-Fontana stain – Black colour
Lipofuscin-Ziehl-Neelsen stain – Pink
Hemosiderin (Iron)-Perl's stain – Dark blue
Formalin pigment – Bleached by alcoholic picric acid.

Q. What are the special stains for calcium?
Ans. Von Kossa stain (Black colour of calcium) and Alizarin red (Red colour of calcium).

Q. What are the special stains for amyloid?
Ans. The various special stains for amyloid are: Methyl violet (metachromatic stain) - rose pink colour of amyloid, crystal violet (metachromatic stain) - pink colour of amyloid, Congo red with polorising microscopy - apple green birefrengence.

Q. What are the diseases in which epithelioid cell granulomas are seen?
Ans. These are tuberculosis, tuberculoid leprosy and sarcoidosis.

Q. What is the best stain to demonstrate lepra bacilli?
Ans. Lepra bacilli are best stained with Fite-Faraco stain.

Q. What are the causes of fatty change liver?
Ans. Fatty change liver occurs due to protein deprivation, alcohol intake, chloroform poisoning, phosphorus poisoning, eclampsia, CVC liver and hepatitis C.

Q. What are the various types of amyloid?
Ans. The various types of amyloid are AA, AL, AA - secondary amyloidosis, AL - primary amyloidosis, multiple myeloma, transthyretin (TTR) - familial amyloidosis and β_2 microglobulin - dialysis associated amyloidosis.

Q. What diseases predispose to secondary amyloidosis?
Ans. Diseases resulting in necrosis and tissue breakdown like tuberculosis, chronic ulcerative colitis, Crohn's disease, bronchiectasis and lung abscess.

Q. What are the types of Pathological Calcification?
Ans. The types are:
(a) Dystrophic calcification occuring in dead/damage tissues and
(b) Metastatic calcification in living tissues due to hypercalcaemia.

Q. What is the difference between coagulative and liquifactive necrosis.
Ans. In coagulative necrosis, tissue architecture is maintained though cellular details are lost. In liquifecative necrosis no tissue architecture can be identified and it is replaced by pus.

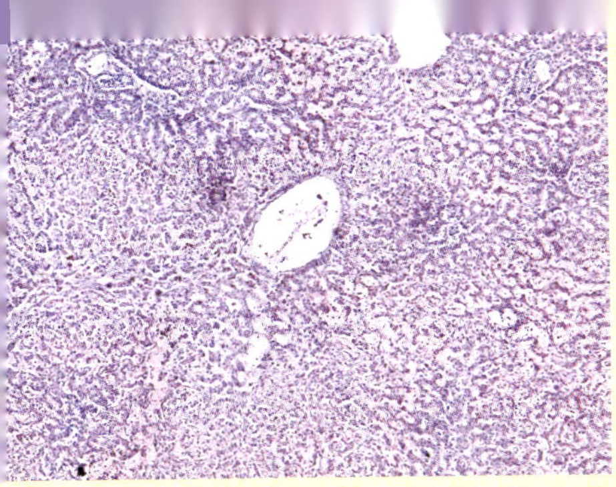

4

Fluid and Hemodynamic Derangements

EDEMA

Edema is defined as accumulation of excess fluid in the interstitial tissues. It may be:

- protein rich *exudate* if inflammatory in origin (due to increased permeability), or
- protein poor *transudate* if due to circulatory, hemodynamic or osmotic factors.

Pulmonary edema

- Occurs with increased hydrostatic pressure in pulmonary circulation as in venous congestion due to left sided heart failure resulting in transudate (Fig. 4.1).
- It can also occur in shock and in diffuse alveolar damage and pulmonary hyper-sensitivity reactions, in which conditions the fluid is an exudate.
- Fluid accumulates in the alveolar septae, which along with the congested vessels causes septal widening.
- The fluid then escapes into alveolar lumina, seen as acellular eosinophilic coagulated material.
- Inflammatory reaction is absent.

Cerebral edema

- Seen in encephalitis, meningitis and near focal lesions like abscess, tumour etc.
- Fluid collects around the cells and in perivascular Virchow-Robin spaces resulting in a clear wide space around the cells and vessels (Fig. 4.2).
- The fibrillar matrix is also loose due to fluid in the interfibrillar spaces.

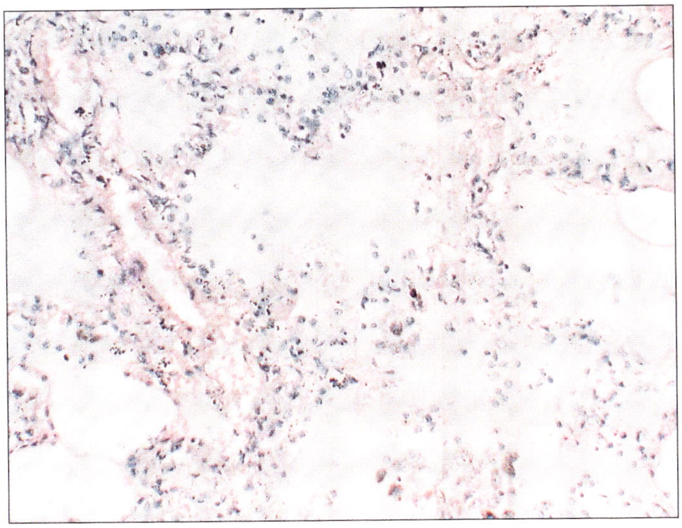

Fig. 4.1 Pulmonary edema – Alveoli filled with fluid without inflammatory cells (transudate).

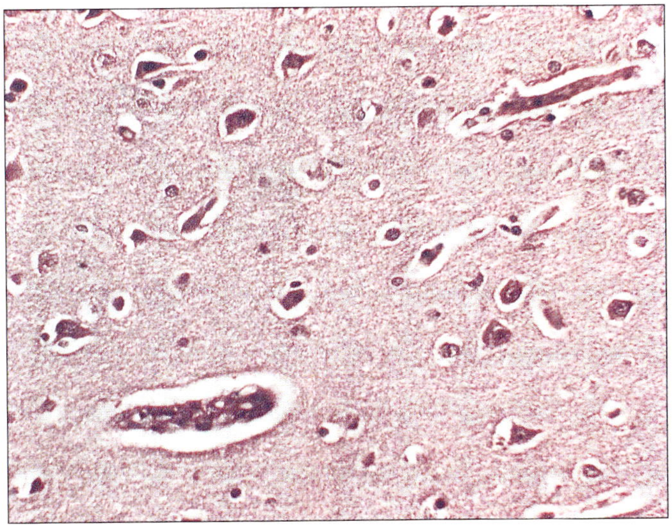

Fig. 4.2: Cerebral edema seen as clear space around vessels and cells.

CONGESTION

Passive venous congestion (Chronic venous congestion – CVC) occurs due to prolonged impairment of venous drainage. Edema is always associated.

CVC liver (nutmeg liver):

Grossly, the liver surface (on cut section) shows alternating dark and light areas - "nutmeg" appearance. The congested areas correspond to dark zones and fatty and normal tissue provide the light zones (Fig. 4.3).

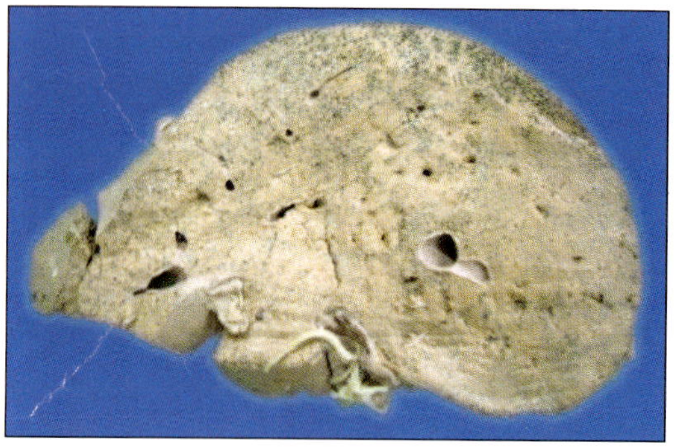

Fig. 4.3: Cut section of nutmeg liver showing dark & pale mottling.

Microscopically

- Liver shows normal architecture.
- Each lobule shows zonal alterations.
- The central veins and the surrounding sinusoids are dilated and congested (Fig. 4.4).

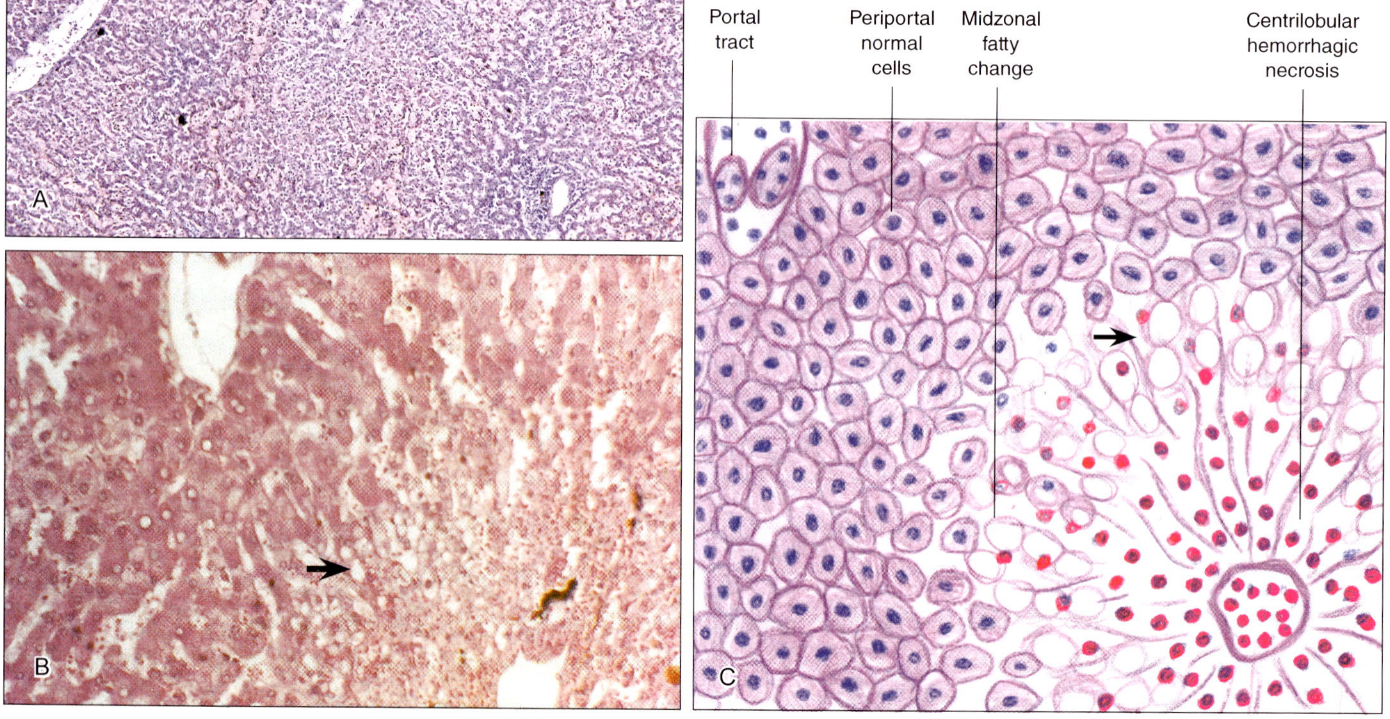

Fig. 4.4: A. CVC liver showing centrilobular congestion with normal periportal liver cells. B. and C. CVC liver showing the 3 zones. Central vein is at lower right with centrilobular congestion. Arrow (↑) demonstates the fatty change in hepatocytes. Periportal liver cells are normal.

- If severe, microhaemorrhages and pressure atrophy or necrosis of centrilobular hepatocytes may be associated.
- The midzonal hepatocytes (with sublethal hypoxia) show fatty change (Fig. 4.4 B and C).
- Periportal zone shows normal hepatocytes (Fig. 4.4).
- These alternating congested, fatty and normal zones causes the characteristic "nutmeg" appearance grossly on cut surface.

CVC spleen (Banti's spleen):

- Grossly the spleen is markedly enlarged (Fig. 4.5) due to marked expansion of the red pulp, widely separating the lymphoid follicles of the white pulp.

Microscopically

- The sinusoids are dilated and congested, with fibrosis of the septae.
- Perivascular haemorrhages result in organisation with hemosiderin laden macrophages and fibrosis (siderotic nodule, Gamna Gandi Bodies) (Fig. 4.6).
- Giant cell reaction and calcification may also occur (Fig. 4.6).

CVC lung (brown induration)

- Shows edema in the alveoli.
- In addition, there is congestion of septal vessels, microhaemorrhages, hemosiderin laden alveolar macrophages (heart failure cells) and septal fibrosis (Fig. 4.7 and 3.4).

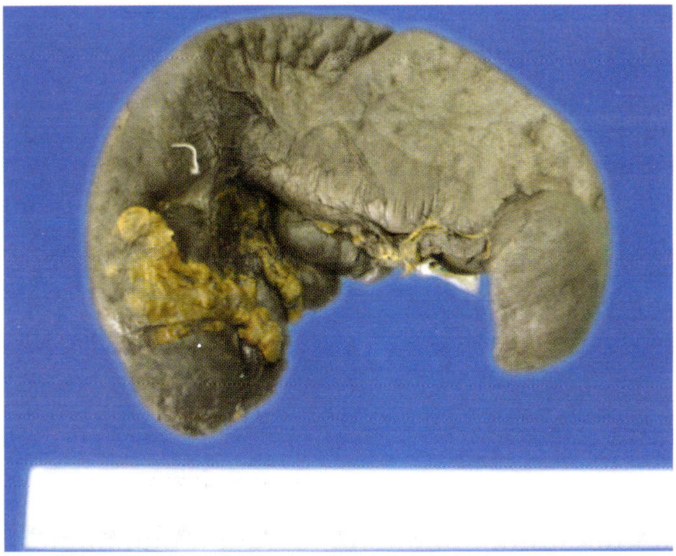

Fig. 4.5: Markedly enlarged spleen due to chronic venous congestion.

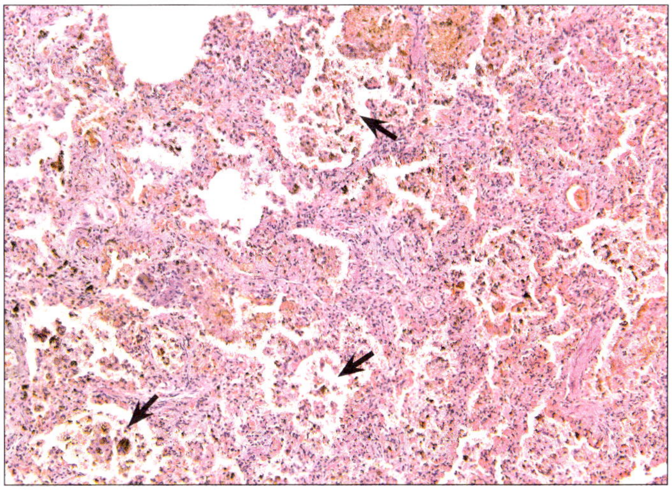

Fig. 4.7: CVC lung – edematous septae with congested capillaries and alveoli with hemosiderin laden macrophages (↑) (heart failure cells).

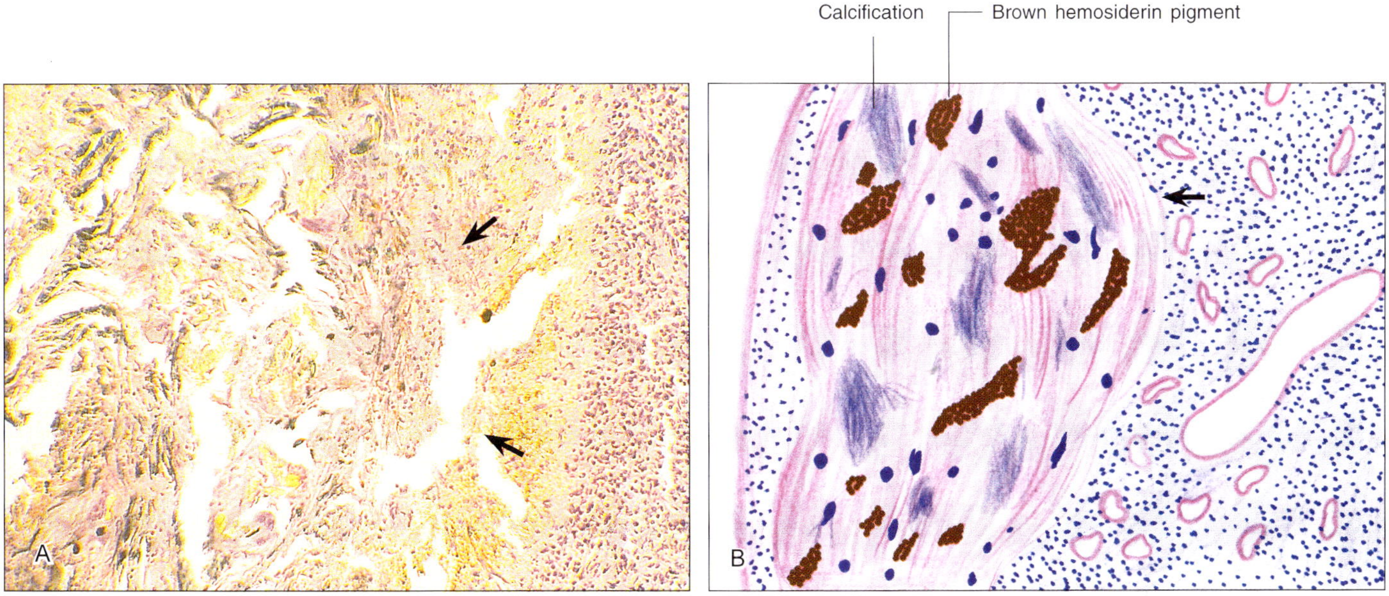

Fig. 4.6: A. and B. Banti's spleen – Siderotic nodule (Gamna Gandi body) (↑) with calcification is seen.

- The congestion and edema of CVC is to be differentiated from pneumonia (inflammation in alveoli) by the absence of inflammatory cells.
- However, CVC lung is a favourable soil for bronchopneumonia to set in.

THROMBOSIS

Thrombosis is defined as an intravascular mass of blood constituents, formed in intact circulation.

Recent thrombus

- Formed of clumped platelets, fibrin strands and entangled RBC.
- It is attached to the vessel wall at the point of initiation of thrombogenesis (Fig. 4.8).
- It may or may not occlude the entire lumen.

Organised canalised thrombus

- Organisation occurs with the entry of phagocytic cells and granulation tissue from the vessel wall into the thrombus (Fig. 4.9).
- The resultant scar tissue and its shrinkage as well as inter-communication of the newly formed vessels may result in recanalisation (also contributed to by associated fibrinolysis).

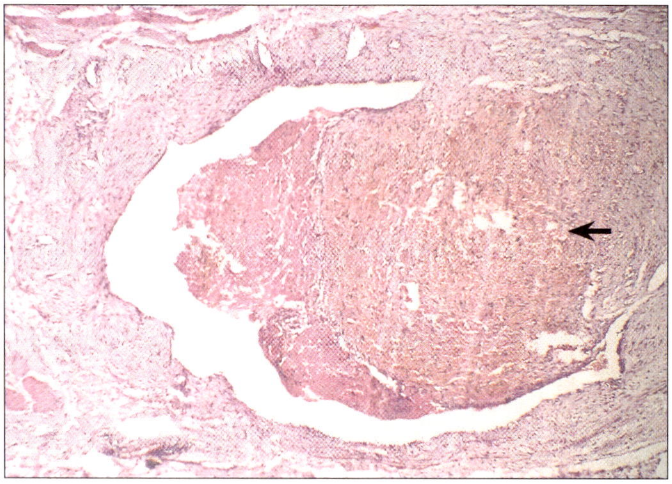

Fig. 4.8: Recent thrombus (non-occlusive) – fibrin & blood components (↑) adherent to vascular wall at site of origin.

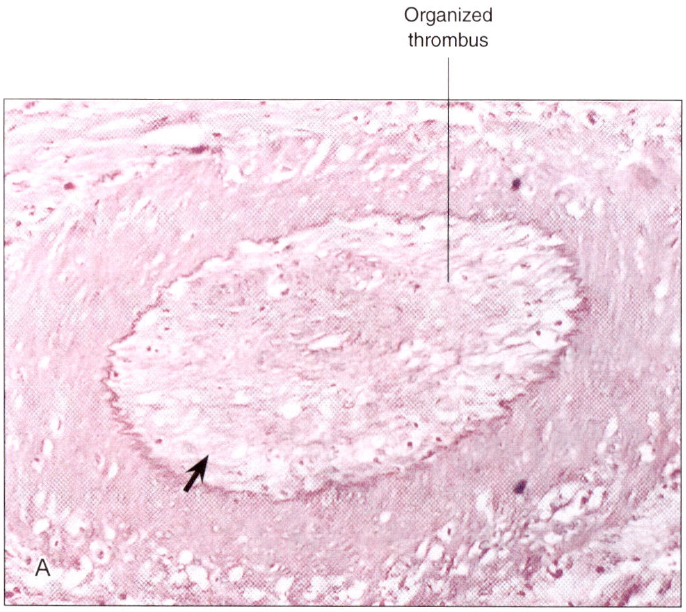

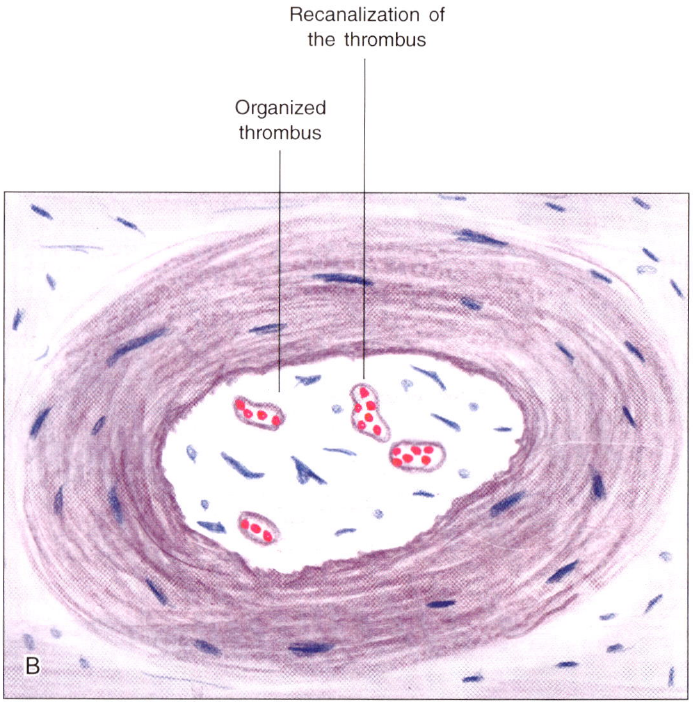

Fig. 4.9: A. and B. Organised canalised thrombus (occlusive) in an artery (↑)

INFARCTION

An infarct is defined as an area of ischaemic necrosis. This could be due to occlusion of its arterial supply (as is common in heart, kidney and spleen) or its venous drainage (torsion of bowel loop, testis, ovary). It may be:

- Pale if due to obstruction of end artery, in the absence of dual or collateral supply and in dense solid organs (e.g. spleen, kidney, heart) (Fig. 4.10).
- Red (haemorrhagic) if due to venous obstruction or in loose organs (e.g. intestines), or if there is dual blood supply (e.g. lungs).

Infarct kidney

- Usually a wedge shaped, subcortical pale infarct (Fig. 4.10).
- The infarcted area shows coagulative necrosis (maintained architecture with loss of cellular and nuclear details) (Fig. 4.11).
- At the junction of the infarct and normal tissue is the reactive zone of congestion, haemorrhage and inflammation (↑) (Fig. 4.11).
- With time, organisation by granulation tissue occurs, resulting in a scar.

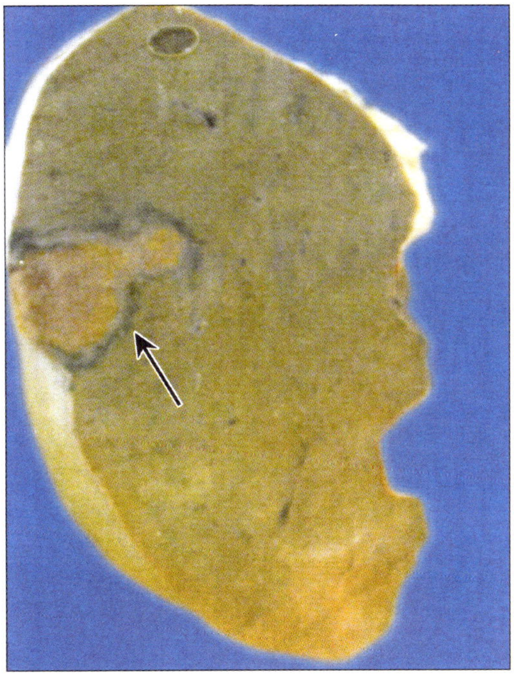

Fig. 4.10: Splenic infarct – subcapsular wedge shaped pale area ↖ surrounded by zone of hyperemia.

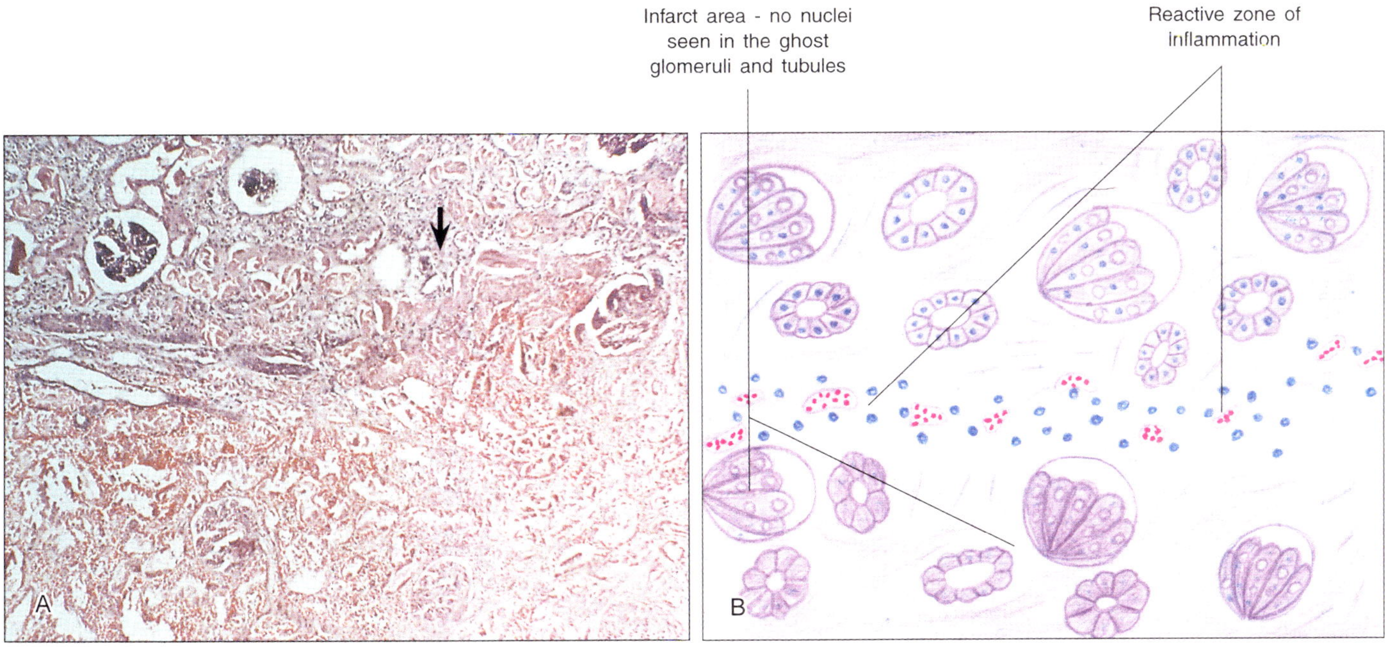

Fig. 4.11: A. and B. Infarct kidney. Infarct at bottom of figure and normal kidney at the top with reactive zone in the middle (↑).

VIVA-VOCE

Q. How will you differentiate between transudate and exudate?

Ans.

	Transudate	Exudate
• Specific gravity	< 1.012	> 1.016
• Protein content	< 2.5 g%	> 2.5 g%
• Associated with inflammation	No	Yes
• Inflammatory cells are present	No	Yes

Q. What are the causes of nutmeg liver (CVC liver)?

Ans. The various causes are congestive heart failure, obstruction to inferior vena cava and hepatic vein thrombosis.

Q. What is a Gamna Gandi body?

Ans. Gamna Gandi body is an organising hemorrhage, forming a nodule with dystrophic calcification and hemosiderin pigment in spleen.

Q. Why is CVC lung also called brown induration.

Ans. In CVC lung, there are “heart failure cells” – macrophages with brown hemosiderin pigment, turning the lung into brown coloured lung. Associated fibrosis results in firmness and induration.

Q. In an infarct in spleen, heart or kidney, why is the infarct wedge shaped?

Ans. Sudden blockage of a small artery by thrombosis/embolus results in coagulative necrosis of the wedge shaped/ triangular area supplied by the capillaries of the artery.

Q. In an infarct what is the demarcation between the infarct and normal tissue?

Ans. The reactive zone (seen as dark band) between the viable and infarcted zones is because of dilated vessels and inflammation.

Q. What is the fate of an infarct in a solid organ like heart/spleen or kidney?

Ans. The triangular infarcted areas gets replaced by granulation tissue which eventually becomes a fibrotic scar.

Q. In which organs is the haemorrhagic infarct seen?

Ans. Haemorrhagic infarct is seen in organs with double blood supply like lung. In small intestine, obstruction to venous drainage (torsion of bowel loop), results in haemorrhagic infarct (gangrene).

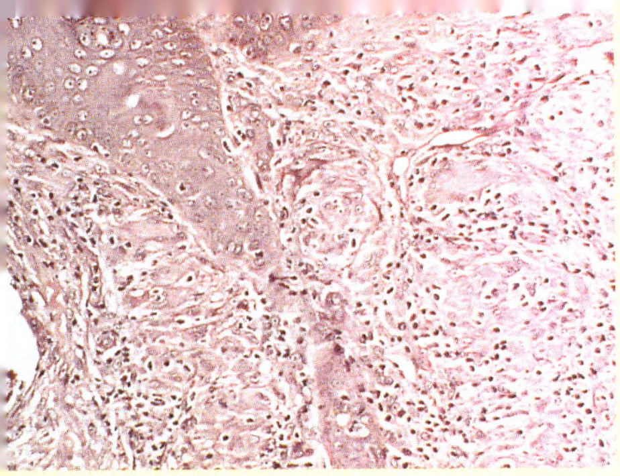

5

Infectious Diseases

Though many organisms have preferred sites of localisation (organotropism) and cause damage in specific organ systems, some infections affect any or several tissues.

BACTERIAL DISEASES

Tuberculosis

Tuberculosis can occur in almost all tissues but most commonly involves lung, intestines and lymph nodes. It is diagnosed by the presence of the typical epithelioid cell granulomas (see Fig. 2.14) with Langhan's giant cells and caseous necrosis (see Fig. 3.13) and is confirmed by demonstration of the acid fast bacilli by Ziehl Neelson staining (Fig. 1.7).

Leprosy

Leprosy preferentially affects skin and peripheral nerves and based on the immune status of the patient, manifests as two polar (plus intermediate) forms.

(a) ***Tuberculoid leprosy.*** Skin biopsy shows noncaseating epithelioid cell granulomas in the dermis, including the superficial Grenz zone and the dermal nerve twigs (Fig. 5.1). These are surrounded by a good number of lymphocytes. Organisms are few on acid fast (Fite Faracco) staining.

(b) ***Lepromatous leprosy.*** Dermis shows collections of foamy histiocytes (Lepra cells) with few lymphocytes (Fig. 5.2A and B). Grenz zone is spared, with thinning and atrophy of the epidermis. Stain for AFB reveals numerous organisms inside lepra cells, often as stacks or globi (Fig. 5.2C).

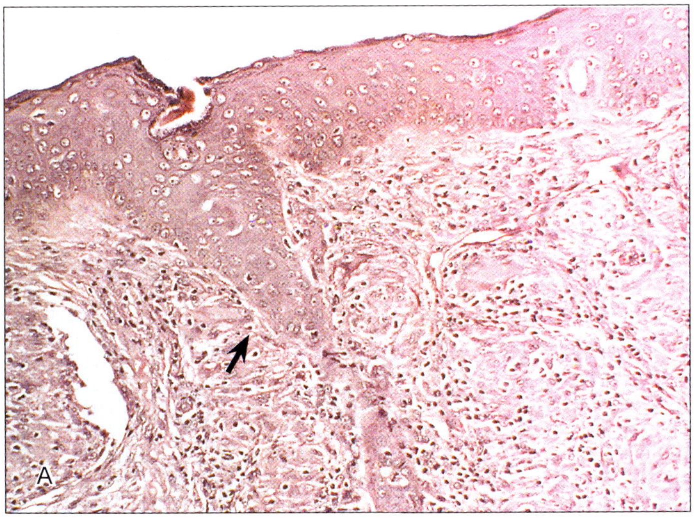

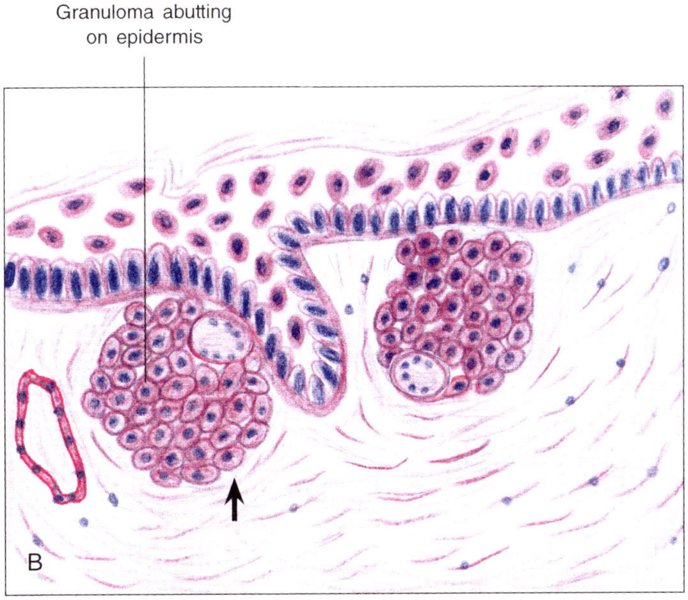

Fig. 5.1: A. and **B.** Tuberculoid leprosy with granulomas abutting on epidermis (↑).

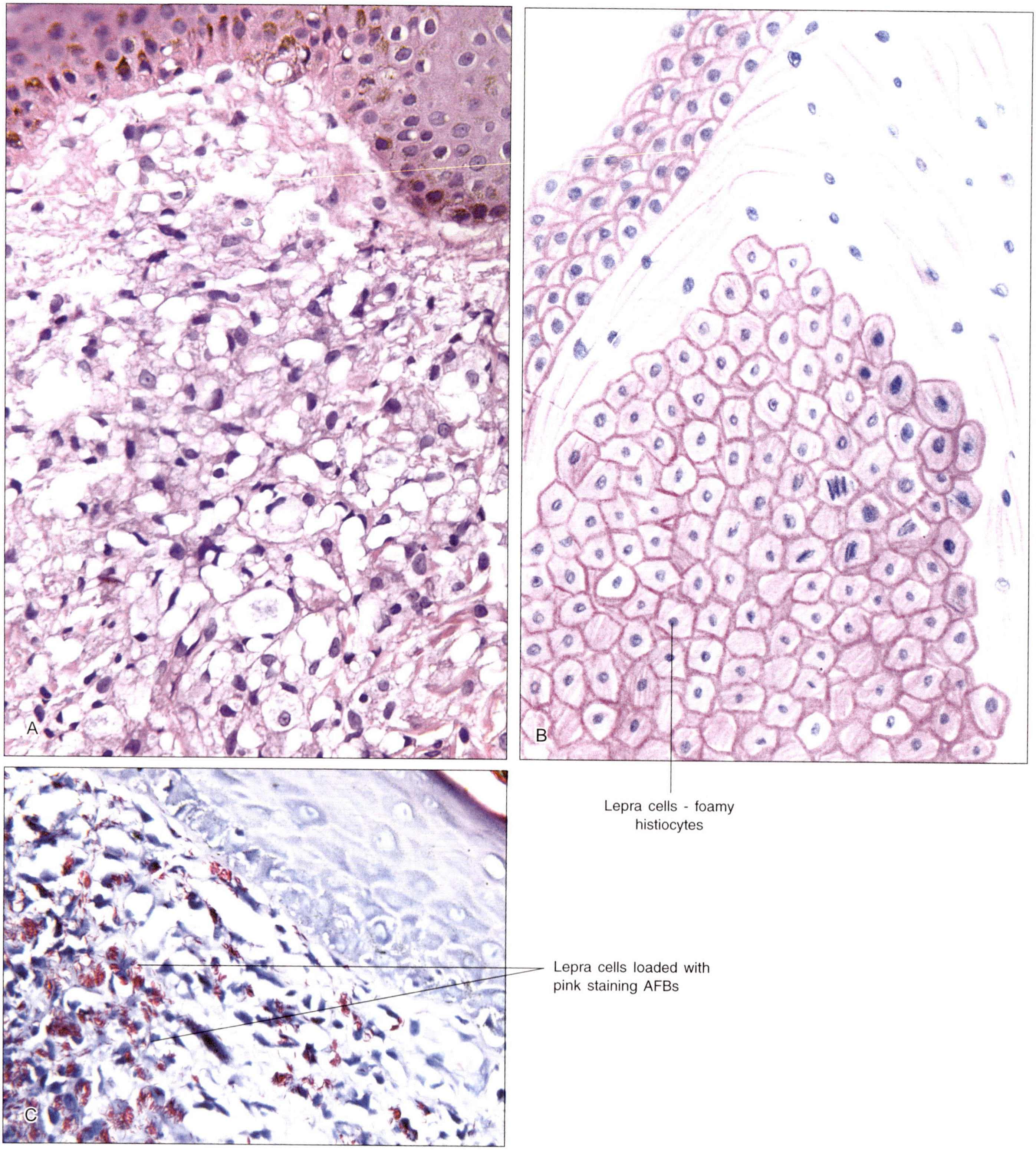

Fig. 5.2: A. and B. Lepromatous leprosy with foamy macrophage granulomas with clear Grenz zone. C. Fite stain demonstrates large number of pink staining AFBs in Lepra cells in a case of Lepromatous leprosy

Actinomycosis

Actinomycosis is caused due to gram positive aerobic bacteria with a tendency to grow in mycelial network and filaments, simulating fungi. They are normal commensals, which cause infection due to local conditions that favour them, like devitalisation, anaerobic mileu etc., and lead to formation of deep sinuses discharging yellow (sulphur) granules.

Section from infected site shows central colonies of organism with peripheral radiating filaments. The inflammatory reaction is acute, non-specific (Fig. 5.3).

FUNGAL DISEASES

Many of the fungal infections occur in debilitated or compromised hosts and may result in widespread dissemination and deep systemic involvement. The tissue reaction may range from acute inflammatory to chronic granulomatous.

Fungi are identified by their morphology on H&E and special stains (PAS, methanamine silver) (Fig. 5.4) and by culture studies.

Candida – nonbranching pseudohyphae and buds.

Mucormycosis (Rhizopus) – Broad non-septate hyphae of irregular width with wide angled branching.

Aspergillus – Septate branching hyphae with occasional conidia (fruiting bodies). If severe, colonies can form fungal balls.

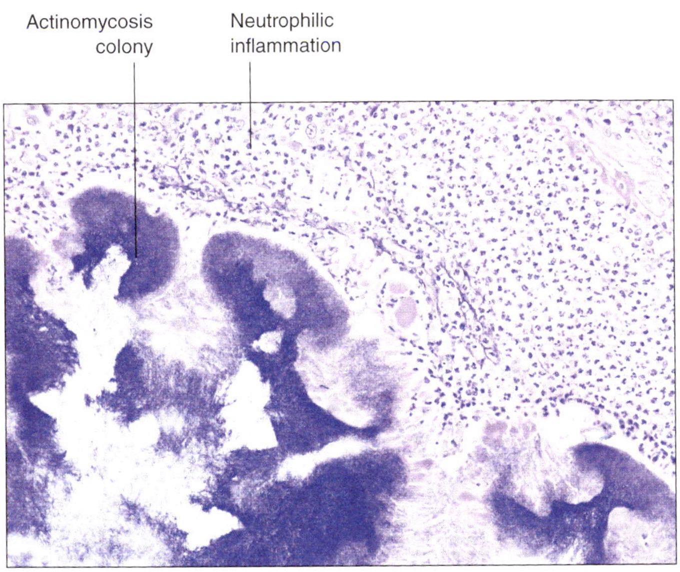

Fig. 5.3: Actinomycosis colony surrounded by acute inflammatory response of neutrophils

Cryptococcus – Round yeast forms with single budding. These have an unstained mucinous capsule which stains brightly with mucicarmine stain.

Histoplasma – Tiny yeast forms (2-4 μ) found inside histiocytes.

Chromomycosis – Pigmented budding yeasts.

Rhinosporidium – Large spherules with endosporulation (Fig. 5.5).

PARASITIC DISEASES

Common protozoal infections in man include amoebiasis, malaria (Fig. 14.1–14.4) and kala-azar (Fig. 14.6). Many helminthic infections occur in man but most of them like ascaris, enterobius etc. are intestinal (luminal) in habitat. Only a few have tissue migrating life cycles.

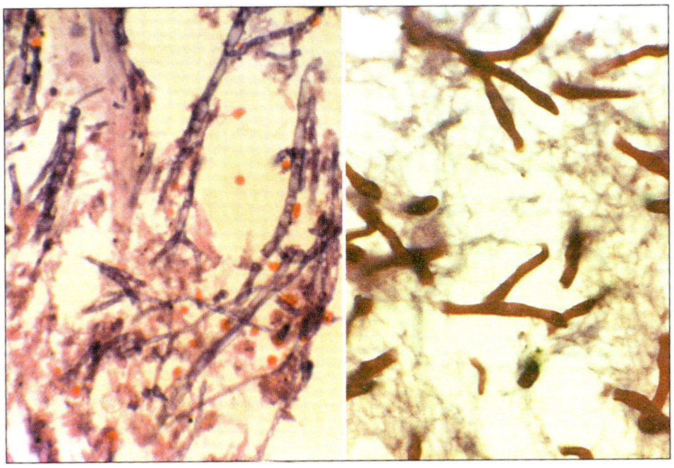

Fig. 5.4: Fungal hyphae in H&E. PAS stain on right of figure staining them magenta coloured.

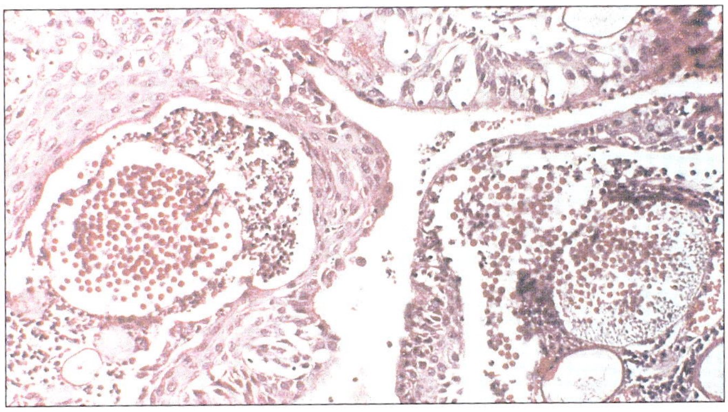

Fig. 5.5: Rhinosporidiosis – Thick walled spherules with endospores in a nasal lesion.

Filariasis

Filariasis – lymph node (see also micro-filaria, Fig. 14.5). Adult filarial worm is seen in lymphtic channels near the lymph node. It is identified by the body wall and the gravid uterus bearing the microfilariae. If dead, it may calcify or elicit an intense inflammatory reaction with eosinophilic predominance around it (Fig. 5.6). The node shows reactive hyperplasia with capsular fibrosis.

Cysticercosis

Cysticercosis occurs when man becomes intermediate host for Taenia solium. The larvae – cysticercus cellulosae – present as subcutaneous or intramuscular nodules though they may localise in any organ including brain. They are seen as pearly white, translucent cysts up to 1.5 cms in diameter with an invaginated scolex with hooklets (Fig. 5.7). When the larva dies and disintegrates, it elicits an inflammatory reaction.

Hydatid Disease

Hydatid Disease is due to larval form of Echinococcus granulosus. These occur in deep viscera, especially liver, mesentry and lung as large cysts several cms in diameter (Fig. 5.8). The pearly white opaque cyst wall shows the characteristic laminated membrane, lined on the inner surface by the germinal layer which, with time, gives rise to small brood capsules (scolices which grossly form the hydatid sand) (Fig. 5.9). It is surrounded by the host reaction of inflammation with giant cells, eosinophils and fibrosis.

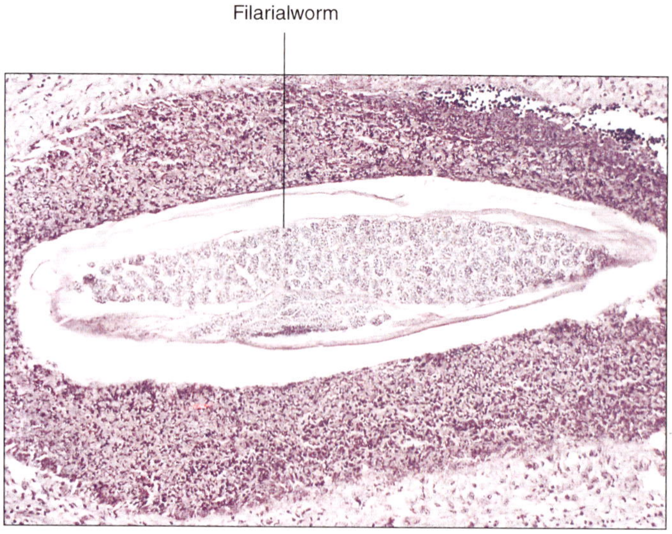

Fig. 5.6: Adult female gravid filarial worm with surrounding inflammation and fibrosis.

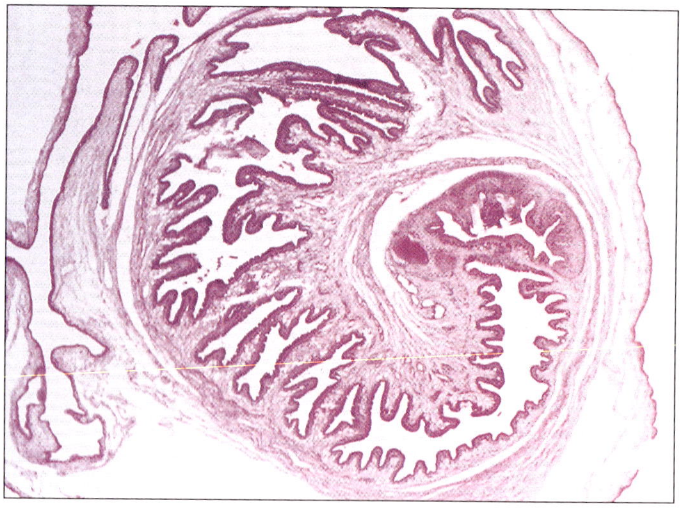

Fig. 5.7: Scolex of cysticercus cellulosae.

Fig. 5.8: Hydatid cysts in mesentry. Note the pearly white (like white of an egg) membrane lining the cysts (↑). The white membrane is lined by scolices.

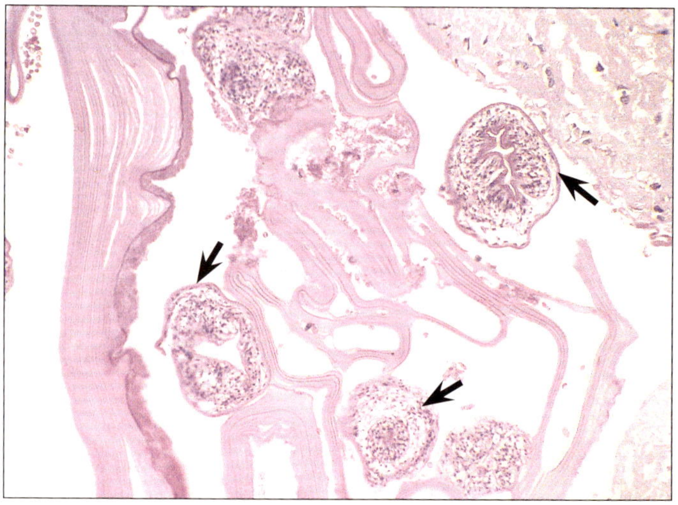

Fig. 5.9: Laminated membrane and scolices (arrows) in hydatid cyst.

VIVA-VOCE

Q. Which diseases are caused by acid fast bacilli?
Ans. Tuberculosis and leprosy

Q. Which are the tissues involved in rhinosporidiosis?
Ans. Rhinosporidiosis mainly involves the mucosal surfaces of nose, nasopharyx and conjuctiva.

Q. In which diseases, histoplasmosis occurs?
Ans. Histoplasma infection occurs in immunocompromised states like - HIV infection, corticosteroid therapy and immunosuppressive therapy.

Q. Are cysticercosis and hydatid disease common in India?
Ans. Yes, both diseases are seen in our country. Cysticercosis forms nodules under the skin, intramuscular and brain. Hydatid disease involvcs liver, lung and mesentry.

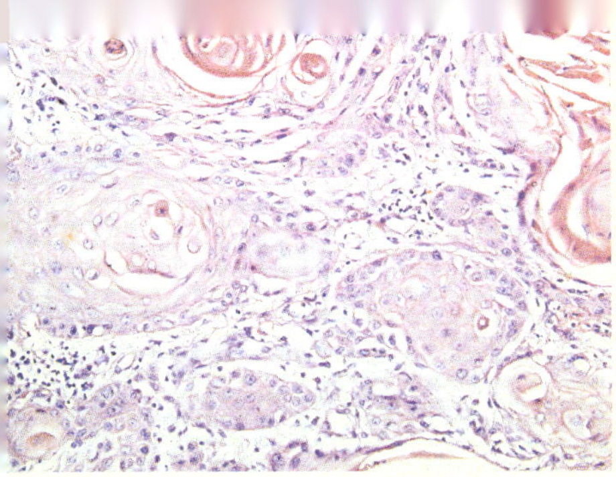

6

Growth Disorders and Neoplasia

GROWTH DISORDERS

Hyperplasia is increase in tissue mass due to increase in number of constituent cells. It is reversible and in response to a stimulus. It can be seen in skin and mucosal squamous epithelium as increase in keratin and prickle cell layers; and in glandular epithelium (GIT, endometrium) as multilayering and crowding of glands.

Hypertrophy is increase in tissue mass due to increase in size (and cytoplasmic organelles) of the constituent cells. It is seen in muscle tissue (skeletal, cardiac, myometrial etc.) which has limited proliferative capacity (Fig. 6.1). It is reversible and in response to a (physical) stimulus (e.g. pregnant uterus, work overload).

Metaplasia is replacement of one type of mature tissue by another, by altered differentiation of the primitive or basal cells. The commonest type is squamous metaplasia of columnar epithelium (tracheobronchial, endocervical) or urothelial transitional epithelium in response to inflammation and chronic irritation. Others are intestinal metaplasia of gastric mucosa, osseous metaplasia in scars etc.

Squamous metaplasia cervix

In this lesion the columnar lining of the everted endocervix gets replaced by stratified squamous epithelium (Fig. 6.2). Metaplastic zone is identified by the presence of endocervical glands under the squamous epithelium. Gland lining may also show metaplasia. Some degree of chronic inflammation is also associated.

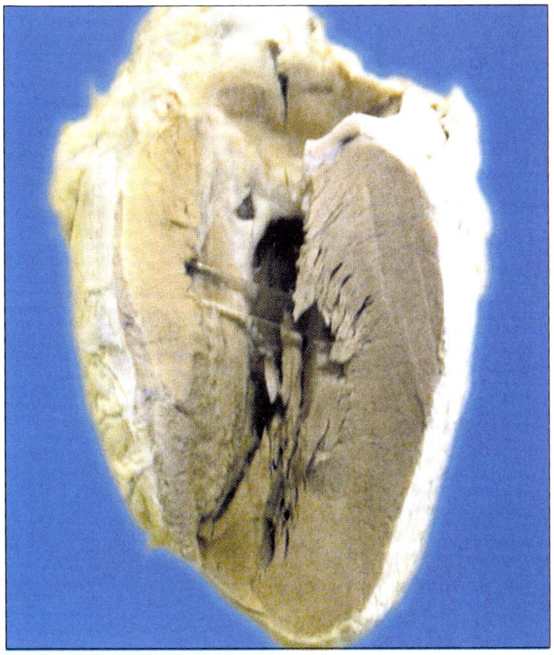

Fig. 6.1: Left ventricular hypertrophy.Ventricular wall is markedly thickened and therefore the ventricular cavity is narrowed.

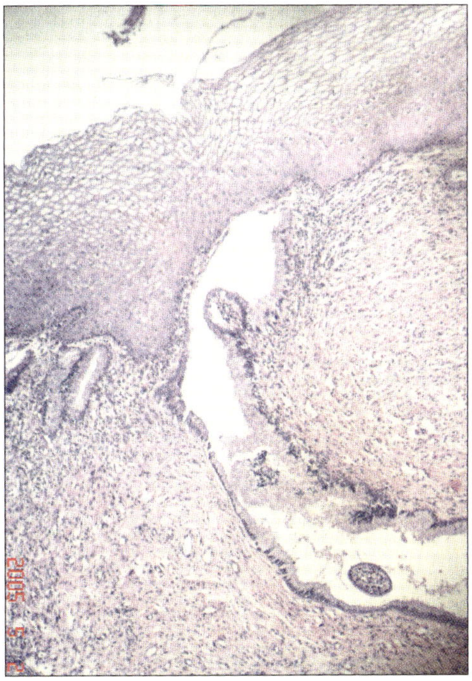

Fig. 6.2: Squamous metaplasia of endocervical lining and of gland opening.

Dysplasia

Dysplasia is abnormal maturation as seen in squamous and glandular epithelia, resulting in cytologic and nuclear alterations like loss of polarity, nuclear enlargement, hyperchromasia, persistence of mitotic activity even in maturing superficial layers of epithelium (Fig. 6.3). Common sites of dysplasia are in the metaplastic cervical and bronchial epithelia and in the regenerating colonic epithelium in ulcerative colitis. Dysplasia carries a definite premalignant potential.

Carcinoma in-situ

Carcinoma in-situ (Intraepithelial neoplasia) is the most severe form in the spectrum of dysplasia and implies the earliest (pre-invasive) stage of carcinoma. This is encountered in epithelia (bronchial, cervical) where dysplasia is documented to be premalignant. It is characterised by involvement of the full thickness of epithelium by dysplasia and by presence of abnormal mitotic figures (Fig. 6.4).

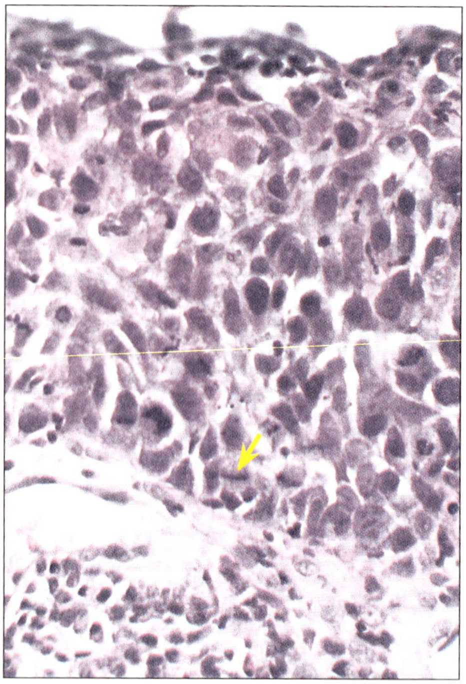

Fig. 6.4: Carcinoma in-situ – Full thickness dysplasia with severe nuclear changes and mitosis (↑)

NEOPLASIA

Neoplasia (or new growth) implies an abnormal mass of tissue whose growth exceeds and is uncoordinated with normal growth, and continues irrespective of its causative stimulus being withdrawn.

Tumours are classified:

(a) by the cell or tissue of origin, and

(b) as *benign* and *malignant*, predictive of their behaviour, as reflected by histological appearance.

On the whole, benign tumours are cytologically made up of normal looking cells (well differentiated) whereas malignant tumours show varying degrees of ***anaplasia*** (dedifferentiation) in the form of pleomorphism (variation in size and shape of cells and nuclei), hyperchromatic large nuclei, prominent nucleoli, higher nuclear– cytoplasmic ratio, tumour giant cells, abnormal mitotic figures etc. (Fig. 6.5). Another feature indicative of a malignant tumour is its spread including local ***infiltration*** and distant ***metastasis*** (see Fig. 6.21, 6.22, 6.23).

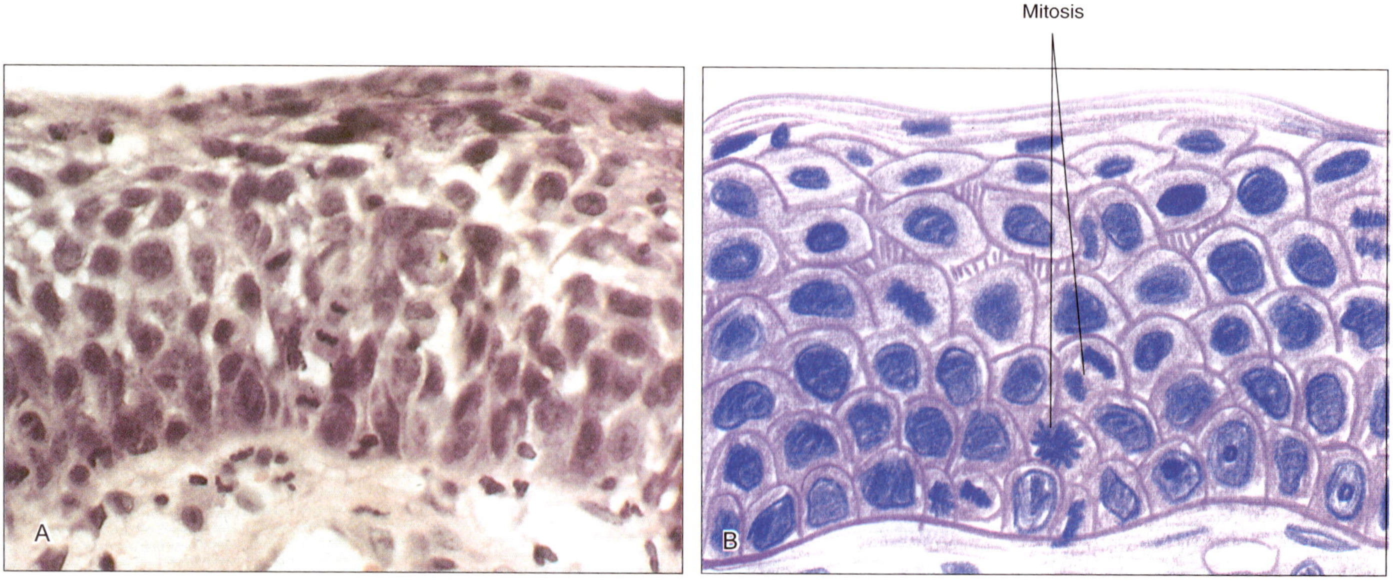

Fig. 6.3: A. and B. Squamous epithelium of the cervix showing dysplasia – nuclear variation, mitosis and loss of polarity.

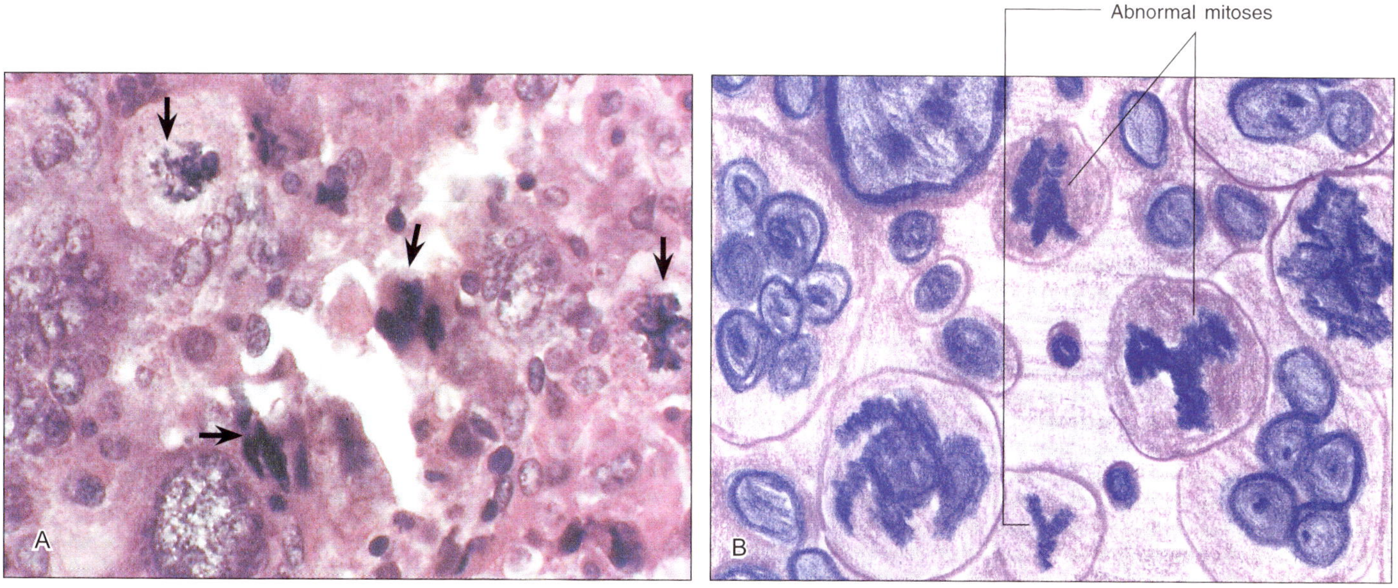

Fig. 6.5: A. and B. Features of anaplasia – showing cell pleomorphism, nuclear pleomorphism and abnormal mitosis (↑).

COMMON EPITHELIAL TUMOURS

Epithelial tumours arising from specialised epithelium of different organs occur in respective systems. However, the common epithelial tumours are:

BENIGN

Papilloma

Papilloma is an outgrowth of proliferated epithelium with complex branching fibrovascular stalk, e.g. squamous papilloma of skin, oral and genital mucosa (Fig. 6.6); transitional papilloma of nose and sinuses; ductal papilloma of breast; papilloma of colonic epithelium. The lining is hyperplastic but cytologically normal with normal polarity maintained. Mitosis, if present, is normal.

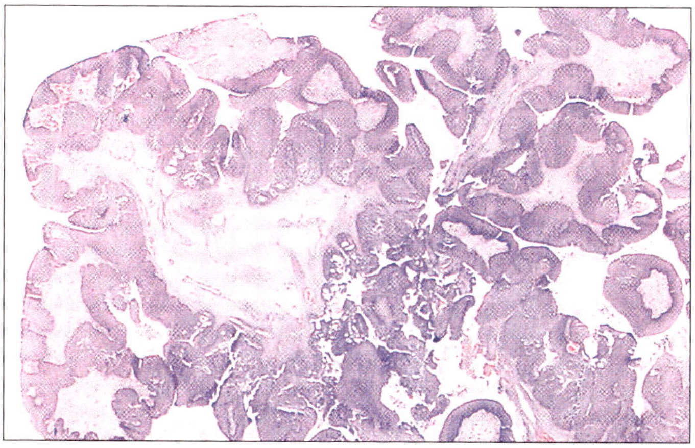

Fig. 6.6 Squamous papilloma – papillae lined by normal to hyperplastic squamous epithelium.

Adenoma

Proliferation of glandular epithelium to form tubular structures (e.g. adenomatous polyp of intestine (Fig. 6.7), adenoma of sweat ducts etc.) or of parenchymatous organs (kidney, endocrine glands etc.). Grossly they may be solid, nodular, polypoidal or cystic. Cells lack any feature indicative of anaplasia.

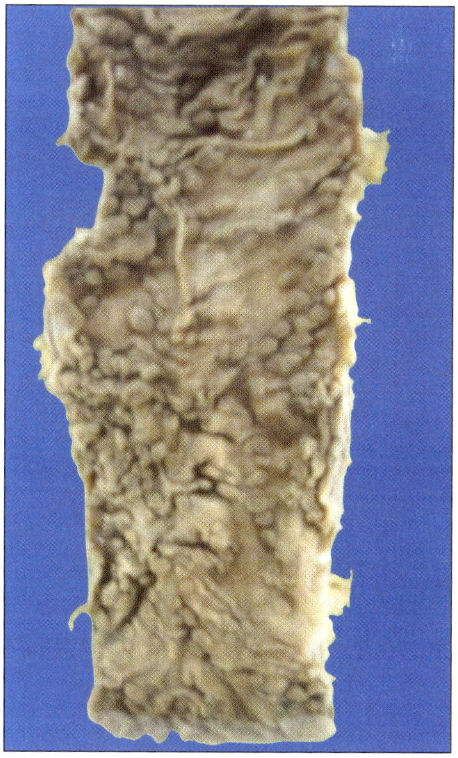

Fig. 6.7: Numerous polyps (pedunuclated) in a case of polyposis coli. These polyps are adenomas of large intestine.

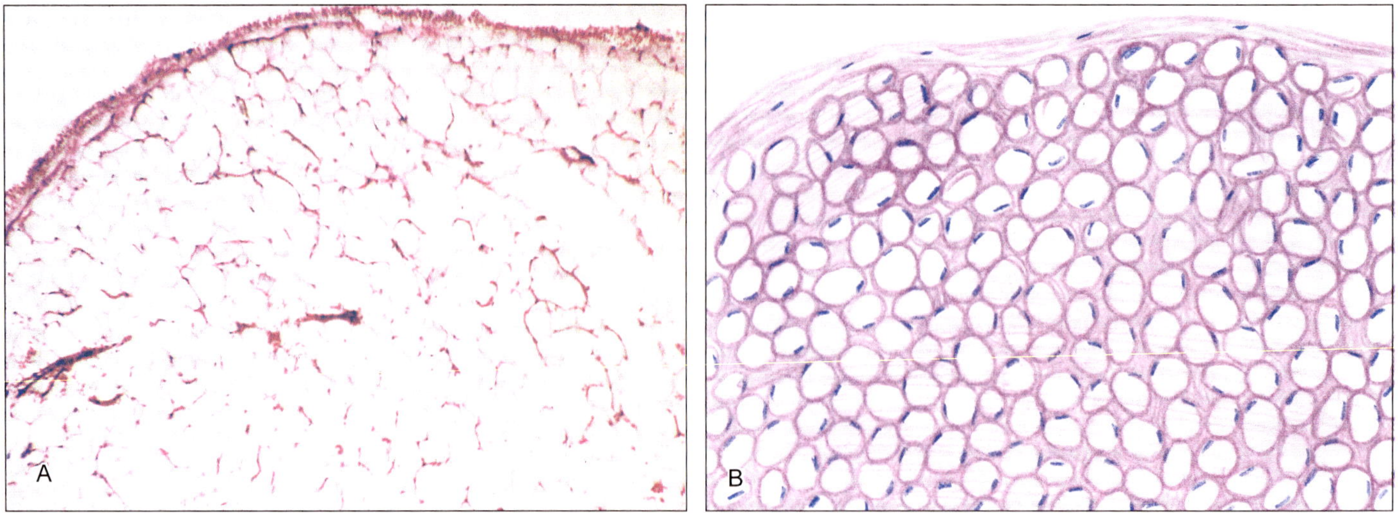

Fig. 6.13: A. and B. Lipoma made up of mature fat cells. Capsule seen on top of figure.

Angioma

Angioma is a vascular tumour often present at birth (malformation or true neoplasm). Though benign, they are not encapsulated. They may be of three main types:

(a) **Capillary hemangioma**, common in superficial tissues, is made up of numerous small vascular channels with plump endothelial lining. Many may contain R.B.C. (Fig. 6.14A and B).

(b) **Cavernous hemangioma**, often seen in visceral organs, has large cavernous channels with thin fibrous walls and filled with blood (Fig. 6.14C and D). Lack of a muscle coat differentiates these channels from arteries and veins.

(c) **Lymphangioma**, is often congenital (cystic hygroma in the neck). These are made up of small and large lymphatic channels, containing eosinophilic plasma with lymphocytes and no RBC.

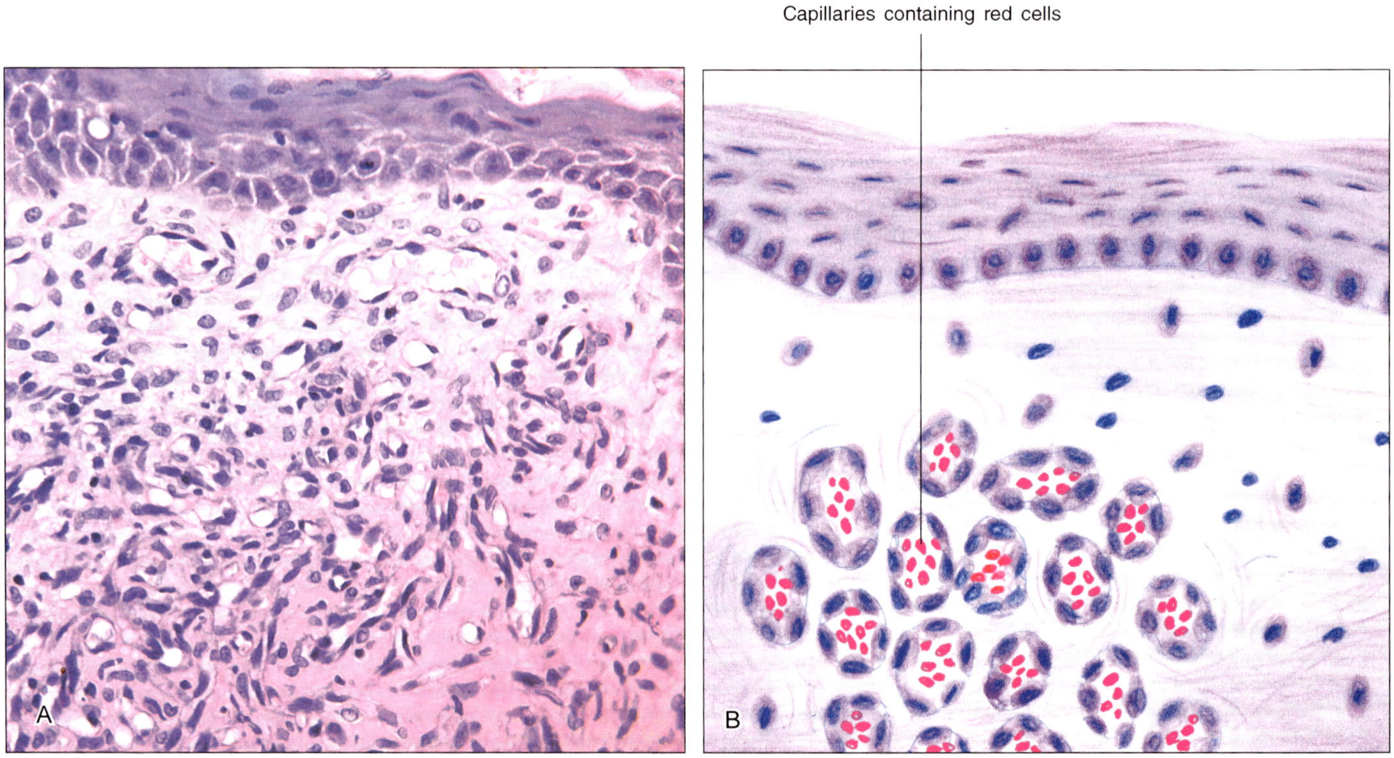

Fig. 6.14: A. and B. Capillary hemangioma shows numerous small vascular channels with plump endothelial cells.

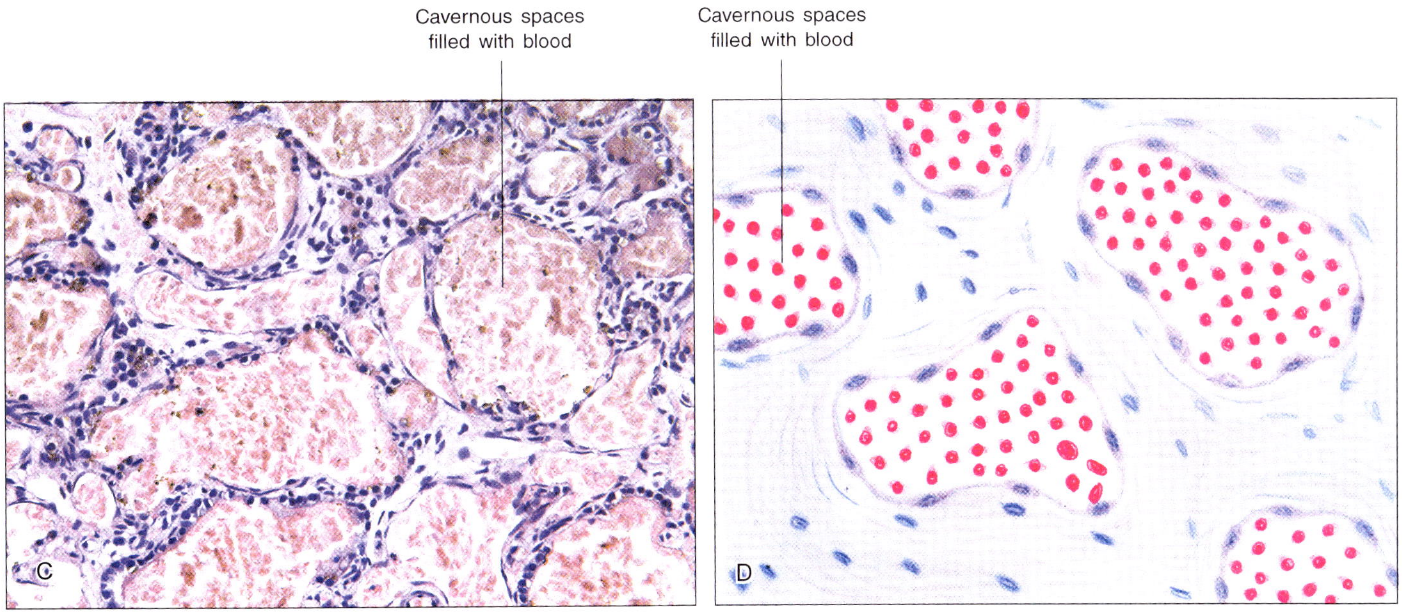

Fig. 6.14: C. and D. Cavernous hemangioma shows large spaces filled with blood and walls are thin.

Neurofibroma and neurilemmoma (schwannoma)

Neurofibroma and neurilemmoma (schwannoma): Neurofibroma and neurilemmoma are common in superficial soft tissues. They are formed of elongated spindle cells with elongated nuclei, set in a fibrillary background. The cells and nuclei may have a wavy configuration (neurofibroma) or may show palisading of nuclei into regimented rows (neurilemmoma).

LEIOMYOMA

Leiomyoma is commoner in muscular visceral organs (like uterus, GIT etc.) than in the soft tissues. Uterus is the commonest site. It is not capsulated but there is a cleavage between the leiomyoma and surrounding myometrium (Fig. 6.15).

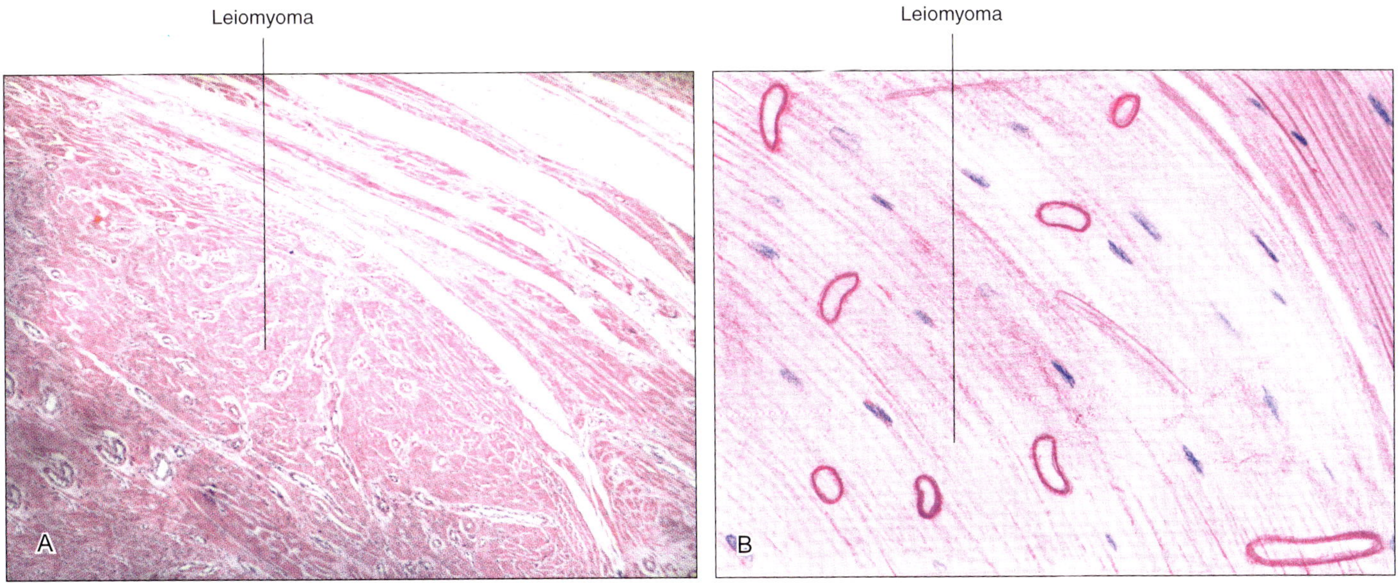

Fig. 6.15: A. and B. Leiomyoma is composed of bundles of smooth muscle and there is a cleavage between the tumour and surrounding myometrium.

MALIGNANT MESENCHYMAL TUMOURS (SARCOMAS)

Malignant mesenchymal tumours (or *sarcomas*) are basically made up of spindle cells with anaplastic features (Fig. 6.16). Poorly differentiated sarcomas are difficult to classify by cell type but better differentiated sarcomas can be typed as *fibrosarcoma* (collagen fibrils formation), *leiomyosarcoma* (myofibrils), *liposarcoma* (lipoblasts with fat vacuoles in cytoplasm), *chondrosarcoma* (hyaline cartilaginous matrix), *osteosarcoma* (osteoid laid down by tumour cells) etc. Various markers like desmin, vimensin and CD34 are used to differentiate each other.

SPECIAL TUMOURS

Some tumours do not strictly fall into epithelial or mesenchymal tumours because of:

(a) neoplastic proliferation of both epithelial and stromal components (e.g. ***fibro-adenoma*** of the breast in which both ductal elements and stromal elements proliferate (Fig. 6.17, 6.18). These are encapsulated (Fig. 6.17).

(b) arising from primitive cell rests (pluripotent cells) which are capable of differentiating into more than one tissue type of one germ cell layer e.g. ***Wilms tumour*** of the kidney, capable of forming several tissues of mesodermal origin (see Fig. 23.15, 23.16);

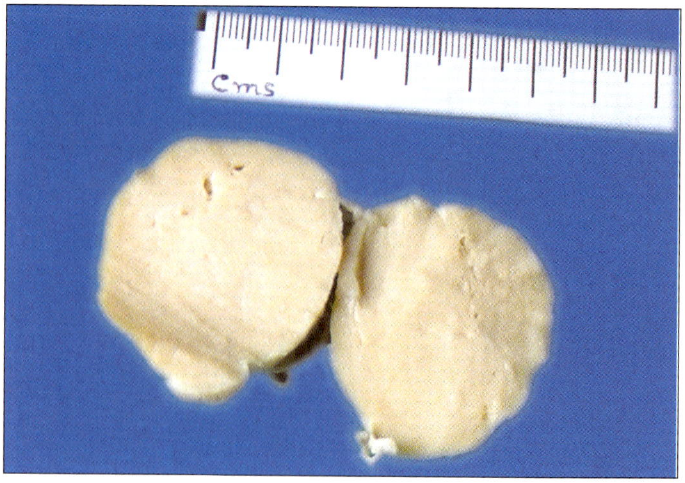

Fig. 6.17: Fibroadenoma breast: Note the circumscription and encapsulation.

(c) ***Teratoma*** of the gonads arising from totipotent cells which can form any tissue from any or all 3 germ cell layers viz. ecto-, meso- and endoderm. There are islands of skin with appendages (ectodermal), fat tissue, muscle tissue (mesodermal), columnar epithelium (endodermal). (Fig. 6.19).

(d) ***Intradermal nevus.*** It is a benign proliferation of melanocytes. The nevus cells are present in superficial dermis as clusters of small cuboidal cells, with melanin pigment in their cytoplasm. Though the

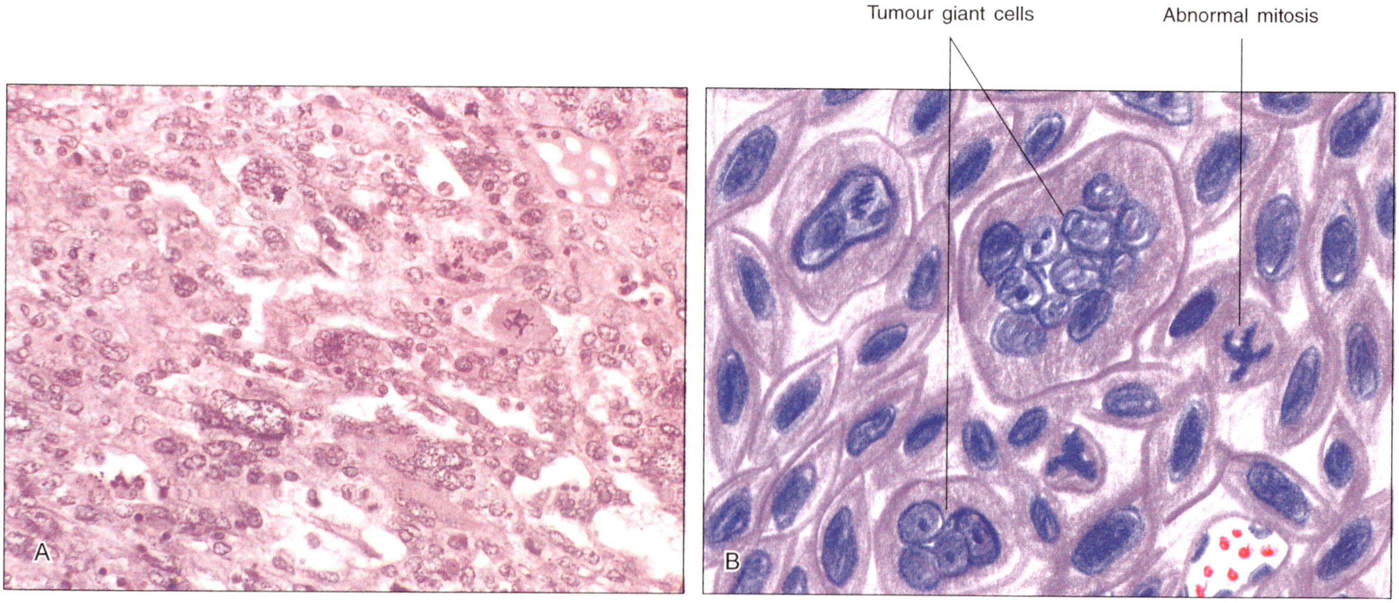

Fig. 6.16: A. and B. Sarcoma – Spindle cell tumour with features of anaplasia. Variation in cell size and shape, giant cells, mitosis and hyperchromatic nuclei.

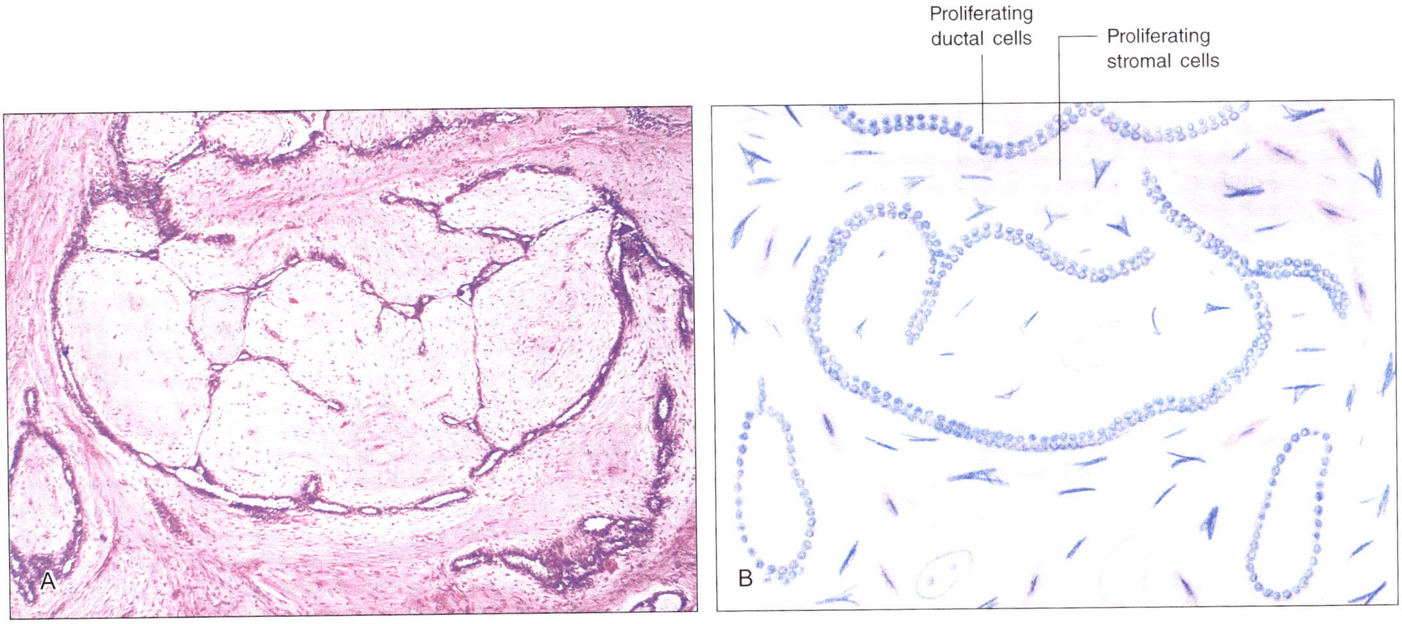

Fig. 6.18: A. and B. Fibroadenoma breast. There is proliferation of both ductal and stromal elements.

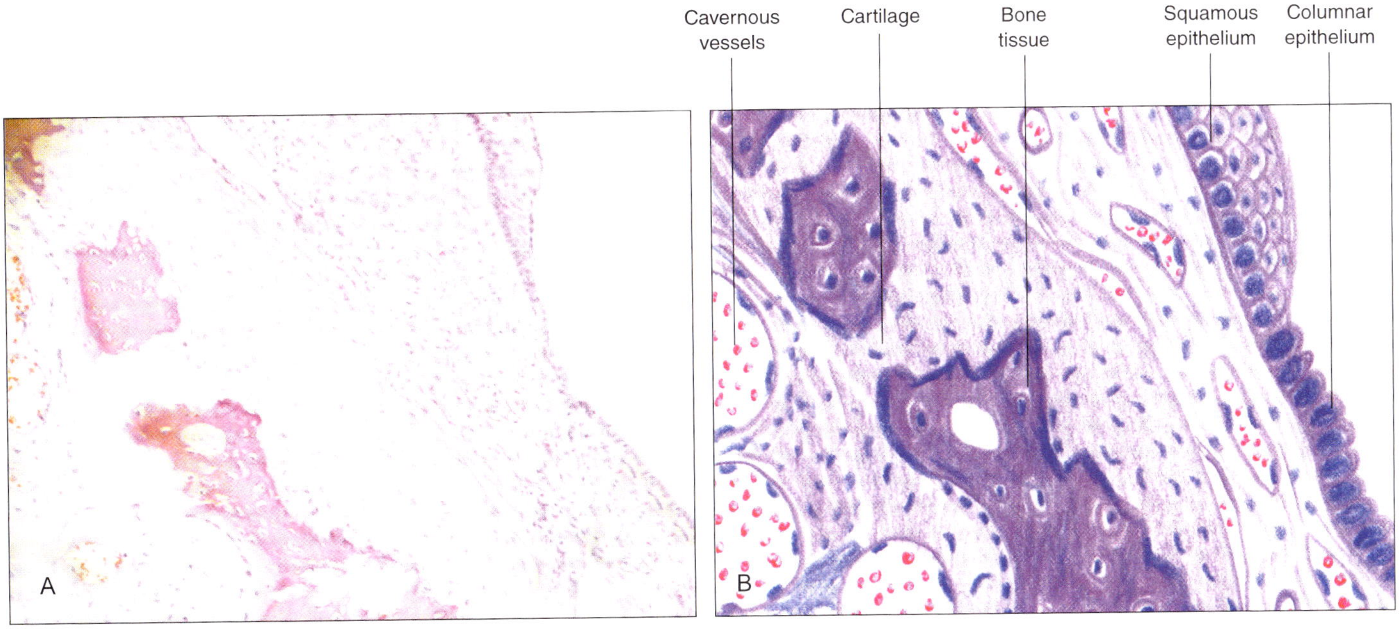

Fig. 6.19: A. and B. Teratoma ovary shows squamous and columnar epithelia, bone tissue, cavernous vessels and cartilage tissue

cells are present in dermis, lesion does not have well defined margins and may extend into deeper dermis, it is a benign lesion devoid of mitotic activity and pleomorphism (Fig. 6.20).

SPREAD OF MALIGNANT TUMOURS

Spread and metastasis are the behavioural hallmarks of malignant tumours. Spread may be:

(a) ***Local infiltration*** into surrounding tissues. In tumours that appear to have a capsule, microscopy reveals infiltration of capsule by the malignant cells.

(b) ***Lymphatic spread*** is more often seen in carcinomas as tumour emboli inside lymphatic channels. The channels are identified by their flattened lining and thin wall devoid of muscle coat. This spread results in metastasis to draining lymph nodes (Fig. 6.21). These deposits first occur in subcapsular sinuses and may later replace the entire node.

(c) ° occurs more often in sarcomas. Venous channels are the portal of entry for tumour cells to form tumour emboli. Lungs, liver, bones and brain are the common sites of metastatic deposits (Fig. 6.22, 6.23).

(d) ***Seeding of body cavities*** like the peritoneum (by

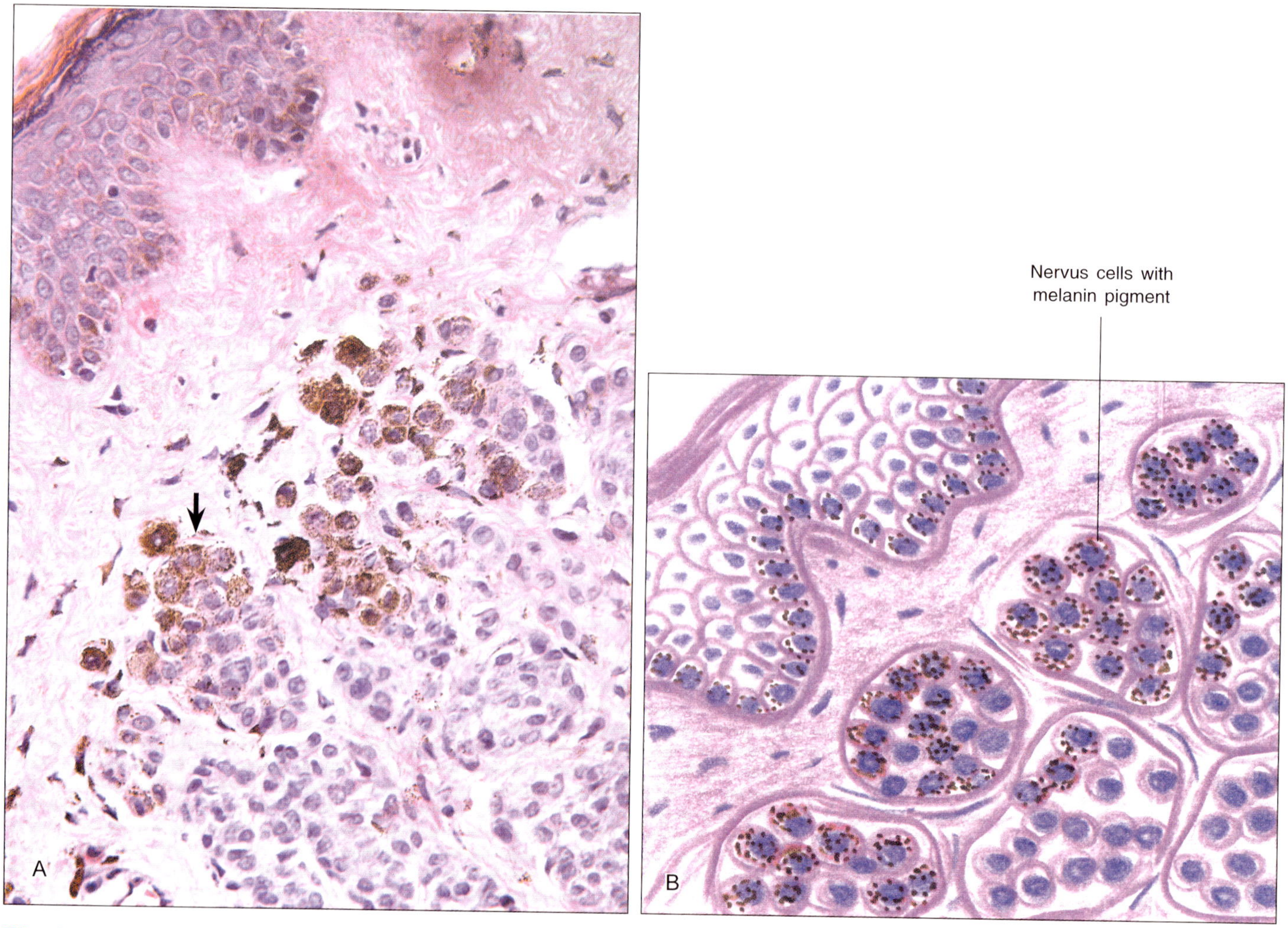

Fig. 6.20: A. and B. Intradermal nevus. Nests of nevus cells with melanin in the superficial nests (↑).

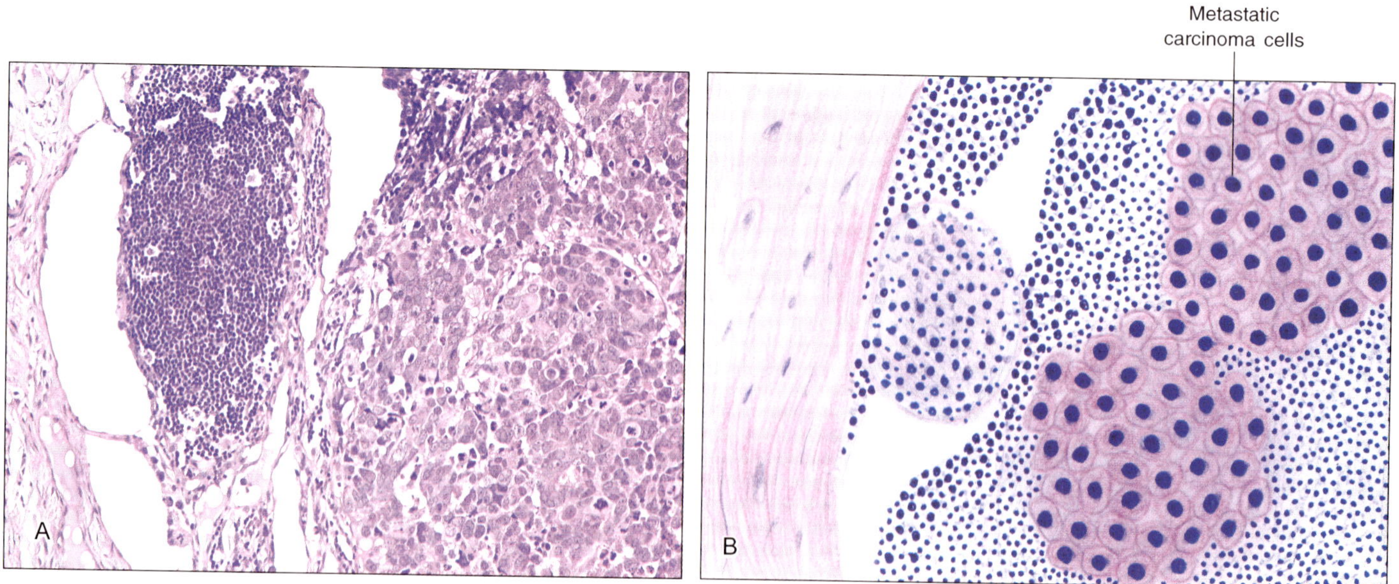

Fig. 6.21: A. and B. Deposit of metastatic carcinoma in lymph node on the right. On the left capsule of lymph node and lymphoid tissue is seen.

ovarian and GIT malignancies) and pleura (by lung cancers as well as by metastatic tumours to the lung) results in dissemination of malignancy. The malignant cells can be demonstrated cytologically in the pleural effusion and ascitic fluid by aspiration.

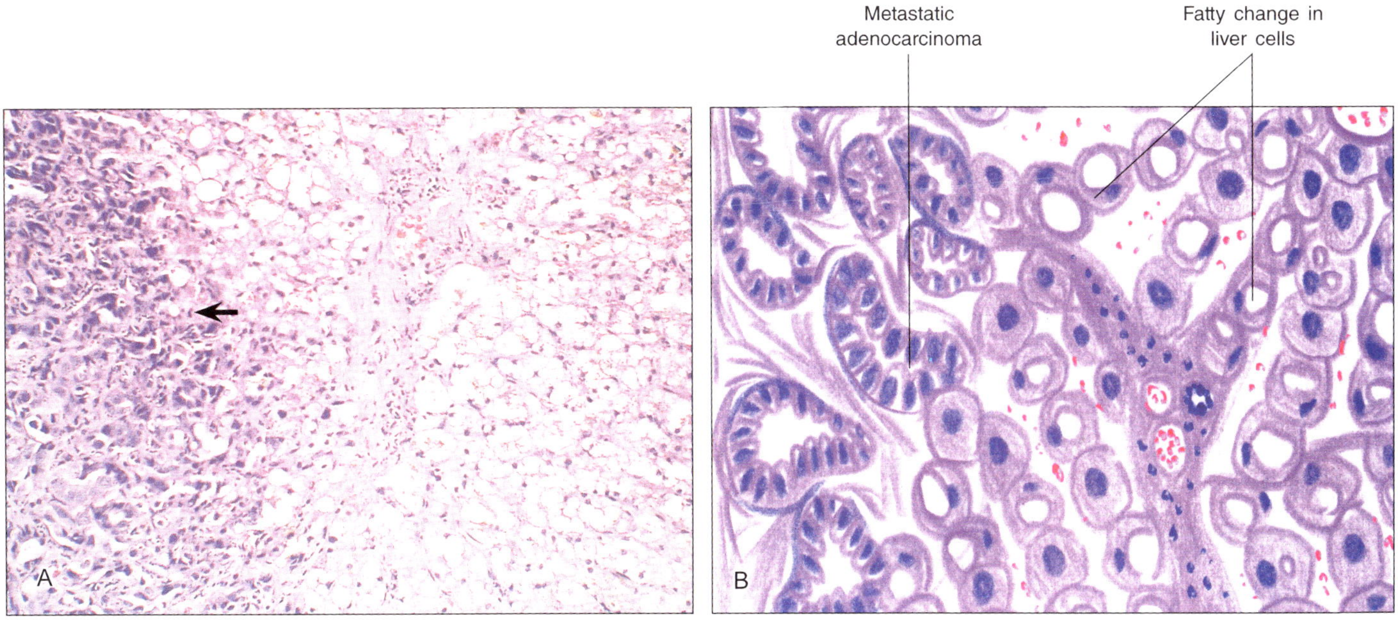

Fig. 6.22: A. and B. Adenocarcinoma (←) deposit (at left of figure) in liver which shows fatty change.

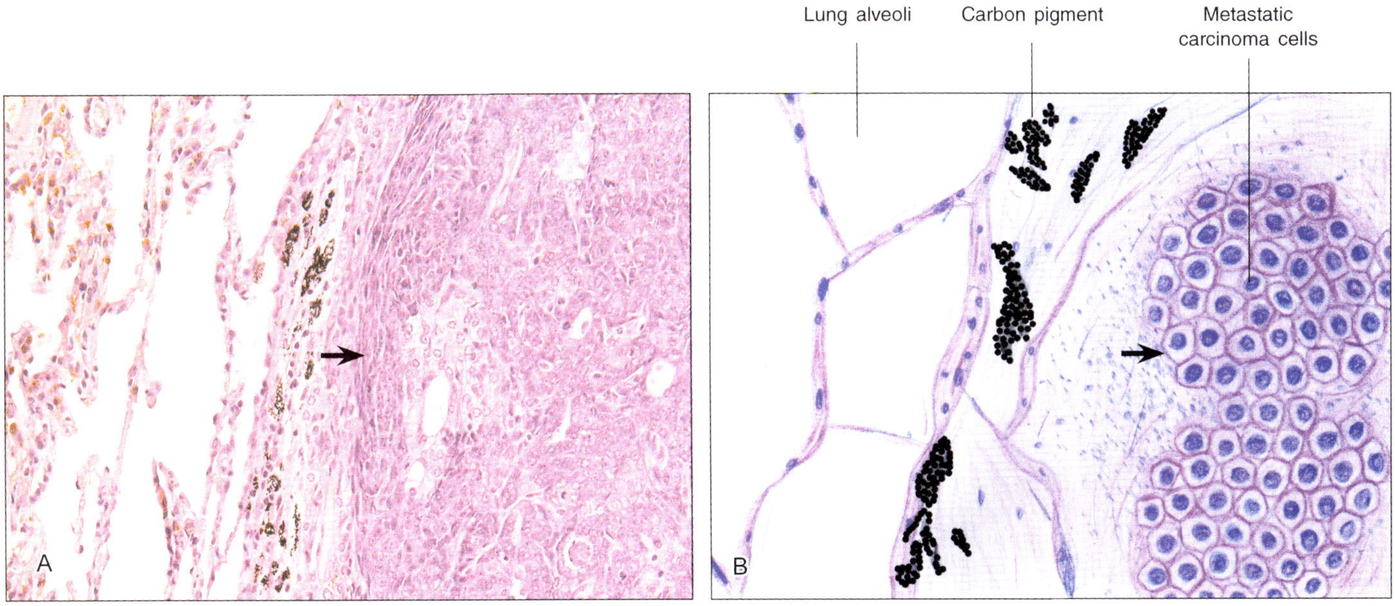

Fig. 6.23: A. and B. Metastatic carcinoma in Lung. On left side lung alveoli and black carbon pigment are seen. On the right is metastatic tumour deposit (↑).

VIVA-VOCE

Q. Give an example of hyperplasia?

Ans. Endometrial hyperplasia is not uncommon. The endometrial glands are hyperplastic with increase in number and multi-layering of the lining cells. If atypical, may transform to adenocarcinoma.

Q. Give examples of metaplasia of epithelium?

Ans. In endocervix and bronchi, there is change of columnar epithelium to stratified squamous epithelium. In the urinary bladder, transitional epithelium may undergo metaplasia to stratified squamous epithelium.

Q. What is connective tissue metaplasia?

Ans. In certain situations like myositis ossificans, there is metaplasia of fibroblasts to osteoblasts which results in bone formation.

Q. Give an example of epithelial dysplasia which can progress to carcinomia.

Ans. Squamous epithelium of cervix progresses to dysplasia, then to carcinoma in situ (intraepithelial neoplasm) and finally to invasive carcinoma.

Q. Which benign tumour is not encapsulated?

Ans. Hemangioma and Nevus are not encapsulated.

Q. Name the common sites of squamous cell carcinoma in India?

Ans. 1. Cervix - due to HPV virus. 2. Oral cavity, tongue - due to tobacco chewing 3. Bronchus - due to smoking

Q. Name a malignant tumour which does not metastasize?

Ans. Basal cell carcinoma of skin infiltrates locally, but does not metastasize.

Q. How will you differentiate between various malignant mesenchymal tumours?

Ans. Special stains like fat stain (for liposarcoma), Masson's trichrome (for fibrosarcoma) and PTAH (for rhabdosarcoma) are used. Besides, various markers like vimentin, smooth muscle actin, CD34 can be employed in immunohistochemistry.

Q. In which tumour, one comes across proliferation of both epithelial and stromal elements?

Ans. Fibroadenoma of breast.

Q. Give examples of lymphatic spread of malignant tumour?

Ans.
- Carcinoma breast – axillary lymph nodes.
- Bronchogenic carcinoma – tracheobronchial lymph nodes.
- Oral cancer – cervical lymph nodes

Q. Give examples of hematogenous spread of malignant tumours?

Ans.
- Carcinoma breast – lung
- Rectal carcinoma – liver
- Osteosarcoma of bones – lung
- Prostate carcinoma – bones (pelvis and spine)

Q. Name the mesenchymal tumors which spread by lymphatic route?

Ans.
- Rhabdomyosarcoma
- Clear cell sarcoma
- Alveolar soft part sarcoma
- Synovial cell sarcoma

Q. Name some malignant tumors with suffix 'oma' and not suffix as carcinoma/sarcoma.

Ans.
- Dysgerminoma
- Seminoma
- Chordoma
- Hepatoma (also known as hepatocellular carcinoma)
- Hypernephroma (renal cell carcinoma)

Q. Name some pediatric tumors which are blastomas.

Ans. Nephroblastoma (Wilms tumor), Hepatoblastoma, Retinoblastoma

Q. Name EBV associated tumors:

Ans.
- Hodgkin's lymphoma
- Burkitt's lymphoma
- Extranodal NHL/T cell lymphoma
- Lymphomatoid granulomatosis
- Nasopharyngeal carcinoma
- Follicular dendritic cell sarcoma
- Primary effusion lymphoma

Q. What is the most important feature characteristic of malignant tumor.

Ans. Metastatic spread. This never occurs in benign tumours.

Q. What are the common sites for hematogenous metastasis.

Ans. Lungs, liver and bones.

Q. What do the terms grading and staging mean in a malignant tumour.

Ans. Grading is based on histological cellular and architectural features of differentiation/anaplasia. Staging is based on the extent of spread. Both are important prognostic factors.

SECTION C
Haematology

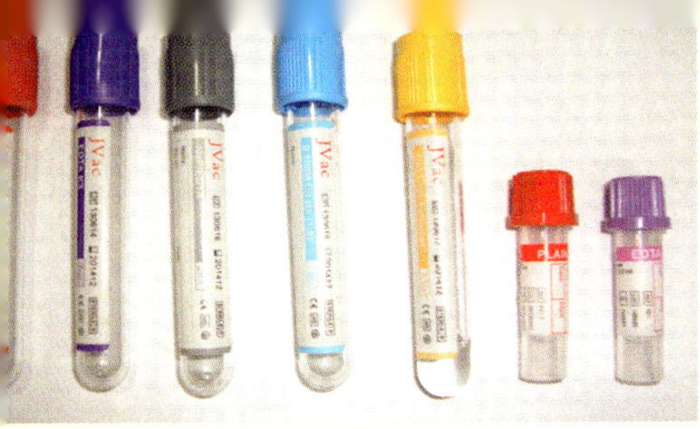

7

Anticoagulants and Blood Collection

ANTICOAGULANTS

Whole blood is required for various haematologic tests. Commonly used anticoagulants are:

- EDTA
- Sodium citrate solution
- Heparin
- Double Oxalate
- Sodium fluoride

EDTA

Disodium/tripotassium salts are commonly used. These remove free calcium ions from blood by chelation, thus preventing coagulation of blood. *Tripotassium* EDTA *being more soluble than sodium salt is preferred for cell counters.* Such blood can be used for making peripheral smears till upto 4 hours after collection. Morphologic alterations start to appear in the neutrophils within 30 minutes of collection. Platelets swell and their disintegration causes an artificially produced elevation in count. Red cells become spherocytic/macrocytic.

Uses

- EDTA is suitable for Hb, TLC, platelet count, eosinophil count and RBC count.
- EDTA is used as an anticoagulant for HbF estimation and Hb electrophoresis.
- EDTA is not suitable for coagulation studies.
- EDTA is used in solid form – 2 mg/ml of blood and is added to tubes/vacutainers (with lavender top) (Fig. 7.1).

Sodium Citrate

Sodium citrate binds loosely with free calcium ions to form a calcium citrate complex, thus preventing coagulation of blood.

Uses

(a) For coagulation studies – 3.8% Trisod. citrate pentahydrate or 3.2% Trisodium citrate dihydrate solution-1 part mixed with 9 parts of blood 1:9 (0.5 ml:4.5 ml.).

(b) For E.S.R. by Westergren method – Sodium citrate solution is used in a ratio of 1:4 (0.5 ml : 2 ml of blood).

Heparin

Heparin acts as an antithrombin thus inhibiting coagulation of blood. Heparinised syringe is made by taking 1 drop of heparin to wet the inner surface of the syringe and then blood is collected in it.

Uses

(a) For osmotic fragility tests for diagnosis of spherocytosis.

(b) For red cell enzyme studies like G-6-PD and PK deficiency.

Disadvantage

Since it causes clumping of platelets and leucocytes, it should not be used for cell counters. Smears made from heparinised blood show pink background (not good for red cell and white cell morphology).

Double Oxalate

A mixture of Potassium and Ammonium oxalates in the ratio of 2:3 was used previously for various hematologic tests and has now been replaced by EDTA. Potassium salt causes shrinkage of RBCs while Ammonium salt causes swelling of RBCs and therefore double oxalate salts are preferred over single oxalate. This causes morphologic changes in white and red cells and therefore is not in use these days. It was used as 2 mg/ml of blood.

Sodium Fluoride

It is used for blood sugar assay. It is an inhibitor of red cell glycolytic enzymes.

COLLECTION OF BLOOD

Adequate patient preparation, specimen collection and handling are essential pre-requisites for accurate testing and result. Samples, after a correct labelling with the name, age etc. of the patient, investigation required should be sent to the laboratory at the earliest possible since most of the tests should be performed within 1–2 hours.

For blood chemistry tests, it is preferable to fast overnight (6 p.m. to 8 a.m. next day) to ensure that the patient is in the basal state. This minimises the effects of ingested substances on the results of various tests. Patients should be made aware that fasting does not include abstaining from water.

The blood should be collected in a multidraw in glass/ plastic vacutainers which have a coloured top (Fig. 7.1) e.g.:

(a) Purple/lavender top	EDTA
(b) Green top	Heparin
(c) Light blue top	Sodium citrate for coagulation
(d) Grey top	Fluoride
(e) Red top	Non-additive for serum
(f) Yellow top	Citrite for blood culture

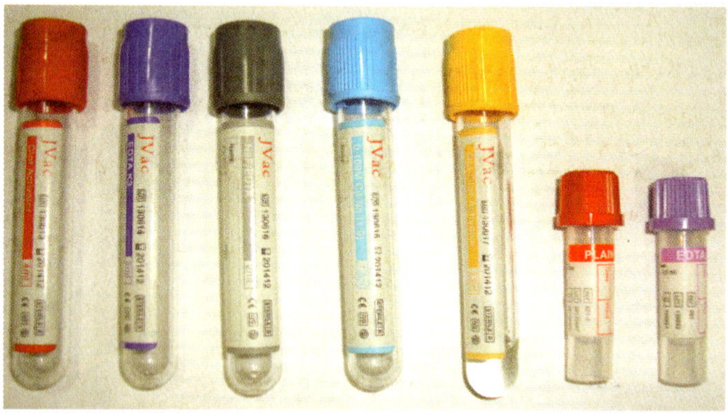

Red Grey Lavender Light blue Yellow Red Purple

Red – No chemical – For serum determinations
Grey – Sodium Fluoride – For glucose determination
Lavender – Potassium EDTA – For whole blood hematology and immunology
Light blue – 3.2% sodium citrate – For coagulation studies
Yellow – Citrite for blood culture
Red & purple – Pediatric vacutainers

Fig. 7.1: Vacutainers for blood specimen collection. The stopper colour indicates the chemical in the tube and accordingly used for vairous tests.

Collection should be done in the proper ratio of anticoagulant: blood for specific tests e.g. for coagulation studies ratio of anticoagulant to blood is 1 : 9 (sodium citrate - anticoagulant).

Labelling. Specimen identification and labelling should be done at the bedside immediately after collection.

Laboratory requisition form. This form should be filled in and should give the brief signs and symptoms of the patient. The clinician must write if the patient is HIV, Hepatitis B, or Hepatitis C positive so that the lab personnel can take adequate precautions. Information regarding the patient having indwelling catheter or on certain drugs must be given to the pathologist.

Blood may be withdrawn by 3 methods:

A. **Venous** blood from antecubital vein using a vacutainer/syringe.
B. **Capillary** blood from a finger/heel.
C. **Arterial** blood from an artery.

Method for Venous Blood

- Clean the antecubital area of the arm using alcohol swab.
- Apply a tourniquet at the upper arm and close the fist. This makes the vein prominent.
- Insert the needle of the syringe into the vein. Presence of the needle into the vein is indicated by the appearance of blood in the hub of the needle.
- Slowly apply suction on the syringe and release the tourniquet. Open the fist as blood comes into the syringe. As the required amount of blood is collected in the syringe, withdraw the syringe with the needle from the vein keeping a spirit swab at the skin puncture.
- Pour blood into a EDTA vial/citrate vial except a few drops.
- Pour one drop each onto 3 slides and make 3 peripheral smears as given in Fig. 10.1.

Vacutainer (Vacuum Tube) Method

- Follow the first 2 steps of the method for venous blood.
- The appropriate vacutainer tube is placed in a reusable plastic holder and a disposable needle is attached by screwing the threaded needle hub-top the holder. The tube is then inserted into the holder until the top of its stopper is level with the marked guideline which causes the tube to recede.
- Place the patient's arm in a slightly vertical position. When using the vacutainer, venipuncture must not be performed in a horizontal plane as backflow of blood can result.

- The needle is inserted into the vein as in syringe technique and the base of the collection tube is pushed forward breaking the vacuum seal. Time is allowed for the vacuum tube to fill.
- Open the fist, release the tourniquet and withdraw the needle with the syringe.
- If multiple tubes have been requested, the tourniquet is released before collection of each tube. The needle remains in the vein, the tube is removed and the other tubes are attached as needed.

Method for Capillary Blood

Finger Prick Method

- Wipe the tip of the ring finger, using alcohol swab and let the area dry up.
- Give a prick with a sterile disposable lancet/needle on the lateral side of the tip of the finger and gently squeeze the finger so that free flow of blood starts.
- Discard the first two drops.
- Free flowing blood may be collected in haemoglobinometer pipette – 0.02 ml each for Hb, TLC, platelet count etc.
- Smears are made from the drops collected on the slides.

Heel Prick Method

In an infant, gently rub the heel to warm it. Clean the lateral/medial part of the heel (plantar surface) using alcohol. Give a prick on medial/lateral part of plantar surface. Collect blood for Hb/TLC and make the peripheral smears.

Arterial Blood

Arterial blood is usually collected from femoral artery for blood gas analysis. Pulsations of the femoral artery are felt below the inguinal ligament. Disposable needle and syringe are used for blood collection.

WHOLE BLOOD, SERUM, PLASMA

Whole Blood

Used for haemogram (Hb, ESR, platelet count, reticulocyte count, peripheral smear evaluation), osmotic fragility, HbF estimation, Hb electrophoresis, Coombs test etc. It is also used for biochemical investigations like sugar, urea, etc.

Serum

Serum is obtained when blood is allowed to clot in a tube with a red top or in a vial. Within one hour the clot retracts and serum can be extracted. Move a thin clean bamboo stick along the attachment of clot to the test tube, the clot retracts and straw coloured serum admixed with RBCs is extracted. Pour serum in another tube, centrifuge it at 3000 RPM for 15 minutes. RBCs settle down and clear serum is decanted off in a clean test tube.

Serum is devoid of fibrinogen and major fraction of clotting factors like XI, VIII, IX, X, V, VII and II which have been used up in clotting process.

Uses

- For estimation of S. bilirubin, creatinine, uric acid, S. proteins, albumin, globulin, A/G ratio and enzymes.
- For electrophoresis of proteins, lipoproteins and immunoglobulins.
- For estimation of various serum enzyme levels – S. alkaline phosphatase, S. acid phosphatase, Asparate (SGOT) and Alanine aminotransferase (SGPT).

Plasma

Plasma is obtained following centrifugation of the **anticoagulated** blood e.g. citrated blood collected for coagulation studies is centrifuged at 3000 RPM for 20 minutes. RBCs form the sediment and the supernatant is the plasma.

Uses

- For coagulation studies – PT, APTT.
- For assay of FDP, D-dimer.
- For assay of various factors – VIII, IX.
- For confirmation of haemoglobinemia where plasma is coloured red as in Paroxysmal nocturnal haemoglobinuria (PNH) and Paroxysmal cold haemoglobinuria (PCH).

VIVA-VOCE

Q. What gauge needle should be used for collection of venous blood?

Ans. A 20-22G needle is suitable for collection of venous blood. If thinner needles of 23, 24G are used, there may be haemolysis of blood resulting in haemoglobinemia, rendering the specimen unfit for various haematological and biochemical investigations.

Q. Why should we not squeeze the finger while collecting blood?

Ans. Prick should be deep enough for free flow of blood or gentle squeezing to start the flow of blood. Squeezing the finger tip hard results in tissue fluids diluting the blood, thus lowering the haematological values.

Q. Why initial 1-2 drops of blood (in a finger prick method) are discarded?

Ans. Initial drops of blood get contaminated with the antiseptic (ethyl alcohol) and therefore discarded.

Q. Which is the preferred anticoagulant for haemogram (Hb, TLC, PCV, Retic count, Platelet count, DLC and peripheral smear assessment)?

Ans. EDTA – Potassium salt is the anticoagulant of choice for cell counters and manual methods.

Q. Why is ring finger preferred for capillary blood?

Ans. Ulnar side of the tip of ring finger is comparatively less innervated and therefore prick is less painful.

Q. Why is liquid anticoagulant – sodium citrate solution not used for Hb, TLC, PCV, Platelet count, etc.?

Ans. Addition of liquid anticoagulant dilutes the blood altering Hb, TLC, haematocrit etc., therefore, powder form of EDTA salt is used.

Q. Why are double oxalates no longer used as anticogulant for Hb/TLC/Platelet count etc.?

Ans. Oxalates induce morphologic alterations in white and red cells and therefore smear morphology cannot be studied.

Q. What are the differences between plasma and serum?

Ans.

Plasma	Serum
1. Plasma is obtained by centrifugation of the anticoagulant added blood.	Serum is obtained when blood undergoes clotting.
2. It contains all clotting factors except calcium ions.	It does not contain fibrinogen, prothrombin F.V, VII, VIII, IX, X, XI and XII which have been used in clotting.
3. It is used for coagulation studies like PT, APTT, TT.	It is used for estimation of various biochemical parameters and serum enzymes like SGOT, SGPT, S. alk phosphatase, S. uric acid, S. electrolytes etc.

Q. What are the tests in which Sodium Citrate solution is used as an anticoagulant?

Ans. 3.2% Trisodium citrate solution is used for

(a) ESR - in the 1 : 4 (blood) ratio.

(b) Coagulation studies in the 1 : 9 (blood) ratio.

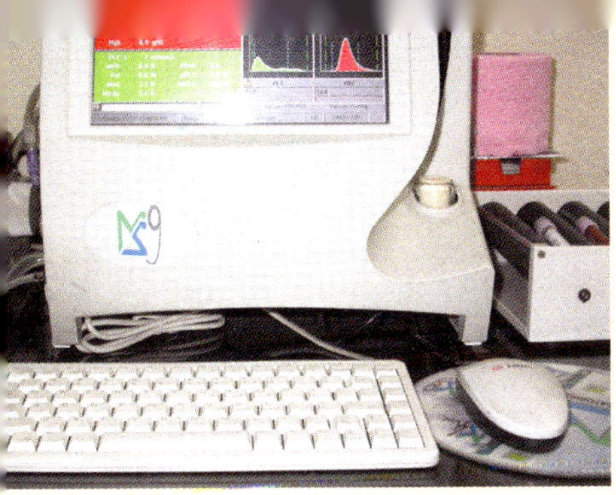

8

Haemoglobin Estimation

Estimation of red cell mass can be made by measuring haemoglobin – Hb. Various methods are available for Hb estimation; Sahli's, cyanmethemoglobin and the haematology analysers (cell counters).

SAHLI'S METHOD

This is the most popular colour matching method for Hb estimation.

Apparatus

It consists of a square tube with markings of Hb% on one side and percentage on the other side; 100% = 14.5 gm%. Comparator has a flat surface of a standard brown colour. Hb pipette has mark of 0.02 ml (20 cumm) (Fig. 8.1). A dropper is used to put N/10 HCl and distilled water into the square tube. Hb meter with square tube and flat comparator surface is preferable to the round tube.

Principle

Blood is added to N/10 HCl which converts Hb into acid haematin. Brown colour of acid haematin is matched against the brown colour of the comparator.

Technique

- Add N/10 HCl with a dropper into the square Hb meter tube upto mark 3 gm%.
- Fill Hb pipette with 0.02 ml of blood and wipe off the excess blood at nozzle of the pipette with moistened cotton. Blood may be taken from a EDTA tube or from a finger prick.
- Blow off the blood in the pipette into the Hb meter tube. Rinse the pipette by drawing in and discharging the blood – acid solution at least twice.
- Withdraw the pipette from the solution and rinse it with 2-3 drops of HCl so that Hb-acid solution sticking to the pipette goes into the tube. Withdraw the pipette. Allow acid to act on the RBCs for 10 minutes to lyse the red cells and convert Hb to acid haematin.
- Mix acid haematin with a glass rod provided with the Hb meter set.
- Match colour of the solution with that of the comparator in the natural light. If it is darker, add distilled water

Sahli's comparator - square

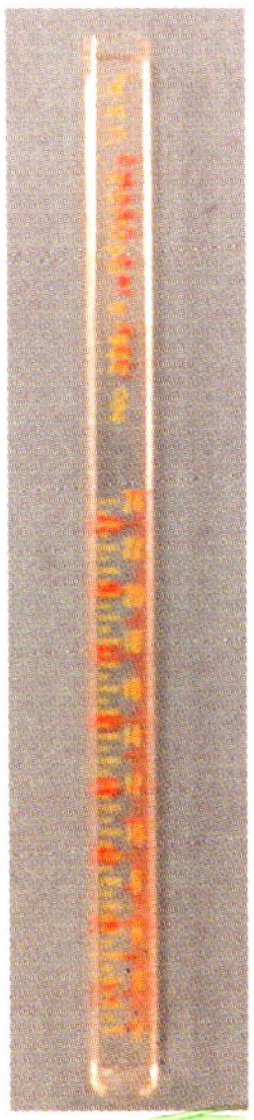

Sahli's hemoglobin tube - square

Hb pipette

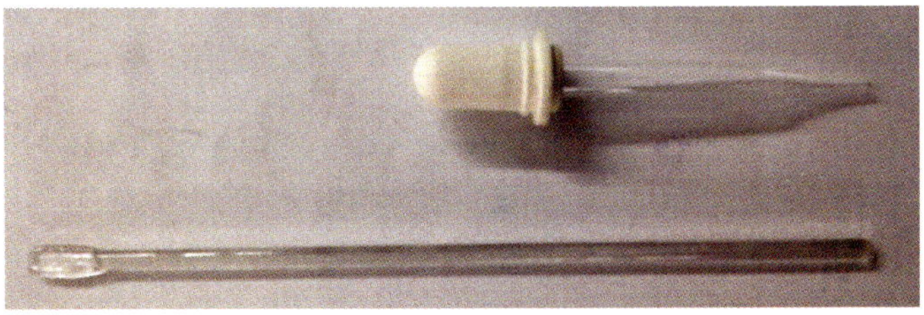

Glass rod as stirrer and dropper

Fig. 8.1

with a dropper and stir the solution with a glass rod. This process is continued till the colour of the solution matches the comparator colour.

- Take out the stirrer from the solution but keep it in the upper inside of the tube and take the reading from the upper meniscus in gm%.

Sources of error

(a) If blood in EDTA tube is not mixed properly before filling the pipette, low/high Hb value may be obtained depending on whether mainly the plasma or the sedimented RBCs are taken in the pipette.

(b) If Hb pipette has not been calibrated accurately at 0.02 ml, erroneous Hb value will be obtained.

Disadvantages

(a) Since it is a colour matching technique there may be visual error in matching.

(b) After 10 minutes, colour of acid haematin starts fading; lower Hb value is obtained if reading is taken thereafter.

(c) Acid does not convert all haemoglobins into acid haematin, therefore Hb value obtained is slightly lower than the actual Hb of the individual.

Normal Range

Males	13-18 gm%
Females	11-16 gm%
Newborns	14-19 gm%

Significance of Hb Value

Low Hb values. Low Hb values are obtained in various types of anaemias. Lower the Hb, more severe is the anaemia. Anaemia may be deficiency anaemia, hemolytic anaemia etc. Peripheral smear evaluation helps in typing the anaemia.

High Hb values. High Hb values (more than 17 gm) are observed in polycythemia rubra vera – PRV and secondary erythrocytosis; the latter is encountered in cases with kidney tumours, leiomyoma uterus, high altitude, cases of hypoxia – chronic pulmonary disease, congenital heart disease and cigarette smoking.

Other methods of Hb estimation

1. Cyanmethaemoglobin – HiCN method.
2. Alkali haematin method.
3. Oxyhaemoglobin method.
4. Cell counter/autoanalyser.

CYANMETHAEMOGLOBIN METHOD

Principle

Hb is oxidized to methaemoglobin by potassium ferricyanide. MetHb in turn is converted to a stable cyanmethaemoglobin by Potassium cyanide. Colour of this solution is compared against a standard of known Hb value colorimetrically.

$$\text{– Hb (Fe++)} \xrightarrow{\text{Pot. Ferricyanide}} \text{Hb (Fe+++)}$$

Met Hb

$$\text{– Hb (Fe+++)} \xrightarrow{\text{KCN}} \text{Hb (Fe+++) CN}$$

Met Hb Cyanmethaemoglobin

Apparatus

Photoelectric colorimeter with a green filter or at a wavelength of 540 nm (Fig. 8.2).

Reagents

Drabkin's Solution – Composition

Potassium cyanide	100 mg
Potassium ferricyanide	400 mg
Potassium dihydrogen phosphate	280 mg
Sterox SE	1 ml
Water to	2 litres

Method

1. Take 5 ml. of Drabkin's solution in a test tube.
2. Add 0.02 ml of blood to it using a Hb pipette (as in Sahli's method). Rinse the pipette twice by drawing in

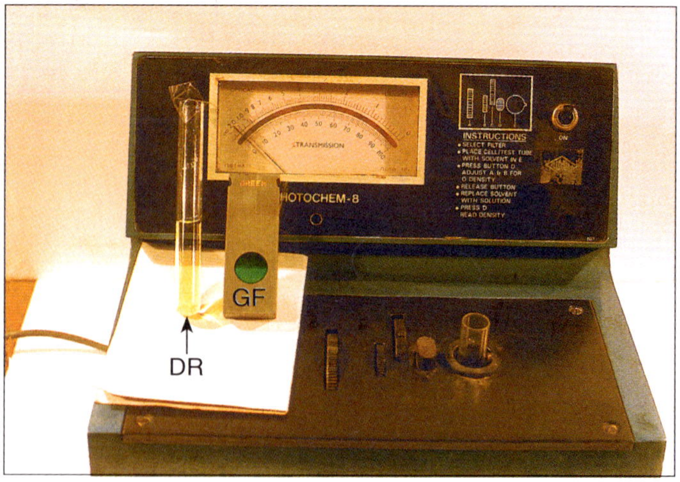

Fig. 8.2: Colorimeter with Drabkin solution (DR) and green filter (GF) or at wavelength 540 – cyanmethemoglobin method.

Drabkin solution. Mix blood with Drabkin's solution thoroughly.

3. Wait for 10 minutes.
4. Switch on the colorimeter with a green filter/540 nm and wait for 5 minutes.
5. Adjust OD at 0 using Drabkin solution as blank.
6. Pour test solution into the cuvette and note down OD of the test sample.
7. OD of the standard cyanmethemoglobin solution is taken against the blank.

$$Hb = \frac{\text{OD of test sample} \times \text{conc.of std.}^{*} \times 250^{**}}{\text{OD of std.} \times 1000^{***}} \text{ gm\%}$$

* Conc. of standard is given for each standard e.g. 50 mg/100 ml.

** Since 0.02 ml of blood has been added to 5 ml Drabkin, dilution is 1 in 250.

*** Divide by 1000 to get the value in gm%.

OD-Hb Table (see table 8.1)

OD-Hb table can be prepared by diluting the standard in 1 in 2, 1 in 4, 1 in 8 (with distilled water) and taking the OD against blank – Drabkin solution. A graph is plotted between OD and the corresponding Hb value; a straight line is obtained. From the standard curve, a table

Table 8.1: OD-Hb Table

Cyanmethaemoglobin Method							
OD	***Hb***	***OD***	***Hb***	***OD***	***Hb***	***OD***	***Hb***
		.224	7.0	.398	12.6	.575	18.2
		.230	7.2	.405	12.8	.582	18.4
		.236	7.4	.412	13.0	.589	18.6
.066	2.0	.242	7.6	.418	13.2	.596	18.8
.072	2.2	.249	7.8	.424	13.4	.602	19.0
.078	2.4	.256	8.0	.430	13.6	.609	19.2
.084	2.6	.262	8.2	.437	13.8	.616	19.4
.091	2.8	.268	8.4	.444	14.0	.622	19.6
.098	3.0	.274	8.6	.450	14.2	.628	19.8
.104	3.2	.281	8.8	.456	14.4	.635	20.0
.110	3.4	.288	9.0	.462	14.6		
.116	3.6	.294	9.2	.468	14.8		
.123	3.8	.300	9.4	.474	15.0		
.130	4.0	.306	9.6	.480	15.2		
.136	4.2	.313	9.8	.486	15.4		
.142	4.4	.320	10.0	.492	15.6		
.148	4.6	.326	10.2	.499	15.8		
.154	4.8	.332	10.4	.506	16.0		
.160	5.0	.338	10.6	.512	16.2		
.166	5.2	.344	10.8	.518	16.4		
.172	5.4	.350	11.0	.524	16.6		
.178	5.6	.356	11.2	.530	16.8		
.185	5.8	.362	11.4	.537	17.0		
.192	6.0	.368	11.6	.543	17.2		
.198	6.2	.374	11.8	.549	17.4		
.204	6.4	.380	12.0	.555	17.6		
.210	6.6	.386	12.2	.561	17.8		
.217	6.8	.392	12.4	.568	18.0		

of OD with corresponding Hb value is made. OD of the test samples is taken and the corresponding Hb value is recorded from the Table (Table 8.1). It is advisable to check the Table readings with a new standard every week and a new Table made.

Advantages

1. Being a colorimetric method, visual error of matching the colour is eliminated.
2. Hb value obtained is accurate since all Hbs except sulfhemoglobin are converted into cyanmethaemoglobin.
3. Cyanmethaemoglobin is a stable compound and colour does not alter with time.
4. Certified cyanmethaemoglobin standards are available.

Disadvantages

1. KCN is a very potent poison and therefore bottle should be labelled as POISON and stored safely.
2. Any turbidity in the Drabkin solution alters OD greatly and therefore inaccurate Hb values are obtained.
3. In India National Quality Control Programme is being run by AIIMS, New Delhi.

Precautions

1. Never pipette Drabkin solution by mouth; always use a suction bulb/autodispenser.
2. Hb standard used should preferably be the one approved by International Committee for Standardization of Hematology.

Other Methods of Hb estimation

1. ***Oxyhaemoglobin method*** – 0.04% liquid ammonia (Ammonium hydroxide) is used which lyses the red cells. O.D. of oxyhaemoglobin solution so obtained is taken at 540 nm in a colorimeter.
2. ***Alkaline haematin method*** – Strong alkali like N/10 NaOH is used and the colour of alkaline haematin is compared against a standard.
3. ***Haldane's method*** – In this method, RBCs are lysed and carbon monoxide is added to convert Hb to carboxy-haemoglobin whose colour is compared with that of a standard.

Hb, CELL COUNTS AND ABSOLUTE VALUES BY HAEMATOLOGY AUTOANALYSER

Haematology autoanalyser (cell counter) (Fig. 8.3, 9.4, 9.5)

- Red cells are lysed by the lysate provided and the colour is matched against the inbuilt standard colour and the Hb value is obtained. Most of the cell counters utilise a cyanide free bio-degradable reagent.
- RBCs and platelets are analysed using the DC-detection method.
- White cells are analysed by flow cytometry using a semiconductor laser.
- DLC is based on cytochemical stains. Abnormal cell information is provided by the advanced cell counters.
- Haematocrit is calculated by cumulative pulse height detection method.
- The various parameters obtained include Hb, PCV, TLC, Plt, DLC, MCV, MCH, MCHC, red cell distribution width (RDW) red cell diameter, platelet diameter and 3-part/5-part differential count.
- Cell counters also display histograms of red cells, white cells and platelets (Fig. 8.3, 9.4, 9.5).
- Such systems are accurate provided standardisation of these analysers is carried out frequently; however, standards are expensive.

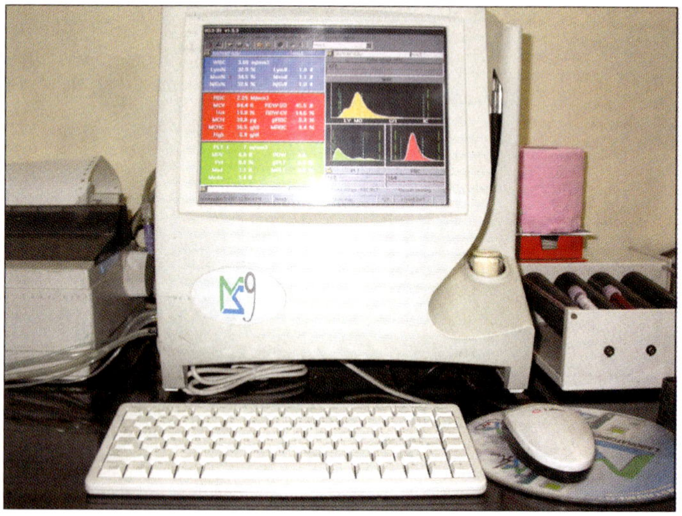

Fig. 8.3 Hematology autoanalyser for Hb, TLC, Plt count, MCV, MCH, MCHC and DLC.

VIVA VOCE

Q. What are the various methods available for Hb estimation?

Ans. These are:

- Acid haematin – Sahli's method
- Alkali haematin method – KOH/NaOH is used
- Oxyhaemoglobin method – NH_4OH is used.
- Cyanmethaemoglobin method – Drabkin solution is used.
- Automated haematology analysers.

Q. What are the various uses of Hb pipette?

Ans. Hb pipette can measure 0.02 ml (20 cumm) of blood and therefore can be used wherever different dilutions are required e.g.

- For TLC – 0.4 ml Turk's fluid in a small test tube, add 0.02 ml blood (using Hb pipette), resulting in a dilution of 1 in 20.
- For RBC count – 4 ml RBC fluid + 0.02 ml blood – dilution 1 in 200.
- For platelet count – 0.4 ml platelet count fluid + 0.02 ml blood – dilution 1 in 20.
- For eosinophil count – 0.2 ml Dunger's fluid + 0.02 ml blood-dilution 1 in 10.
- For sperm count, CSF cell count etc.

Q. What is cyanmethaemoglobin?

Ans. In cyanmethaemoglobin method, Drabkin solution containing KCN + K3Fe(CN)6 is used. K3Fe(CN)6 being an oxidising agent converts Hb(Fe++) to Met Hb(Fe+++) and KCN converts Met Hb to Cyanmethaemoglobin (a stable compound).

Q. What are the advantages of Cyanmethaemoglobin method over Acid Haematin method?

Ans. (a) It is a colorimetric method, so personal error of matching the colour of acid hematin method is eliminated.

(b) CyanmetHb is a stable compound and its colour does not change while acid haematin colour starts fading after 10 minutes and a lower Hb value is obtained, if reading is taken later on.

(c) In cyanmethaemoglobin method, all Hbs except sulfhaemoglobin are converted to cyanmet Hb while in acid haematin method carboxy Hb, carbamino Hb and sulfhaemoglobin are not converted into acid haematin, therefore, a lower Hb value is obtained.

Q. What precautions are needed in the cyanmethaemoglobin method?

Ans. Drabkin solution should not be turbid, wavelength of 540/green filter is to be used, Hb standard should be an inter-national/WHO standard for accuracy.

Q. Why is reading taken from upper meniscus?

Ans. In coloured solutions, reading is taken from the upper meniscus and in colourless liquids (e.g. water), it is taken from the lower meniscus.

Q. Why should the stirrer not be taken out of Hb meter tube?

Ans. Whenever stirrer is taken out, small amount of acid haematin sticking to the glass rod is lost, thus lowering the Hb value. Therefore, it should just be lifted up from the solution in the upper part of the tube, while taking the reading.

Q. In Sahli's method, why do we wait for 10 minutes after mixing blood with acid?

Ans. So that RBCs are lysed and Hb gets converted into acid haematin completely.

Q. In Sahli's Hb meter apparatus, why are square tube and flat comparator glasses preferred?

Ans. It is easier to compare adjoining flat surfaces e.g. square tube with acid haematin with flat brown surface on either side. Error due to curvature is avoided.

Q. Why is N/10 HCl used in Sahli's method?

Ans. Brown colour of the comparator glass is equivalent to the colour of acid hematin produced using N/10 HCl for a blood sample of 14.8 gm%. Test solution is compared against it. Therefore no other strength of HCl should be used.

Q. In cell counters, what is the chemical used (cyanide free) for estimation of haemoglobin?

Ans. Sodium Lauryl Sulphate (SLS) is used and it rapidly converts Hb into detectable chromogen.

Q. Name some tumors which cause rise in hemoglobin values?

Ans.
- Leiomyoma uterus
- Renal cell carcinoma
- Liver tumors (hepatocellular carcinoma)
- Cerebellar hemangio-blastoma

Q. Cut off value of hemoglobin for polycythemia vera?

Ans.

Males	18.5 g/dl
Females	16.5 g/dl

(Hb > 17 g/dL in men, Hb > 15 g/dL in females which if associated with a documented and sustained increase of atleast 2 g/dL from an invididuals baseline value that cannot be attributed to correction of iron deficiency)

Q. Mutation associated with polycythemia?

Ans. JAK 2 v617F (occurs in > 95% patients)
JAK 2 exon 12 mutations

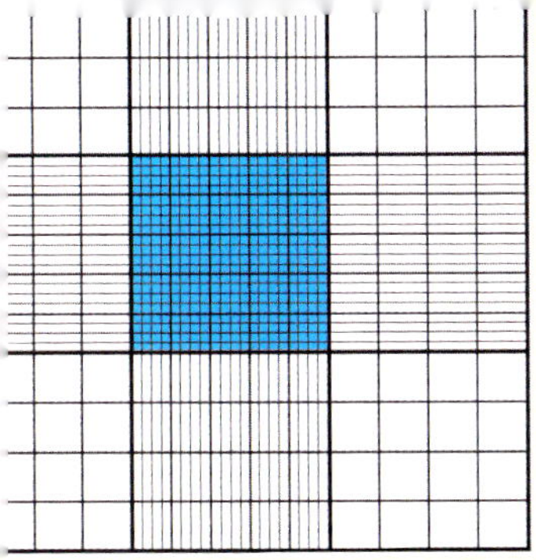

9

Cell Counts

Cellular elements constitute 45% of the blood volume. Red cells, white cells and platelets get altered in various disease states and therefore their assessment is an essential investigation in work up of various diseases.

TOTAL LEUCOCYTE COUNT – TLC

Leucocytes in the blood can be measured by a manual method using a Neubauer chamber or by using an electronic cell counter. The former method is still widely used.

Principle

Whole blood is diluted with WBC fluid that hemolyses the red cells. Nucleated cells – WBCs stained by Gentian violet are counted in a **Neubauer chamber**.

Equipment

Hemocytometer set consisting of WBC pipette (Thoma pipette) and improved Neubauer chamber with cover slip.

WBC pipette has a white bead in the bulb and markings of 0.5, 1 and 11 (Fig. 9.1).

Improved Neubauer chamber has a shiny surface which makes the lines very clearly visible even after charging it. It has a total area of 3 mm × 3 mm with central ruled area of 1 mm × 1 mm. The central area consists of 25 groups of 16 small squares separated by bold lines. Corner 1 mm × 1 mm squares have 16 smaller squares each, which are used for TLC (Fig. 9.2). Depth of the chamber is 0.1 mm.

Fig. 9.1: WBC pipette, white bead (↑)

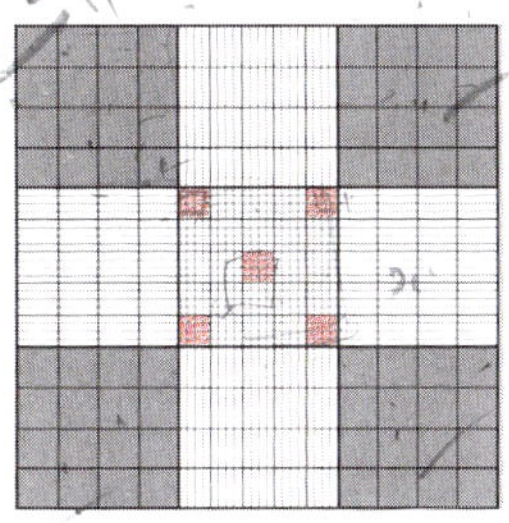

Fig. 9.2a Large corner squares (shown grey) for TLC. 5 small squares in central square (shown red) for RBC count.

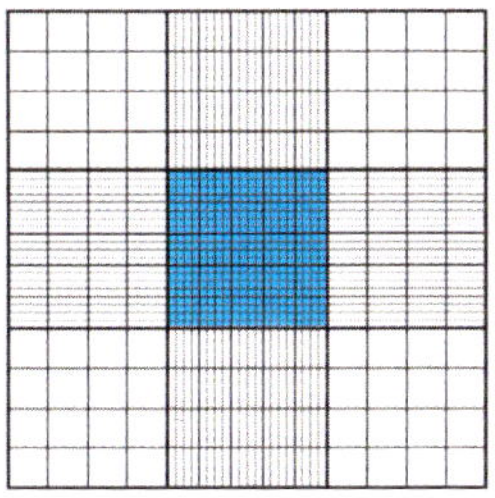

Fig. 9.2b Central 1 × 1 mm (shown blue) for platelet count.

WBC Fluid (Turk's Fluid)

Composition

Glacial acetic acid	– 2 ml to lyse RBCs
1% Gentian violet	– 5 drops to stain WBC nuclei
Add water to	100 ml

Method

- Mix the blood gently by shaking the vial so that cells and plasma mix well.
- Fill blood in the WBC pipette upto mark 0.5 and wipe off excess blood on the sides of the pipette nozzle.
- Fill the pipette with Turk's fluid upto mark 11 by drawing the fluid from the bottle.
- Rotate the pipette slowly so that blood and fluid mix thoroughly in the bulb of the pipette; mixing is facilitated by the white bead present in the bulb.
- Discard 1 drop WBC fluid since fluid upto mark 1 has not mixed with blood.
- Clean the chamber and place the thick cover slip on the ruled area.

- Charge the chamber by placing the tip of the pipette just under the cover slip and fluid flows under it by capillary action till the counting chamber is just filled.
- Wait for 2-3 minutes for cells to settle.
- Examine the ruled area under micro-scope using a low power objective. White cells are easily recognised since their nuclei are stained by gentian violet.
- Count white cells in 4 corner large squares (1 × 1 mm each – Fig. 9.2a).

$$\text{TLC} = \frac{N \times 20}{4^{*} \times 0.1} = N \times 50$$

depth of the chamber = 0.1 mm

dilution = 1 in 20

*4 corner squares (grey coloured) are counted.

N – Number of WBCs in 4 large squares

Sources of error

(a) ***Errors due to equipment*** – These errors are because of the inaccuracies of the graduations of the pipettes and depth of the ruled area. Therefore, use of a certified standard (ISI) equipment is suggested.

(b) ***Errors due to nature of the sample*** – When blood is taken from an EDTA vial, the sample should be mixed thoroughly, otherwise high/low counts may be obtained if mainly sedimented cells/plasma is taken. Clots in the blood entangle cells giving fallacious results.

(c) ***Operator's errors***
- improper charging of the chamber;
- mistaking dust particles for cells;
- overflowing of the chamber with mixture going into the moat.

(d) ***Field errors*** – Unequal distribution of cells in the counting chamber; can be corrected by counting large number of cells.

Nucleated red cells are not lysed and counted with WBCs. If nucleated red cells are more than 4/100 WBCs in the DLC, a correction for n RBCs should be made.

$$\text{Corrected TLC} = \frac{\text{TLC} \times 100}{100 + \text{Number of n-RBCs/100 WBCs}}$$

Normal range of TLC

Adults	4000–11000 cells/cumm	($4–11 \times 10^9$/L)
At birth	8000–28000 cells/cumm	($8–28 \times 10^9$/L)
Childhood	6000–15000 cells/cumm	($6–15 \times 10^9$/L)

Leucocytosis

TLC more than 11000/cumm. This is observed in:
- pregnancy
- exercise
- leukemoid reaction
- diabetic and uremic coma
- infectious mononucleosis
- bacterial and viral infections
- leukemias – CML, CLL and acute leukemias

When TLC is very high a dilution of 1 in 100 or 1 in 200 using RBC pipette may be necessary for accurate count.

Leucopenia

TLC less than 4000/cumm. This is observed in:
- aplastic anemia
- hypersplenism
- typhoid, paratyphoid fever
- drug induced leucopenia
- radiation and cytotoxic therapy
- megaloblastic anemia
- subleukemic leukemia

When there is marked leucopenia, it is advisable to use 1 in 10 dilution for greater accuracy by taking blood upto mark 1 instead of 0.5.

Other Methods of TLC

Using Hb pipette

Take 0.4 ml of Turk's fluid in a small test tube and add 1 Hb pipette – 0.02 ml of blood into it and mix. Dilution is 1 in 20. Charge the chamber with a dropper.

Cell counters

(page 69).

RED CELL COUNT

Estimation of red cell mass can be made by RBC count, Hb estimation and haematocrit. All three are important in evaluating any case of anaemia and also for the calculation of absolute values.

Equipment

(a) Red cell pipette with a red bead in the bulb and markings of 0.5, 1 and 101 (Fig. 9.3).

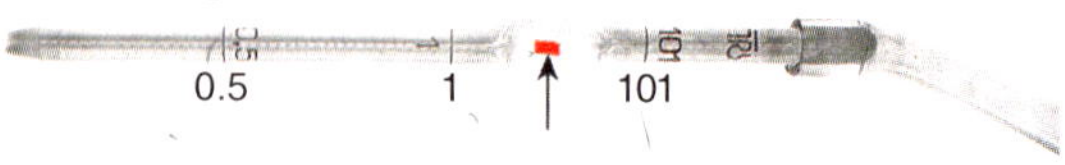

Fig. 9.3: RBC pipette, red bead (↑).

(b) Improved Neubauer chamber (Fig. 9.2).

Diluting fluid

(a) ***Hayem's fluid***

Mercuric chloride	0.5 gm
Sodium chloride	1.0 gm
Sodium sulfate	5.0 gm
Distilled water	200 ml

Filter the solution and keep it at room temperature. Mercuric chloride prevents the growth of bacteria, while sodium chloride and sodium sulfate provide iso-osmolality. However, RBCs tend to agglutinate especially in cases of dysproteinemia. Therefore, Dacie's fluid is recommended.

(b) ***Dacie's fluid (formol – citrate solution)***

Sodium citrate dihydrate	5.0 gm	Stock solution
Formalin	1 ml	
D. water to	100 ml	

Stock solution is diluted 1 in 10 before use.

Method

- Draw EDTA blood to exactly 0.5 mark of RBC pipette. Wipe the tip of the pipette with wet cotton to remove excess of blood on the sides of the tip.
- Dip the tip of the pipette in the diluting fluid and draw it upto mark 101, past the bulb.
- Rotate the pipette in its long axis to ensure thorough mixing of blood and diluent; facilitated by the red bead in the bulb.
- Place the cover slip on the cleaned ruled area of the Neubauer chamber.
- Discard the first drop from the pipette since blood and diluent are not mixed in the long nozzle of the pipette. Charge the chamber till it is completely charged by the capillary action.
- Allow the cells to settle in the chamber for 2-5 minutes.
- Locate the central ruled area for red cell counting by examining under low power objective.
- Count RBCs using high power objective in the 5 red squares (Fig. 9.2) and add them together – N.

$$\text{RBC count} = \frac{N}{1/5 \times 1/10 \times 1/200}$$

$$= \text{counted cells} \times 10000$$

1/200 – dilution of blood

1/10mm – depth of the chamber

1/5 mm^2 area counted (5 × 1/5 × 1/5mm^2)

Normal range

Adult male	4.5–5.5 million/cumm	($4.5–5.5 \times 10^{12}$/L)
Adult female	3.8–5.2 million/cumm	($3.8–5.2 \times 10^{12}$/L)
At birth	4.0–6.0 million/cumm	($4.0–6.0 \times 10^{12}$/L)

Increased red cell count

(a) ***Physiologic*** – newborns.

(b) ***Polycythemia rubra vera*** – a chronic myelo-proliferative disorder.

(c) ***Secondary polycythemia***

- due to dehydration
- hypoxia - at high altitude
- renal cell carcinoma
- uterine myomas
- hemangioblastoma of cerebellum
- phaeochromocytoma

(renal cell carcinoma to phaeochromocytoma: increased erythropoietin production by kidney)

Decreased red cell count

- anaemias
- haemodilution

Sources of error

As given for WBC count.

Other errors in RBC count

- Hayem's solution does not lyse the WBCs which appear granular and need differentiation from RBCs in cases of leukemias where TLC is very high.
- Whenever possible, both sides of the chamber should be filled and count carried on both sides and mean of the two taken.

Other Methods

1. ***Using Sahli's Hb meter pipette***, 0.02 ml blood is added to 4 ml of RBC fluid with a dilution of 1 in 200.
2. ***Cell counters*** (page 69).

PLATELET COUNT

Principle

Anticoagulated blood is diluted with a diluent that hemolyses the red cells leaving platelets e.g. in 1% Ammonium oxalate. However, in Dacie's fluid and Rees-Ecker fluid RBCs are not lysed and threfore these can be used for RBC count also.

Diluting Fluids

1. ***Brecher-Cronkite fluid*** – 1% Ammonium oxalate solution is filtered and stored at 4°C.
2. ***Dacie's fluid***

• Sod. citrate dihydrate	5 gm
• Formalin	1 ml
• 0.2% brilliant cresyl blue	0.1 ml
• D. water to make	100 ml

Stock solution is diluted 1 in 10 before use.

3. ***Rees-Ecker fluid***
   - Sodium citrate 3.8 gm
   - Brilliant cresyl blue 50 mg
   - Formalin 0.2 ml
   - D. water to make 100 ml

   Brilliant cresyl blue stains platelets pale blue.

Equipment

Improved Neubauer chamber, WBC pipette, RBC pipette.

Method

- Fill blood upto mark 0.5 on WBC pipette.
- 1% Ammonium oxalate diluent is filled upto mark 11 of WBC pipette thus making a dilution of 1 in 20.
- Charge the chamber as given for TLC count.
- Place the charged chamber in a moist petri dish (wet filter paper at the bottom) for 5 minutes so that the platelets settle down.
  - Platelets are counted in the central 1 × 1 mm square (Fig. 9.2b). Platelets are recognised more readily if the focus of light microscope is altered carefully with the fine adjustment and if illumination is reduced by closing the iris diaphragm. Condenser should be lowered. Platelets appear as highly *refractile* particles.

$$\text{Platelet count} = \frac{\text{No. of plt. counted} \times \text{dilution}}{1 \times 1 \text{ sqmm} \times 1/10 \text{ mm (depth)}}$$

$$= \frac{N \times 20}{1/10}$$

$$= N \times 200 \text{ platelets/cumm}$$

Normal Range

1,50,000–4,00,000 platelets per cumm (150-400 × 10^9/L).

Sources of Error

1. If agglutinated platelets are seen in the Neubauer chamber, count should not be carried out on such a specimen.
2. Always review the platelets in a well stained peripheral smear.
3. Sources of error as observed in TLC/RBC count.

Thrombocytopenia

Plt. count is less than 1,00,000/cumm. Its causes are :

- acute ITP
- chronic ITP
- DIC (Disseminated intravascular coagulation)
- drug induced thrombocytopenia
- all causes of pancytopenia like aplastic anemia, hyper-splenism, megaloblastic anemia, acute leukemias etc.
- Dengue fever

Thrombocytosis

Plt. count more than 4,00,000/cumm occurs in essential thrombocythemia, CML, post hemorrhage, post surgery, haemolytic anaemia and iron deficiency anaemia.

OTHER METHODS OF PLATELET COUNT

- Cell counter (page 69)
- Using Hb pipette. Take 0.4 mL of Brecher-Cronkite fluid in a small test tube. Add 0.02 ml of blood into it. Mix the two. Charge the Neubauer chamber. Count the platelets in the 4 corner bing squares (of TLC). Platelet count = N × 50.

ABSOLUTE EOSINOPHIL COUNT (AEC)

AEC is an accurate assessment of eosinophils in blood and is useful in diagnosis, treatment and follow-up of cases of eosinophilia.

Dunger's Fluid

- Eosin – 200 mg dissolved in 10 ml of distilled water. It stains the granules of eosinophils as orange red.
- Water – 80 ml. It lyses the red cells and white cells except eosinophils which are more resistant.
- Acetone – 10 ml, to fix the eosinophils. Filter and keep the fluid in a refrigerator.

Equipment

Improved Neubauer chamber, WBC pipette.

Method

- Take blood in a WBC pipette upto mark 1.
- Fill the pipette with Dunger's fluid upto mark 11 so that dilution is 1 in 10.
- Mix the fluid and blood by rotatory movement of the pipette and mixing is facilitated by the white bead in the bulb of the Thoma pipette.
- Charge the Neubauer chamber as is done for TLC count and wait for 5 minutes for eosinophils to settle down.
- Count the eosinophils in 4 corner squares as for TLC (Fig. 9.2a) using a low power objective within 1/2 hour. Eosinophils are recognised by their bright red granules.

$$\text{AEC} = \frac{N \times 10}{4 \times .1}$$

- dilution = 1 in 10.
- depth of chambr 0.1 mm
- 4 squares of 1 × 1 mm are counted.

AEC = number of eosinosphil in 4 squares × 25.

Normal Range

40-450 cells/cu mm (0.04–0.45 × 10^9/L)

High AEC

High AEC is observed in:
- parasitic diseases like worm infestations
- allergic conditions
- eosinophilic leukemia
- idiopathic hyper eosinophilic syndrome
- tropical eosinophilia
- other secondary causes of eosinophilia.

AEC using Fuch's Rosenthal Chamber

This is preferred to the Neubauer chamber since the ruled area is 16 sq.mm and depth is 0.2 mm (Neubauer chamber depth is 0.1 mm) and therefore more cells are counted increasing the accuracy of the count.

Other method of AEC

- Cell counter (page 69)

Sources of error

As for RBC/WBC count.

COMPLETE BLOOD COUNTS (CBC) (HAEMOGRAM) (CELL COUNTER)

Complete blood counts include the following:
- Hb
- TLC
- RBC count
- Plt. count
- DLC
- PCV/haematocrit
- Reticulocyte count
- Peripheral smear examination for red cell morphology, platelet morphology, parasites and any atypical cell.

All the above tests can be carried out on a 2 ml EDTA sample along with 2 peripheral smears.

Automated cell counters. These are single button-switch equipments and aspirate the blood sample with an autoprobe wiping facility. The screen displays the parameters along with 3 histograms for WBCs, RBCs and platelets (Fig. 9.4). The various parameters obtained in the cell counter report are:
- Hb
- MCV
- MPV
- Haematocrit (Hct)
- MCH
- RDW
- TLC
- MCHC
- Platelet count
- PDW
- Differential count 3 part or 5 part
- Reticulocyte count

The report also demonstrates histograms of WBCs, red cells and platelets (Fig. 9.5).

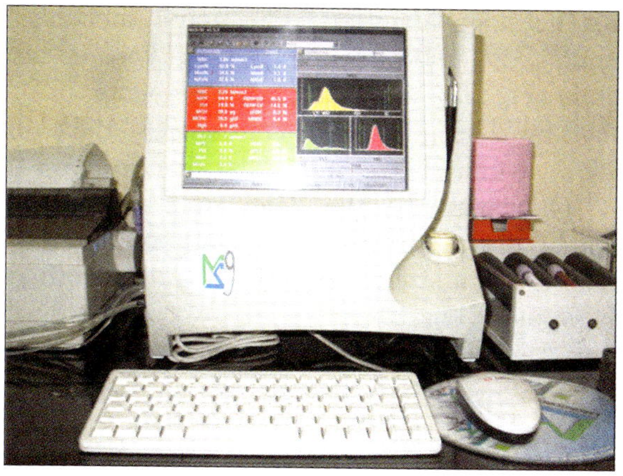

Fig. 9.4 Hematology autoanalyser for Hb, TLC, Plt count, MCV, MCH, MCHC and DLC.

Haemoglobin and haematocrit. Hb is obtained using a cyanide free reagent (Sodium Lauryl Sulphate). The counter calculates the mean MCV which gets multiplied by red cell count to give the haematocrit (Hct). Though packed cell volume (PCV) and Hct are used interchangeably; PCV is obtained by centrifuging the blood sample.

Red Cell Parameters and Histogram

The red cell parameters are haemoglobin, red cell count and MCV. MCH and MCHC are also displayed indicating the hemoglobin content of the red cells (Fig. 9.5).

Red cell histogram displays *Red cell distribution width (RDW)* in the form of standard deviation (SD) or coefficient of variation (CV). The bell-shaped curve indicates the degree of variation in the cell size i.e., anisocytosis. RDW-CV is normally between 10.4 to 15.2% (RDW-SD is 35.5 to 49.5 fl) (Fig. 9.5). RDW > 16 indicates anisocytosis of red cells and evaluation of the peripheral blood film is essential to look for spherocytes, fragmented red cells, tear drop cells, target cells and polychromatophils.

Some of the important diagnostic red cell values are:
- MCV < 80 fl, MCH < 25 RBC count > 5 million and RDW < 16; – microcytic anaemia, thalassemia trait.
- MCV < 80 fl, MCH < 25 and RDW high – iron deficiency anemia.
- MCV > 100 fl – macrocytic anaemia.

WBC histogram. The WBC histogram is based on the size of cells in femtolitres on the x-axis and the relative frequency of the cells on the *y* axis. It displays 3 peaks—the first one of lymphocytes (30–60 fl), the second one of middle cells and the third one of large cells (115–150 fl) corresponding to neutrophils. Absolute counts of lymphocytes, middle cells and neutrophils are also displayed. The middle cell count (78–114 fl) includes eosinophils, monocytes, blasts, promyelocytes, myelocytes and metamyelocytes.

5-part differential count is obtained in the present

Q. How do you clean the sides of the pipette nozzle?

Ans. – By wiping the sides with wet cotton.
– Never touch the tip of the nozzle as the blood-fluid mixture/blood will be drained off by capillary action.

Q. What are the differences between WBC and RBC pipette?

Ans. – Markings are .5, 1 and 11 in WBC pipette; .5, 1 and 101 in RBC pipette.
– Dilution is 1 in 20 in WBC pipette; 1 in 200 in RBC pipette.
– White bead in WBC pipette; red bead in RBC pipette.

Q. What are the sources of error in cell counts – manual method?

Ans. See page 66, 67 and 68.

Q. How do you clean the Neubauer chamber?

Ans. After use, the chamber should be rinsed in water and wiped clean with a lint-free cloth and dried. Lint or gauze should not be used to clean the chamber as it may scratch the chamber and lint particles may stick to it. Do not touch the ruled area as fingerprints are not easily removed and hamper accurate cell counts. Always hold the chamber from the sides.

Q. How do you clean the WBC/RBC/Hb pipette?

Ans. These pipettes are cleaned by filling them with distilled water and blowing it out twice. Finally, acetone is sucked into the pipette and blown out. Acetone removes water from it and dries it completely. In a dry pipette bead rolls freely while in wet pipette, it does not.

Q. Why is 1 drop of fluid from WBC/RBC pipette discarded?

Ans. Diluting fluid in the nozzle of the pipette is not mixed with blood and therefore needs to be discarded.

Q. What is the significance of increased Red cell distribution width (RDW)?

Ans. RDW indicates the variation in cell size and therefore is a pointer of degree of anisopoikilocytosis. Normal RDW-CV is < 16.

Q. What is the significance of platelet volume (PV).

Ans. Platelet volume indicates the size of platelets. PV > 12 fl is suggestive of presence of giant platelets which are observed in Bernard-Soulier syndrome, regenerating platelets in Dengue fever and in myeloproliferative disorders.

Q. What is the other name of WBC pipette?

Ans. Thoma pipette.

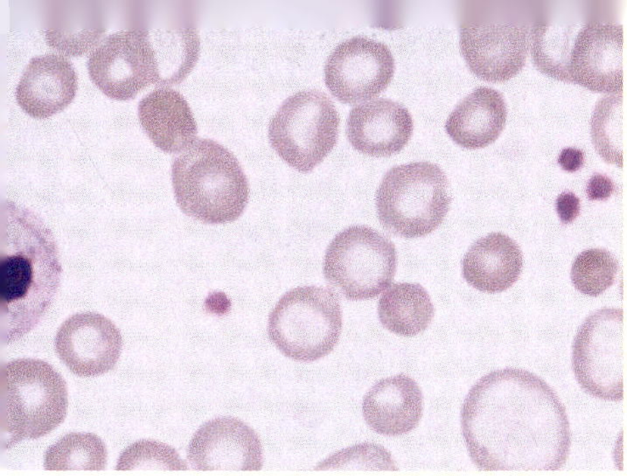

10

Peripheral Smear and Differential Leucocyte Count

PERIPHERAL SMEAR

Peripheral smear (peripheral blood film – PBF) is the most important investigation in haematology. It provides information about red cells – their number, shape, size and variations in morphology to diagnose different types of anaemias and other hematologic disorders. Differential leucocyte count – DLC is very important in diagnosis of various haematologic and non-haematologic diseases. Assessment of platelet number, their aggregates and morphology is helpful in diagnosis of various bleeding disorders. Moreover, smear evaluation is a check on the values obtained from automated cell counters. For evaluation of a peripheral smear (PS) it is essential to have a nicely made and stained PS.

How to make a PS

- Take one drop of venous blood from the syringe as the blood is collected from the antecubital vein for various haematologi-cal/biochemical investigations. A drop of blood can be taken from a finger prick/heel prick in infants. This drop of blood is put on a cleaned slide 1 cm from the end.
- Take another slide with a smooth edge – spreader and place the edge over the drop so that blood spreads along the edge.
- Keep the spreader slide at approximately 30°-40° angle (Fig. 10.1) and make a smear with a forward movement of the spreader. Smear should be 2.5 to 3.5 cm in length and spreader should preferably have smaller edge than the slide on which smear is being made.
- Air dry the smear.
- Make at least 2 smears of each sample.

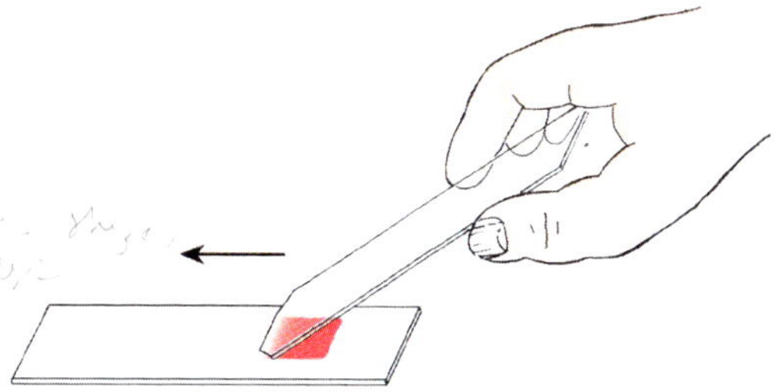

Fig. 10.1: How to make a peripheral smear

Sources of Error

- If the slide is greasy, smear has blank oval areas, hence the need for a thoroughly cleaned slide.
- If the spreader edge is not smooth, ragged tail of the smear is formed, which has majority of neutrophils while rest of the smear reveals paucity of neutrophils – called "tailing of the smear". Irregular distribution of cells does not give accurate DLC and, therefore, spreader should have a smooth edge.

FIXATION OF THE SMEAR

- Smears should be fixed within 4 hours to get good staining of cells and avoid background staining of plasma. Take methanol in a Coplin jar. Give 4-6 dips to the smear in methanol. Let it air dry.
- Methanol of the prediluted Leishman stain for 2 minutes fixes the smear and post dilution stain for 15-30 minutes actually stains the PS.

STAINING OF THE SMEAR

Staining of the smears is carried out using *Romanowsky stains* which stain red cells, white cells, platelets and parasites.

Staining with Leishman's stain

- Place the PS on the staining rack.

- Pour the stain on the slide with a dropper and count the drops and cover the whole slide with the stain.
- After 2 minutes, pour double the number of drops of buffer water (Sorensen's phosphate buffer, pH 6.8) or distilled water on the slide and mix buffer with stain, using a dropper.
- Let the slide be stained by this mixture for 15-30 minutes. Exact time to be decided for each batch of stain.
- Pour running water from one side of the slide so that the stain scum is drained off the slide and no more stain is left on the slide (Fig. 10.2).
- Pick up the slide and keep it slanting for it to dry up.
- The slide is ready for examination.

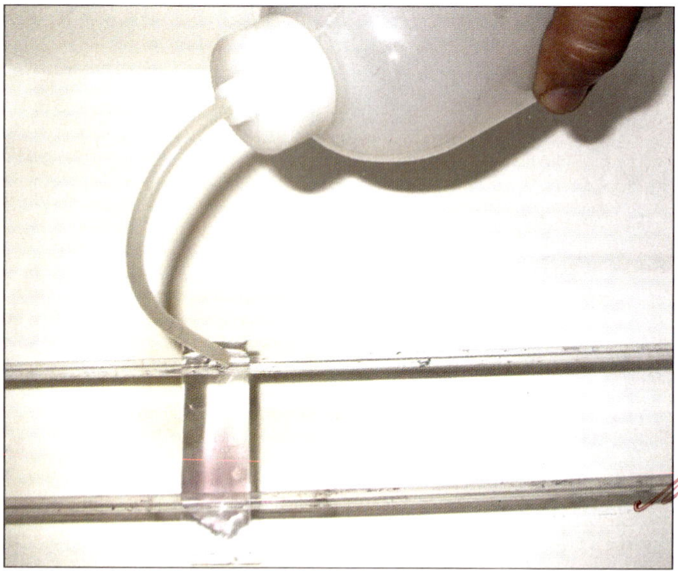

Fig. 10.2: Washing the stain off the smear by pouring water on one side of the slide.

Sources of error

- If the pH of the buffer is too acidic, then red cells stain pink, and WBCs stain very light.
- If the pH of the buffer is too basic, red cells stain blue and WBCs take a bluish black hue. Hence, for proper staining, buffer with correct pH 6.8 should be used.
- Sometimes red cells demonstrate holes in them. These are due to air bubbles because of air drying in humid weather (July-August). To overcome this, during these months, smear should be dried up quickly by waving it vigorously in air.

ROMANOWSKY STAINS

These stains consist of mixture of methylene blue, eosin and methylene blue oxidation products – azures which are formed by interaction and chemical treatment of the stain. These products are responsible for different shades of staining e.g. red cells - pink; eosinophilic granules - red-orange; basophilic granules - bluish black; neutrophilic granules - lilac (azurophilic granules combine with azures of the stain); nuclear chromatin - purple black; white cell cytoplasm - faint purple.

Following are the commonly used stains:
- Leishman stain
- Giemsa stain
- Wright's stain
- Jenner's stain
- Jenner-Giemsa stain

Leishman stain

Leishman stain powder	1 gm
Methanol (acetone free)	500 ml

Mix the two. Warm the mixture to 50°C for 15 minutes in a conical flask. Filter the stain and the stain is ready for use after 2 days.

Giemsa stain

Giemsa stain powder	1 gm
Glycerol	66 ml
Methanol (acetone free)	66 ml

Dissolve Giemsa stain in glycerol at 60°C for 2 hours. Cool it. Add 66 ml of methanol (acetone free) and mix. Keep it at 37°C for 1 week to ripen. Stain is filtered before use.

Buffer water (Sorensen's phosphate buffer)

Solution A

Pot. dihydrogen phosphate - 9.08 gm/litre

Solution B

Dibasic Sod. phosphate - 9.47 gm/litre

For pH 6.8	Solution A	50.8 ml
	Solution B	49.2 ml

Mix the two solutions to get 100 ml of buffer water.

Giemsa staining

- Fixation of the smears - 8-10 dips in methanol in a Coplin jar.
- Dry the slides and then pour the diluted (1 in 10) stain for 20-30 minutes. Exact dilution and time of staining to be determined for each batch of stain.
- Wash the slide (as in Leishman staining) and dry it.

EVALUATION OF A PERIPHERAL SMEAR

Peripheral smear (PS) is the single most useful investigation which gives lot of information about red cells, white cells, platelets, abnormal cells and haemoparasites.

Steps

- Apply very thin layer of oil all over the smear and examine it under low power objective to look for:
  - quality of PS
  - uniformity of staining.
- ***Area for DLC*** – tail and edges of the smear should be avoided while doing DLC, since monocytes and neutrophils predominate in these areas. However, this area is better suited for parasites like microfilaria and malarial parasites, since these being heavier than red cells are carried to the tail by the spreader slide. DLC should be carried out in thin part of the smear next to tail and moving the slide as shown in Fig. 10.3 till a minimum of 100 cells have been counted.
- ***Area for red cell morphology*** – choose an area where red cells are evenly distributed and there is slight overlap of RBCs. Tail, head and edges of the smear should be avoided.

  The best area is between tail and body of the smear (Fig. 10.3).

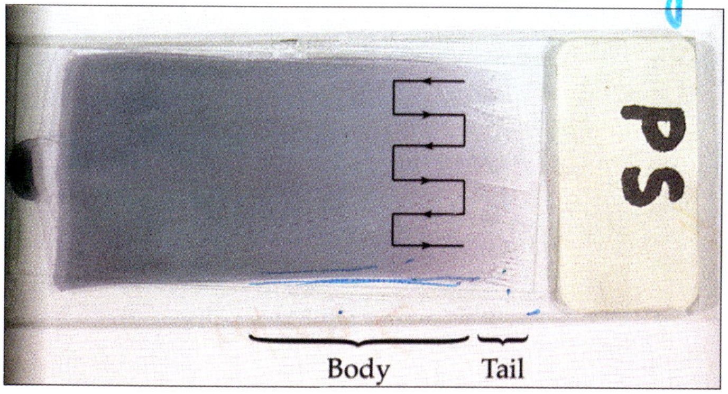

Fig. 10.3: P.S. demonstrating body and tail of the smear. Area for DLC earmarked is close to tail.

- Examine this area in oil immersion lens by putting a drop of oil onto the slide.

  Look for:
  - (i) red cell morphology
  - (ii) platelet clumps
  - (iii) record the different types of white cells.
- Move the slide sideways and then horizontally and count at least 100 white cells (Fig. 10.4).

N	N	L	N	L	L	N	L	E	M
N	N	N	M	L	L	E	N	N	N
N	L	N	N	N	L	L	M	N	N
N	N	N	N	L	N	N	N	L	N
N	L	N	L	L	N	N	N	N	E
N	N	M	N	N	L	N	M	N	N
L	N	N	L	N	L	N	M	N	N
L	N	N	N	N	N	E	N	N	N
L	L	L	N	N	N	N	L	N	N
N	L	L	N	N	N	N	N	N	L

N – Neutrophils L – Lymphocytes M – Monocytes
E – Eosinophils B – Basophils

Fig. 10.4: Differential count on the smear; by counting 100 cells

Normal Range of DLC

Neutrophils	50-75%
Lymphocytes	25-45%
Monocytes	3-8%
Eosinophils	1-6%
Basophils	0-1%

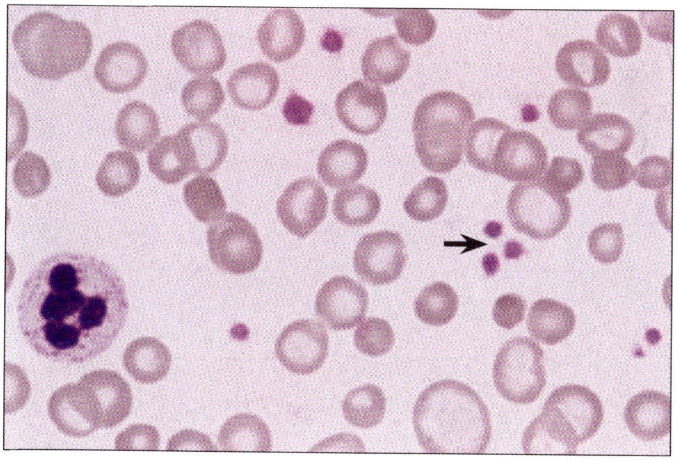

Fig. 10.5: Normal P.S. demonstrating red cells, a neutrophil, and platelets (↑).

ALTERATIONS IN DLC

Alterations in DLC are a manifestation of the underlying disease process and therefore accurate DLC is of great clinical significance while making treatment decisions. Some of the DLC alterations are discussed hereunder.

Neutrophilia

More than 75% neutrophils in peripheral blood (neutrophilia) is usually accompanied by leucocytosis of 15000-30000/cumm (Fig. 10.6). Neutrophils in bacterial infections demonstrate toxic granules. These granules are strongly peroxidase positive and actually represent lysosomes. Sometimes, neutrophils demonstrate Dohle bodies which are round-oval structures, 1-4 microns in size, in the peripheral part of cytoplasm of a neutrophil. These are believed to be part of the vestigial cytoplasm left from earlier cellular stages. These are observed in toxic conditions like scarlet fever, septicemia, pneumonia, burns and exposure to cytotoxic drugs.

Common causes of neutrophilia

(i) ***Acute bacterial infections*** due to staphy-lococcus, streptococcus, pneumococcus, gonococcus and meningococcus like
- lobar pneumonia
- bronchopneumonia
- pyogenic meningitis
- cellulitis

- infected burns
- diphtheria
- acute salpingitis

(ii) ***Acute inflammatory diseases*** like
- acute rheumatic fever
- acute appendicitis

(iii) ***Acute stress states*** like
- post surgery
- post haemorrhage
- myocardial infarction

(iv) ***Chronic myeloproliferative disorders*** like
- CML (chronic myeloid leukemia)
- polycythemia vera (PV)

At times, high neutrophilia is accompanied by the presence of immature white cells like metamyelocytes, myelocytes and promyelocytes and such a condition is called *Leukaemoid reaction*; this needs to be differentiated from CML as given in the table 16.3. In leukemoid reaction TLC is high and blasts are < 1%, without basophilia.

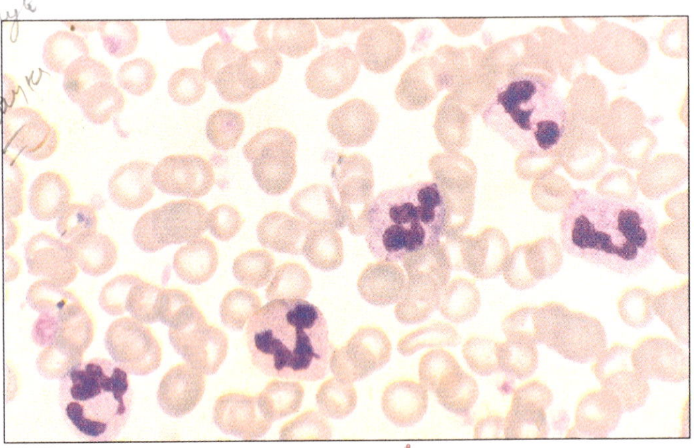

Fig. 10.6: Neutrophilia

Neutropenia

Reduction in neutrophils results in relative increase of lymphocytes; however, severe neutropenia results in leucopenia. Some of the conditions are:

(i) ***infective diseases*** like typhoid, para-typhoid, influenza and Rocky mountain spotted fever;

(ii) ***physical agents*** - radiation;

(iii) ***chemicals*** - benzene;

(iv) ***antimetabolite drugs*** - cyclophos-phamide, methotrexate etc.;

(v) ***haematologic disorders*** like megaloblastic anaemia, aplastic anaemia, subleukaemic leukemia, cyclic neutropenia and chronic granulomatous disease of childhood.

Lymphocytosis

In lymphocytosis, mature lymphocytes are usually more than 45% in peripheral blood (Fig. 10.7). Common causes of lymphocytosis are:

(i) ***chronic infective conditions*** like tuberculosis, syphilis and brucellosis;

(ii) ***viral diseases*** like infectious mononucleosis, infectious lymphocytosis, measles, chicken-pox and viral fevers;

(iii) ***neoplastic conditions*** like CLL (chronic lymphocytic leukemia), NHL spillover.

Infectious mononucleosis is characterised by the presence of transformed lymphocytes (virocytes) which are blastoid, monocytoid and of plasmacytoid forms.

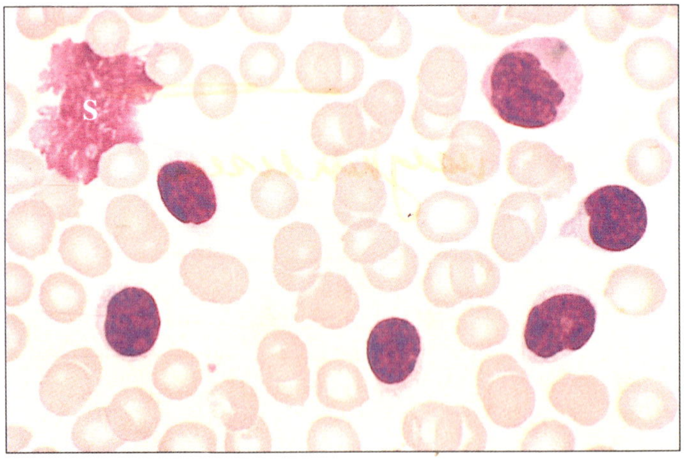

Fig. 10.7: Lymphocytosis

Eosinophilia

A wide range of disorders are responsible for an increase in eosinophils in blood (Fig. 10.8) as well as in many organs like lung, CNS and skin and may result in organ dysfunction. Eosinophilia is observed in:

(i) ***allergic states*** like bronchial asthma, hay fever and urticaria;

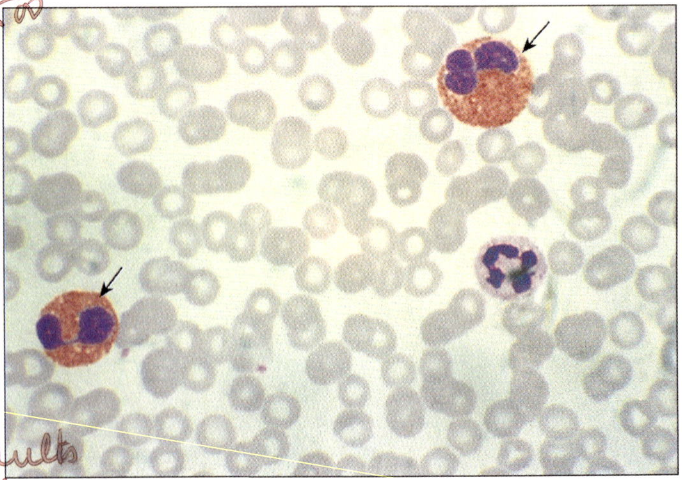

Fig. 10.8: Eosinophilia – 2 eosinophils (↑) and 1 neutrophil. Eosinophils with bilobed nuclei and coarse orange-red granules.

(ii) ***parasitic infestations*** like filariasis, round worm, hook worm infestation and echinococcosis;
(iii) ***dermatoses*** like pemphigus, atopic dermatitis and eczema;
(iv) ***haematologic disorders*** like hyper-eosinophilic syndrome and Hodgkin's disease;
(v) miscellaneous conditions like pulmonary eosinophilia, *tropical eosinophilia* and *Loeffler's syndrome.*

Monocytosis

Increased number of monocytes (Fig. 10.9) is observed in:
(i) ***parasitic conditions*** like malaria and kala-azar;
(ii) ***infective conditions*** like subacute bactrial endocarditis, tuberculosis, syphilis and typhus;
(iii) ***neoplastic states*** like acute monocytic leukemia AML – M5; acute myelo-monocytic leukemia AML – M4 and chronic myelo-monocytic leukemia.

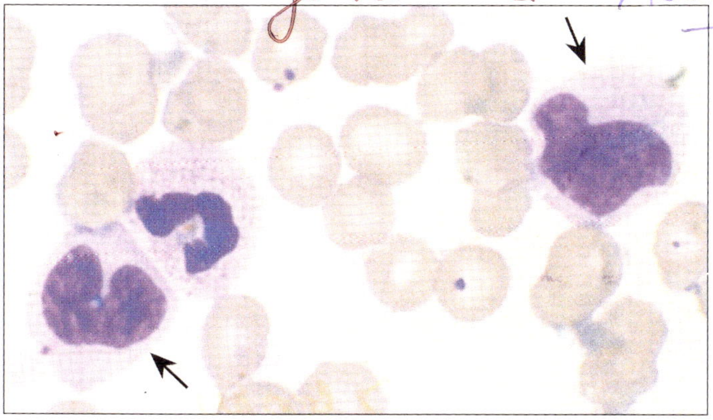

Fig. 10.9 Monocytosis. Monocytes with reniform nuclei and glassy chromatin (↑) with one neutrophil.

Basophilia

In a normal individual basophils are less than 1% in peripheral blood. Increase in basophils is found in CML, myelofibrosis, basophilic leukemia and urticaria pigmentosa (Fig. 10.10).

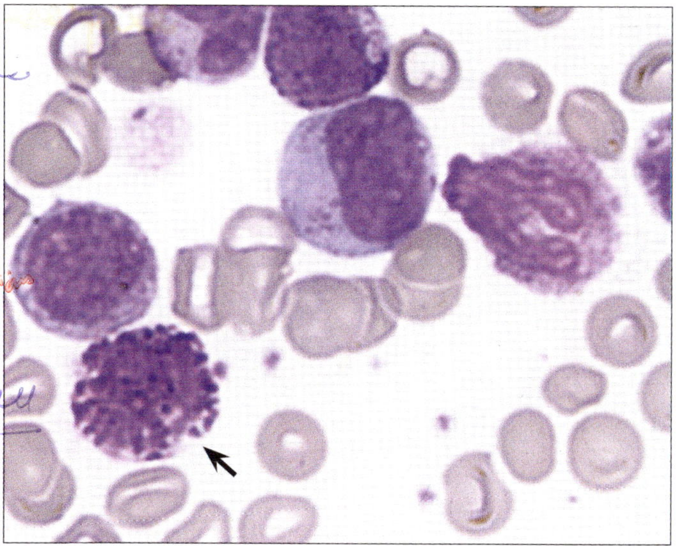

Fig. 10.10: Peripheral blood film from a case of CML shows basophils (↑) with nucleus covered by dark basophilic granules.

VIVA VOCE

Q. What is tailing of the smear?
Ans. If the edge of the spreader is not smooth, the smear shows streaks which contain large number of neutrophils and platelets. In rest of the smear neutrophils are diminished.

Q. What is a **thick smear** and what is its use?
Ans. Thick smear is made by spreading a drop of blood on the slide in an area of about 2 cm diameter and letting it dry. This smear is given 2-4 dips in tap water till red coloured solution comes out (dehemoglobinisation of the smear). Then the smear is fixed in methanol and stained with Giemsa/Leishman stain. Thick smear is of use in quick detection of malarial parasite.

Q. What parasites can be identified in peripheral smear?
Ans. Malarial parasite, microfilaria and sometimes L.D. bodies which may be free or inside a monocyte in fulminant cases of kala-azar.

Q. How can an assessment of platelets be made on PS?
Ans. In a smear, platelets are usually present in clumps. Platelets are singly scattered all over the smear if smear is made from EDTA blood or in cases of platelet function disorder where aggregation is defective. In a normal person, there are 3-5 platelets for every 100 RBCs. Fewer than 3 platelets/100 RBCs is suggestive of thrombocytopenia and platelet count should be carried out.

Q. In which cases plasma stains the smear blue?

Ans. In hypergammaglobulinemia (M. myeloma, W. macroglobulinemia), plasma stains blue and colours the background and is usually associated with rouleaux formation of RBCs.

Q. What stains the neutrophilic granules?

Ans. Neutrophilic granules are stained purple by the azures of methylene blue.

Q. What is the use of buffer for diluting the stain?

Ans. Romanowsky stain diluted with phosphate buffer pH 6.8 imparts a reddish hue to red cells and differential staining of granules of granulocytes.

Q. What are toxic granules?

Ans. These are coarse granules (strongly peroxidase positive, represent phago-some), observed in bacterial infections like pyogenic meningitis, enteric fever etc.

Q. What is the evidence of bacterial infection in infants?

Ans. Increase in the number of band forms of neutrophils suggests a bacterial infection. This helps in differentiating bacterial diarrhoeas from viral diarrhoeas, since the latter ones may not require any antibiotic therapy.

Q. What is lymphoid leukemoid reaction?

Ans. There is lymphocytosis in peripheral blood and there may be atypical lymphocytes (virocytes). Causes are:

- infectious mononucleosis
- measles, chickenpox
- viral fevers

Q. What are virocytes?

Ans. Virocytes are transformed lymphocytes with blastoid/monocytoid/plasma-cytoid features observed in viral fevers e.g. infectious mononucleosis, flu and measles etc.

Q. What is agranulocytosis?

Ans. Agranulocytosis is severe neutropenia resulting in susceptibility to bacterial infections.

Q. What other information is provided by neutrophils?

Ans. (a) Hypersegmentation (more than 5 lobes) of the nucleus is a feature of megaloblastic anemia (Fig. 11.2).

(b) Drumstick (Fig. 30.4) on the nucleus is indicative of second X chromosome (corresponding to Barr body in buccal smear) in females.

Q. What are the causes of basophilia?

Ans. Basophilia is observed in chronic myeloid leukemia, myelofibrosis, basophilic leukemia and mastocytosis

Q. Do automated hematology analysers provide DLC?

Ans. Yes, automated hematology analysers (cell counters) provide a DLC which is accurate in 5-part differential cell counter. Newer hematology analysers provide information about atypical cells also.

Q. What are the blood findings in Dengue fever.

Ans. In dengue fever, hematocrit is higher in proportion to Hb, thrombocytopenia and transformed lymphocytes are seen. In recovery phase, giant platelets are observed in the PS which indicate regenerating platelets.

Q. How do you fix the smear white staining with (a) Leishman stain and with (b) Giemsa stain.

Ans. (a) Leishman stain - Leishman stain poured on the slide for first 2 minutes acts as a fixative since the stain contains methanol.

(b) Giemsa stain - Slides are dipped in methanol before pouring stain on the slides.

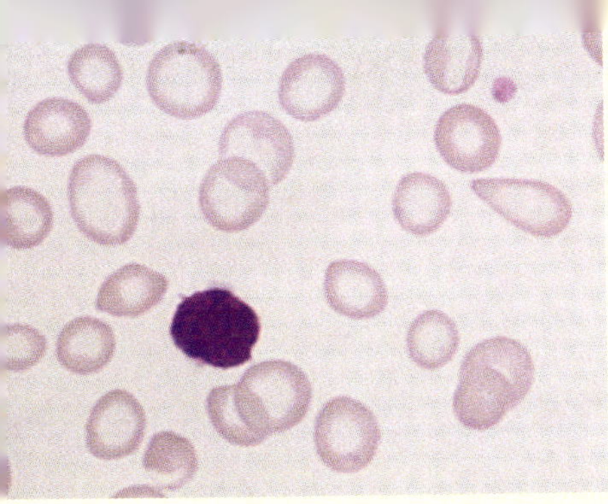

Red Cell Morphology and Anaemias

11

To assess the red cell morphology, a well made and stained peripheral smear – PS is essential. Smear gives information about the size, shape of RBCs and their variations, and the extent of hemoglobinisation. These features help in characterising different types of anaemias. Various terminologies are used to describe red cell features. Some of these are:

Normal

Red cells are biconcave discs with a diameter of 7.2–7.7 microns (normocytic) with central one-third pallor (normochromic) (Fig. 11.1).

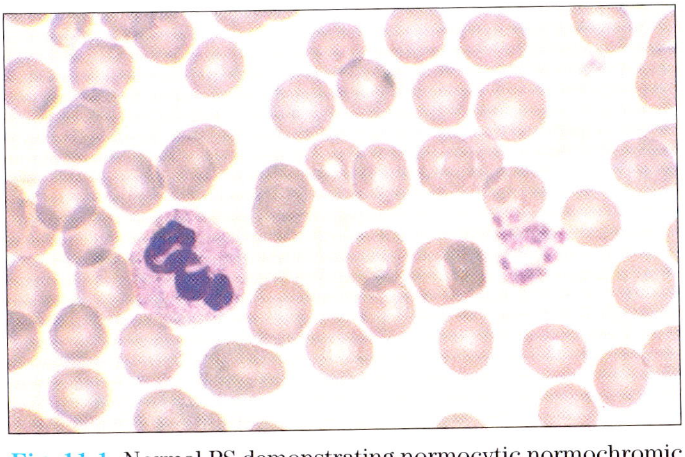

Fig. 11.1: Normal PS demonstrating normocytic normochromic red cells.

Macrocytosis

Macrocytes are larger red cells with a diameter of more than 7.8 microns and MCV of more than 100 fl. Macrocytes in Vit. B12 and Folic acid deficiency are usually oval in shape and are called *macroovalocytes* (Fig. 11.2).

Microcytosis

These RBCs have a diameter of less than 7.2 microns and MCV is less than 80 fl. Microcytosis associated with hypochromia i.e. increased area of central pallor is observed in iron deficiency anaemia (Fig. 11.3) and thalassemia major (Fig. 11.4) and minor.

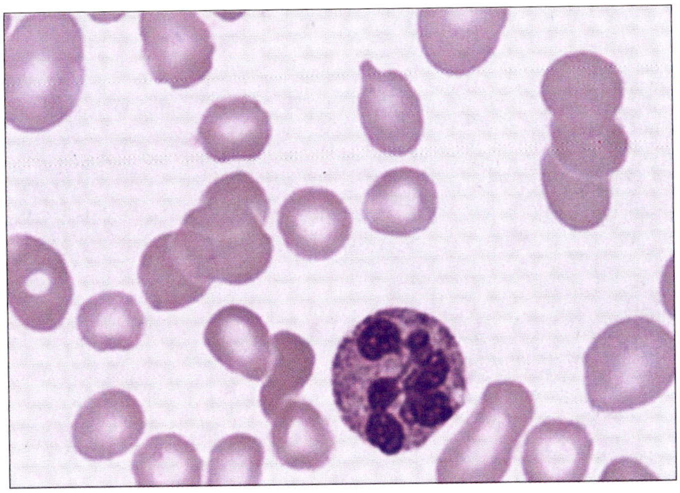

Fig. 11.2: Macrocytic anemia showing anisopoikilocytosis, and macroovalocytes with a single tear drop cell (T). There is a large hypersegmented neutrophil.

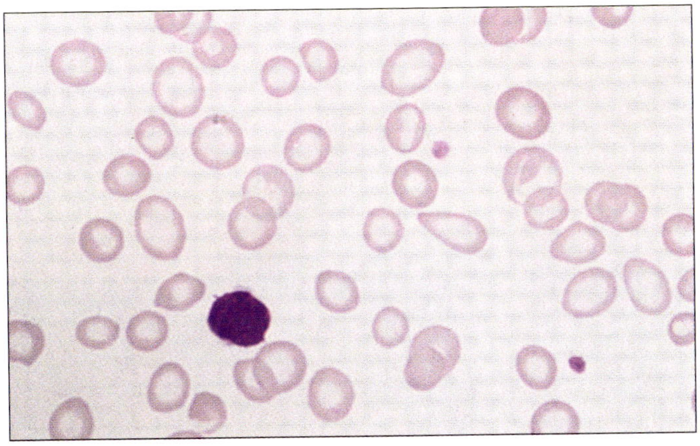

Fig. 11.3: Microcytic hypochromic anemia - mild degree of anisopoikilocytosis with microcytic RBCs demonstrating more than 2/3 pallor - Iron deficiency anemia.

Anisocytosis

It denotes variation in the size of red cell population (Fig. 11.4); however very mild variation in cell size is normal and clinically insignificant.

Poikilocytosis

It denotes variation in the shape of red cell population e.g. tear drop cells, oval cells, helmet cells etc. (Fig. 11.4). Sickle shaped RBCs are observed in sickle cell disease (Fig. 11.5).

Spherocytosis

In a smear, spherocyte is recognised as a smaller deeply staining cell. The central pallor is not observed (Fig. 11.6). These are present in hereditary spherocytosis and autoimmune hemolytic anemia.

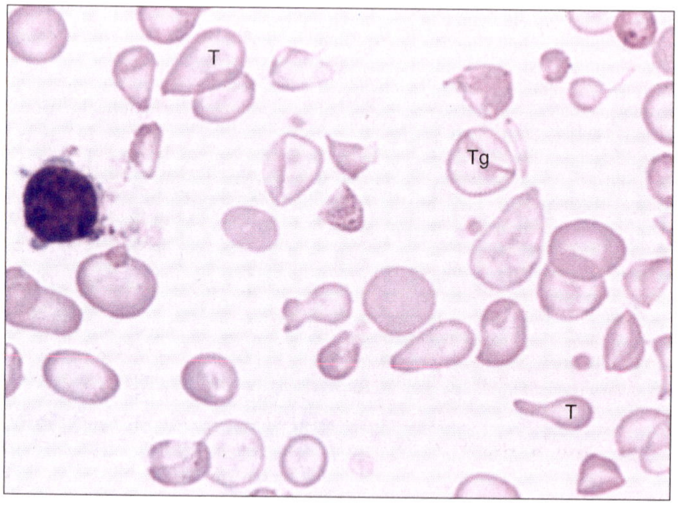

Fig. 11.4: Marked degree of anisopoikilocytosis with microcytic hypochromic red cells, tear drop cells (T), target cells (Tg) – Thalassemia major.

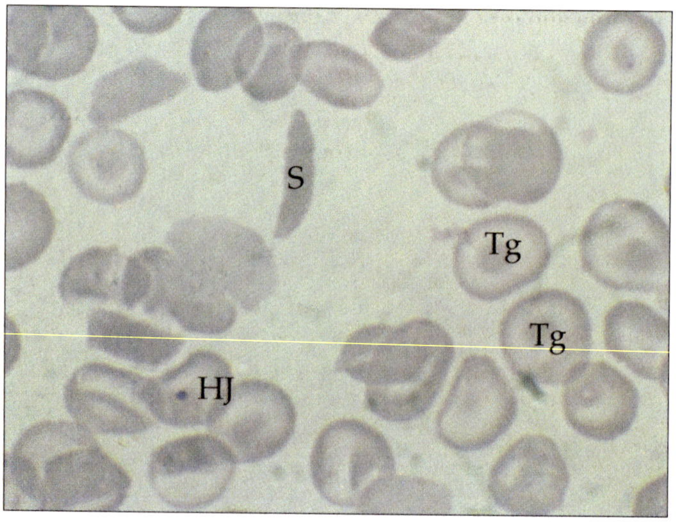

Fig. 11.5: Sickle cell anemia demonstrating anisopoikilocytosis, large number of target cells (Tg) and few boat shaped sickle cells (S) seen. Occasional RBC shows Howell-Jolly body (HJ).

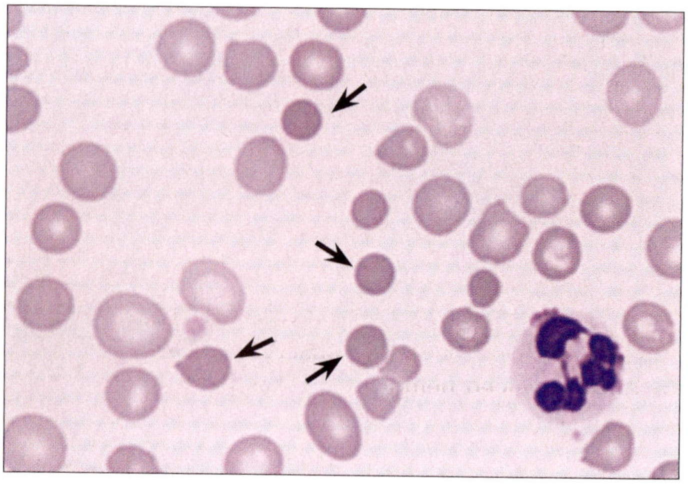

Fig. 11.6: Moderate degree of anisocytosis with few microspherocytes (↑) lacking central pallor in a case of Hereditary spherocytosis.

Target cells

Target cells possess redistributed Hb so that only the periphery and the central regions of the cell appear hemoglobinised (Fig. 11.5). When the cell Hb is reduced and the cell membrane surface area remains the same, Hb is redistributed producing a target cell. Target cells are found in sickle cell anemia, thalassemia major, hemolytic anaemias, post-splenectomy and liver disease.

Sickle cells

These are thin, elongated, slightly curved red cells (Fig.11.5); or elongated cells with irregular outlines and are seen in a sickle cell disease. Sickling is induced in low oxygen state (Fig. 11.7 and 11.8).

Schistocytes (fragmented cells)

These are irregular shaped, triangular and spiculated cells. These cells are in the process of fragmentation. Such cells are the characteristic feature of microangiopathic hemolytic anemia and DIC.

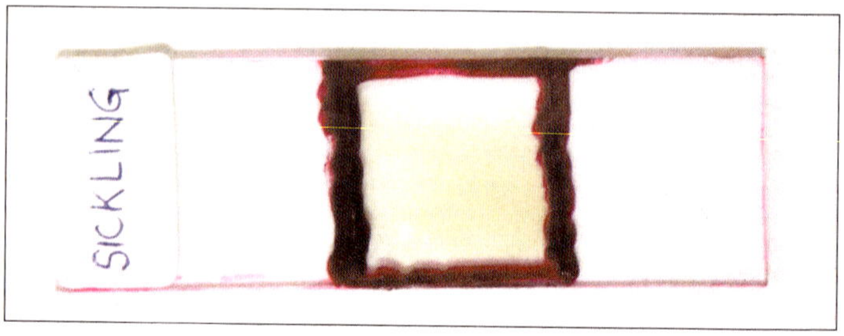

Fig. 11.7: Sickling preparation. The coverslip is placed on the blood + 2% sod. metabisulfite mixture and sealed with nail polish.

Acanthocytes

These red cells possess irregular large coarse spicules having sharp ends. Such cells are seen in abetalipoproteinemia and liver disease. In the latter, there is a marked increase in cholesterol content and cholesterol to phospholipid ratio.

Burr cells

Red cell projections are numerous, uniform in size and regularly spaced. These are observed in cases of uremia, and drug induced hemolytic anemia in infants.

ANAEMIAS

Anaemia refers to a decrease in the total number of circulating red cells with decrease in Hb when compared with normal for that group. In males Hb less than 12g/dl (WHO) and in females Hb less than 10.5g/dl (WHO) is taken as anemia.

Symptomatology of anaemia depends upon the Hb value, change in blood volume, severity of the disease contributing to anemia and also the rate at which these changes occur. Patient complains of fatigue, dyspnoea and angina due to reduced oxygen transport, pallor, tachycardia and sometimes congestive heart failure. Based on morphology, the anaemias have been classified as:

- macrocytic anaemia
- microcytic hypochromic anaemia, and
- normocytic normochromic anaemia

Macrocytic Anaemia

- Hb - decreased.
- TLC is normal/decreased.
- Platelets - normal/reduced; severe macrocytic anemia is associated with *pancytopenia*.
- MCV - more than 100 fl; MCHC - normal 31-36% (g/dl).
- MCH - more than 35 pg.
- PS findings - mild to moderate degree of anisopoikilocytosis; red cells are *macro-ovalocytic* (Fig. 11.2); there is presence of tear drop cells, elongated cells and red cells with inclusions like *Howell jolly bodies* (nuclear remnant), *basophilic stippling* and *Cabot rings*. Few large hypersegmented neutrophils (*macropolys*) are observed (Fig. 11.2). These may be the first manifestation of megaloblastic anemias (Fig. 11.2). Platelets are normal/decreased. Smear may show an occasional late megaloblast.
- S. bilirubin is 1.5-3 mg% because of hemolysis resulting from intramarrow death of megaloblasts – a feature of *dyserythropoiesis*.

Microcytic Hypochromic Anemia

- Hb - decreased.
- TLC - normal.
- Platelets - normal/increased.
- MCV - less than 80 fl; MCHC - less than 31 g/dl.
- MCH - less than 30 pg.
- PS findings - red cells are smaller than normal and central pallor is half/more than half of the red cell diameter (normal RBCs have a central one-third pallor). Such a picture is seen in iron deficiency anemia and thalassemia major (Fig. 11.3).

(a) ***Iron deficiency anemia (IDA)*** – Smear reveals mild to moderate degree of anisopoikilocytosis with microcytosis. RBCs demonstrate mild to severe degree of hypochromia. In severe hypochromia, cells reveal only a thin rim of Hb at the periphery - *ring/pessary cells*. Few tear drop cells and elliptical cells—pencil cells are also present (Fig. 11.3). DLC is usually normal; however, in cases in which iron deficiency is because of hookworm infestation, there may be associated eosinophilia. IDA needs differentiation from Thalassemia major (Table 11.1).

(b) ***Thalassemia major*** – (See also table 11.1) A hemolytic anemia, quite common in our country demonstrates moderate to severe degree of anisopoikilocytosis with many target cells, besides microcytic hypochromic red cells. There is presence of stippled red cells, few fragmented cells and nucleated RBCs (Fig. 11.4). Smear also demonstrates polychromasia reflecting a high reticulocyte count. Serum bilirubin is increased. HbF is raised to 20-90%; marrow iron stores are increased. This should be differentiated from iron deficiency anemia (Table 11.1).

Dimorphic Anaemia

In India and other developing countries, patients manifest multiple deficiencies of B_{12}, folic acid, iron and other vitamins. In such cases, RBCs demonstrate a dual population of macrocytes and microcytic hypochromic RBCs. In some cases, macrocytes with hypochromia are demonstrable.

Sickle Cell Anaemia

Smear reveals a moderate to severe degree of anisopoikilocytosis with large number of target cells. There is presence of fragmented red cells, nucleated RBCs and sickle cells. Red cells are normochromic to mildly hypochromic. Sickle cells are densely staining cells varying in shape from short oval to long elliptical or narrow curved sickle cells with pointed ends (Fig.11.5). In case of doubt, sickling preparation can be made to confirm sickle cell anaemia.

Table 11.1: Iron deficiency anemia and thalassemia major

	Iron deficiency anemia	Thalassemia major
Cause	Iron deficiency	Hereditary hemolytic anemia (gene defect)
P. smear		
• target cells	occasional	many
• anisopoikilocytosis	mild	moderate to severe
• nucleated RBCs	rare/absent	present
Retic. count	normal	high
BM Iron	nil	marked increase
Biochem. findings		
• S. Fe	marked ↓↓	markedly ↑↑
• % transferrin saturation	< 16%	> 40%
• S. ferritin	< 15 ng/ml	300-3000 ng/ml
• S. bilirubin	normal	mild increase
• Urine - urobilinogen	normal	increased
Other hemat tests		
• HbF	nil	20-70%
• Clin. features	pallor	hepatosplenomegaly with pallor
• Bone changes	nil	Present with hair on end appearance in skull

Demonstration of Sickling

In sickle cell disease and trait, red cells contain HbS which, under low oxygen tension, forms tactoids resulting in sickling of RBCs. Time taken for sickling to develop depends upon the amount of HbS and degree of low oxygen tension. In sickle cell disease, sickling develops within $^1/_2$ hour while in trait it is demonstrable, usually within 4 hours.

Method

- Prepare a 2% sodium metabisulfite solution.
- Take 2 slides marked as test and control and put 1 drop of the solution on both slides.
- Add less than ½ drop of patient's blood to the test slide and normal blood to control slide.
- Mix the solution with the blood added.
- Put a cover slip on each slide.
- Seal the edges of the cover slip with nail polish (Fig. 11.7).

Examine the slide immediately, after 15 minutes, ½ hour, 1 hour, 2 hours, 4 hours and 12 hours for development of sickling.

Result: Red cells assume a *filamentous, sickled and holly leaf* appearance in sickle cell disease and trait (Fig. 11.8).

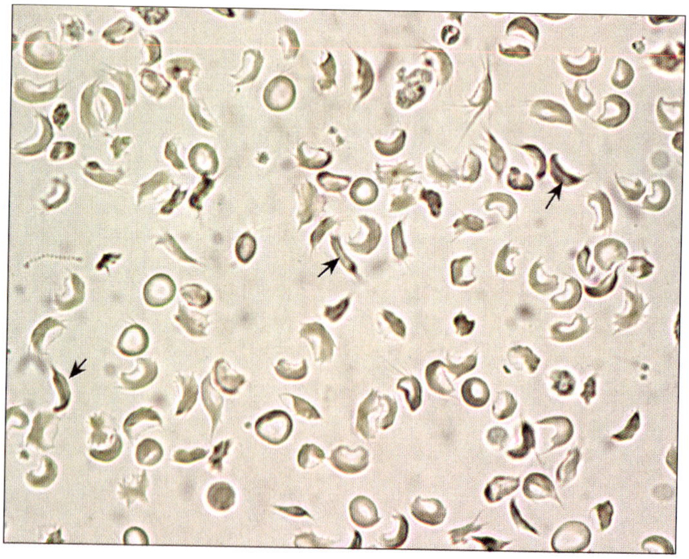

Fig. 11.8: Sickling preparation. Red cells assume sickle/ elongated shape following incubation with 2% sod. metabisulfite solution.

Screening for HbS

In many countries it is considered expedient to screen bood donors and patients for general anaesthesia from high risk ethnic groups (particularly where there is a risk of prolonged stasis).

Donor screening for HbS is a legal requirement in Brazil and Saudi Arabia.

Because of the high morbidity associated with HbS, population screening projects are being carried out.

Sickle Cell Test – Microtyping system (Gel card)

HbS on interacting with the reducing agent in the gel tansform into sickle cells which are highly inflexible and thus cannot pass through gel and are trapped in the gel forming a red line (in SS). A negative reaction indicates absence of HbS; strong ++++ indicates presence of HbS, probably homozygous, while weak positive reactions of + to ++ indicates low percentage of HbS in heterozygotes (HbS trait).

Hereditary Spherocytosis

An autosomal dominant hemolytic anemia characterised by jaundice, anemia and splenomegaly. Smear demonstrates anisocytosis of variable degree featuring spherocytes, (being biconvex, lack central pallor) (Fig. 11.6). There is polychromasia suggestive of high reticulocyte count. These spherocytes undergo hemolysis even at 0.7-0.9% saline demonstrating a shift to right in the osmotic fragility curve.

Normocytic Normochromic Anaemia

Such type of anemia with normal red cell indices is encountered in post-hemorrhagic anemia and in marrow suppression.

Glucose-6-Phosphate Dehydrogenase Deficiency (G-6-PD Deficiency)

G-6-PD catalyses the conversion of G-6-Phosphate into Ribulose-5-Phosphate. A deficiency of this enzyme reduces the ability of RBCs to withstand the effects of various oxidising drugs/agents, resulting in hemolytic anaemia (Fig. 11.9).

Deficiency of this enzyme results in lack of reduced glutathione GSH-GSH and NADPH leading to accumulation of peroxides (which cannot be reduced to water). Peroxides oxidise Hb to MetHb which gets precipitated as Heinz bodies resulting in lysis of the red cells in reticuloendothelial cells.

Since it is a **sex linked disease**, males and homozygous females suffer. In G-6-PD deficiency, hemolysis may be precipitated under following conditions:

- favism, due to consumption of fava beans;
- drug-induced hemolytic anaemia; drugs which may result in hemolysis are:
  - antimalarials - primaquine, quinine and chloroquine
  - sulfa drugs
  - nitrofurans
  - acetylsalicylic acid and acetanilid
- high fever
- severe infection

Screening Tests for G-6-PD Deficiency

1. Methemoglobin reduction test (MRT).
2. Ascorbate cyanide test.
3. Fluorescence spot test.

It is important to get the test for G-6-PD deficiency done before primaquine is administered since in a G-6-PD deficient patient it may result in severe acute hemolysis, acute renal failure and even death.

Methaemoglobin reduction test (MRT)

In this test Hb is converted into MetHb by adding sodium nitrite. If the enzyme levels are normal, MetHb is reduced to Hb in the presence of a reducing dye – Methylene blue; otherwise, MetHb remains, which is of brown colour. A positive and a negative controls are also set up.

In males, brown colour of solution - deficiency positive.

In homozygous females, brown colour of solution - deficiency positive.

In heterozygous females, intermediate colour (between red and brown) is observed.

Quantitative assay of G-6-PD can be carried out.

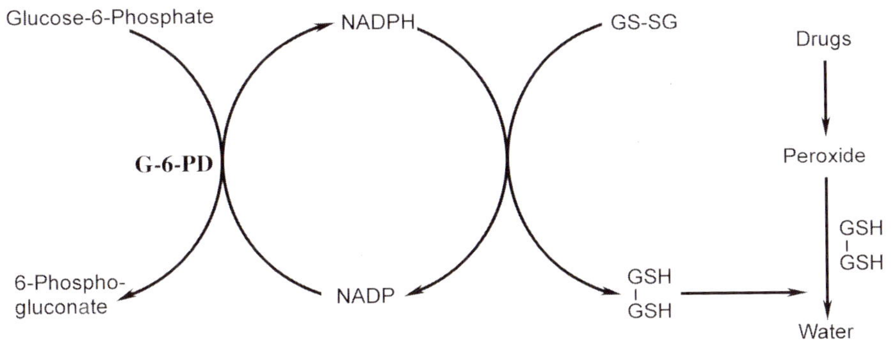

Fig. 11.9: Role of G-6-PD in metabolism of drugs with oxidative effects producing peroxide which is rendered non-toxic by GSH.

Thalassemia Major

Thalassemia major is characterised by increased HbF levels and accelerated hemolysis of RBCs because of the accumulated free alpha chains inside the red cells. Quantitative estimation of HbF is carried out by alkali denaturation method or HPLC.

Alkali denaturation test for HbF

This test is based on the fact that normal Hb i.e. HbA gets denatured on exposure to alkali, but HbF is resistant and is not destroyed; therefore assessed in a hemolysate solution. HbF is also resistant to weak acids.

Thalassemia trait – HbA_2 estimation

In case of thalassemia trait, HbA_2 is assessed. It is elevated to 3.6 to 9% (normal levels being 1-3.5%) and is diagnostic. Thalassemia trait is prevalent in all parts of the country.

It is estimated by

- High performance liquid chromatography (HPLC) - a sensitive method (Fig. 11.10).

However, it should be kept in mind that HbE moves electrophoretically and chromatographically in the same zone as HbA_2, but HbE encountered in HbE trait/HbE thalassemia/HbE homozygous is usually more than 10% while HbA_2 is always less than 10%.

Peak Name	Calibrated Area %	Area %	Retention Time (min)	Peak Area
F	0.8	---	1.10	20533
Unknown	---	0.7	1.23	19289
P2	---	4.0	1.30	102432
P3	---	3.4	1.70	87764
Ao	---	85.6	2.46	2202559
A2	5.4*	---	3.67	140057

Total Area: 2,572,634

F Concentration = 0.8 %
A2 Concentration = 5.4* %

*Values outside of expected ranges

Analysis comments:

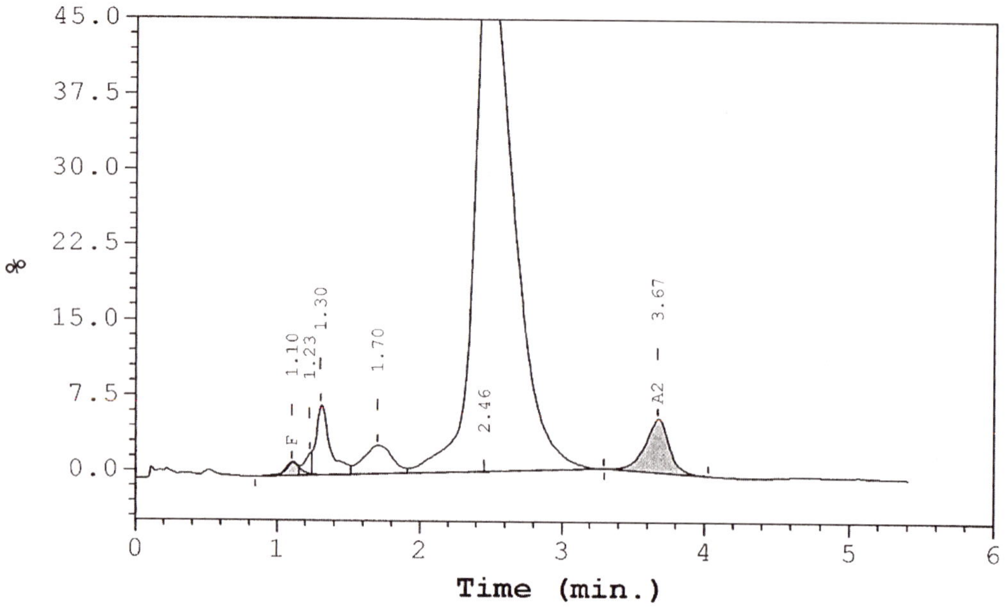

Fig. 11.10: HPLC demonstrating HbA, HbA_2 and HbF. HbH_2 is > 3.6% (< 9%), suggesting thalassemia trait

Hb Electrophoresis

Various abnormal Hbs have different electrophoretic mobility and, therefore, get isolated from HbA on electrophoresis using Tris buffer at pH 8.6 and carrying out electrophoresis in starch agarose gel poured on the 7.5 × 2.5 cm glass slide. The electro-phoresed slide is stained with Amido Black. HbD and HbS move in the same region and are differentiated from each other by carrying out Sickling test. HbE and HbA_2 move in the same region but can be differentiated quantitatively as explained above. HbF, D, S, Q India, E, C move slower than HbA (Fig. 11.11).

Diagnosis of PNH by gel method

Paroxysmal nocturnal hemoglobinuria (PNH) is characterised by intermittent intravascular hemolysis. Red cells lack DAF (Decay accelerating factor CD55) and MIRL (Membrane inhibitor of reactive lysis CD59). Monoclonal antibodies to anti-DAF and anti-MIRL are incorporated into the gel.

If DAF and MIRL are present (in a normal person), then agglutination occurs. On the other hand, lack of DAF and MIRL (in PNH cases) there is no agglutination and the negative test indicates that the patient is positive for PNH. Diagnosis is also made by positivity of **Ham's acidified serum** test. Following an attack of intravascular hemolysis, hemoglobin is reabsorbed by tubular cells where it is converted into hemosiderin and **hemosiderinuria** is demonstrated in the urine deposit in these cases.

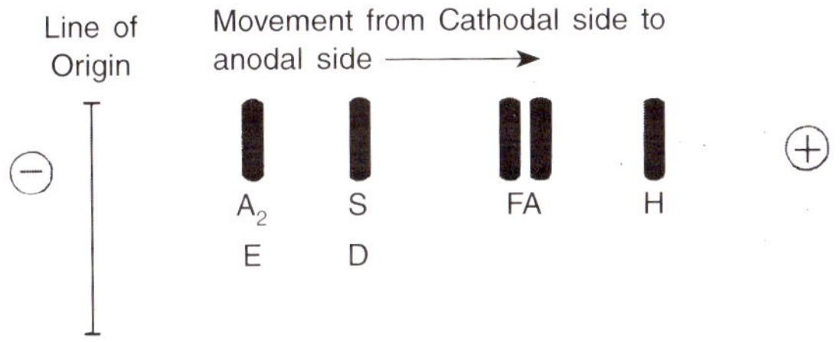

Fig. 11.11: Hb mobility on starch Agarose electrophoresis-Tris-EDTA-Borate buffer ph-8.6

VIVA VOCE

Q. Enumerate the conditions in which target cells are seen.

Ans. Target cells are present in haemoglobinopathies, chronic liver disease and change in lipid/protein ratio. Haemoglobinopathies like sickle cell disease, HbC, HbD, HbE disease and thalassemias demonstrate target cells.

Q. In which conditions are microcytic hypochromic red cells seen and how to differentiate the type of anemia?

Ans. In iron deficiency anaemia and thalassemia major/minor. In the former, S. ferritin is very low, <15 microgram/L, and B.M. iron is nil while in the latter, S. ferritin is very high, BM iron is increased and HbF is 20-90% (Table 11.1).

Q. What are dyserythropoietic anaemias?

Ans. This is a group of diseases in which erythropoiesis is abnormal and early normoblasts fail to mature to intermediate normoblasts which in turn do not mature to late normoblasts. Many of these normoblasts die in BM. The most frequent cause is megablastic anaemia, the others being thalassemias and sickle cell disease.

Q. What are deficiency anaemias?

Ans. Anemias due to deficiency of iron, B12, folic acid, vitamin C, protein and zinc.

Q. Which parasitic infections cause deficiency anaemias?

Ans. Hookworm infestation is a common cause of iron deficiency anemia and D. latum infection causes B12 deficiency.

Q. What is aplastic anaemia?

Ans. Anemia due to aplasia of hemopoietic precursors and resulting in pancytopenia. Aplastic anaemia may be drug/ chemical/ radiation induced or idiopathic.

Q. Is urobilinogen normally excreted in urine?

Ans. Urobilinogen is normally excreted 2-4 mg/24 hours and it imparts a pale yellow colour to the urine. It is increased in hemolytic anaemias.

Q. Besides sickling, what other tests clinch the diagnosis of sickle cell disease?

Ans. Hb electrophoresis at pH 8.6 demonstrates a slow moving Hb band and reduced solubility of HbS.

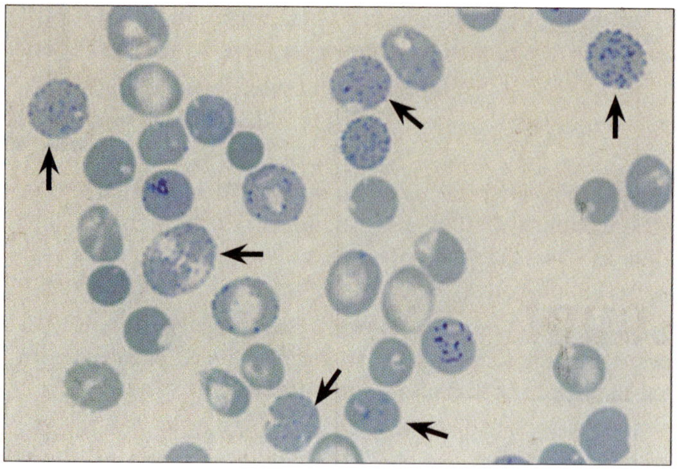

Fig. 12.2 HbH inclusions. Red cells demonstrating dot like blue inclusions (↑) in a reticulocyte preparation using brilliant cresyl blue solution.

seen as single or multiple rounded inclusions in G-6-PD deficiency patients following exposure to oxidising drugs/ chemicals. Biting of the Heinz body with part of the red cells by the macrophages of spleen results in bite call hemolytic anaemia.

Normal Range

Normal	0.5-2%
Cord blood	1-7%

High Reticulocyte Count

Retic count indicates the erythropoietic activity of the bone marrow and red cell production. Stimulation of erythroid elements results in increased reticulocyte release *e.g.* in:

- hemolytic anaemias
- hemolytic crisis
- following therapy in iron/folic acid/B_{12} deficiency anaemias. In such situations, highest counts are observed on 6th/7th day of therapy and reflect marrow response to hematinics.

Low Reticulocyte Count

Reduced retic count (<0.5%) is observed in diminished erythropoietic activity states like:

- aplastic anaemia
- pure red cell aplasia
- Fanconi's anaemia
- aplasic crisis due to Parvo virus in Hereditary spherocytosis and Sickle cell disease.

Reticulocyte Correction for Anaemia

Suppose retic count in an adult patient with 7.5 gm Hb is 2%, it does not reflect a true marrow response.

Corrected R. count

$$= \frac{\text{Patient's Hb} \times \text{Estimated R. count}}{\text{Normal Hb value for that age}}$$

$$= \frac{7.5 \times 2}{15}$$

$$= 1\%$$

Reticulocyte Count on Automated Cell Counters

Retic count can be carried out using an argon laser based flow cytometer. Retics are stained directly with Auramine 0 – a fluorescent dye and are passed through a laser beam (Fig. 9.5). The automated method is more precise.

VIVA VOCE

Q. What is a supravital stain?

Ans. The stain which colours the living cells but outside the body e.g. red cells of peripheral blood stained by BCB – Brilliant cresyl blue.

Q. Name the dyes used for reticulocyte count.

Ans. The dyes which stain the RNA of red cells are Brilliant Cresyl Blue and New Methylene Blue.

Q. What further information does Reticulocyte count smear provide?

Ans. R. count smear demonstrates HbH inclusions and Heinz bodies. The former are seen in alpha-thalassemias while the latter are observed in Heinz body anaemia and G-6PD deficiency anaemia during hemolytic episodes.

Q. How is Reticulocyte count useful in cases of anaemia?

Ans. (a) R count is increased in hemolytic anaemia, it is low in megaloblastic anaemias and very low in aplastic anaemia and pure red cell aplasia.

(b) In deficiency anaemias, as the therapy is instituted, the marrow responds and the R count increases on 6th/7th day. R count in such cases is indicative of response to therapy.

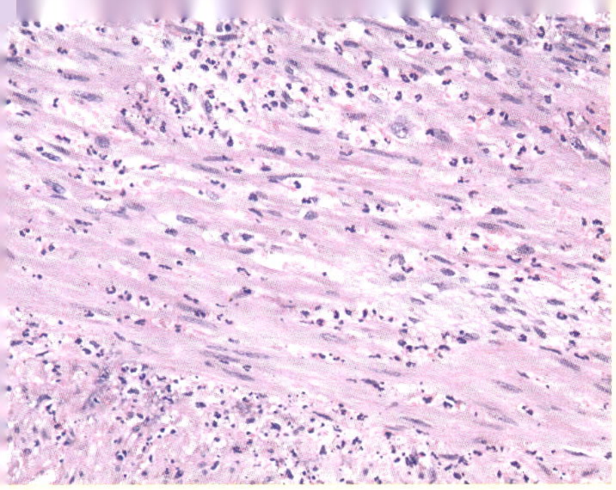

13

Haematocrit, Red Cell Indices, Erythrocyte Sedimentation Rate and LE Cell Test

HAEMATOCRIT (PACKED CELL VOLUME) ESTIMATION

Hematocrit is the % volume of red cells (when packed) in a given sample of blood. It gives an estimate of relative volume of cells and plasma *e.g.* in a case of anaemia red cells get reduced and hence haematocrit is diminished. It is useful for evaluating absolute values like MCV and MCHC. The 3 methods used are (a) using Wintrobe's tube and (b) using capillary tube and (c) using automated hematology cell counters.

Wintrobe's Method

Principle

Anticoagulated whole blood is centrifuged and the volume of red cell mass denotes the haematocrit. It is expressed as percentage.

Steps

- Collect 2 ml blood in an EDTA vial.
- Take a Wintrobe's tube (110 mm in length, internal diameter 2.5 mm and calibrated at 1 mm intervals to 100 mm with bold markings from top as 0, 10, 20, 30, ... 100 for ESR and 100, 90, 80, ... 10, 0 for PCV (Fig. 13.1a).
- Shake the blood sample so that plasma and cells are mixed properly.
- Take blood in a Pasteur's pipette (dropper with a long nozzle) from the tube and place the end of the nozzle to the bottom of the lumen of W. tube (Fig. 13.1b). Press the teat of the P.pipette very slowly and simultaneously start

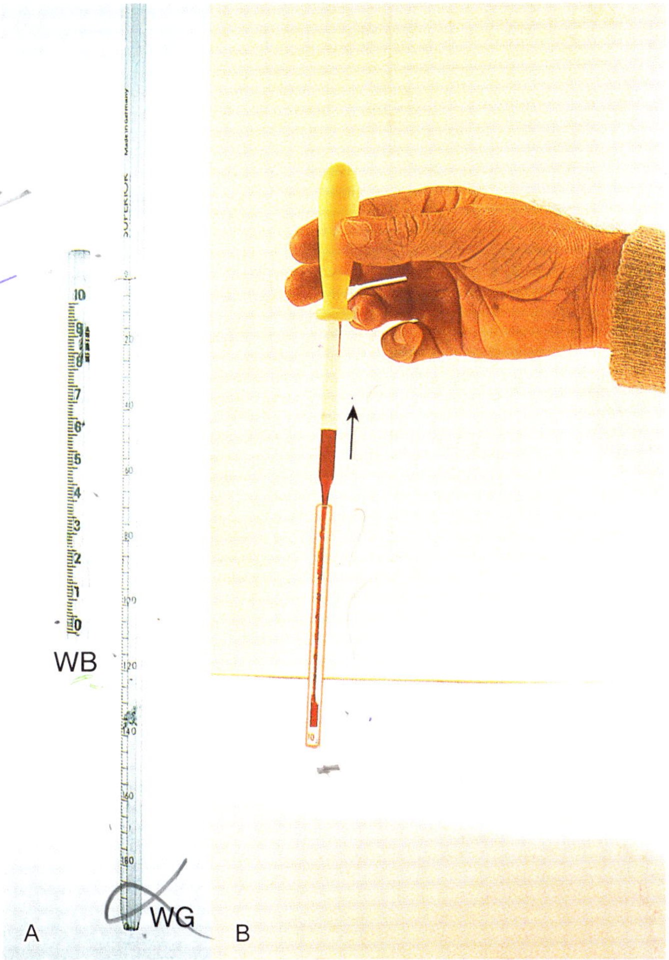

Fig. 13.1: (A) Wintrobe tube (WB) and Westergren pipette (WG) (open at both ends); (B) Filling a Wintrobe tube using a Pasteur pipette.

withdrawing it from the tube so that blood fills bottom and gradually reaches the top at 100 marking. There should not be any air bubble in the blood column.

- Centrifuge the tube at 3500 RPM (2000-2400g) for 30 minutes.
- Take out the W. tube and read the column of packed cells on PCV scale *e.g.* 0 from bottom upwards.

Microhaematocrit Method

Principle

A capillary tube is incompletely filled with whole blood by capillary action. The end of the tube is then sealed with a sealing material; the tube is centrifuged at high speed and the red cell column is measured.

Equipment

Microhematocrit centrifuge and capillary tubes – plain and heparinised (Fig. 13.2).

Method

- Fill 3/4th of the plain capillary tube by dipping one end of the tube in the EDTA blood. (heparinished capillary tube to be used to fill from a free flowing finger prick).
- Plug the end of the tube with sealing wax/putty. Care should be taken that there is no air gap between sealing material and blood.
- Place the tube flat in the microhematocrit centrifuge so that sealed end is in contact with the outer rim of the centrifuge head. Close and latch the outer cover of the centrifuge.
- Set the speed at 10,000 RPM for 5 minutes.
- After 5 minutes, remove the capillary tube and record the hematocrit by placing the capillary tube in the microhematocrit reader scale.

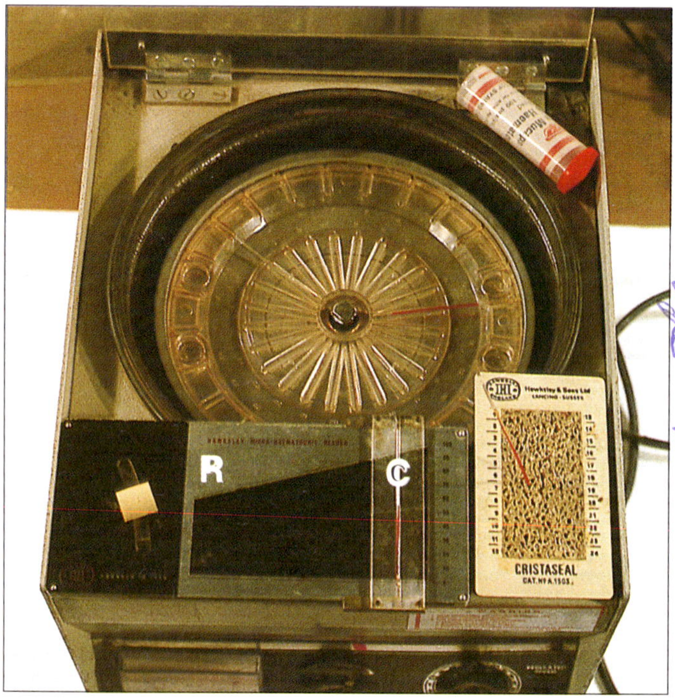

Fig. 13.2 Microhematocrit centrifuge, capillary tube (C), sealing putty and microhematocrit reader (R).

Advantages

Only small quantity of blood is needed which can be collected from finger prick/heel prick in infants.

Precautions

- Microhaematocrit reading should be taken quickly, as slanting of red cell column occurs if tubes are left in a horizontal position for more than 5 minutes.
- Take care not to include buffy coat while recording the PCV.
- While filling the capillary tube from a finger prick, squeezing the finger should be avoided as this causes dilution of the blood with tissue fluid resulting in a lower PCV.

Sources of Error

- Prolonged stasis of blood due to tourniquet results in hemoconcentration and false high results may be obtained.
- Muscular activity results in elevation of red cells, white cells and platelets, thus hematocrit may be higher than the actual.
- When EDTA concentration is more than 2 mg/ml of blood, errors in PCV result.

Normal Range

Males	40-55%
Females	35-48%
Infants	45-60% (cord blood)

Variations in Haematocrit

Increased PCV – in Polycythemia rubra vera and secondary polycythemic states.

Decreased PCV – in anemic states.

Additional Information from the Method

1. ***Plasma column***
   - clear/straw coloured – normal state
   - yellow – jaundice
   - turbid – hyperlipidemias
   - red – hemoglobinemia as in PNH
2. ***Buffy coat*** – On careful examination of the Wintrobe tube after centrifugation of the blood, a thin greyish white layer is visible on top of the packed red cell

column (Fig. 13.3). It represents the packed WBCs and platelets. Thickness of the buffy coat increases in cases with high WBC count – in CML, CLL and acute leukemias.

Buffy coat preparation is made for LE cell test (Fig. 13.5).

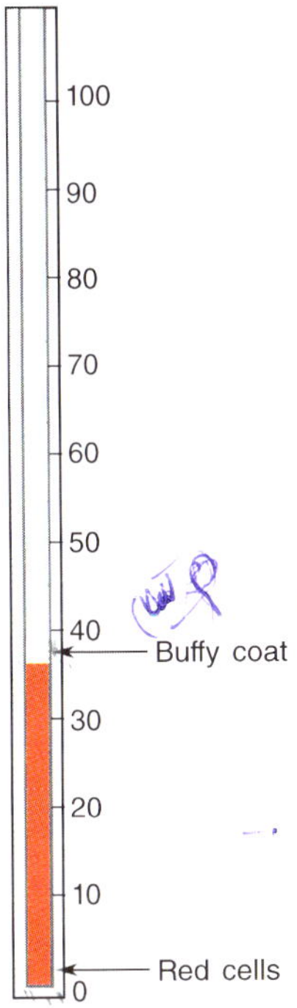

Fig. 13.3 Wintrobe tube with packed red cells and buffy coat.

Hematocrit estimation in cell counters

Hematocrit in the cell counters is calculated from red (Fig. 9.5) cell count and MCV as hematocrit = RBC count × MCV. Hematocrit reflects the concentration of red cells and is three times the Hb value, e.g. hematocrit in a person with Hb of 12 gms, is nearly 12 × 3 = 36.

RED CELL INDICES (ABSOLUTE VALUES)

Red cell indices are very useful in characterisation of anaemias. The three important indices are MCV, MCH and MCHC. All the indices are given by cell counters (Fig. 9.5).

Mean Corpuscular Volume MCV (Fig. 9.5)

$$\text{MCV} = \frac{\text{PCV} \times 1000}{\text{RBC count in millions}}$$

$$= 0.45 \times 1000/5 = 90 \text{ fl}$$

Normal range: 82-98 fl.

MCV increases (>100 fl) in macrocytic anaemia and decreases (<80 fl) in microcytic hypochromic anaemia. Anaemias are now classified as per the MCV.

Mean Corpuscular Haemoglobin Concentration – MCHC (Fig. 9.5)

It is the ratio of hemoglobin to the volume of packed cells (haematocrit). MCHC is acually a measurement of haemoglobin concentration in the red cell taking volume into account.

$$\text{MCHC} = \frac{\text{Hb}}{\text{PCV}} = \frac{15}{0.45} = 33\% \text{ (g/dl)}$$

Normal range: 31-36% (g/dl).

MCHC is decreased in hypochromic anaemia (in iron deficiency anaemia), remains nearly normal in macrocytic anaemia (though MCH is increased because of large sized red cells).

Mean Corpuscular Hemoglobin – MCH (Fig. 9.5)

MCH is the amount of Hb in the red cell. If a normochromic red cell is large, MCH is raised (in macrocytic anaemia); and if it is small, MCH is reduced.

$$\text{MCH} = \frac{\text{Hb} \times 10}{\text{RBC count}} = \frac{15 \times 10}{5} = 30 \text{ pg.}$$

Normal range: 28-32 pg.

MCH is decreased in hypochromic anemia and increased in macrocytic anemia.

In **macrocytic anemia**, since the RBC is larger but normochromic, therefore MCH increases because it does not take into account MCV of the RBC. However, MCHC remains same because it takes volume of the red cells into account which is increased because of the larger RBC and Hb per cell is proportionate to volume and hence MCHC (Hb/PCV) remains nearly same.

ERYTHROCYTE SEDIMENTATION RATE (ESR)

Estimation of ESR is a widely used test in clinical practice. The rate of fall of RBCs in plasma is influenced to a great extent by the rouleaux formation, plasma viscosity and ratio of red cells to plasma.

Stages of Sedimentation

Sedimentation occurs in 4 stages:

1. **Rouleaux formation** – This occurs in first 15 minutes and minimum sedimentation occurs.
2. **Formation of fine threads** – This occurs in next 15 minutes because of globulin and fibrinogen.
3. **Rapid fall** – Protein network along with red cell mass falls in next 15 minutes.
4. **Packing phase** – Packing of RBCs occurs during the last 15 minutes.

Factors Affecting ESR

1. **Plasma globulin and fibrinogen** – Alpha 1 and alpha 2 globulins and fibrinogen reduce the potential of red cells facilitating rouleaux formation. Plasma viscosity correlates with acute phase reactants, total proteins, albumin and gamma globulin.
2. **Number, size and density of red cells** – When cells are in normal plasma, rouleaux formation is minimal and sedimentation is slow. However, if asymmetric macromolecules increase, the negative charge on surface of RBCs is reduced and the rate of rouleaux formation increases. Spherocytes and sickle cells do not exhibit rouleaux formation even in the presence of moderate anemia and, therefore ESR, is normal or diminished in H. spherocytosis and Sickle cell disease.
3. **Technical factors** – ESR tube must be perpendicular. Deviations as small as 3% from absolute vertical can increase the ESR by 30%.

Methods

The four methods commonly employed are: Westergren's, Wintrobe's, MicroESR method and automated method.

WESTERGREN'S METHOD

- Collect 2 ml of blood in 0.5 ml of 3.8% Trisodium citrate pentahydrate solution (1 in 4 parts of blood).
- Mix the two and withdraw blood by rubber teat attached on top of Westergren's pipette upto 0 mark (at top). Westergren's pipette is 30 cm in length, 2.5 mm in diameter and is calibrated as 0 to 200 mm from top to bottom (Fig. 13.1A).
- Place the pipette on rubber cork of the Westergren's stand and make it vertical (Fig. 13.4) using the adjustable levelling screws and detach the rubber teat.
- Measure the height of plasma column after 1 hour. This gives the ESR in mm in the 1st hour.

Normal Range

Men	0-10 mm	1st hour
Women	0-20 mm	1st hour

Advantages

This is a more sensitive and accurate method as compared to Wintrobe's method because the column is longer, i.e. 200 mm.

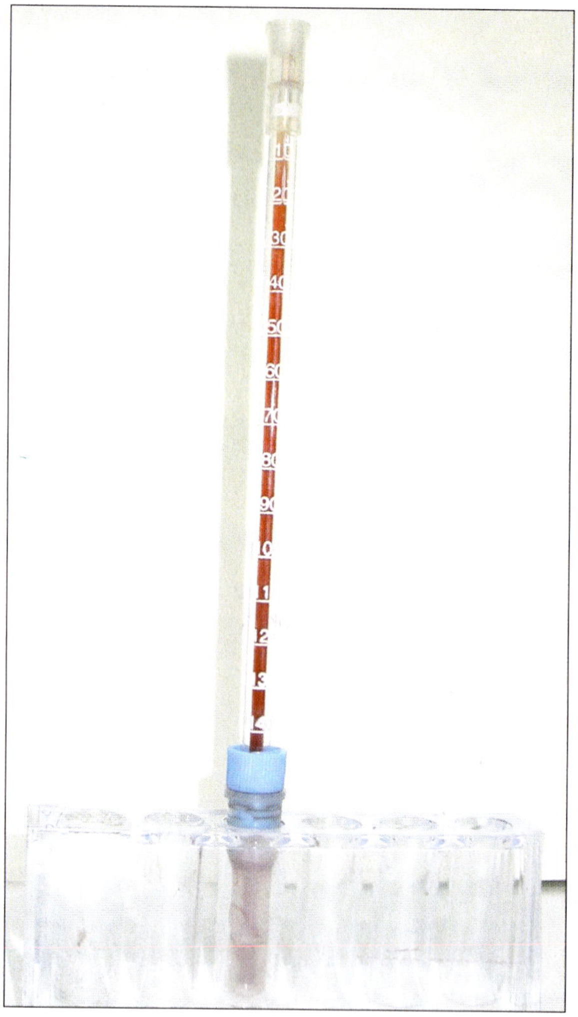

Fig. 13.4 Modified Westergren's method

WINTROBE'S METHOD

Wintrobe's tube is used for estimation of ESR first and then the tube is centrifuged for estimation of haematocrit.

Method

- Collect 2 ml blood in an EDTA vial.
- Fill Pasteur pipette having a long stem.
- Tip of the P.pipette is taken to the bottom of the W. tube and blood is slowly filled into the tube; the pipette is slowly withdrawn (Fig. 13.1) and blood is filled upto top mark of 0/100.
- Keep the tube in a vertical position for 1 hour in the Wintrobe tube stand and note the fall in red cells from top mark of 0.

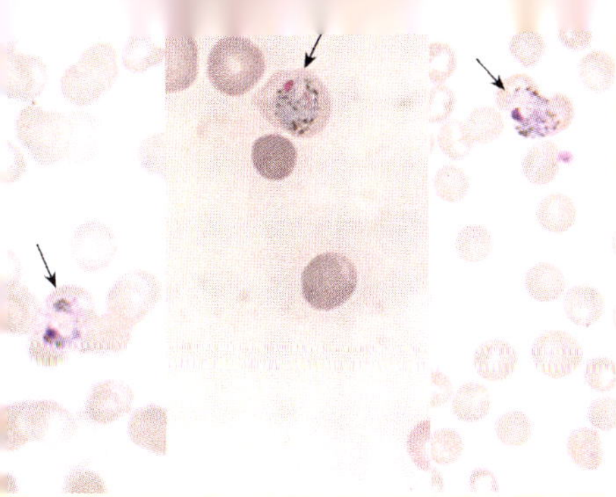

14

Haemoparasites

Parasites are frequently detected in peripheral blood in Indian patients. Indian subcontinent is endemic for both malaria and filariasis. Both the diseases can be diagnosed by careful examination of a well made and stained peripheral smear.

MALARIA

Malaria is clinically characterised by high fever with chills and rigors; these paroxysms of fever last for 4-16 hours followed by afebrile period lasting 1-2 days depending upon the type of malaria. Febrile paroxysms coincide with the erythrocytic schizogony of the malarial parasite. Hyperplasia of the reticuloendothelial system results in splenomegaly, which is slate grey to black in colour because of deposition of hemozoin pigment in the reticuloendothelial cells.

Collection of Blood Smears

Peripheral blood smears should be made 2-6 hours after the peak of the febrile paroxysms, as the number of parasites is more during this period.

Both thin and thick smears made from a finger prick are stained with Giemsa/Leishman stain. Thin smear is examined first and if malarial parasites are not found, then thick smears should be evaluated.

PLASMODIUM VIVAX

In the peripheral blood trophozoites, schizonts and gametocytic stages are present.

Trophozoite

In the ring form, a blue ring with a red nucleus is present, while in a growing form, ring becomes irregular in a large RBC with development of Schuffner's dots (Fig. 14.1).

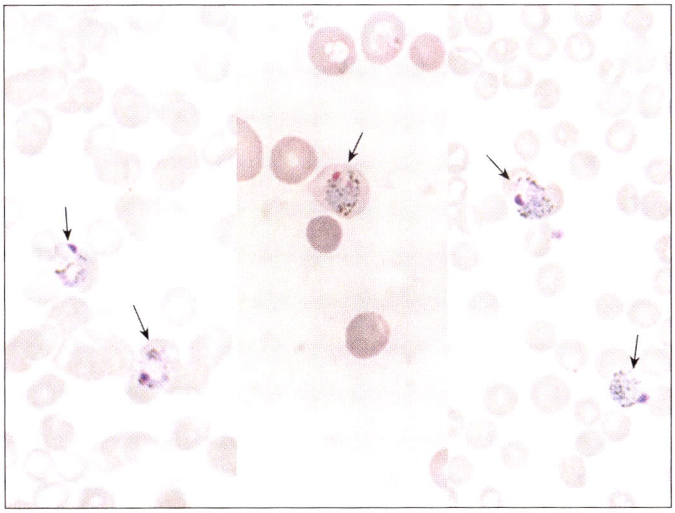

Fig. 14.1: Malarial parasite P. vivax – Schizont stage, nucleus is red and the ring shaped body is blue. Schuffner's dots are red, malarial pigment stains brown.

Schizont

It is larger (9-10μ size) and almost fills an enlarged RBC. There are reddish Schuffner's dots in the RBC.

Gametocyte

Gametocyte is much larger than a schizont; the female gametocyte has eccentric red nucleus (Fig. 14.2) and is blue in colour with Schuffner's dots while the male has pale blue cytoplasm with large and diffuse pale red nucleus and plenty of Schuffner's dots.

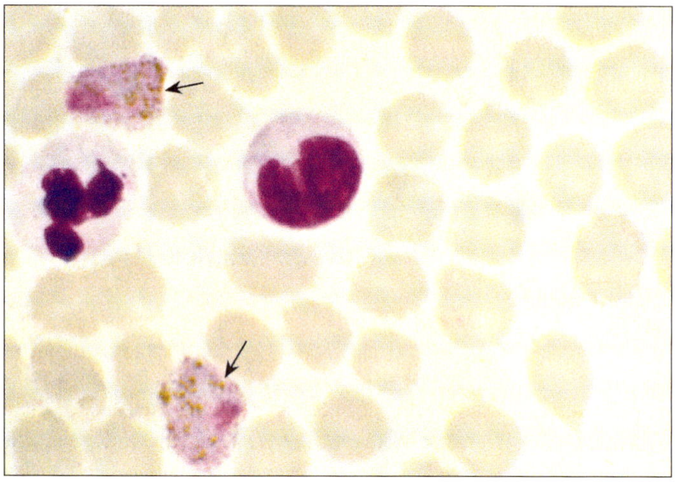

Fig. 14.2: Gametocytes of P.vivax with eccentric red nucleus and Schuffner's dots.

PLASMODIUM FALCIPARUM

In the peripheral blood only ring stage and gametocytes are present. Schizonts are not present in blood since schizogony takes place in tissues.

Trophozoite stage

Rings are 1-1.5μ in size, blue in colour with a red nucleus. The rings have a regular outline. Some of the RBCs demonstrate 2-3 rings and some rings have 2 nuclei (Fig. 14.3).

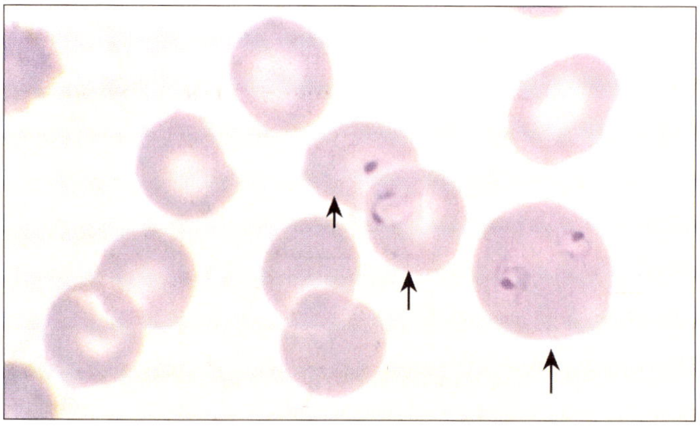

Fig. 14.3: Ring stage of P.falciparum with one RBC showing 2 rings.

Gametocyte Stage

Gametocytes are crescentric (Fig. 14.4) and only a thin red cell border is recognised. Female gametocyte is blue with a central, compact red nucleus and malarial pigment in cytoplasm. Male gametocyte is paler in colour and has a diffuse lightly stained nuclear material in the central zone.

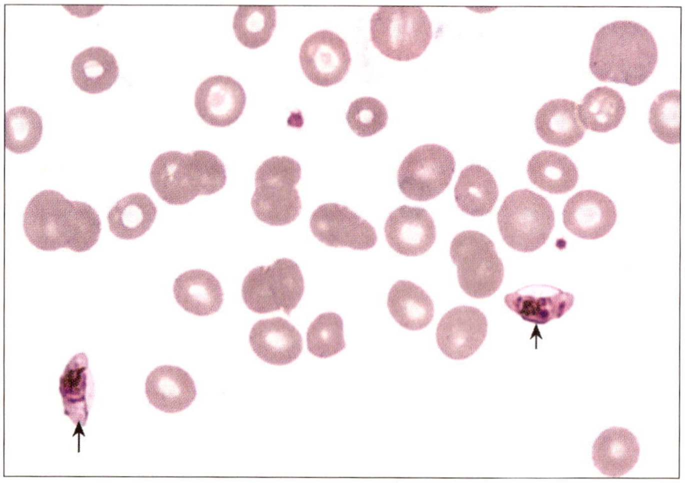

Fig. 14.4: Crescentric gametocytes of P.falciparum with brownish hemozoin pigment close to nucleus.

Thick Film for MP

RBC outlines are not visualised since dehemoglobinisation has already been carried out. Only malarial parasites with distorted morphology are made out. Thick film is a concentration method for malarial parasite and one microscopic field is equivalent to 40-50 microscopic fields of a thin smear. However, thin film is essential for morphology and thus characterizing the type of malarial parasite. Thick film method is preferred for mass surveys for a quick diagnosis. It is better to make both thin and thick films on the same slide.

Malarial Pigment

Due to parasitemia of RBCs, red cell physiology is disturbed. Globin part of the hemoglobin is broken down and resynthesized into parasite protein and the unutilized part is hemozoin – a brown pigment which is present in malarial parasite (Fig. 14.4) and also results in pigmentation of various organs – liver, spleen, brain, etc.

Natural Protection from Malaria

People deficient in **Glucose-6-Phosphate dehydrogenase** have some protection against malaria since Plasmodium cannot survive inside the RBC because it needs G-6-PD enzyme for survival.

In **sickle cell disease**, the Plasmodium infects the RBC and induces quicker sickling and sickled RBCs with parasite inside them are sequestered by the reticuloendothelial cells of the spleen, thus providing protection against malaria.

Blood Alterations in Malaria

These include high reticulocyte count due to hemolytic component, more so in falciparum malaria, monocytosis and anemia in chronic malaria. Anemia progressively becomes moderately severe due to hypersplenism.

Rapid test for Malaria – Microtyping test (Gel card) (Malaria antigen detection test)

Plasmodium produces an enzyme Plasmodium LDH (pLDH). 10 µl of fresh/frozen/dried whole blood is taken. RBCs are lysed and pLDH from parasitised RBCs is released. Presence of pLDH is detected using monoclonal antibodies against specific epitopes of pLDH (Immunochromatographic test - Optimal). Some of the tests are based on Histidine rich protein-2 (HRP2) of the P. falciparum. HRP2 ramains longer in circulation than LDH and therefore more cases are false +ve even after treatment (immunochromatographic test - Optimal). Positive test indicates active Plasmodium infection and differentiates P.falciparum from P.vivax and other malarial infections. Test is quick, specific, sensitive and ideal for field conditions.

This test is useful to differentiate between various Plasmodium species and also to determine strains of Plasmodium resistant to therapy by repeating the test 48 hours after treatment.

FILARIASIS

Wuchereria bancrofti is confined to tropical and subtropical regions. In India, the disease is confined to the regions along the banks of big rivers and sea coast. Adult worms localise in the lymphatic vessels and lymph nodes (Fig. 5.6) causing obstruction to lymph flow resulting in lymphedema and elephantiasis. Embryos of W. bancrofti (microfilaria) pass through lymph nodes, lymphatics and reach circulating blood and demonstration of *microfilaria* (Fig. 14.5) in peripheral blood is diagnostic of filariasis.

Collection of Blood Sample

Smears for demonstration of microfilaria should be made preferably between 10p.m. and 2 a.m. or **midnight smears**. The microfilariae can be demonstrated in:

(a) ***Peripheral smear***.
(b) ***Thick blood smear***.
(c) ***Unstained wet preparation*** – Two drops of blood are taken on a slide and a cover slip is placed. Microfilaria are made out by their movements causing agitation of the wet smear and can be confirmed by examining under a low power objective.
(d) ***Concentration method*** – Take 5 ml blood in EDTA vial. Centrifuge at 2500 r.p.m. for 5 minutes. Remove the plasma. Take the sediment of cells and make 4-6 smears. Air dry, fix in methanol and stain with Romanowsky stain.

Alternatively 5 ml blood + 10 ml D. water is taken and the mixture is shaken vigorously till blood is completely hemolysed. Centrifuge the tube at 2500 r.p.m. for 15 minutes. Deposit is examined for microfilariae.

Morphology of microfilaria

Microfilaria of W.bancrofti shows the hyaline sheath which is longer than the larval body. Somatic cells appear as granules and extend from head to the tail end except the terminal tail sheath – a distinguishing feature of W.bancrofti microfilaria (Fig. 14.5). Filariasis evokes a blood and tissue eosinophilia.

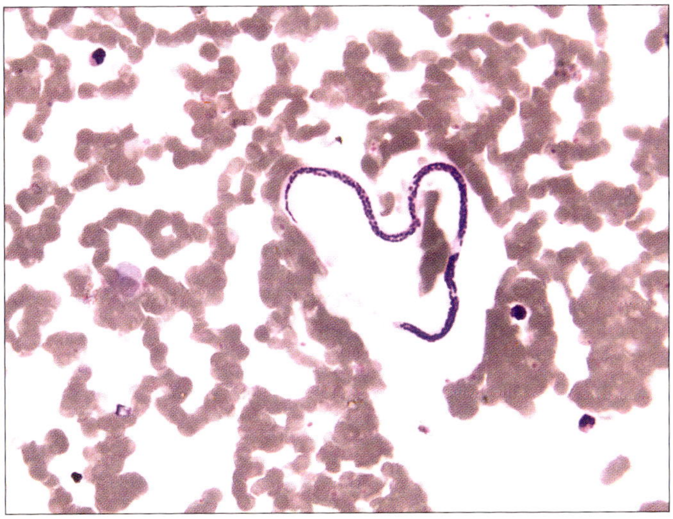

Fig. 14.5: Microfilaria of W.bancrofti – Peripheral smear

TRYPANOSOMES

These affect mainly the African subcontinent. These are flagellate protozoa having a narrow body and are mobile.

LEISHMANIA DONOVANI

Kala-azar is endemic in Bihar. Amastigote forms – L.D. bodies are observed in reticulum cells in the bone marrow and spleen (Fig. 14.6). L.D. body has a nucleus and a kinetoplast. Rarely L.D. bodies are seen free or in monocyte in peripheral blood when parasitemia is very high.

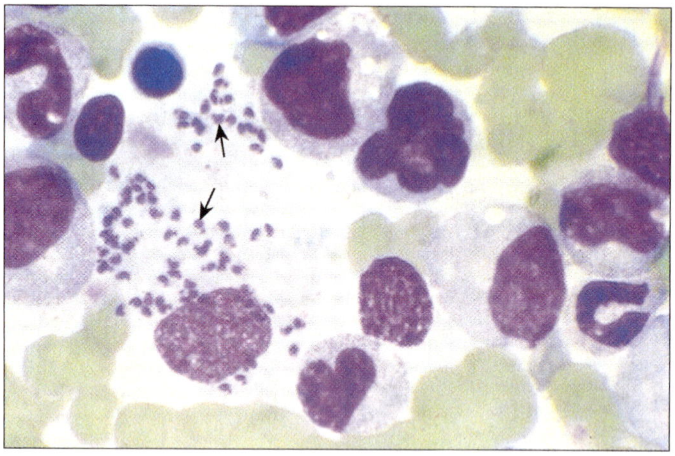

Fig. 14.6A: Bone marrow aspirate showing intracellular and extracellular L.D. bodies.

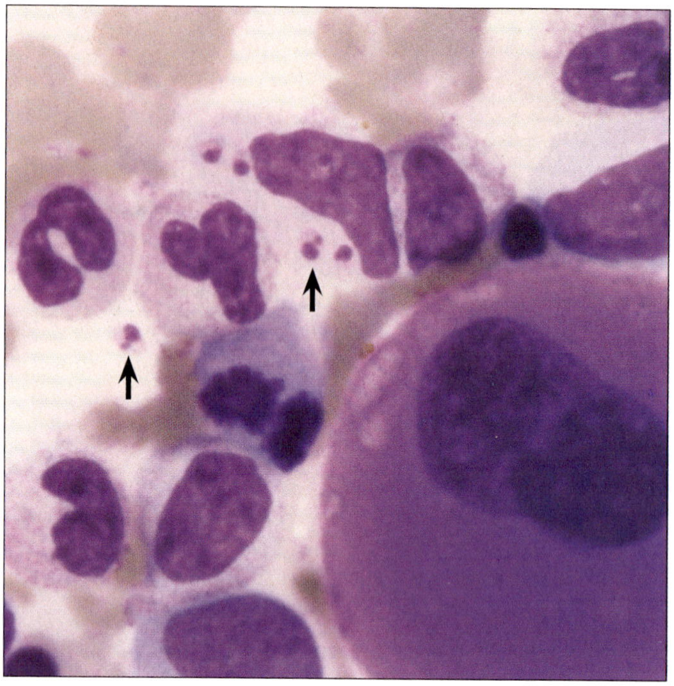

Fig. 14.6B: L.D. bodies (↑) demonstrate nucleus and the smaller kinetoplast.

VIVA VOCE

Q. Why is RBC larger in P.vivax infection?

Ans. P.vivax parasite enters reticulocytes which are larger while P.falciparum affects RBCs of all ages.

Q. Why is the nucleus of M.P. red?

Ans. Nucleus of M.P. is made up of RNA and stains red with Romanowsky stains.

Q. What are the clinical forms of falciparum malaria?

Ans. Clinical manifestations may include cerebral malaria, blackwater fever, algid malaria and hemolytic disease.

Q. What is the blood picture in malaria and filariasis?

Ans. In malaria there is monocytosis while in filariasis there is eosinophilia.

Q. What is the difference in the microfilariae of W.bancrofti, Loa-loa and B. malayi?

Ans. In Loa-loa and Brugia malayi, nuclei extend upto the tail tip, while in W.bancrofti, nuclei do not extend upto the tail tip.

Q. What is the advantage of malaria antigen detection test?

Ans. Falciparum malaria test is based of PLDH and immunochromatography. It is easy, requires only 1 drop of blood and takes only 15–20 minutes. The test is quite sensitive and being used for field studies. Microscopy is not required. However, microscopic detection of malaria is the Gold standard.

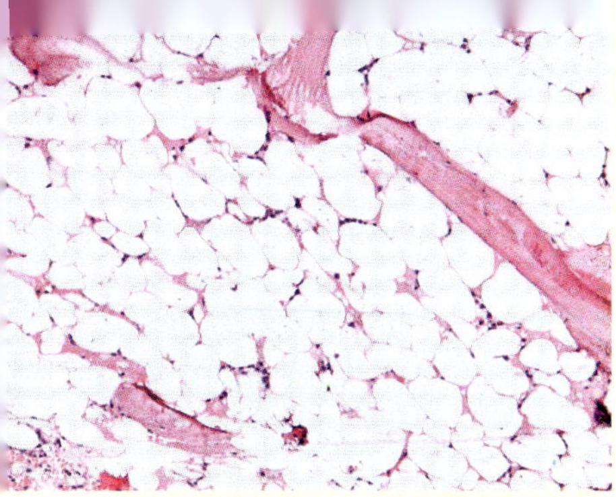

15

Bone Marrow Examination

Bone marrow evaluation is essential in certain diseases to confirm/rule out a hematologic disorder. Marrow may be obtained by:

(a) bone marrow aspiration
(b) bone marrow trephine biopsy.

Bone marrow aspiration is easy, simple and safe.

Sites for Bone Marrow Aspirate

Sites for bone marrow aspirate (BMA) are sternum, posterior superior iliac spine, iliac crest, anterior superior iliac spine and spinous process of lumbar vertebra (Fig. 15.1). Upper end of tibia is the ideal site for marrow aspirate in infants.

Needles

Needles commonly employed for marrow aspirate are Salah needle (Fig. 15.2) and Klima needle.

Method

(a) Patient is made to lie in lateral position and the legs are flexed and thighs are taken against abdomen, so that posterior superior iliac spine becomes prominent.

(b) Skin covering posterior superior iliac spine and surrounding area is cleaned with iodine, followed by alcohol and the area is draped, taking aseptic precautions.

(c) 5 ml of 1% xylocaine is injected into the skin overlying the posterior superior iliac spine and also into the periosteum.

(d) A small 3 mm cut is given with a sterile blade on the skin. Guard on the *needle* is adjusted taking into account the thickness of the subcutaneous issue.

(e) *Salah needle* along with its stylet and guard (Fig. 15.2) is introduced through the skin cut into the bone with a rotatory clockwise and anti-clockwise movement. Needle is pushed through the cortex into the medullary bone and the resistance gives way as needle enters the medullary cavity. Guard prevents further pushing in of the needle.

(f) The stylet is withdrawn and a 10 ml syringe is attached to the needle. Suction is applied to draw 0.2 to 0.4 ml of marrow into the syringe. Suction is stopped. Do not aspirate more marrow, as it may result in dilution of the marrow.

(g) Needle and syringe together are withdrawn and marrow is poured onto the slides placed at an angle of 30° so that blood present in marrow is drained off.

(h) Using a spreader slide, smears of marrow are made and the particles of marrow are carried to the end of the slide. The process of pouring marrow, and making the slides should be very quick so as to avoid clotting of marrow. Good marrow smears contain *marrow particles* as well as *trails* of particles. Atleast 6 smears are made.

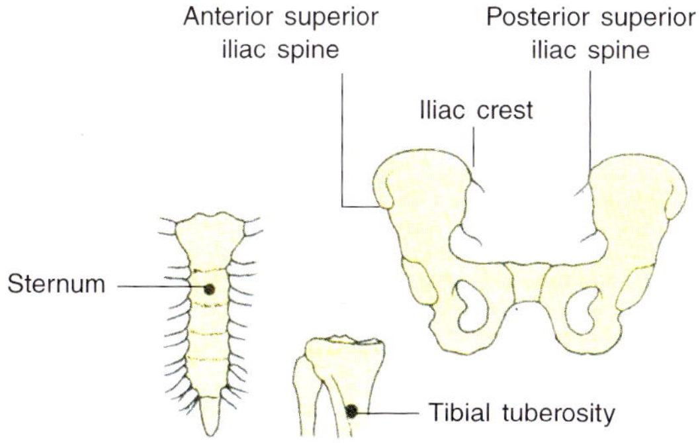

Fig. 15.1: Sites of bone marrow aspiration

Fig. 15.2: Salah Needle with stylet (S) and guard G.

(i) 2 smears are fixed in methanol for 10 minutes and stained with Giemsa stain. Iron stain is carried out on 1 smear to assess iron stores. Rest of the smears are used for cytochemistry/immunophenotyping etc. as per the requirement of the case.

Clot Sections of the Marrow

The clotted marrow should be put in a vial with 10% formalin. It is processed like tissue biopsy and sections should be taken and stained with hematoxylin and eosin. Such sections containing marrow provide additional information of the marrow cellularity and topography of the cells just like a trephine biopsy of the marrow.

EVALUATION OF BONE MARROW ASPIRATE

Marrow smears are screened first under a *scanner objective* to look for the presence of *marrow particles*. Most of the marrow particles are present in the tail of the smear and trails made by these particles provide enough cells to study their morphology and carry out a differential count on the smears.

Cellularity

Cellularity of the marrow is assessed from the marrow particles by visual evaluation of fat : cells, keeping in mind that in children marrow is highly cellular with less than 25% fat, while in adults, fat constitutes 40-50%. With advancing age there is progressive increase in fat with concomitant reduction in cells. Marrow is reported as hypercellular, normocellular or hypocellular as assessed by scanner and low power objectives.

M:E ratio

At least 500 marrow cells are counted and percentages of different cells calculated. M:E ratio gives the proportion of myeloid and erythroid cells and reflects hyperplasia, hypoplasia or normal number of myeloid and erythroid cells. Normal M:E ratio is 3:1-15:1.

Erythropoiesis

Erythroid cells are examined for maturation, dyserythropoiesis and type of reaction – normoblastic/megaloblastic/micronormo-blastic.

Myelopoiesis

Myeloid cells are evaluated for any maturation arrest, granulation – lack of it/hypergranulation, number of blast cells, degenerative changes like vacuolations in cytoplasm of myeloid cells.

Megakaryopoiesis

Megakaryocytes are examined in the marrow particles and in the cell trails. Besides number of megakaryocytes, it is important to assess budding of platelets from megakaryocytes and also relative number of promegakaryocytes to megakaryocytes.

Other Cells and Abnormal Cells

Smears are examined for reticulum cells, lymphocytes, plasma cells, metastatic tumour cells, any abnormal cells, parasite (Leishmania Donovani) and fungus (Histoplasma capsulatum), if any.

Iron Stores

Iron stores are assessed by Perl's stain (Fig. 15.3).

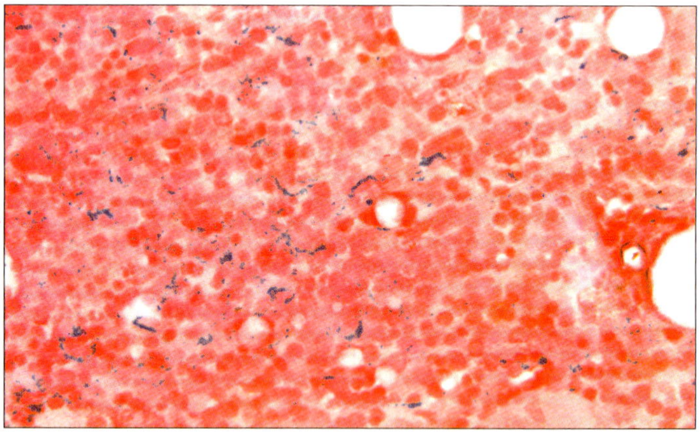

Fig. 15.3: Bone marrow fragment demonstrating increased iron stores. Perl's stain (Prussian blue reaction).

ASSESSMENT OF IRON STORES

Iron after absorption from small interstine is carried to the sites of iron storage – the main site being bone marrow. In the bone marrow, iron, in the ferric form as hemosiderin, is present in the reticulo-endothelial cells and free in the marrow. Iron can be demonstrated by prussian blue reaction.

Method (Perl's Stain) – Prussian Blue Reaction (Fig. 15.3)

1. Take freshly made bone marrow smear which has marrow fragments, since iron is demonstrable only in these marrow particles.
2. Fix the smear in methanol for 15 minutes and dry it.
3. Mix equal quantities of 2% Potassium ferrocyanide and N/5 HCl immediately before use in a Coplin jar.
4. Place the fixed marrow smear in the staining solution for 30 minutes.
5. Wash the slide in running tap water for 15 minutes, followed by distilled water.

6. Counterstain the slide with 1% nuclear fast red or 0.1% neutral red which stain the nuclei red.
7. Examine the slide and look for marrow particles using a scanner objective.
8. Examine the marrow particles in low power objective and then in high power objective for iron granules in reticuloendo-thelial cells and free iron.

Grading of Iron Stores

Grading of iron stores can be done as follows:

(a) ***Nil*** – No iron containing macrophage/no free iron; in iron deficiency anemias.

(b) ***Decreased*** – Occasional macrophage containing granules, seen on high power.

(c) ***Normal*** – Hemosiderin granules are present as free and in reticulum cells in marrow fragments. Seen in low power.

(d) ***Increased*** – Hemosiderin granules are abundant inside the reticular cells and extracellularly (Fig. 15.3).
- in hemolytic anemia
- in anemia of chronic renal failure
- in multitransfused patients *e.g.* in thalassemia, aplastic anemia (hemosiderosis)
- in megaloblastic anemia.
- in sideroblastic anemia.

Examine the normoblasts for iron granules – *sideroblasts* – in oil immersion lens.

(a) ***Normal sideroblasts*** – 1-3 pinpoint size of granules in cytoplasm of late normo-blasts.

(b) ***Abnormal sideroblasts*** – 1-10 pinhead size of granules in late and intermediate normoblasts *e.g.* in megaloblastic anemia.

(c) ***Ring sideroblasts*** – Coarse > 5 granules arranged in a perinuclear ring pattern *e.g. in sideroblastic anemia.*

Iron stores should be assessed in bone marrow films in all cases, since it is a quick, accurate and practical method of assessing iron stores and serves as a guide for chelation therapy in thalassemics and for differentiating iron deficiency (hypochromic) anemia from thalassemia.

INDICATIONS FOR BONE MARROW ASPIRATION

- ***Red cell disorders*** – Megaloblastic anemia, pure red cell aplasia, pancytopenia.
- ***White cell disorders*** – Subleukemic/aleukemic leukemia, all acute blastic leukemias for FAB typing.
- ***Megakaryocytic disorders*** – ITP and other thrombocytopenias.
- ***Myeloproliferative disorders*** – Polycythemia vera, Chronic myeloid leukemia, Idiopathic thrombocythemia.
- ***Myelodysplastic syndromes***
- ***Storage disorders*** – Gaucher's and Niemann-Pick's disease.
- ***Parasitic disorders*** – Kala-azar.
- ***Plasma cell disorders*** – M. Myeloma, Waldenstrom's macroglobulinemia.
- ***For iron stores***
- ***For metastatic deposits*** – Ca breast, prostate, lung, kidney, etc.
- ***For histocytic disorders*** – Langerhans cell histiocytosis, Hemophagocytic syndrome.
- Non-Hodgkin lymphoma involvement

Dry Tap

In aplastic anemia and myelofibrosis, marrow is not obtained and needle and syringe are dry – dry tap. In aplastic anemia marrow has been replaced by fat while in myelofibrosis marrow has been replaced by fibrous tissue.

BONE MARROW TREPHINE BIOPSY

Marrow trephine biopsy provides a core of bone with marrow spaces. Needles used for obtaining bone marrow biopsy are: Jamshidi needle (Fig. 15.4), Westerman-Jensen needle and Islam needle. As the core of the bone marrow is obtained, it is rolled between two glass slides to obtain marrow *imprint* smears. These smears are representative of the marrow and excellent for study of morphology and for special stains. Biopsy is decalcified, processed and multiple sections obtained are stained with Hematoxylin and eosin stain (Fig. 15.5A), reticulin stain, Masson's trichrome stain for fibrous tissue and immunocytochemical stains in acute leukemias.

Sites

- Posterior superior iliac spine is the preferred site.
- Anterior superior iliac spine
- Spinous process of vertebra.

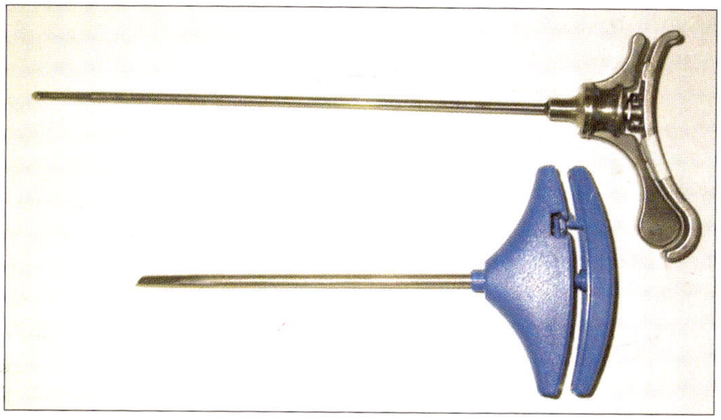

Fig. 15.4: Jamshidi needles for bone marrow trephine biopsy. (a) All steel autoclavable needle, (b) Disposable needle with plastic handle

Indications

- Aplastic anemia (Fig. 15.5 B).
- Myelofibrosis.
- Hypoplastic acute leukemia, AML-M7.
- For detection of micro metastasis in cancer cases. Marrow positive for metastatic deposit indicates disseminated malignancy i.e. stage IV.
- For lymphoma involvement. Hodgkin and Non-Hodgkin
- In myeloproliferative disorders to study reticulin and the proliferative cell lines for typing.
- Pre and post bone marrow transplantation in acute leukemia, CML and multiple myeloma etc.
- In cases of PUO – for tuberculous granuloma.
- MDS.
- AIDS.
- Chronic lymphoproliferative disorders
- For detection of bone marrow necrosis

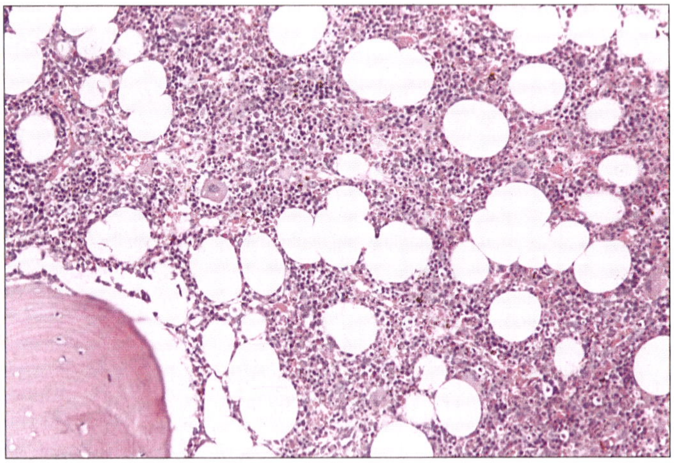

Fig. 15.5 A: Bone marrow biopsy. Normal BMB showing cellular marrow with myeloid, erythroid cells with scattered megakaryocytes.

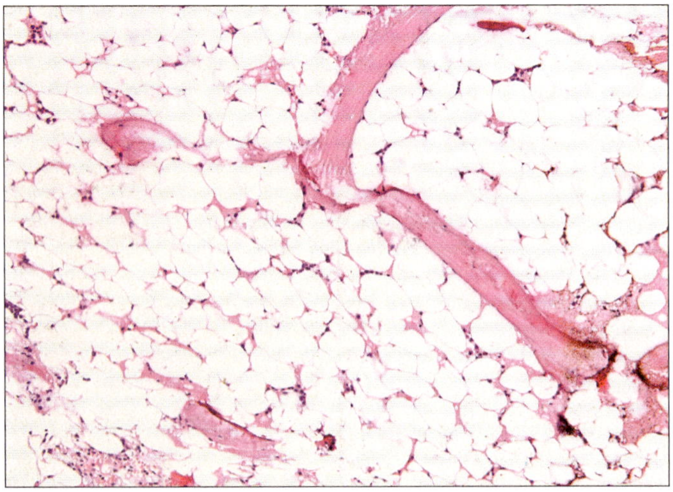

Fig. 15.5 B: Aplastic anemia. Bone marrow biopsy shows marked increase in fat in the marrow spaces since the hemopoietic cells have been replaced by fat and therefore marrow aspirate is a dry tap.

ERYTHROPOIESIS

In the bone marrow, islands of erythroid precursors are seen as collections around reticulum cells which supply iron to developing normoblasts. Erythropoiesis involves:

- hemoglobinisation of normoblasts
- pyknosis and extrusion of nuclei
- reduction in size from early normoblast to red cell.

The various stages of erythropoiesis are given hereunder:

Pronormoblast (Proerythroblast)

- round cell, basophilic cytoplasm
- 10-16μ size, centrally placed nucleus with closely meshed chromatin, 2-5 nucleoli.

Early Normoblast (Early erythroblast)

- round cell, 8-18μ in size, N:C ratio 2:3
- cytoplasm less basophilic than that of pronormoblast
- nucleoli not seen, chromatin is coarse (Fig. 15.6).

Intermediate (polychromatic) Normoblast (Intermediate erythroblast)

- 8-12μ in size.
- Cytoplasm is polychromatic because of hemoglobinisation of cytoplasm
- nuclear chromatin is deep staining and coarse (Fig. 15.6)

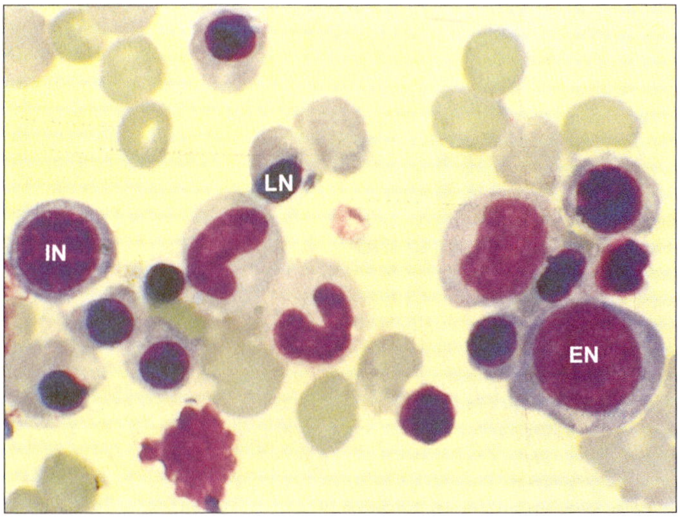

Fig. 15.6: Normal bone marrow with early (EN) intermediate (IN) and late normoblasts (LN).

Late (orthochromatic) Normoblast (Late erythroblast)

- 8-10μ, round cell

- pyknotic eccentric or partially extruded nucleus (Fig. 15.6)
- well hemoglobinised cytoplasm.

Reticulocyte – can be demonstrated on supravital staining (reticulocyte count – Fig. 12.1).

REACTION OF MARROW

(a) Normoblastic

Normal maturation of red cell precursors (Fig. 15.6).

(b) Megaloblastic

Early, intermediate and late megaloblasts are larger than their counterpart normoblasts with more open nuclear chromatin (sieve like) and asynchrony between nuclear and cytoplasmic maturation with nuclear maturation lagging behind (Fig. 15.7). Intermediate and late megaloblasts demonstrate features of dyserythropoiesis like nuclear budding and multiple Howell Jolly bodies. Megablastosis is observed in B_{12} and Folic Acid deficiency.

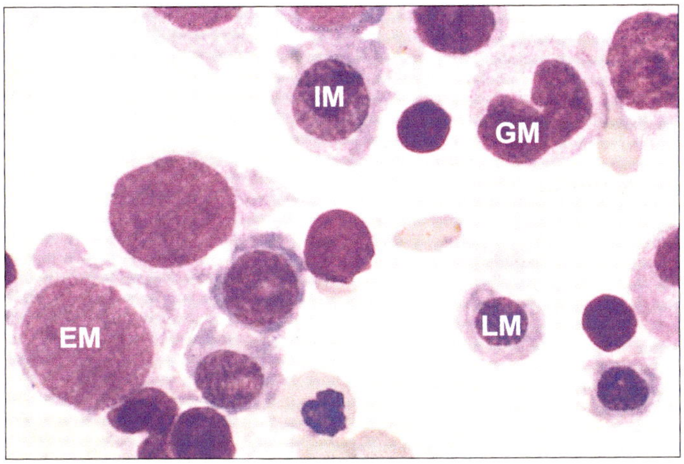

Fig. 15.7: Megaloblastic Anemia. Bone marrow showing early (EM), intermediate (IM) and late megaloblasts (LM) which are larger than normoblasts and have open sieve like chromatin. Giant metamyelocyte (GM) is seen.

(c) Micronormoblastic

Normoblasts are smaller than the usual size. There is persistent basophilia of cytoplasm with fraying of cytoplasmic borders. This is observed in iron deficiency anemia where bone marrow iron is nil.

(d) Macronormoblastic

The erythroid precursors are larger than the corresponding normoblasts, but smaller than megaloblasts and the nuclear chromatin is also intermediate between those of megaloblasts and normoblasts, observed in nutritional deficiency of Vit. B_{12}, Fe, and folate and also in partly treated megaloblastic anemias.

MYELOPOIESIS

Normal granulocyte production in BM involves:

- Cells and nuclei from myeloblast onwards become smaller as maturation takes place.
- Granulation appears in promyelocytes which progressively diminishes until metamyelocyte stage and then granulation remains constant.
- Specific granules are observed from myelocyte stage.
- Nuclear chromatin becomes progressively more coarse and deeply stained.

The various stages in myelopoiesis are:

(a) Myeloblast

15-25μ, centrally placed round nucleus with a characteristic reticular chromatin network with 3-5 nucleoli (lymphoblast usually has 1-2 nucleoli).

(b) Promyelocyte

12-20μ, round central/eccentric nucleus with a chromatin pattern coarser than in myeloblast with 2-4 nucleoli. Cytoplasmic granulation is observed.

(c) Myelocyte

12-15μ, nucleus is flattened on one side with chromatin coarser than in promyelocyte with absence of nucleoli; fine cytoplasmic granules are present (Fig. 15.8).

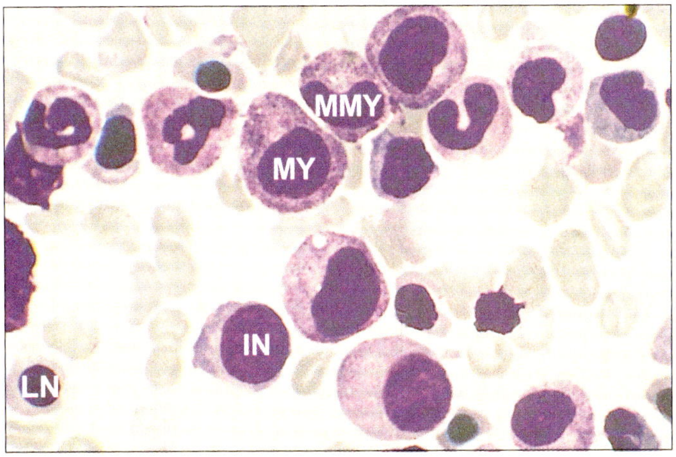

Fig. 15.8: Normal bone marrow showing myeloid precursors myelocytes (My), metamyelocytes (MMy) and band forms (B). A few intermediate (IN) and late mormoblasts (LN) are also seen.

(d) Metamyelocyte

10-15μ, eccentric nucleus which is kidney shaped, chromatin pattern is coarser than that of myelocyte, numerous fine granules in cytoplasm (Fig. 15.8).

Table 16.1 Lymphoblast and Myeloblast

Lymphoblast	Myeloblast
• Nuclear chromatin – coarse	fine
• Cytoplasm – scanty	Scanty to moderate
• Nucleoli – 1-2	3-5
• Auer rod –ve	+ve

Cytochemistry in Acute Leukaemias

Typing of blast cells is essential before instituting chemotherapy, since treatment regimens for lymphoblastic and myeloblastic leukemias are entirely different. At times, it is difficult to differentiate AML from ALL just on morphology, in such cases *cytochemical stains* are carried out.Cytochemical stains help in typing the blast cells (Table 16.2).

Table 16.2 Cytochemistry in acute leukemias

Stain	AML	ALL
Peroxidase	+	–
Sudan Black B	+	–
Non-Specific esterase	+ in M_4 & M_5	
	AML	–
PAS	– in blasts	+
	(+ in erythroblasts of M_6)	Block positivity

Myeloperoxidase Stain

Myeloperoxidase staining is based on the fact that azurophilic granules of mature and immature cells of myeloid series contain peroxidase enzyme in their cytoplasm and intensity of positivity increases with maturity. Benzidine is oxidised by hydrogen peroxide, in the presence of peroxidase present in myeloblasts and other cells of myeloid series. Blue granules (Fig. 16.3B) are seen in the thin rim of cytoplasm of blast cells. This stain is positive in M_1, M_2, M_3, M_4, M_5 and M_6 blasts and Auer rods in AML.

- Lymphoblasts and erythroblasts are negative (Fig. 16.3A).
- Useful to differentiate between AML and ALL.

Sudan Black B stain

This stain demonstrates phospholipids – as black granules in myeloblasts and other cells of myeloid series. Staining pattern is same as for Myeloperoxidase stain. Rarely, lymphoblasts show fine black granules due to the presence of mitochondrial phospholipid.

- Useful to differentiate between AML and ALL.

Periodic Acid Schiff (PAS) stain

Carbohydrate is oxidised to aldehyde which gives a positive magenta colour with basic fuchsin. In lymphoblasts of ALL, large magenta granules – "Block Positivity" (Fig. 16.4) is demonstrated. Myeloblasts and monoblasts do not reveal block positivity. However, erythroblasts of AML-M_6 demonstrate positive staining. Developing granulocytes react positively in all stages of development, with mature neutrophils reacting most strongly. Monocytes contain few fine, scattered granules. Megakaryocytes and platelets are intensely positive.

- Useful to differentiate between AML and ALL.

Non-Specific Esterase stain

This stain demonstrates lysosomal non-specific esterase activity of monoblasts and differentiates them from myeloblasts and lymphoblasts. The most widely used

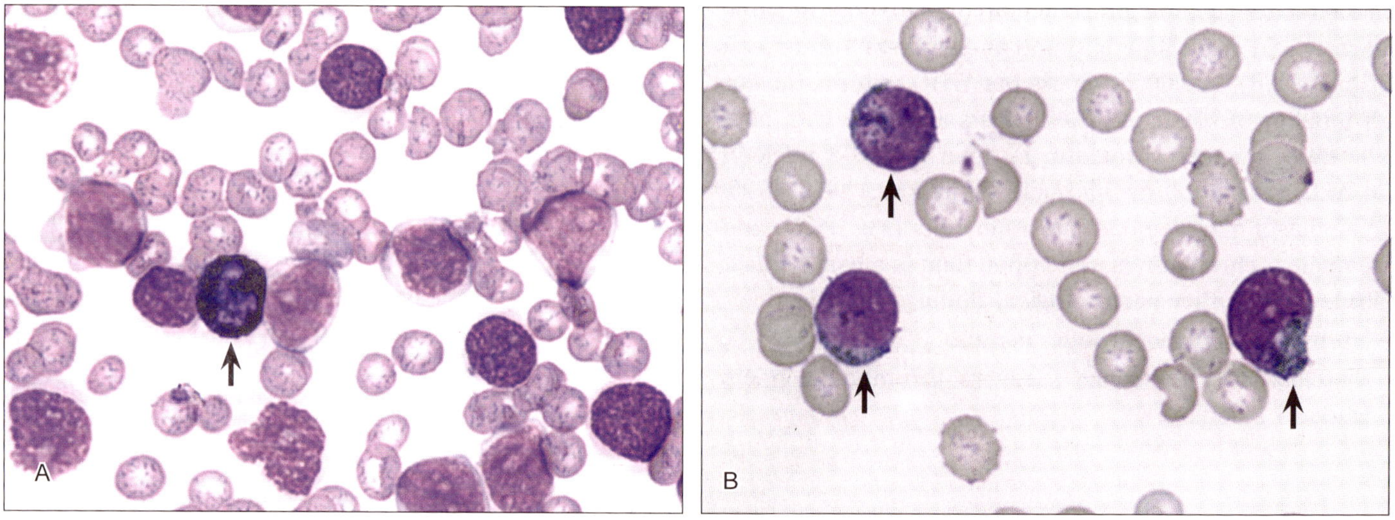

Fig. 16.3: Myeloperoxidase stain. A. Blast cells in ALL are negative and one neutrophil is positive showing blue granules (↑). B. AML-blast cells demonstrate dark blue granule positive with peroxidase stain (↑).

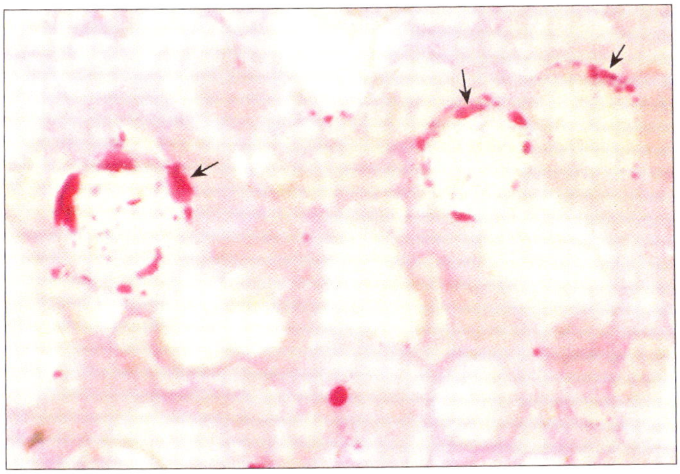

Fig. 16.4: PAS stain. Blasts demonstrate magenta coloured coarse granularity – block positivity in ALL.

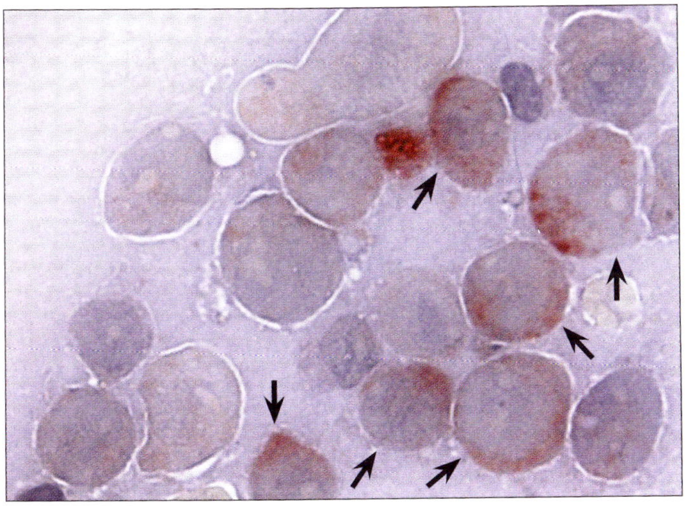

Fig. 16.5: Non-specific esterase stain. Monoblasts and promonocytes from a case of AML-M5 demonstrate positivity (↑).

substrate is alpha-naphthyl acetate. Positivity is indicated by dark red cytoplasmic granules in monocytes, histiocytes and megakaryocytes (Fig. 16.5).

- Useful to confirm AML-M_4 and M_5.

  Marker studies: Monoclonal antibodies are useful in differentiating cases which cannot be diagnosed on cytochemistry. CD13, cAnti-MPO (cytoplasmic antiMPO) and CD33 are positive in AML while CD61 is diagnostic of AML-M_7. To assess the level of differentiation of ALL - CD10, HLA-DR, CD19 are useful. T-ALL blasts demonstrate positivity with cCD3. *Flow cytometry* is useful for characterization of various acute leukaemias.

CHRONIC MYELOID LEUKAEMIA (CML)

CML is a clonal stem cell disorder and is associated with Philadelphia (Ph) chromosome – a unique cytogenetic abnormality. The molecular abnormality is BCR-ABL and is diagnostic of CML. There is leucocytosis in the range of 50,000 to 5 lacs per cumm.

P.S. findings

- Marked leucocytosis.
- Myeloid cells of all stages from blast to mature polymorphs. However, the predominant immature cell is **myelocyte**. In a classical case the picture is

Blasts	1-5%
Promyelocytes	2-8%
Myelocytes	15-30%
Metamylocytes	15-25%
Band forms	5-15%
Neutrophils	40-70%
Basophils	1-8%
Eosinophils	2-10%
Monocytes	2-10%

  with **basophilia**, **eosinophilia** and **thrombocytosis** (increased platelets) (Fig. 16.6).
- Normocytic normochronic anemia.
- At times it needs differentiation from leukemoid reaction. (Table 16.3).

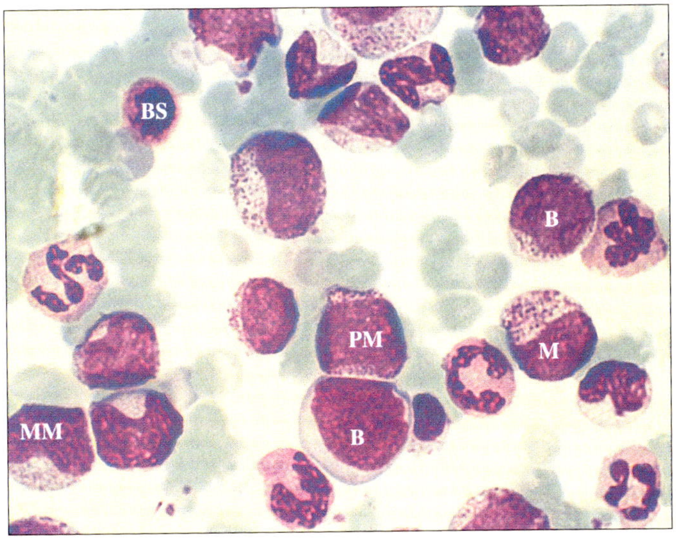

Fig. 16.6 CML - showing leucocytosis, metamylocytes (MM), myelocytes (M), promyelocytes (PM), a blast cell B and a basophil (BS).

Table 16.3 Leukemoid Reaction and CML	
Leukemoid Reaction	**CML**
• TLC – 10,000-50,000	50,000-5,00,000
• Basophilia –ve	+ve
• Eosinophilia –ve	+ve
• NAP score – ↑ – (150-350)	↓ (0-40)
• Ph chromosome –ve	+ve
• Cause of leukemoid reaction present	No cause
• No splenomegaly	Moderate to massive splenomegaly
• BCR-ABL negative	BCR-ABL positive

Neutrophil Alkaline Phosphatase

Alkaline phosphatase is present in the cytoplasm of neutrophils. This enzyme is located in the specific (secondary) or tertiary granules which give a positive reaction.

NAP Score

Based on the intensity and number of blue granules in neutrophils' cytoplasm, individual cells are scored as follows:

0 : Negative.
1 : Diffuse pale blue cytoplasm with occasional granules.
2 : Moderate blue granules.
3 : Unevenly distributed blue granular precipitate.
4 : Uniform, strongly positive, numerous coarse granules.

100 consecutive neutrophils are counted and the sum of their scores is determined.

Normal range

Adults	25-100
Newborn infants	150-300

High Scores are found in:

- leukemoid reaction (Fig. 16.7)
- myelofibrosis
- polycythemia rubra vera
- idiopathic thrombocythemia
- pregnancy
- Down's syndrome

Low Scores are found in:

- PNH
- CML (Fig. 16.7)
- Hereditary hypophosphatasia

CHRONIC LYMPHOCYTIC LEUKAEMIA (CLL)

CLL is a malignancy of mature lymphocytes in the elderly. It is of insidious onset and may be detected incidentally or the patient may present with generalised lymphadenopathy. There is leucocytosis in the range 20,000 to 5 lacs per cumm.

P.S. findings

- Marked leucocytosis
- Mature lymphocyte is the preponderant cell (Fig. 16.8).
  Polys – 2-30%
  Lymphos – 70-98%
- Normocytic normochromic anemia.
- Platelets are normal initially and as the disease advances, thrombocytopenia and anemia develop.
- Smear demonstrates **smudge** cells – lymphos, which rupture while making the P.S. because of delicate nuclear membrane (Fig. 16.8) and are seen as smudgy nuclear material.
- Lymphocytes in CLL are CD19/CD20 positive and are monoclonal.

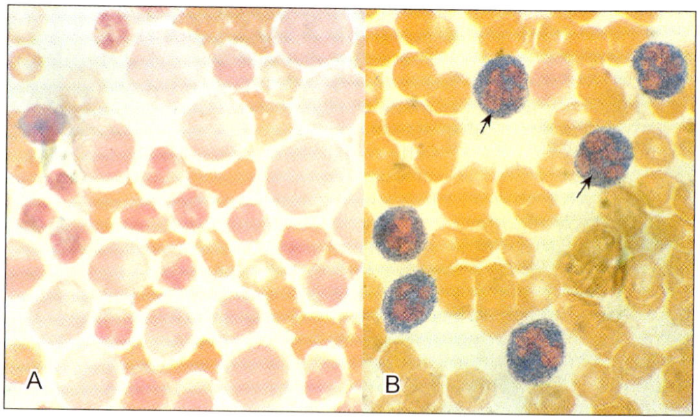

Fig. 16.7: (A) CML – Neutrophils are negative for NAP, only one neutrophil is positive 1+. Low NAP score 10. (B) Leukemoid reaction – Neutrophils are positive 4+. High NAP score 356.

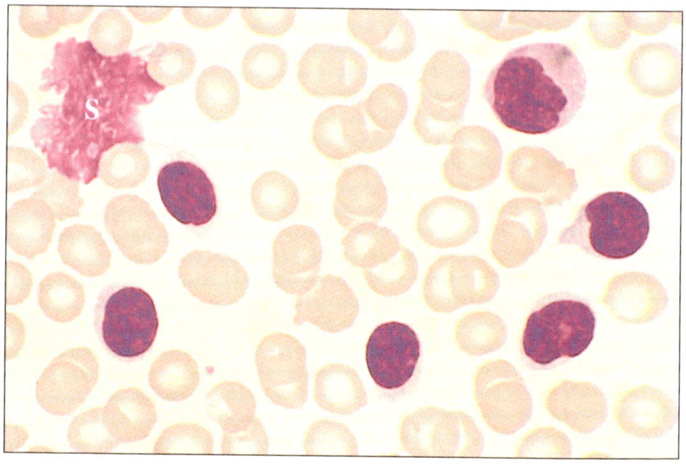

Fig. 16.8: CLL. Smear shows lymphocytic leucocytosis and a single smudge cell – S

VIVA VOCE

Q. Which is the most useful cytochemical stain in differentiating AML and ALL?
Ans. Myeloperoxidase stain is positive in most of the subtypes of AML and helps in differentiating it from ALL.

Q. How do you differentiate between lymphoblast in ALL and myeloblast in AML?
Ans. See Tables 16.1 and 16.2.

Q. What is aleukemic leukemia and how is it diagnosed?
Ans. In aleukemic leukemia blast cells are not present in the peripheral blood; however, marrow shows more than 20% blast cells, and is diagnostic.

Q. Which acute blastic leukemia has good prognosis?
Ans. ALL has better prognosis as compared to AML.

Q. What is the phenotype of CLL?
Ans. CLL is a neoplastic process of B-lymphocytes and this fact is used to differentiate it from lymphocytosis.

Q. Which chronic leukemia has worse prognosis?
Ans. CML has worse prognosis than CLL.

Q. Which chronic leukaemia is more common?
Ans. CML is more frequent than CLL in India.

Q. What is the difference in the age incidence of CML and CLL?
Ans. CML is the disease of 30-50 years while CLL is a disease of the elderly >60 years. CML is also seen in children and young adults.

Q. What is the difference between FAB and WHO classification of AML?
Ans.
- The cut off %age of blasts in the bone marrow is 20% in WHO, while it is 30% in FAB classification.
- Various subtypes of AML in WHO classification give an indication of prognosis and are based on cytogenetic abnormalities.

Q. What are the prognostic factors in acute myeloid leukemia.
Ans. Cytogenetic and molecular abnormalities determine the prognosis in many cases of AML.

Q. What is the diagnostic feature of Acute promyelocytic leukemia (AML-M3).
Ans. PML-RARA molecular abnormality is the diagnostic feature of AML-M3.

Q. Which are the diagnostic markers for AML, B-ALL and T-ALL as used in flow cytometry.
Ans. AML – cMPO (cytoplasmic MPO)
B-ALL – cCD79a (cytoplasmic CD79a)
T-ALL – cCD3 (cytoplasmic CD3)

Q. What is the age prevalence of ALL and CLL.
Ans. ALL is a disease of children while CLL is the neoplasm of old age.

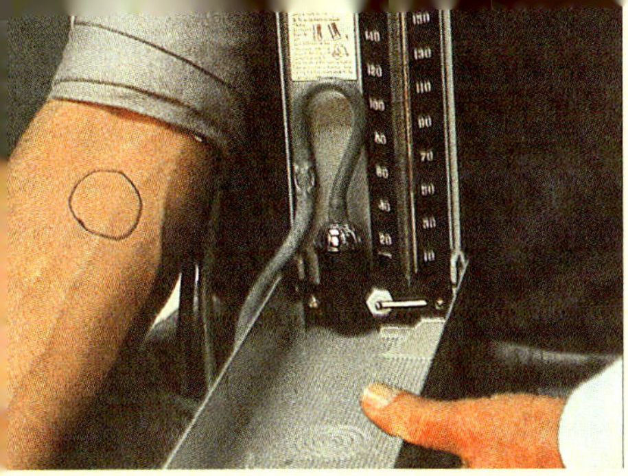

17

Haemostasis

Haemostasis is the mechanism by which bleeding from an injured blood vessel gets stopped. Changes begin with injury to the tissue and blood vessels resulting in the formation of thrombus which seals the injured vessel. During this process, there is activation of extrinsic and intrinsic systems of coagulation along with fibrinolytic system, while the platelet plug initiates the sequence of haemostasis. Any defect in the platelet number/function, coagulation mechanism, fibrinolytic system, antithrombin III, protein C/S would lead to bleeding/thrombotic episodes. While investigating a case of bleeding disorder, it is essential to assess the function of various systems to localise the defect. Following basic investigations are required:

(i) Platelet count and function studies, the latter are carried out on a platelet aggregometer.
(ii) Bleeding time – BT and clotting time – CT.
(iii) Prothrombin Time – PT.
(iv) Activated Partial Thromboplastin Time – APTT.
(v) Thrombin Time – TT.
(vi) D-Dimer test (FDP)

BLEEDING TIME (BT)

A small cut of a standard size and depth is made on the skin and the oozing blood is wiped off with a filter paper. Bleeding stops when the capillaries contract and platelet plug seals the vessel. Therefore BT is a measure of platelet number and function, capillary function and platelet plug formation.

Previously **Duke's** and **Ivy's** methods were used; however, **Template method** is the method of choice.

Template Method for BT

1. Make the patient sit on a chair with an arm rest, so that forearm is exposed and steady on the arm rest.
2. Clean the forearm with alcohol and air dry.
3. Sphygmomanometer cuff is inflated to 40 mm at the upper arm.
4. Place the template 5 cm distal to antecubital crease, avoiding superficial veins.
5. The template, made of plastic, has a longitudinal slit of 9 mm length and thickness of the plastic and the angle of the blade is such that the incision made through the slit is 9 mm long and 1 mm deep. The template is pressed against the skin to flatten the skin surface and the slit is parallel to antecubital crease.
   (In the ***simplate*** test, on pressing the trigger, an incision of 5 mm length and 1 mm depth is made. No pressure is applied to the device.)
6. The blade is introduced into the slit and skin is penetrated and incision made with a smooth rapid movement along the entire length of the slit.
7. A stop watch is started immediately after the incision is made.
8. Another incision is made 1.5-2 cm away from the first one and the other stop watch is started.
9. The skin incisions are blotted with filter paper (Whatman No. 1), without touching the wound edges or skin every 30 seconds until blood stops flowing. Time taken is noted. Carefully appose the edges of the incisions by applying an adhesive strip.
10. Mean of the two readings is the Bleeding Time (BT) for the patient.

Normal range: 2-9 minutes.

Prolonged Bleeding Time

Prolonged Bleeding Time is observed in

- Thrombocytopenia. If platelet count is less than 50,000/ mm^3, BT should not be carried out as bleeding is difficult to stop.
- Platelet function disorders – thrombasthenia, and Von-Willebrand's disease.

- Vascular abnormalities – in pseudoxanthoma elasticum, Ehlers-Danlos syndrome.
- In hemophilia A and B, secondary bleeding may occur from the puncture wound 24 hours after the test even if BT is normal.
- In uremic patients.
- Patient on antiplatelet medication – aspirin.

Hess's Test (Capillary resistance test)

Method

- Inflate a sphygmomanometer cuff placed at upper arm to 80 mm Hg for 5 minutes.
- Release the inflation after 5 minutes. Patient is instructed to lift the arm to shoulder height.
- Gently tap the area below the antecubital fossa with hand.
- Examine the flexor aspect of forearm (below the elbow) in an area of 5 cm diameter (Fig. 17.1).
- In a normal individual, less than 5 petechiae are present.

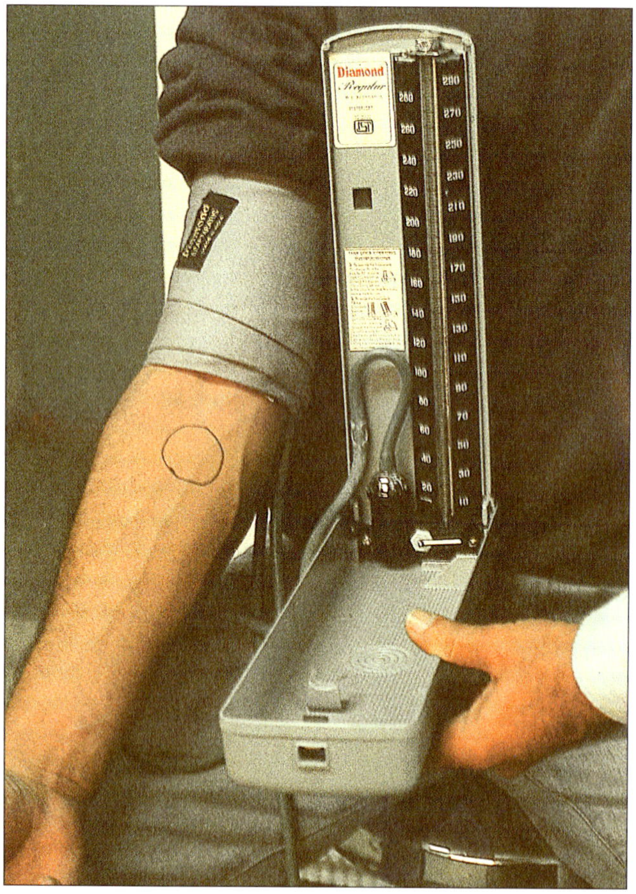

Fig. 17.1: Hess's test.

Positive test

More than 10 petechiae, often numerous, are suggestive of defective capillary resistance which may be due to thrombocytopenia, defective platelet function, thrombasthenia, vascular purpura and scurvy.

WHOLE BLOOD CLOTTING TIME (LEE & WHITE METHOD)

This is not a sensitive test as it fails to detect mild/ moderate procoagulant defects and is, therefore, not recommended as a screening test. APTT is a sensitive test for assessment of coagulation cascade.

Steps

(a) Withdraw 3 ml of venous blood using, aseptic precautions. A stop watch is started, the moment blood appears in the glass syringe. If disposable plastic syringe is used, then the stop watch is put to 'on' when blood is poured into the glass tubes, since activation of clotting process gets initiated as the blood comes in contact with glass.

(b) Deliver 1 ml of blood each into 3 small test tubes (10 cm × 1 cm size) labelled as No. 1, 2 and 3 already placed in a water bath at 37°C.

(c) After 3 minutes, take out tube No. 1, tilt it to 90° to look for clot formation and put back into the water bath. Repeat the same process every 30 seconds.

(d) Note the time when the tube can be inverted without its contents spilling. Record CT.

(e) Now start examining tube No. 2 every 30 seconds, exactly the same way as tube No. 1, till the clot forms and record the time.

(f) As the clot forms in the 2nd tube, start inverting the 3rd tube till blood clots. Stop the watch. Record the time from the moment blood enters the syringe/glass tube to the clotting in the 3rd tube. Take mean of the CT of tubes 2 and 3.

Precautions

(a) Size of the tubes should be uniform and preferably 1 cm in diameter.

(b) Tubes should be totally clean, since any substance coating the inner surface will affect CT.

(c) When CT is markedly prolonged as in severe hemophilia, it may take even upto one hour for clotting to occur.

Normal range : 4-11 minutes at 37°C.

Significance. CT is a rough, insensitive indicator of intrinsic pathway of coagulation and is prolonged only when there is severe deficiency of Factor VIII (98% deficiency), IX or fibrinogen (afibrinogenemia) and in heparin therapy. Normal value of CT is obtained in mild to moderately severe hemophilia A and B and it does not exclude major factor deficiency. A sensitive measure of the efficiency of intrinsic pathway of coagulation is activated partial thromboplastin time with kaolin (APTT/ PTTK).

Following CT, the tubes should be left in the water bath and examined after one hour for *clot retraction*.

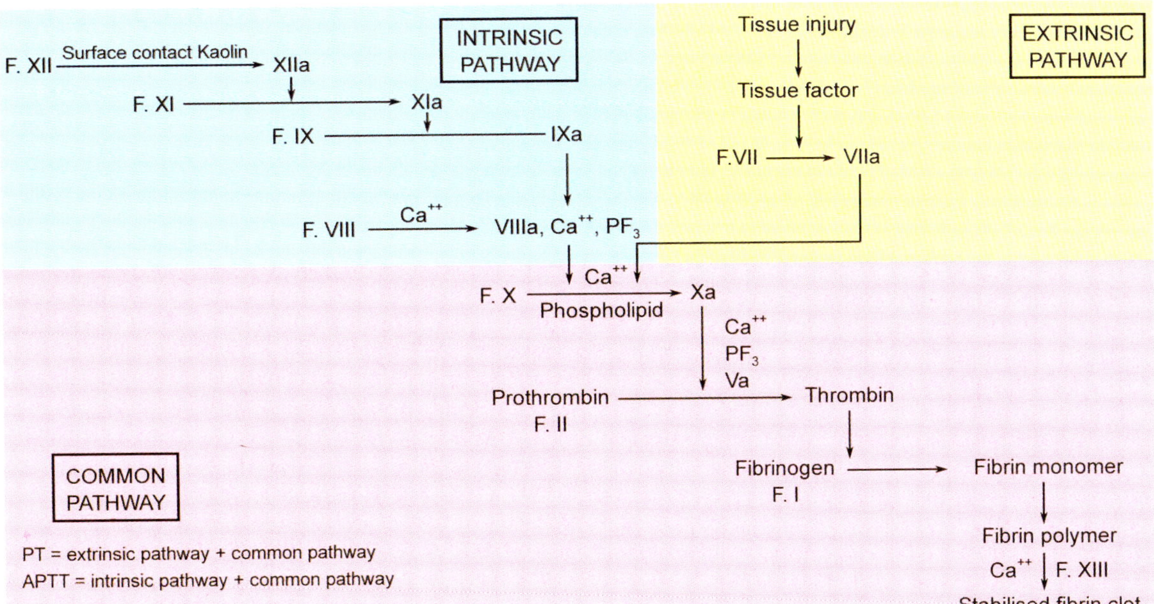

Mechanism of Coagulation

COLLECTION OF BLOOD FOR COAGULATION STUDIES

A clean venous puncture is made and 4.5 ml blood (1 : 9 ratio) is collected in 0.5 ml of 3.2% Trisodium citrate dihydrate solution (or 3.8% trisodium citrate pentahydrate) and the two are mixed. After collection, blood should be placed in a refrigerator at 4°C till it is centrifuged to collect plasma. Centrifugation should be carried out in a refrigerated centrifuge.

Precautions

1. Venous blood collected should be free of tissue fluid.
2. Sample should not be hemolyzed by the vein puncture or by delivering the blood forcibly through the needle into the vial.
3. An exact 9:1 ratio should be employed while collecting 4.5 ml blood in 0.5 ml of sodium citrate solution. Any variability of plasma : anticoagulant ratio affects the results of coagulation studies. Vacutainers that draw 4.5 ml blood in 0.5 ml citrate ensure exact 9:1 ratio.
4. Glassware should be clean.
5. Siliconized syringes are useful where research studies are contemplated.

QUICK'S ONE STAGE PROTHROMBIN TIME (PT)

Principle

PT test is an indicator of the efficiency of *common pathway and extrinsic coagulation pathway,* in which preformed thromboplastin is added to the test plasma in the presence of calcium and the time taken for clotting of plasma is noted. The main factors involved in the pathway are V, VII, X, II and I. Deficiency of any one of them leads to prolongation of PT. The test is also sensitive to the presence of heparin in blood and to low fibrinogen levels. The test can also be used for control of anticoagulant therapy.

Reagents

(i) Citrated test plasma – Collect 4.5 ml venous blood of the patient in 0.5 ml Tri sodium citrate solution (1:9 parts of blood) in a test tube. Centrifuge the blood sample at 3000 r.p.m. for 15 minutes and collect the supernatant plasma in a clean test tube.

(ii) Citrated control plasma – From a normal person same way as in (i).

(iii) Thromboplastin reagent – It is made by suspending thromboplastin tablets in saline (commercially available thromboplastin preparations with detailed instructions) or acetone dried brain powder suspended in saline.

(iv) Calcium chloride solution (0.025 M).

(v) Waterbath at 37°C, stopwatch or a coagulometer.

Method

(i) Place all the reagents and test tubes (75 × 12 mm) at 37°C for 15 minutes.

(ii) Deliver 0.1 ml of plasma into one test tube and add 0.1 ml of thromboplastin suspension to it and keep the tube in 37°C waterbath.

(iii) After 1 minute, add 0.1 ml of calcium chloride solution to the tube and start the stop watch and submerge the lower end of the tube in waterbath.

(iv) The tube is gently tilted to look for fibrin clot. As soon as the fibrin strands appear, record the time.
(v) The procedure is repeated in duplicate for the same sample.
(vi) One control normal plasma should be taken to assess PT of control sample.

Normal range : 10-16 seconds.

Any prolongation of PT beyond 3 seconds of the control value is taken as abnormal *e.g.* if control value is 12 seconds; 16 seconds is an abnormal reading.

Reporting

PT	–	patient	–	16 seconds
	–	control	–	12 seconds

International Normalized Ratio (INR)

PT is indicative of the working of the extrinsic coagulation pathway. Patients with thrombotic tendency like deep vein thrombosis require anticoagulant therapy like Warfarin (Coumadin) which is a vitamin K antagonist and results in fall in vitamin K dependent factores II, VII, IX, X, Protien C and S. and therefore, an increase in PT occurs. Monitoring of therapy is carried out by assessing PT and INR (International Normalised Ratio).

Since thromboplastins differ in sensitivity and therefore, there is variaiton in the PT test. WHO recommended that each thromboplastin should have ISI (International sensitivity index) value. PT obtained using different thromboplastins are then compared by calculating INR. INR is the ratio of the patient PT compared to mean PT (normal) raised the power of the ISI.

$$\text{INR} = \left[\frac{\text{Prothrombin time of patient in seconds}}{\text{Mean PT for normal plasma in seconds}}\right]^{\text{ISI}}$$

This converts PT performed by different methods to a uniform scale despite the use of different thromboplastins.

INR has helped in comparing the PT of patients with the use of different thromboplastins and also the different types of coagulometers.

Automated coagulometers give the PT and INR of the sample tested simultaneously.

INR is of use to monitor the effectiveness of Warfarin (an oral anticoagulant) in cases of deep vein thrombosis, atrial fibrillation, cardiac valve replacement, acute myocardial infarction and in anti-phospholipid anibody syndrome and the INR should be 2–3.

In cases of Warfarin therapy, PT/INR vary when the patient starts taking oral contraceptives, barbiturates, vitamin K, aspirin and antibiotics.

Now, portable coagulometers are available and the patient can do home monitoring while on oral anticoagulant therapy.

Significance

Prolonged PT is seen in:

(a) liver disease
(b) fibrinogen deficiency-congenital
(c) obstructive jaundice
(d) haemorrhagic disease of the newborn
(e) therapy with anticoagulant drugs like coumarin derivatives
(f) disseminated intravascular coagulation.

Indications

(i) PT is mandatory before a *liver biopsy* is performed since *liver disease* is likely to impair synthesis of various factors like II, V, VII or X resulting in a prolonged PT; a contraindication for liver biopsy.
(ii) PT is used to *monitor oral anticoagulant* therapy. Anticoagulant therapy is considered efficacious if PT exceeds the control to $1^1/_2$ to 2 times the control value.
(iii) As a screening test while investigating cases of *bleeding diathesis.*

Precautions

(a) Ratio of anticoagulant to blood should be 1:9. Any alteration in their proportion will alter PT values – like 3.5 ml blood in 0.5 ml citrate solution leads to overdilution of coagulation factors and excess citration.
(b) Waterbath temperature should be 37°C and all reagents and tubes should remain in waterbath.
(c) In cases with high hematocrit >55% plasma is less than normal per unit volume of blood and therefore less anticoagulant is required.
(d) Always ensure that there is no clot in the blood sample.
(e) Test plasma should be tested within 2 hours of collection.

Other Methods

Automated Coagulation Analyzers.

Coagulometer is an instrument in which the coagulation time of a particular plasma after addition of thromboplastin/phospholipid is measured by the instrument. The basis of the test is turbidimetry/optical method (nephelometry)/ball method (Fig. 17.2).

(a) **Turbidimetry (optical method)**. It relies on the scattering of light and measurement of light attenuation. At the start of the test, the sample is transparent and light is scattered uniformly. As the coagulation is activated, the scattered light is

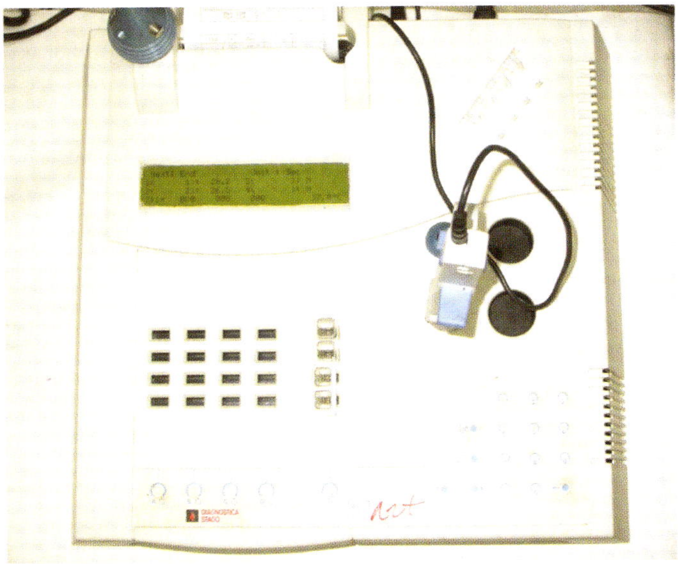

Fig. 17.2: Coagulometer (Semiautomated)

attenuated which returns to a constant level as the coagulation is completed and the time between the two stages is recorded.

(b) **Ball method**. In a rotating tube (in which the plasma and regents have been added) the position of the steel ball is monitored by a sensor. As the plasma coagulates the ball is carried around with the clot and the sensor detects it and stops the clock and the time is recorded.

Semi-automated and fully automated coagulators are now available. Like cell counters, these need to be properly calibrated and monitored.

ACTIVATED PARTIAL THROMBOPLASTIN TIME WITH KAOLIN (APTT/PTTK)

Principle

Platelet substitute – PF_3 (partial thrombo-plastin) is prepared from acetone dried brain/soyabean. Plasma is incubated with kaolin which activates contact factors XII, XI and thus starting the intrinsic pathway of coagulation. Platelet substitute (phospholipid) is the source of platelet factor 3 which in vivo is provided by platelets. Clotting time of plasma is measured after addition of calcium chloride (Ca^{++} source). APTT is an indicator of efficacy of *intrinsic and common coagulation pathway*.

Reagents

- Citrated test plasma.
- Citrated normal plasma.
- Platelet substitute – chloroform extract of acetone dried brain or commercially available phospholipid.
- Kaolin 5 mg/ml (pH 7.35) in barbitone buffer. Other insoluble substances such as silica, ellagic acid can be used.
- Calcium chloride – 0.025 M.

Method

- Place 0.1 ml of plasma into a 75 × 12mm glass tube.
- Add 0.1 ml of thoroughly mixed kaolin suspension to plasma.
- Place plasma kaolin mixture at 37°C water-bath for 10 minutes.
- Mix 2 ml of platelet substitute suspension (phospholipid) with 2 ml of calcium chloride solution and place in the water-bath at 37°C.
- Deliver 0.2 ml of phospholipid – calcium chloride mixture into plasma – kaolin mixture and start the stop watch.
- Time taken for the mixture to clot is recorded.
- Repeat the same for test sample again and time should be within 1 second of the previous reading.
- Record the PTTK time for the control sample.
- The test can be carried out on an automated coagulometer.

Normal range : 26-38 seconds.

Reporting

APTT – patient – 38 seconds
– control – 35 seconds

A time which is 8 seconds more than the normal control is abnormal.

Precautions

As given for PT.

Significance

It is a sensitive method of demonstrating *defects in the intrinsic and common pathway* of coagulation and detects deficiencies of factor VIII, IX (hemophilia A and B), X (Christmas disease), and V. To find out whether patient is suffering from F.VIII or F.IX deficiency, *thromboplastin generation test* or correction studies are carried out. Commercial kits for assays of F.VIII and F.IX are available and helpful in assessing severity of the disease. Requisite management by *cryoprecipitate/recombinant factor VIII preparations* is carried out.

The test is sensitive to reduction of F.V, VIII, IX, X and XI and detects decrease of factor levels to less than 20-30% of normal. However, APTT is normal if factor levels are >35% of normal.

Common causes of a prolonged APTT are:

- Hemophilia A, Hemophilia B.
- Von Willebrand's disease.

- Disseminated intravascular coagulation.
- Liver disease.
- Heparin therapy.
- Vit K deficiency.
- Oral anticoagulant therapy.
- Massive transfusion with plasma depleted red blood cells.

TEST FOR FIBRINOGEN/FIBRIN DEGRADATION PRODUCTS – FDP/D-DIMER

In DIC (Disseminated intravascular coagulation), there is activation of extrinsic or intrinsic coagulation pathway to produce intravascular fibrin deposits resulting in depletion of coagulation factors and thrombocytopenia leading to bleeding. This is accompanied by activation of fibrinolysis secondarily thus accentuating bleeding. Fibrin degradation products are increased in DIC, fibrinolysis and in primary fibrinolytic states.

Causes of DIC

- Pre-eclampsia
- Abruptio placentae
- Retained placenta/dead foetus
- Cirrhosis liver
- Snake bite
- Amniotic fluid embolism
- Fat embolism
- Post-operative pulmonary embolism
- AML - M3
- PNH
- Sepsis, gram –ve shock
- Heat stroke

In cases of obstetric complications, tissue thromboplastin released from placental tissue activates the extrinsic pathway to activate F.X thereby initiating the coagulation sequence. DIC in septicemias is because of the release of endotoxins from gram –ve bacteria activating F XII, which initiates intrinsic pathway. In AML-M_3, leukemic promyelocytes liberate tissue thromboplastin leading to DIC.

Fibrin monomers polymerise in the microvascular system leading to thrombic platelet entrapment resulting in thrombo-cytopenia.

In addition, plasmin inactivates F V, VIII, IX and XI.

Lab Findings in DIC

- Thrombocytopenia because of utilization of platelets in microthrombosis.
- PT ↑, APTT ↑ because of ↓ fibrinogen and plasmic digestion of various factors
- FDP +
- Thrombin time (TT) ↑ because of ↓ fibrinogen

Principle of the test for presence of FDP/D-Dimer

Latex particles are coated with specific antibodies to purified FDP. Serum/plasma of the patient is taken and latex particles (coated with Ab) are added. Presence of agglutination suggests the presence of FDP in the serum. Different dilutions of the serum are used to semi quantitate the FDP levels. D-Dimer assay is a better method.

Kits are commercially available with instructions and reagents.

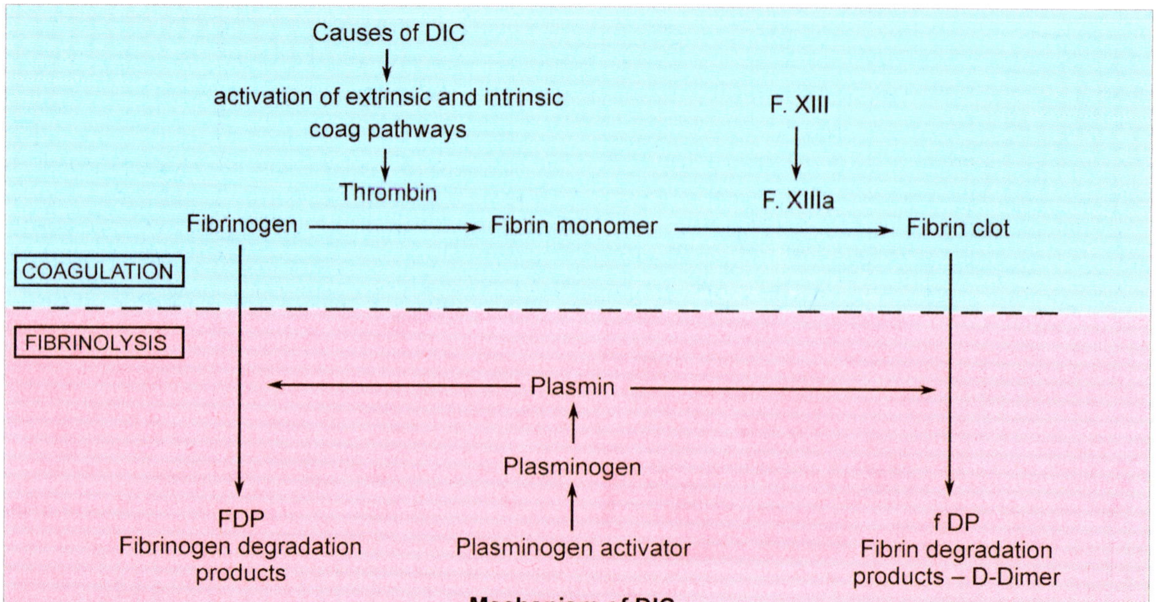

Mechanism of DIC

Assessment of Fibrinolytic System

Euglobulin lysis time. Euglobulin fraction of plasma contains plasminogen, plasminogen activators and fibrinogen. The test is a measurement of fibrinolytic activity.

VIVA VOCE

Q. In BT by template method, why the incision should be parallel to antecubital crease?

Ans. If incision is at right angles to the antecubital crease, the skin edges get retracted and a spindle shaped wound is formed; however, when it is parallel there is no retraction of the skin.

Q. In which conditions is increased capillary fragility observed?

Ans. Increased capillary fragility is observed in senile purpura, Henoch Schonlein purpura, orthostatic purpura, hereditary haemorrhagic telangiectasia (Osler-Rendu-Weber disease), scurvy, and Ehler-Danlos syndrome.

Q. What is the utility of Hess's test?

Ans. This test is a measure of the capillary fragility. This test is positive in conditions of thrombocytopenia, platelet function defects and defects of capillary fragility. In thrombocytopenia, since the platelets are fewer, they are unable to completely plug the inter-endothelial gaps and as the pressure is raised, bleeding occurs from unplugged gaps. This occurs as the platelet count falls below 50000/cumm.

Q. What is the action of aspirin on platelets?

Ans. Aspirin irreversibly blocks the action of platelet cyclooxygenase and hence Arachidonic acid is not converted into endoperoxides and prostaglandins and therefore platelet aggregation does not occur. That is why aspirin is given to patients of coronary artery disease to prevent thrombus formation. This may result in increased bleeding following injury.

Q. Which test is used to monitor oral anticoagulant therapy?

Ans. PT is carried out to monitor oral anticoagulant therapy.

Q. Which test is used to monitor heparin therapy?

Ans. APTT is used to monitor heparin therapy.

Q. Why is it necessary to collect blood : citrate solution in the 9 : 1 ratio?

Ans. When the ratio gets reduced (say, 7 : 1 or 6 : 1), then there is excessive dilution of coagulation factors and also extra citration affects the accuracy of results.

Q. What is the effect of circulating anti-coagulants?

Ans. Inhibitors of coagulation such as heparin or other circulating anticoagulants lead to prolongation of PT and APTT.

Q. What is hereditary haemorrhagic telan-giectasia/Osler-Rendu-Weber disease?

Ans. It is an autosomal dominant condition in which vessels are tortuous, dilated, thin-walled and their ability to contract is diminished. Haemorrhages are commonly observed on face.

Q. What is the cause of senile purpura?

Ans. With advancing age there is reduction in subcutaneous tissue with atrophy of the dermis leaving the small capillaries unsupported and these bleed on trivial trauma and at times spontaneously also. This type of purpura usually involves hands, forearms and neck. Bleeding is usually in the form of ecchymoses. Hess's test is positive.

Q. What are contact factors?

Ans. Contact factors are F.XII, Prekallikrein, F.XI and high mol. wt. kininogen.

Q. What are the fractions of F.VIII?

Ans. VIIIC is the procoagulant protein and its activity is measured by APTT. VWF fraction of F.VIII helps in attachment of platelet to sub-endothelial collagen.

Q. What is the role of kaolin in APTT?

Ans. Kaolin leads to surface contact activation thus initiating the intrinsic system of coagulation from F.XII onwards and that is why the test is called Activated PTT.

Q. What do you understand by partial thromboplastin in APTT?

Ans. Partial thromboplastin is the phospho-lipid (platelet factor 3) which is added to plasma. In vivo, platelets are the source of phospholipid.

(b) Add one drop of washed 20% red cell suspension to each antiserum.

(c) Mix each cell-serum mixture separately with applicator stick and rock the slide gently (Fig. 18.1B).

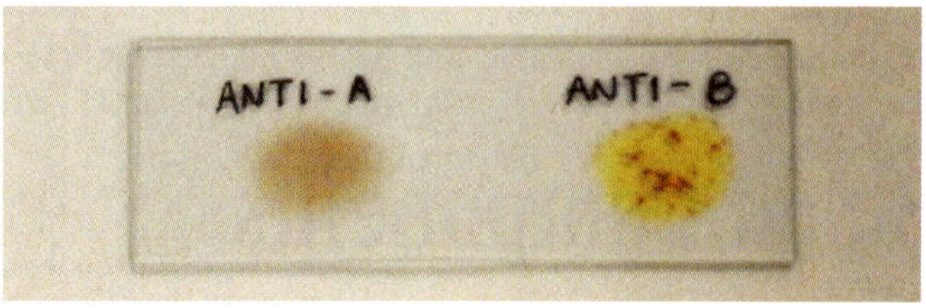

Fig. 18.1B: One drop of washed 20% red cell suspension is added to anti-A and anti-B. Blood is mixed with Anti-A and Anti-B sera. Agglutination in B indicates blood group is B.

(d) Read for "agglutination" macroscopically within 5 minutes and identify the blood group as per table 18.1.

Table 18.1 Interpretation of ABO Grouping

Antibody added	Anti-A	Anti-B	Anti-AB	Result Group
Agglutination	–	–	–	O
	+	–	+	A
	–	+	+	B
	+	+	+	AB

Tube technique for ABO grouping

(a) Take 3 test tubes (65 × 10 mm size), labelled anti-A, anti-B and anti-AB respectively.

(b) Add one drop each of the corresponding serum to each tube *i.e.* anti-A, anti-B and anti-AB sera.

(c) Add 1 drop each of 2% suspension of red cells to the three test tubes and mix the suspensions by gently tapping the tubes.

(d) Centrifuge the tube at 1000 RPM for 1 minute. Dislodge the RBC button by gently shaking the tube.

(e) Transfer one drop of serum-cell suspen-sion mixture onto a glass slide, using a thin bore pasteur pipette. Spread the cells over an area of 2 × 1 cm, using the pipette as a spreader.

(f) Examine the slide under microscope for "agglutination", (Fig. 18.2) and interpret the result for blood group as given in the table 18.1.

Result

Blood group A, B, AB or O is defined.

Controls

Each grouping test should preferably have controls by setting up tests exactly similar to those described above using cells of known groups A, B, AB and O.

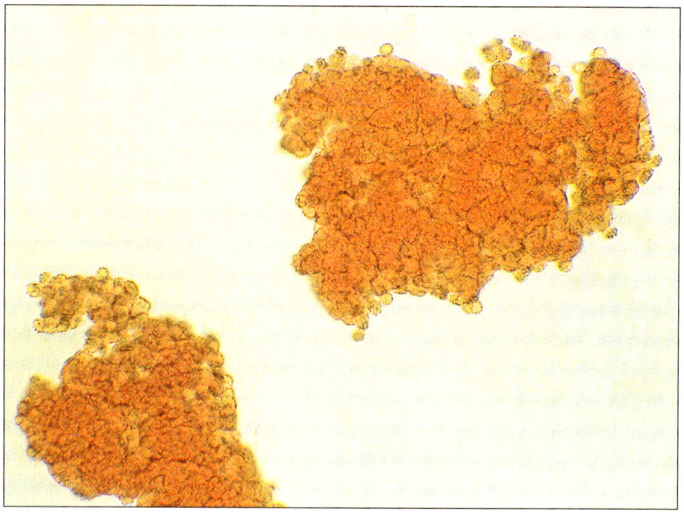

Fig. 18.2: Agglutination of red cells in tube technique method.

Microtyping System (Gel Card)

Microtyping System (MTS) is based on **gel technology**. In these tests gel is held in microtubes contained in a plastic card. Each microtube contains sephadex gel prepared in a buffer solution. The gel contains sodium azide as preservative, group specific antisera or antiglobulin for coombs test etc. which is incorporated into gel at the time of manufacture.

Principle. Cells are poured over the microtube. Incubation at 37°C is carried out followed by centrifugation which pulls the cells down which react with the specific antibody incorporated into the gel resulting in hemagglutination. Agglutinated red cells are too large to pass through the gel matrix which acts as a sieve and are trapped at various places within the gel, forming a line in the microtube indicating positivity of the test.

In case the specific antigen is not present on the red cells, agglutination does not occur .and the red cell pass through the gel forming a pellet at the bottom of the microtube (Fig. 18.3).

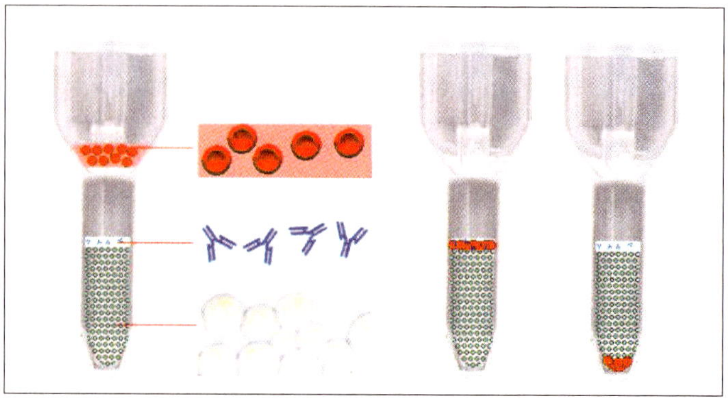

Fig. 18.3: Microtyping gel card. ABO/Rh typing. Red cell reach the bottom of the tube indicating negative test. Positivity of the test is indicated by a red line in the gel.

Advantages

- Greater sensitivity as compared to conventional techniques.
- Technique dependent errors are eliminated.
- No cell washing is required for coombs test.
- Cost effective.

Used for

- Blood grouping and cross matching.
- Coombs test
- For diagnosis of syphilis, measles, diphtheria, parvovirus infection.
- For diagnosis of PNH, sickle cell disease.

A, B, O in Indian population

Prevalence of A, B, AB and O blood groups differs from that in the western population as given in the Table 18.2.

Table 18.2 Blood group distribution

Blood group	Indian population	European population
A	25%	42%
B	37%	9%
AB	5%	3%
O	33%	46%

Rh (D) TYPING

Rh antigen is present- in 85% of human beings → Rh-positive, and those who lack the antigens are Rh-negative.

Slide technique

(a) Place one drop of anti-Rh (D) reagent on a slide. Anti-D reagent should be monoclonal IgM antibody which are commercially available now. Now Anti D_1 + D_2 and (IgM + IgG) anti-D are available which are more sensitive.
(b) Add 1 drop of 20% red cell suspension.
(c) Mix the cell suspension and reagent using a clean stick.
(d) Observe for agglutination after 2 minutes. A positive test (Rh +ve) demonstrates agglutination.

Result

Agglutination indicates Rh +ve blood sample.

Tube technique

(a) Place one drop of anti-D serum in a small test tube.
(b) Add 1 drop of 2% saline suspension of test red cells. Mix the two.
(c) Centrifuge at 1000 RPM. For 1 minute. Gently tap the red cell button.
(d) Take one drop of the mixture on a glass slide, using a thin Pasteur pipette. Spread it with the Pasteur pipette and examine under microscope for agglutination (Fig. 18.2).

Result

Presence of agglutination indicates Rh +ve blood group.

Controls

Known Rh +ve and Rh –ve samples should be employed simultaneously with each set of test cases.

CROSS-MATCHING

Cross-matching is the most important test carried out before a blood transfusion is given. This is carried out to prevent transfusion reactions by detecting antibodies in the recipient's serum that may react with donor's cells. For a thorough cross-matching recipient's serum and donor's red cells are taken and:

(a) saline cross match detects IgM anti-bodies;
(b) albumin technique detects IgG anti-bodies;
(c) enzyme technique detects IgG and some IgM antibodies;
(d) antiglobulin test or Coombs test detects IgG antibodies.

Routine cross-matching

One of the simplest method is:

- Take one drop of recipient's serum in a small test tube.
- Add 5% saline suspension of donor's red cells to the recipient's serum.
- Mix the two.
- Incubate at 37°C for 30 minutes. Centrifuge at 3000 rpm for 1 minute.
- Dislodge the cells gently and examine macroscopically and microscopically for agglutination or lysis.

Result

There is no agglutination or hemolysis in a matched recipient's and donor's samples.

In *mismatching* of donor and recipient, hemolysis/ agglutination occurs.

The procedure as given above may also be carried out between 1 drop of donor's serum and 1 drop of 5% saline suspension of recipient's cells. Incubate at 37°C for 30 minutes. Centrifuge at 3000 rpm for 1 minute. Observe macroscopically and microscopically for agglutination or lysis.

COOMBS (ANTIGLOBULIN) TEST

This test is utilized to demonstrate the presence of IgG antibodies directed against the RBCs. Since IgG antibodies (incomplete antibodies) do not cause agglutination of RBCs, antiglobulin (Coombs) serum is added which combines with IgG antibodies on the surface of RBCs resulting in agglutination of RBCs. It is important to wash the RBCs with saline to remove free gamma globulin, so that when antiglobulin is added, it is not neutralized by other globulins. This test is of two types: direct and indirect Coombs test.

Direct Coombs test

It detects antibodies coated on the surface of red cells, when the sensitization has taken place in vivo.

Method

- Take patient's RBCs from the clot/EDTA blood/citrated blood in a test tube and add normal saline and mix. Centrifuge at 2500 rpm for 5 minutes. Decant the saline.
- Wash RBCs twice more in the same manner.
- After three washings, prepare a 5% saline suspension of RBCs.
- Take 2 drops of saline red cell suspension and add 2 drops of anti-globulin serum and mix well. Incubate at 37°C for 5 minutes.
  Centrifuge at 1000 rpm for 1 minute.
- Dislodge the cell button, gently resuspend the cells and observe for agglutination both microscopically and macroscopically. With each test, one positive control and one negative control is set up.
- Positive control . Take 1 ml Rh +ve EDTA blood and wash with N-saline thrice. To 2 drops of 5% saline suspension, add 2 drops of anti-Rh (anti-D) IgG antibody. Incubate at 37°C for 10 minutes for antibody to get coated on the surface of RBCs. Wash with saline thrice to remove the excess of Ab. Now these RBCs are coated with antibody (control). Take 2 drops of coated RBCs and add 2 drops of antiglobulin serum. Incubate at 37°C. Agglutination should be positive (Fig. 18.4).
- Negative control. Normal individual's RBCs – non-sensitized RBCs serve as a negative control.

Result

Agglutination in the test sample indicates the presence of antibody on the surface of RBCs–positive Direct Coombs Test.

Indications for direct antiglobulin test

In hemolytic disease of newborn (baby's red cells in cord blood are subjected to direct Coombs test) and autoimmune hemolytic anemia. This test demonstrates in vivo attachment of antibodies to red cells.

Indirect Coombs Test

This test is used to demonstrate antibodies that are present in the serum.

- Take 2 drops of patient's serum in a test tube.
- Add 3 drops of 5% "O" cell suspension. These cells are taken from any "O" group person who is Rh +ve.
- Incubate the mixture at 37°C for 10 minutes.
- Wash with n-saline thrice to remove the excess of antibodies.
- Remove the supernatant.

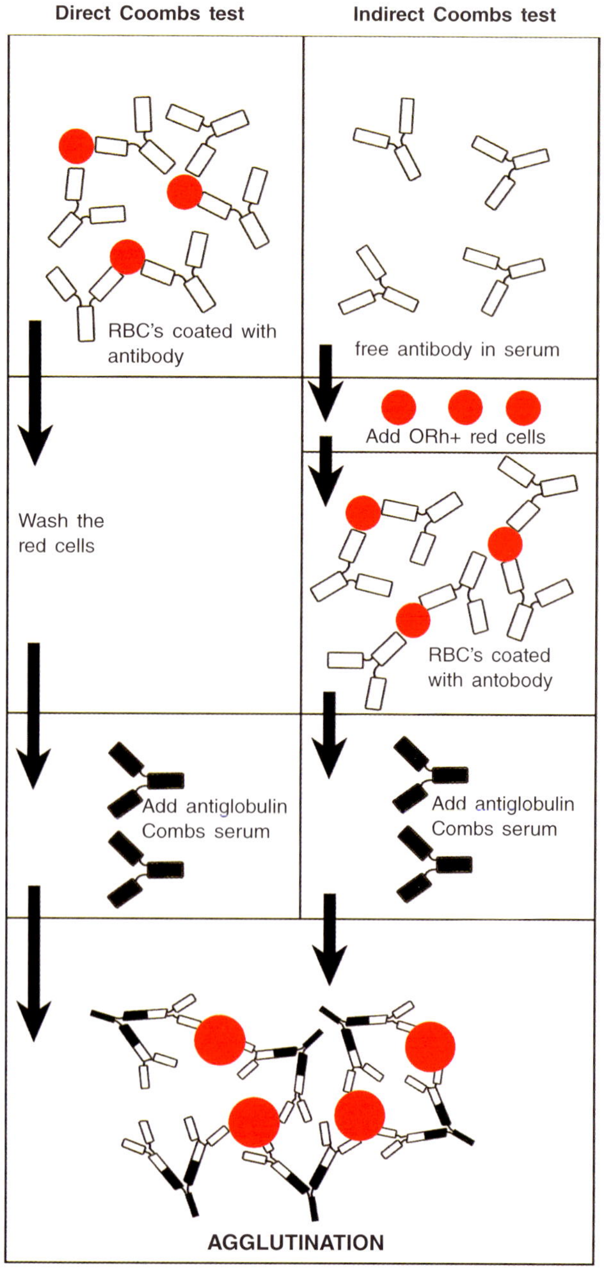

Fig. 18.4: Principle of Coombs test

- Now "O" RBCs are coated with (IgG) anti-Rh antibodies of the patient (if antibodies are present).
- Add 2 drops of Coombs serum (anti-globulin).
- Incubate at 37°C for 10 minutes.
- Centrifuge at 2000 rpm for 1 minute.
- Resuspend the red cells by gentle agitation and examine macroscopically and microscopically for agglutination (Fig. 18.2).

Result

In the positive indirect Coombs test, agglutination of RBCs indicates the presence of antibodies in the test serum.

Indications

In hemolytic disease of newborn-mother's serum is tested to detect anti-Rh antibody and in cross-matching to detect incompatibility of recipient's serum with donor's cells.

Gel card method: this is a sensitive method of detecting antibodies than the conventional Coombs's test.

HEMOLYTIC DISEASE OF THE NEWBORN (HDN)

This is an immune hemolytic anemia affecting the fetus and newborn baby. It occurs when Rh +ve RBCs of the fetus cross placenta in a Rh –ve mother, and induce formation of anti-Rh IgG (anti-D) antibodies in the mother. IgG antibodies cross placenta and lyse fetal red cells resulting in HDN. Usually, during first pregnancy, fetal RBCs cross placenta only at the time of delivery and then IgG antibodies are formed post delivery. In subsequent pregnancies, IgG (formed during previous pregnancy) crosses placenta leading to HDN/hydrops fetalis. Therefore, antenatal assessment of severity of HDN can be made by determining the titre of anti-D in the mother every 4 weeks until 28 weeks, then every 2 weeks.

At the time of delivery, 20 ml of cord blood should be collected (both EDTA and clotted specimens) and it should be subjected to Direct Coombs Test besides A, B, O and Rh(D) grouping. If Direct Coombs Test is positive, maternal blood should be subjected to Indirect Coombs Test to assess the anti-D levels.

For prophylaxis, anti-D is given to Rh negative women within 72 hours of delivery unless the baby is known to be Rh negative. This mops up any Rh+ RBCs of baby which have entered maternal circulation, before immune response is stimulated.

BLOOD TRANSFUSION

Transfusion medicine comprises of blood/blood component transfusion. It is important to collect, store and transfer blood in a proper way.

Collection of blood

Blood is collected in a blood bank under aseptic conditions using *Chitra bag*.

Anticoagulant

CPD – citrate
phosphate
dextrose

or

ACD – citric acid
– sod. citrate
– dextrose

1 unit of blood – 450 ml.

Storage – at 2-6°C in a refrigerator.

Pre-donation check up

- ABO grouping
- Rh-D typing
- Hepatitis BsAg (HBsAg)
- HIV testing
- Test for syphilis
- Hepatitis C antigen
- Malaria

BLOOD COMPONENTS

Various blood components are:

- Whole blood
- Red cell components (Packed red cells)
- Plasma, fresh frozen plasma – FFP
- Platelet concentrates
- Cryoprecipitate

Red Cell Components

Red cells are obtained by centrifuging the blood. In the packed cell unit hematocrit is 55-75%.

These are stored in a refrigerator at 4°C and shelf life is 1 month. White cells are removed as buffy coat and such red cell preparation is preferred.

Indications

- Thalassemia major
- Sickle cell anemia
- Aplastic anemia
- Severe anemia of any cause

Platelet concentrates

These are obtained by centrifugation of platelet rich plasma (PRP), when platelet concentrate and plasma get separated. Platelet concentrates may be obtained from a single donor or pooled plasma. These are stored at 2°C and shelf life is 5 days. Platelets can be obtained from a single donor by platelet pheresis.

Indications

- Thrombocytopenia – Platelet count <20,000/cumm.
- Acute leukemias
- Thrombocytopenia following chemotherapy in various malignancies

Apheresis

Plasma and platelets are separated and collected by using a cell separator. This equipment is used to isolate stem cells (CD34 positive cells)

Plasma

Plasma is collected by centrifugation of blood. Red cells are separated. Plasma can be used in cases of burns.

Fresh frozen plasma (FFP)

Plasma after separation is immediately frozen at –2°C.

Cryoprecipitate

This is obtained by thawing FFP at 4°C. It is rich in F.VIII and F.IX and is used in hemophilia A and B.

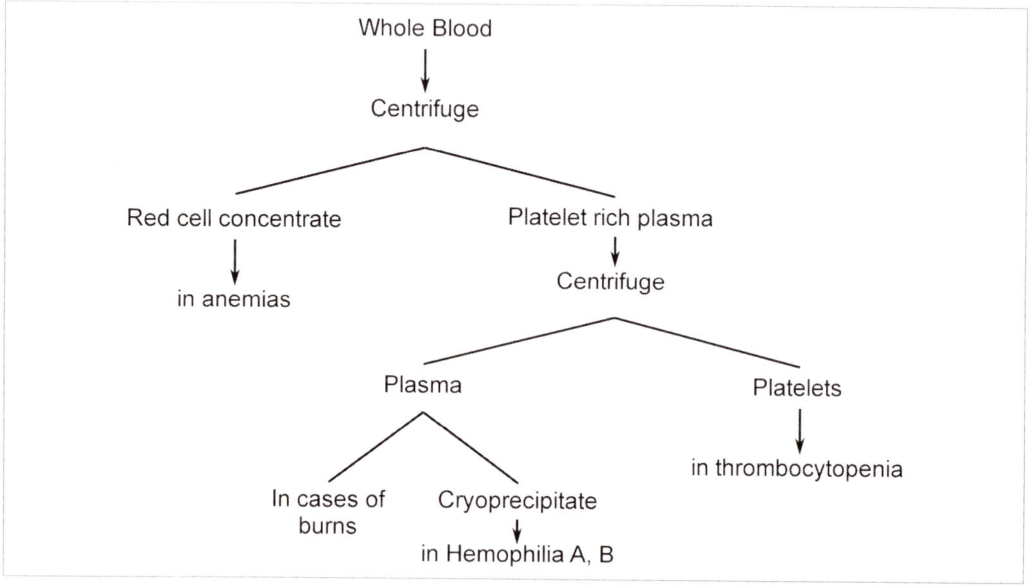

VIVA VOCE

Q. For blood grouping, which method is better – tube or slide method?

Ans. The tube technique is better because the reaction between cells and serum is enhanced because of centrifugation, and therefore weaker antigens like A2 are also detected. Tube method is recommended for both ABO and Rh grouping.

Q. What is the purpose of cross-matching/compatibility test?

Ans. The test prevents transfusion reactions.

Q. How are blood and its components stored?

Ans.
- Blood is stored in a refrigerator at 2-4°C upto 4-6 weeks.
- Platelets can be stored upto 5 days.
- Neutrophils can be stored for 24 hours only.

Q. What is the difference between complete and incomplete antibodies?

Ans. Naturally occurring, anti-A, anti-B antibodies are IgM type – complete antibodies and cause agglutination in saline suspension.

Incomplete antibodies are IgG type and result because of antigenic stimulation and do not cause agglutination in saline suspension, but are detected by Coombs test.

Q. What is Bombay blood group?

Ans. See page 123.

Q. Which blood group has subtypes?

Ans. A has A1 – the stronger antigen and A2 – the weaker Ag. A2 Ag may sometimes be missed, if outdated antisera are used and the patient may be labelled as O. So, to prevent it, add anti-AB serum to patient's red cells. This would agglutinate all Ags except O. Therefore A2 antigen is detected.

Q. What are the causes of Hemolytic disease of the newborn (HDN)?

Ans. HDN is due to (a) ABO disease (b) Rh disease.

Q. What is HDN due to ABO disease?

Ans. This is usually due to baby being A and mother O. Hemolysis is mild and goes undetected unless Coombs test is done on cord serum. Direct Coombs test on cord blood is negative and infants in first pregnancy are affected (unlike HDN due to Rh incompatibility).

Q. What is one unit of blood?

Ans. 450 ml of blood in 63 ml of anticoagulant CPD. (Sod. citrate - Phosphate - Dextrose).

Q. What are blood components?

Ans. Using a cell separator, red cells, white cells and platelets can be separated from blood and given to patients of anemia, neutropenia and thrombocytopenia respectively. Plasma can be used for patients of burns. Other components being fibrinogen, cryoppt. (rich in F.VIII and IX). One unit of blood can be used for different patients.

Q. What are the advantages of the Gel card method for blood grouping?

Ans. Since the monoclonal antibodies are used, the method is very sensitive and weaker antigens also get detected.

Q. Which are the immune hemolytic anemias in which Coombs test is indicated.

Ans.
- Autoimmune hemolytic anemia
- Systemic lupus erythematosus
- Cold agglutinin disease
- Paroxysmalcold hemoglobinuria
- Infectious mononucleosis
- M-DOPA induced immune hemolytic anemia.

Q. What test is employed to detect low level antibodies against red cells?

Ans. Micro-Coombs test

Q. In AIHA what could be present on the surface of RBCs?

Ans. IgG or C'3 may be present on red cell surface and can be detected by Coombs test (anti IgG or anti C3).

SECTION D
Systemic Pathology

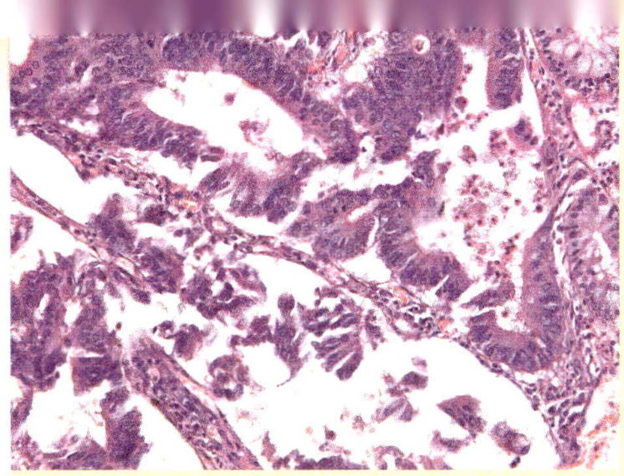

19

Gastrointestinal System

SALIVARY GLAND AND ORAL CAVITY

Squamous cell carcinoma

Squamous cell carcinoma of oral cavity is one of the commonest cancers in India. It is usually well differentiated squamous cell carcinoma with keratin pearls and malignant squamous cells (Fig. 6.8). Verrucous carcinoma is a papillary exophytic carcinoma with good prognosis.

Pleomorphic adenoma

Pleomorphic adenoma (mixed tumour) of salivary gland. Grossly, the tumour is an encapsulated mass 2–5 cm in diameter and is greyish white on cut section with myxoid areas. Tumour is made up of small cuboidal to oval cells with small uniform nuclei (Fig. 19.1). Cells are arranged in groups with focal ductal lumen formation. Stroma shows myxoid change (loose, with scattered spindled cells) and cartilage (glassy, bluish with cells in lacunae) (Fig. 19.1). Compressed salivary gland may be seen at the periphery. Though benign, the tumour is not encapsulated histologically. Cords of cells may be seen extending into surrounding tissue.

STOMACH

Organ identification

Organ is grossly identified by its being a luminal structure (specimen is usually mounted opened) with wide lumen with mucosal folds (rugae) which run haphazardly.

Microscopically stomach is identified by the presence of the 4 layers, with gastric type of mucosa. This shows surface gastric pits (lined by columnar mucous secreting cells with basal nuclei) and the crypts which are densely packed with scant stroma. Crypts show chief cells (with pale cytoplasm) and parietal cells (oxyphil cells with pink granular cytoplasm).

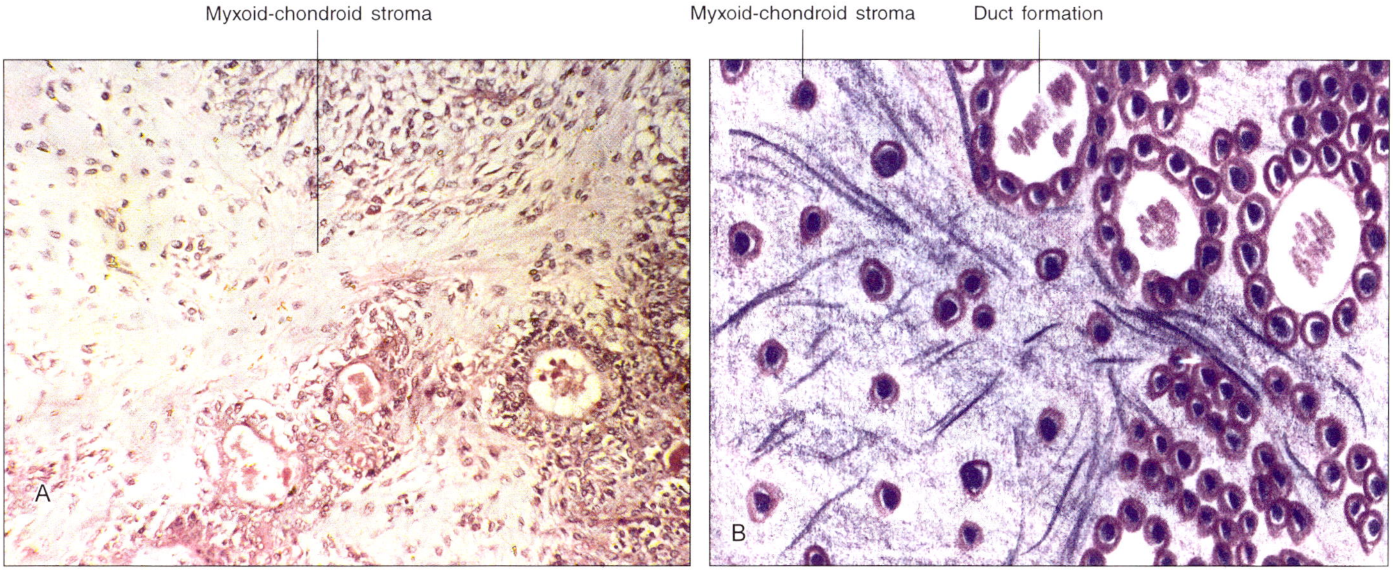

Fig. 19.1: A. and **B.** Pleomorphic salivary adenoma. Cuboidal cells and duct formation in a myxoid – chondroid stroma.

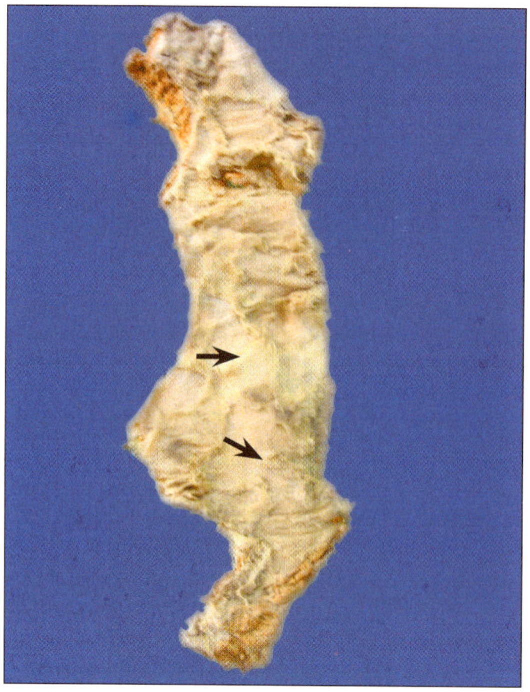

Fig. 19.8: Ascending colon with amoebic ulceration. Large coalesced areas of superficial ulceration with normal intervening mucosa.

Intussusception

Intussusception is the process whereby one loop of bowel telescopes into the segment distal to it (ileoileal or ileocolic) due to peristalsis propelling it forward. Usually a polypoidal lesion is identified at the leading end of the mucosa (Fig. 19.9). It causes acute obstruction and if not relieved promptly it can undergo infarction and gangrene.

Fig. 19.9: Intussusception, opened up to reveal intussusceptum. Note polyp at the tip (→).

Acute Appendicitis

Acute appendicitis is characterized by acute inflammation and ulceration. Neutrophil infiltration in muscle coat is diagnostic (Fig. 2.2, 2.3, 2.4).

Polyps

Polyps are sessile or pedunculated projections into the lumen. The surface is smooth and may get ulcerated. They may be:

(a) ***Non-neoplastic polyps***: In addition to inflammatory pseudopolyps (Fig. 19.7) made up of edematous to inflammed granulation tissue, hamartomatous polyps are seen e.g. juvenile polyp (small, single, rectal in children Fig. 19.10) and Peutz-Jeghers syndrome (larger, pedunculated, multiple, any where in GIT, in adults, associated with risk of malignancies in other organs like breast, lung, pancreas etc.). These polyps have low malignant potential.

Juvenile rectal polyp (Hamartomatous). A round lesion with stalk, it shows dilated rectal glands in lamina propria. Usually, surface is ulcerated and inflammatory infiltration is seen. Glands cytologically resemble normal rectal glands, without atypia (Fig. 19.10).

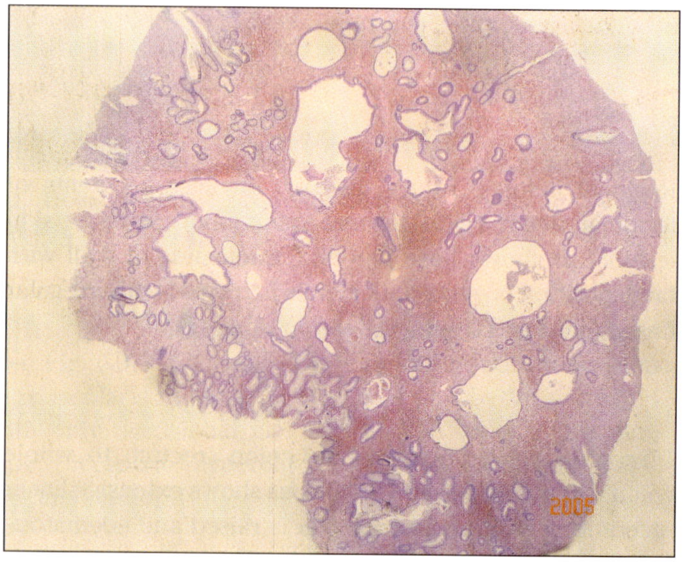

Fig. 19.10: Juvenile rectal polyp with varying sized rectal glands with inflammation in lamina propria.

(b) ***Neoplastic polyps*** are most commonly adenomas. These can be solitary (**Tubular, tubulovillous and villous** – the latter having papillary appearance and higher risk for malignancy); or multiple (Familial Adenomatous Polyposis or Polyposis Coli where over 100 polyps are present and carries an extremely high risk of malignancy) (Fig. 19.11, 19.12). Rarely mesenchymal tumours (leiomyoma, lipoma etc.) can project into the lumen as polyps.

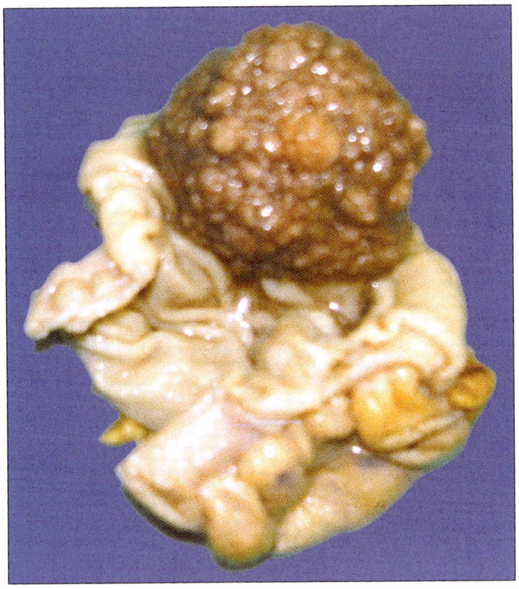

Fig. 19.11: Solitary villous adenoma of colon.

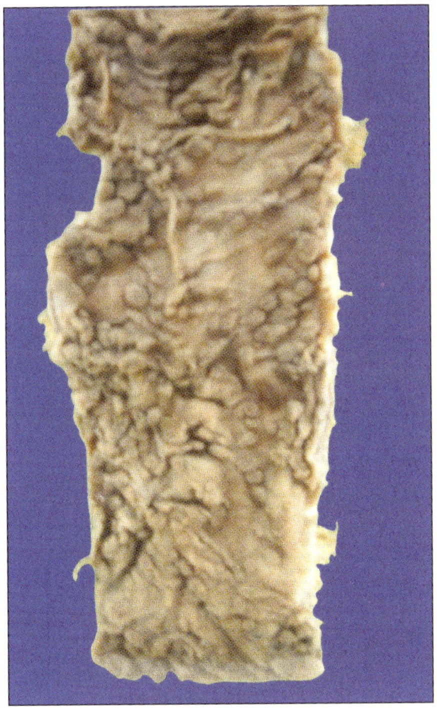

Fig. 19.12: Polyposis coli. Note numerous polyps, some pedunculated. Intervening mucosa is normal.

ADENOCARCINOMA INTESTINE

Adenocarcinoma is rare in ileum and common in the colon. It tends to be proliferative fungating in proximal colon (Fig. 19.13) and ulceroinfiltrative in distal colon (Fig. 19.14).

Adenocarcinoma colon is usually well differentiated, with irregular glands with hyperchromatic cells infiltrating the submucosa and muscle coat (Fig. 19.15). Some lesions may show abundant extracellular mucin (mucin lakes) (Fig. 19.16).

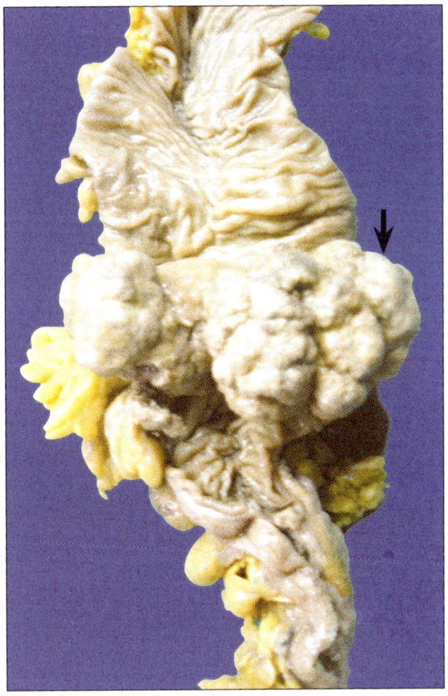

Fig. 19.13: Ileocaecal carcinoma – Proliferative type (↑).

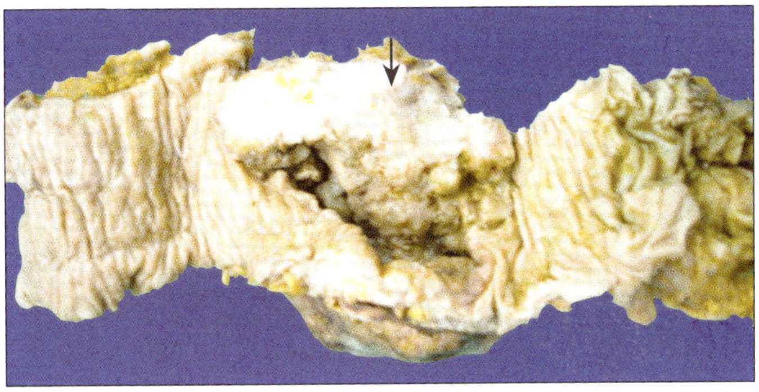

Fig. 19.14: Ulceroinfiltrative carcinoma colon.

Q. What is "Leather bottle stomach"?

Ans. Leather bottle stomach is small capacity stomach due to marked thickening of gastric wall due to diffuse infiltrative type of adenocarcinoma.

Q. In which disease would you find pseudopolyps?

Ans. Pseudopolyps are the mucosal hyperplasia between the ulcerative lesions of large intestine in ulcerative colitis.

Q. Name some risk factors for carcinoma stomach?

Ans. Environmental factors - dietary nitrites, vitamin C and E deficiency, smoking

Genetic factors - Family history, HNPCC, Blood Group A, Familial gastric cancer syndrome (E-cadherin mutation)

Host factors - chronic gastritis, intestinal metaplasia, partial gastrectomy, Barett's esophagus.

Q. Name some risk factors for carcinoma colon?

Ans.
- Environment
  - Increased caloric intake, obesity, smoking, alcohol, ureterosigmoideostomy,
  - Inflammatory bowel disease, pelvic radiation.
- Genetic
  - Hereditary non polyposis cancer syndrome (Lynch syndrome) - mutation in DNA repair gene
  - Familial adenomatous polyposis - mutation in base excision repair gene.

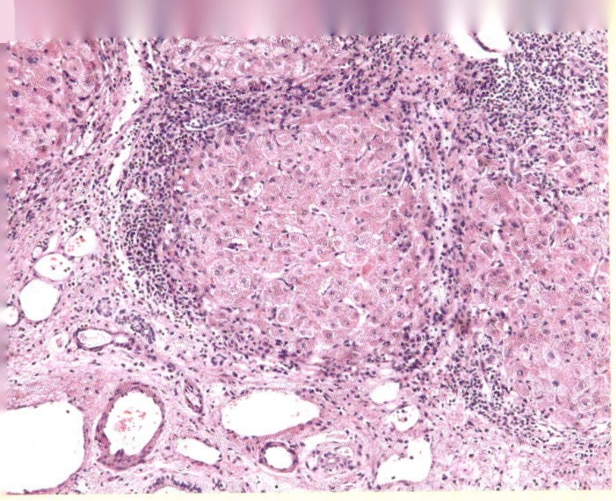

20

Hepatobiliary System

LIVER

Organ identification

Capsulated organ, reddish tan in colour and firm in texture in the normal state. Lobar and lobular venous radicals can be seen on the cut surface.

Microscopically, liver is identified by:

(a) the cords of hepatocytes which are polygonal with abundant pink granular cytoplasm and a central vesicular nucleus with a nucleolus;

(b) the portal tracts showing radicals of hepatic artery, portal vein and bile duct, and

(c) central venous radical which is thin walled.

The portal tracts are the main identifying features when hepatocyte morphology is altered (e.g. extensive fatty change etc.).

Fatty infiltration liver

Fatty infiltration (steatosis). Specimen is usually a slice of liver, identified by the convex diaphragmatic surface and the sharp anterior border. Liver is enlarged, pale, yellowish on cut surface, with a greasy feel. External surface is smooth and devoid of nodularity (see Fig. 3.1, 3.2)

Microscopically fatty liver shows normal architecture and portal tracts. Hepatocytes show varying degrees of steatosis (see Fig. 3.2).

Chronic venous congestion liver

Chronic venous congestion (Nutmeg liver) shows smooth capsule without nodularity. Cut surface shows small (2-3 mm) dark brown areas alternating with pale yellowish areas in a mosaic fashion (see Fig. 4.3, 4.4).

Cirrhosis liver

Cirrhosis is characterised by nodularity on external and cut surface (Fig. 20.1). Cirrhosis is classified as micronodular (nodules upto 3 mm size) or macro nodular (most of the nodules are larger than 3 mm) or mixed. Colour may range from brownish to yellowish (associated fatty change) to rusty (hemosiderin content) to greenish (bile stasis).

Microscopically, it is diagnosed on the basis of pseudolobule formation. Fibrous bands of varying thickness (thinner in alcoholic cirrhosis and broad in post hepatitic cirrhosis) divide the parenchyma into nodules. Inflammation may be prominent in the fibrous bands (post hepatitic cirrhosis) (Fig. 20.2). Liver cells may be normal to fatty. Cholestasis may be prominent as intracellular, canalicular and ductal brown on H&E pigment (biliary cirrhosis) (Fig. 20.2).

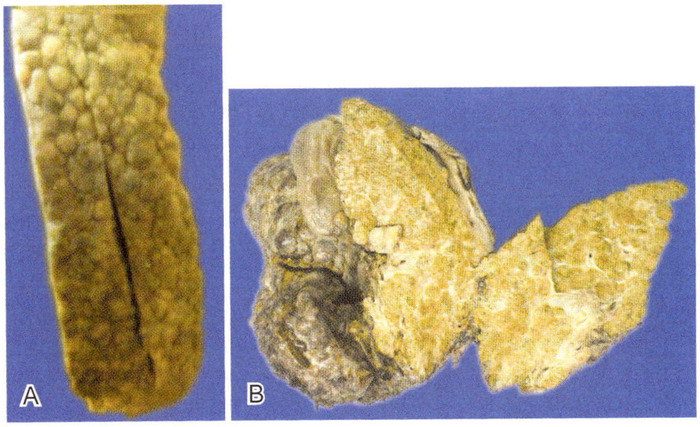

Fig. 20.1: Slice of cirrhotic liver. Note diffuse nodularity on external (A) and cut surface (B).

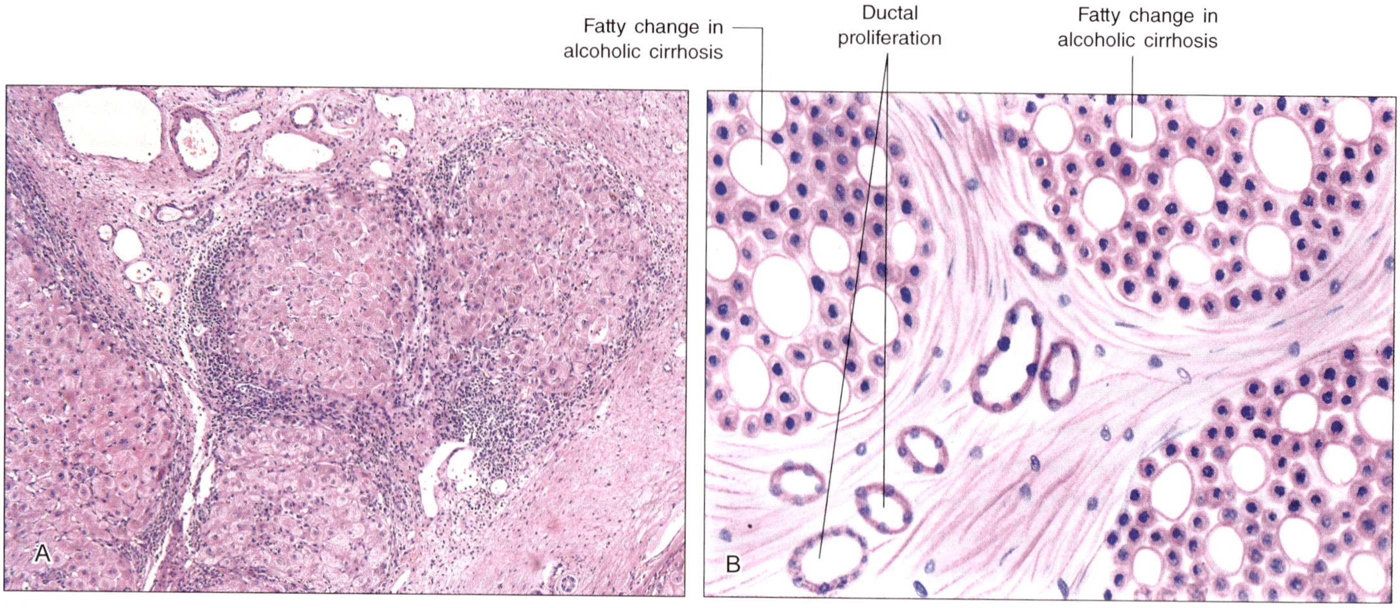

Fig. 20.2: A. and B. Cirrhosis. Fibrous bands and pseudolobules of hepatocytes with inflammatory cells in fibrous tissue and ductal proliferation

Liver abscess

Liver abscess. Pyemic abscesses are usually multiple foci of suppuration, surrounded by a reactive zone of hyperaemia. Amoebic abscess is usually a larger solitary abscess commonly close to the sub-diaphragmatic surface of liver. It contains shaggy necrotic material and lacks the hyperemic zone.

Hydatid cyst

Hydatid cyst is commonly seen in liver. Grossly the cyst is several cms in size and pearly white in colour (Fig. 5.8). It may contain daughter cysts (Fig. 5.9). The surrounding tissue is compressed to form an exocyst.

TUMOURS OF LIVER

Metastatic deposit liver

Metastatic deposits are commoner in liver (Fig. 6.22) than primary hepatocellular carcinoma. Secondaries are characteristically multiple (Fig. 20.3), have central depression due to tumour necrosis and are not related to cirrhosis whereas hepatocellular carcinoma may present as a large single lesion or multiple foci and is often seen in a cirrhotic liver.

Hepatocellular carcinoma

Hepatocellular carcinoma is the commonest primary malignancy of liver. The malignant cells are usually arranged in a sinusoidal or cord pattern and have some resemblance to hepatocytes (polygonal cells with abundant eosinophilic cytoplasm and vesicular nuclei). In addition, they show features of malignancy like pleomorphism, hyperchromasia and increased as well as abnormal mitotic activity (Fig. 20.4).

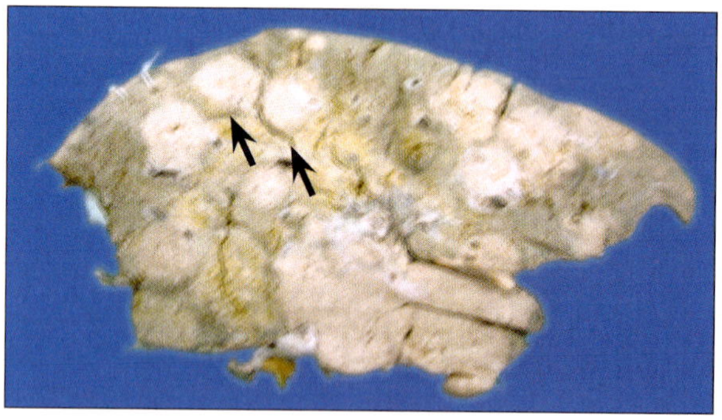

Fig. 20.3: Metastatic deposits in liver seen as multiple grey white nodules (↑).

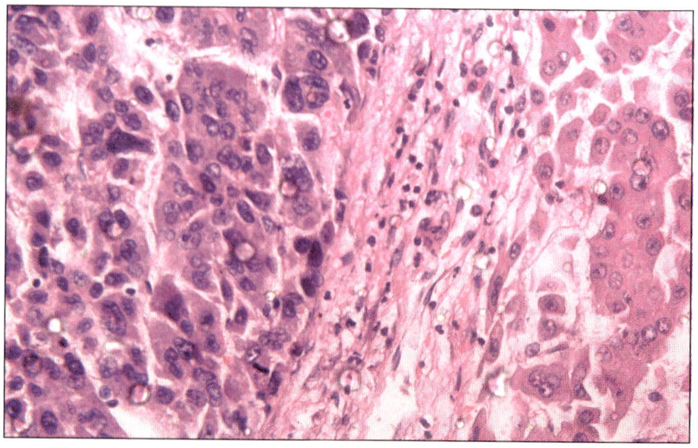

Fig. 20.4: Hepatocellular carcinoma – Malignant lesion on the left showing large polygonal cells and cord pattern with hyperchromatic nuclei. Normal liver cells are on the right

GALL BLADDER

Organ identification

Grossly it has a rounded fundal blind end and a narrow cystic duct end. In the normal state it has a thin wall (1-2 mm), a smooth, transparent peritoneal surface and a velvety appearance of mucosa which is bile stained (green).

Microscopially, it has 3 coats – mucosa, muscle coat and serosa. Mucosa is simple columnar mucus secreting, thrown into villous folds over a loose lamina propria. Muscularis mucosae is not present.

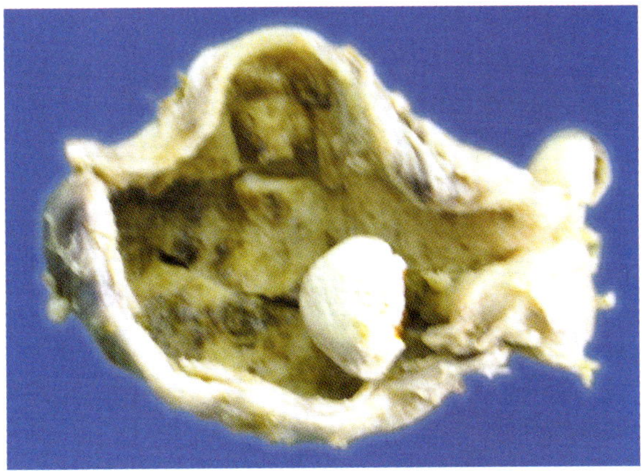

Fig. 20.5: Chronic cholecystitis. Gall bladder wall is thick. There is a single cholesterol stone in lumen.

Chronic cholecystitis

Chronic cholecystitis is characterised by loss of the mucosal velvety appearance and thickening of the wall due to fibrosis. Serosa appears dull and opaque. It is often associated with cholelithiasis (Fig. 20.5).

Microscopically, the normal villous processes are ironed out. Muscle coat is replaced by fibrous tissue. The mucosal lining shows outpouchings into muscle (Rokintansky-Aschoff sinuses). Lymphocytes and plasma cells are seen in all layers. There is fibrosis of serosa also (Fig. 20.6).

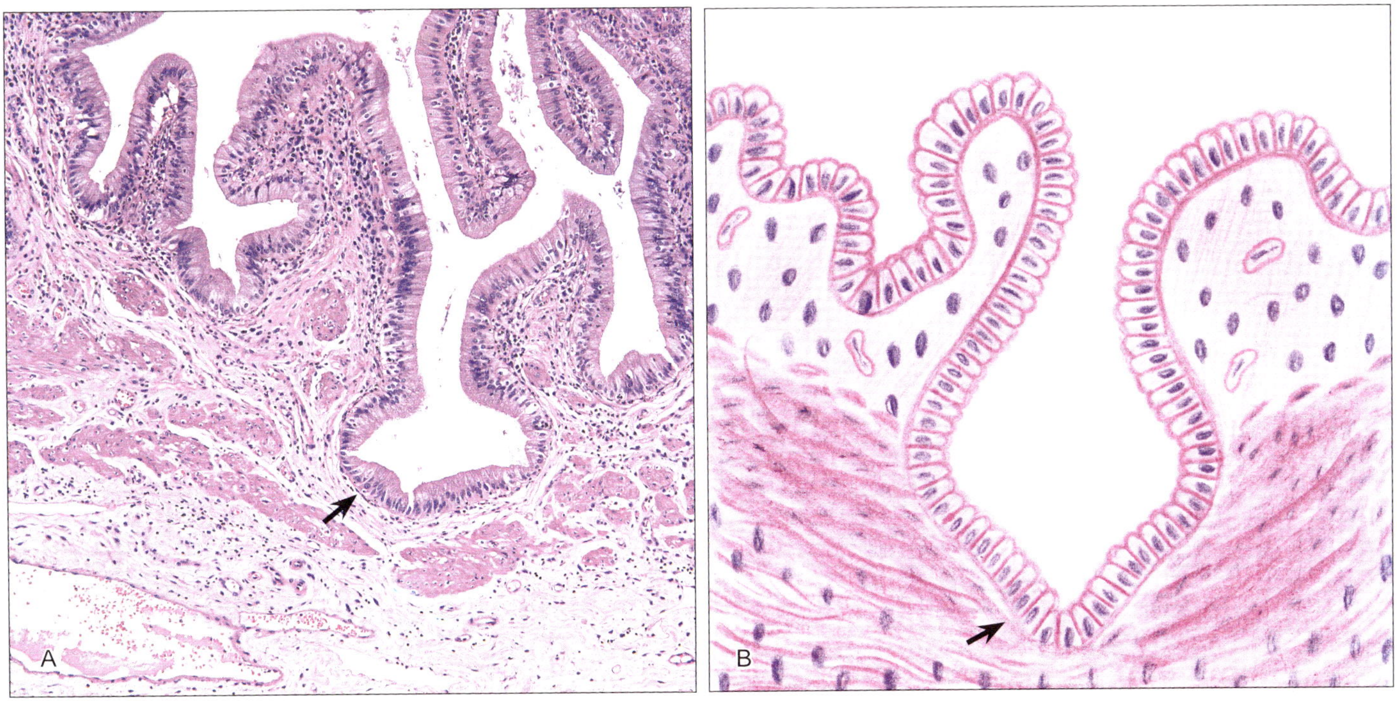

Fig. 20.6: A. and B. Chronic cholecystitis. Inflammation and fibrosis in muscle coat, with Rokitansky Aschoff sinuses (↑).

Mucosa may have yellowish specks at the villus tips due to cholesterol laden foamy histiocytes → ***cholesterolosis*** (Fig. 20.7). Marked dilatation with clear serous to mucinous contents may result in ***mucocele*** of gall bladder (Fig. 20.8).

Cholelithiasis

Cholelithiasis is presence of stones in the gall bladder. Stones may lie loose in the lumen or may be impacted in the cystic duct causing obstruction. They may be solitary yellowish and crystalline (cholesterol stone – see Fig. 20.5) or multiple, faceted and brown black (pigment stones – Figs. 2.8) with variable amounts of calcium salts.

Carcinoma gall bladder

Carcinoma gall bladder may be diffusely infiltrative causing irregular thickening of the wall, or exophytic resulting in a papillary or fungating mass projecting into the lumen (Fig. 20.9).

Adenocarcinoma gall bladder shows glands of varying shapes and sizes infiltrating the muscularis and serosa. Unlike the Rokitansky Aschoff sinuses, these glands are lined by cells with hyperchromatic nuclei and mitotic figures.

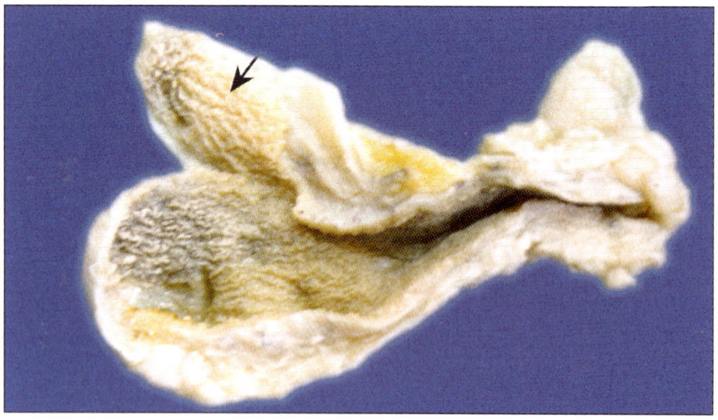

Fig. 20.7: Cholesterolosis–villi yellowish and broad at the tips.

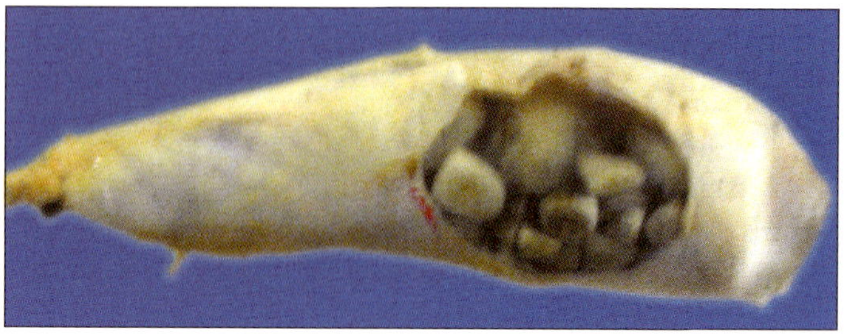

Fig. 20.8: Mucocele – Gall bladder distended with clear mucin and multiple stones.

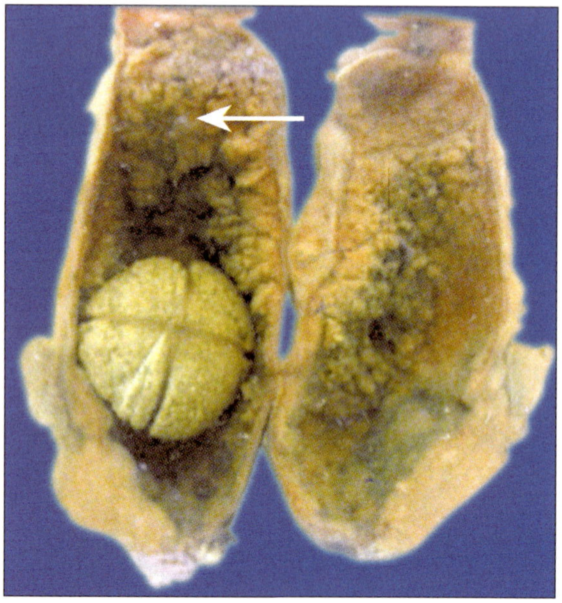

Fig. 20.9: Carcinoma gall bladder with cholelithiasis. Mucosa shows papillary tumour (←).

VIVA-VOCE

Q. What are the causes of fatty change liver?

Ans. The causes of fatty change are alcoholism, phosphorus poisoning, eclampsia, yellow fever, hepatitis C, protein-calorie malnutrition, estrogen and tamoxifen therapy, CVC liver, diabetes mellitus, tuberculosis, hypoxia, and metabolic syndrome.

Q. What are the causes of CVC liver (nutmeg liver)?

Ans. Right sided heart failure, obstruction to inferior vena cava and hepatic vein thrombosis.

Q. In nutmeg liver, why are there light and dark areas?

Ans. Dark areas are because of the venous sinusoidal congestion in the centrilobular zone and light area of midzonal fatty change and periportal normal liver parenchyma.

Q. What are the sequelae of the CVC liver?

Ans. Persistent CVC liver results in hepatic necrosis in the centrilobular zone which gets fibrosed and eventually leading to cardiac cirrhosis.

Q. What are the causes of micronodular cirrhosis?

Ans. Alcoholic cirrhosis, cardiac cirrhosis and biliary cirrhosis are the micronodular cirrhosis with nodules < 3 mm in size.

Q. What are the complications of cirrhosis liver?

Ans. Common complications of cirrhosis are oesophageal varices, ascites and splenomegaly due to portal hypertension, coagulation abnormalities and transformation into malignancy.

Q. Which tumours metastasize to liver?

Ans. Tumours of the GIT, spread to liver, through portal circulation like carcinoma stomach, carcinoma large intestine and carcinoid of intestine.

Q. What is "strawberry gall bladder"?

Ans. Macrophages laden with cholestrol accumulate in the mucosa resulting in yellowish specks at villus tips - strawberry gall bladder.

Q. What are the types of gall stones?

Ans. Pure stones – Cholestrol stones
– Pigment stones
Mixed stones – Commonest, with mixture of cholestrol, bilirubin and calcium.
Combined stones – Nucleus of Pure/mixed stone
– Shell of mixed/pure stone

Q. What are the complications of gall stones?

Ans. The complications are
- Chronic cholecystitis
- Obstruction to biliary tract resulting in colic, jaundice
- Mucocele of gall bladder
- Malignancy gall bladder due to chronic irritation by gall stones
- Empyema gall bladder

Q. What are the microscopic features of alcoholic liver disease?

Ans. Fatty change and Mallory hyaline bodies inside the hepatocytes. Eventually it may progress to cirrhosis liver.

Q. Which gene mutation results in hemochromatosis?

Ans. HFE gene mutation (C282Y)results in hemochromatosis.

Q. Which viral infection predispose to hepatocellular carcinoma?

Ans. Hepatitis B and Hepatitis C predispose to hepatocellular carcinoma.

Q. What is "empyema of gall bladder"?

Ans. Accumulation of pus in the gall bladder due to acute cholecystitis.

Q. What is "hydrops" of gall bladder?

Ans. Accumulation of clear mucinous secretion in obstructed uninflamed gall bladder is denoted as "hydrops".

Q. Name some risk factors for development of hepatocellular carcinoma?

Ans. Chronic hepatitis (hepatitis B, hepatitis C), alcoholism, aflatoxins, tyrosinemia, hereditary hemochromatosis.

Q. What are the stages of alcoholic liver disease?

Ans. The stages are
(a) hepatic steatosis – microvesicular or macrovesicular
(b) alcoholic hepatitis – hepatocyte swelling, necrosis, neutrophilic infiltration, fibrosis
(c) alcoholic cirrhosis – irreversible, micro and macronodular cirrhosis
– later the liver is replaced by scar tissue (Laennec cirrhosis)

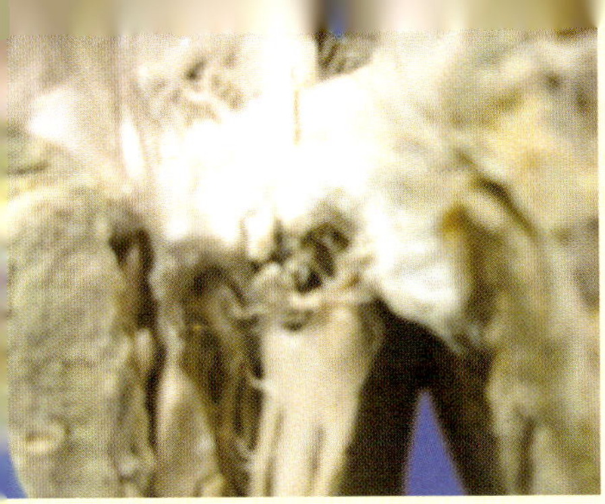

21

Cardiovascular System

ORGAN IDENTIFICATION

Heart

Specimens are usually displayed with the 4 chambers opened. Normal weight of heart is 250-300 gms and any increase in size or weight of the heart is known as *cardiomegaly*. The wall thickness of the ventricles is 0.3-0.5 cm on right side and 1.2-1.5 cms on left side (increase is known as hypertrophy) (Fig. 21.1). Shape of the ventricles is pyramidal with wider base at the atrioventricular valves and the pointed apex at the apex of the heart (increase in lumen with rounding of this shape is known as *dilatation*). The cusps of all the valves are smooth and transluscent. The mitral and tricuspid valves are attached to papillary muscles by chordae tendinae.

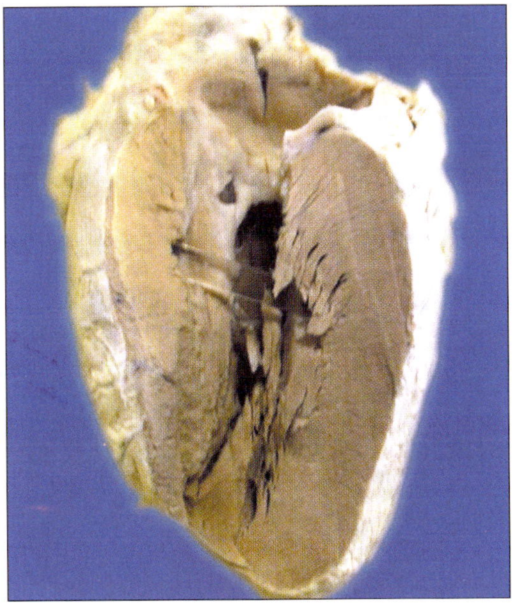

Fig. 21.1: Left ventricular hypertrophy. Note markedly thickened wall narrowing the lumen. Commonest causes are hypertension and aortic stenosis.

Pericardium is normally smooth, glistening and transparent through which myocardium and the epicardial fat are visible.

Aorta is identified by its wide luminal structure, absence of any folds or rugae and presence of foramena of branches on the intimal aspect.

Microscopically, myocardium is made up of branching and anastamosing striated muscle fibres. Aorta has a musculoelastic coat for media in contrast to the muscle coat with elastic lamina seen in muscular arteries.

Rheumatic heart disease

Most important findings are in the valves. Mitral and aortic valves are most commonly affected. The cusps are fibrotic and adherent, causing stenosis. Characteristic vegetations along line of closure are a feature of acute rheumatic fever and may not be present in chronic rheumatic heart disease, as they are replaced by fibrosis. Mitral valve may be converted to a rigid oval opening (fish mouth or button hole shape) (Fig. 21.2). Fibrosis causes decrease in compliance as well as elasticity. Valve incompetence

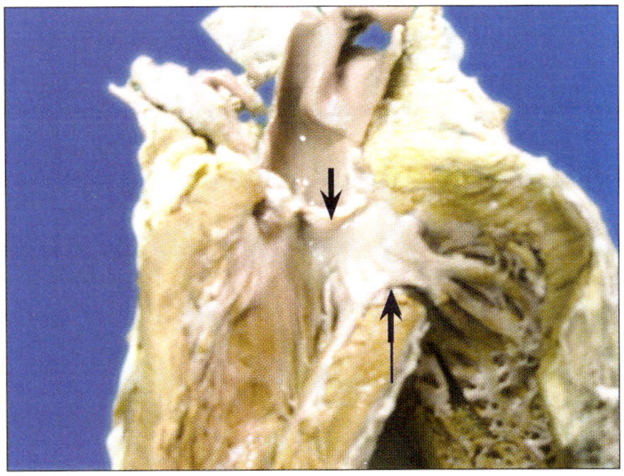

Fig. 21.2: Rheumatic heart disease – Mitral (↑) and aortic stenosis (↓).

is then associated. Aortic stenosis causes left ventricular hypertrophy and incompetence causes dilatation. Chordae tendinae may show shortening and fusion. Left atrium is dilated if mitral stenosis is prominent (Fig. 21.3). Pericardium may show organised serofibrinous pericarditis in the form of shaggy fibrous adhesions (bread and butter appearance).

Rheumatic carditis. This is characterised histologically by **Aschoff bodies**. It is rarely encountered nowadays. It shows an oval collection of inflammatory cells, with fibrinoid material in the centre, usually perivascularly in the myocardium. The cells are lymphocytes and plasma cells along with the characteristic **Anitschkow's cells**. These are large, with abundant amphophilic cytoplasm and a vesicular nucleus with the chromatin arranged as a wavy central band (caterpillar cell). In cross section this central chromatin gives the nucleus an "owl eye" appearance. 2-3 such cells can fuse and form Aschoff giant cells.

Infective endocarditis

In addition to rheumatic fever, a common cause of endocardial vegetations is infective (bacterial) endocarditis. These are friable, bulky vegetations which may destroy the cusps (acute endocarditis) or hang down from them (subacute bacterial endocarditis) (Fig. 21.4).

Fibrinous pericarditis

The pericardial surface shows a rough and shaggy appearance (bread and butter appearance). Common causes are rheumatic fever, uraemia, radiation induced and myocardial infarction.

Myocardial infarct

Cut surface of the infarcted myocardium shows gross changes (most prominent between 3rd and 10th day of infarction). It is a pale infarct i.e. the infarcted area is yellowish grey and soft (Fig. 21.5). It is rimmed by a dark red hyperaemic zone separating it from the normal part of the myocardium. A transmural infarct involves a smaller area of the wall, whole thickness being infarcted except a narrow subendocardial zone. A subendocardial infarct affects only the inner part of the myocardium but may extend over a larger area (often entire circumference) of the wall in a continuous or patchy manner.

On microscopy myocardium is identified by the branching and anastamosing striated muscle fibres. Infarcted area shows coagulative necrosis and is surrounded by inflammation and granulation tissue.

Atherosclerosis Aorta

Atherosclerotic plaques are commonest in abdominal aorta, especially near the ostia of branches. Unruptured

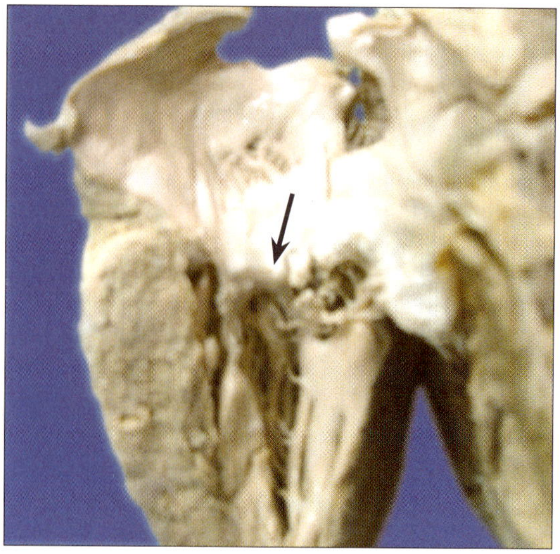

Fig. 21.3: Rheumatic heart disease – Mitral valve is scarred & thickened. Left atrium is dilated.

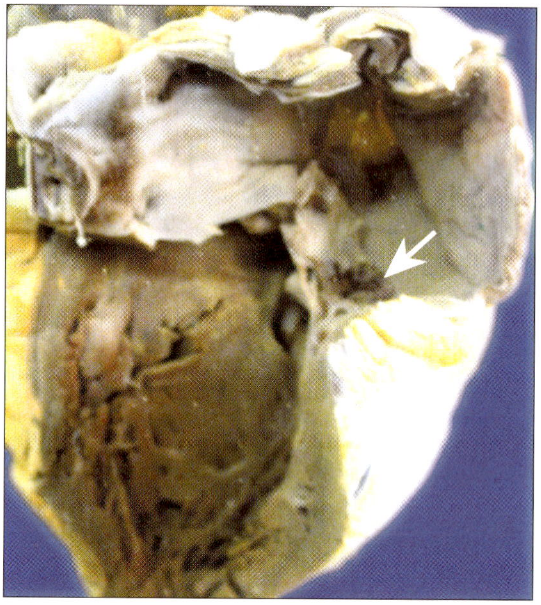

Fig. 21.4: Bulky friable vegetations of infective endocarditis (arrow) on the tricuspid valve cusp.

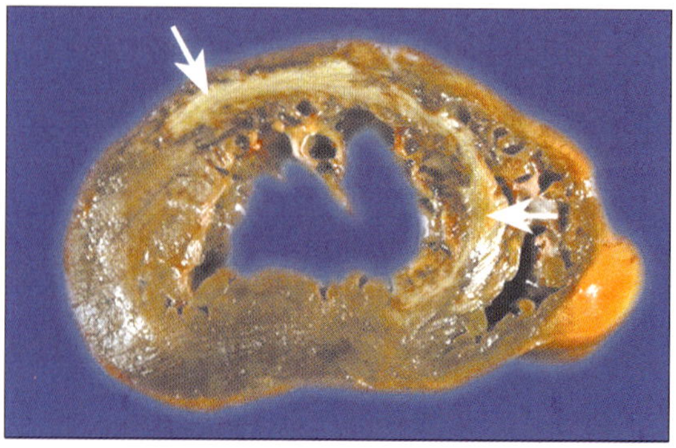

Fig. 21.5: Section across the ventricles to show pale area of infarct in anterior wall of left ventricle and interventricular septum (↘).

plaques are seen on intimal surface as smooth white to yellowish elevations, either as raised plaques 0.5 - 1.5 cms. in size or as coalesced irregular areas (Fig. 21.6). If ruptured, the surface is ulcerated and at these sites the yellowish soft centre of the plaque is visible. Some of the plaques may calcify (white and chalky) or haemorrhage (rusty brown discoloration).

Microscopy section may be of part of the aortic wall or the full section of coronary artery. Lesion is covered by a fibrous cap with a few smooth muscle cells and inflammatory cells. Centre of the lesion shows cholesterol clefts and foamy macrophages along with fibrin and debris (Fig. 21.7). This is surrounded by lymphocytes, smooth muscle cells and histiocytes. Focal calcification may be present. The base and periphery of the plaque show newly formed capillaries. The relative proportion of these components may vary from lesion to lesion. At times, a complication occlusive atheroma is formed (Fig. 21.8).

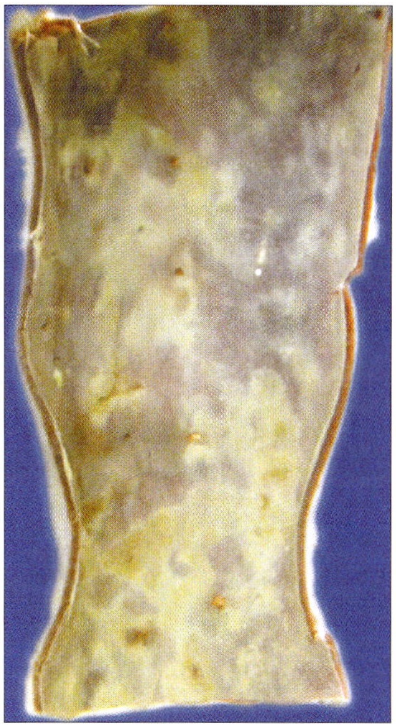

Fig. 21.6: Extensive atherosclerotic (yellowish) plaques in descending aorta.

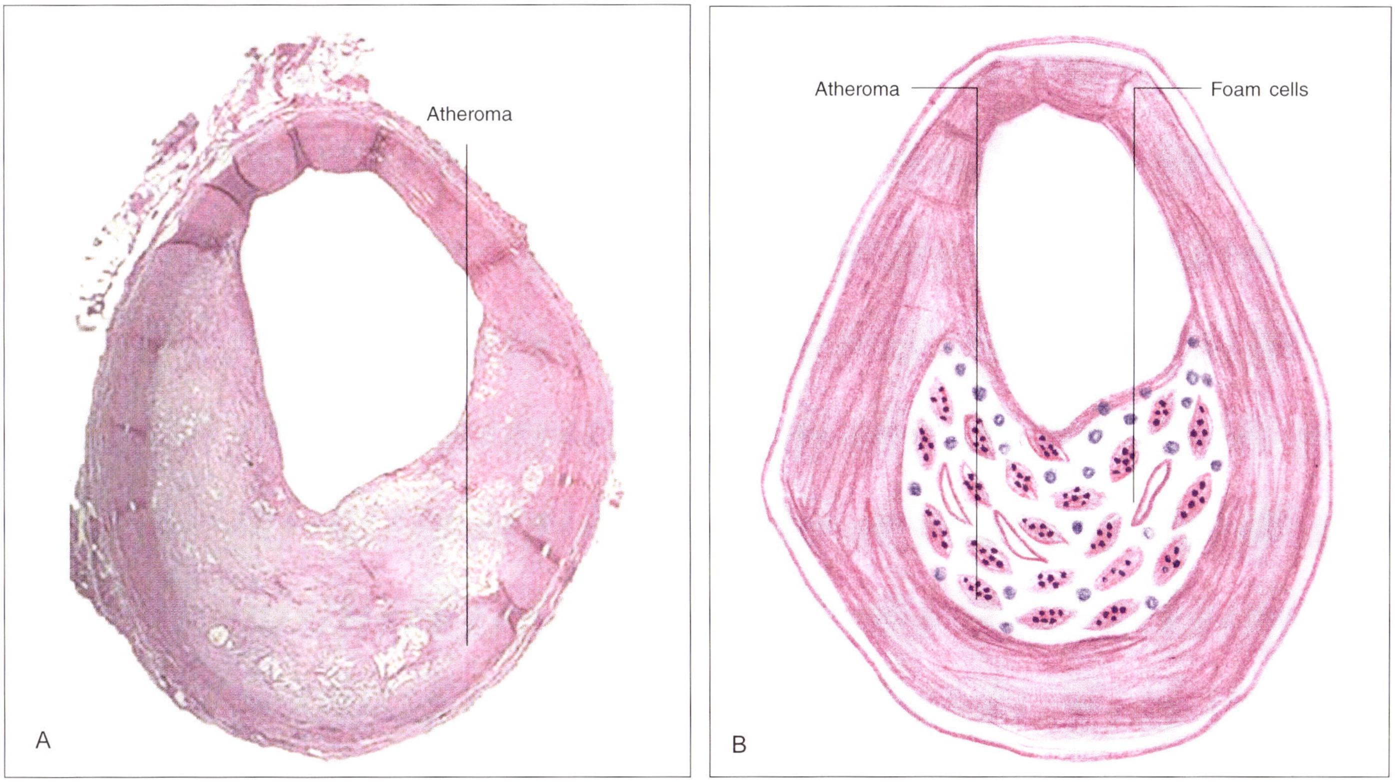

Fig. 21.7: A. and B. Coronary atherosclerosis. Non-occlusive, uncomplicated lesion with fibrous cap, foam cells and inflammatory cells.

Aortic Aneurysm

Aneurysm is dilatation of the vessel. The dilatation may be fusiform or saccular (eccentric outpouching, usually filled by a thrombus). These occur due to weakening of the wall. Atherosclerosis is the commonest cause of aneurysm of abdominal aorta. Syphilitic aneurysm (seen in tertiary syphilis which is now rare) affects the ascending part of the arch of the aorta. This is associated with scarring and wrinkling of the intima (tree barking).

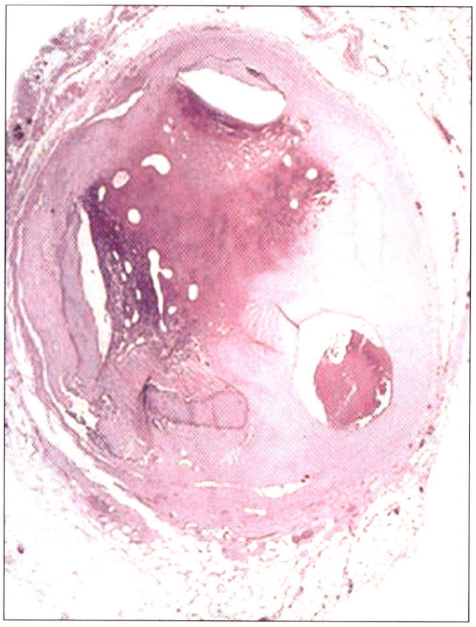

Fig. 21.8: Coronary atherosclerosis. Complicated occlusive lesion.

VIVA-VOCE

Q. What are the gross findings in heart in a case of acute rheumatic fever.

Ans. Vegetations at the contact margins in mitral and/or aortic valves, McCallum's patch in atrial wall and serofibrinous pericardititis.

Q. Name the diseases in which vegetations are present on the valve surface.

Ans. The diseases are
- Rheumatic carditis
- Infective endocarditis
- Non-bacterial thrombotic endocarditis and
- Libman Sach's endocarditis.

Q. What are the causes of "Bread and Butter" pericarditis.

Ans. Serofibrinous pericarditis is observed in rheumatic heart disease, tubercular pericarditis and uremic pericarditis.

Q. What are the causes of left ventricular hypertrophy?

Ans. Left ventricular hypertrophy is observed in
- Hypertension
- Aortic stenosis
- Coarctation of aorta

Q. In which disease are friable valvular vegetations found?

Ans. Infective endocarditis

Q. What are the complication of infective endocarditis?

Ans. Some of the complications of infective endocarditis are
- Renal infarct
- Splenic infarct
- Focal glomerulonephritis
- Dissemination of bacterial vegetations to various organs
- Suppuralive pericarditis

Q. What are the complications of atheromatous plaque?

Ans. The complications include - haemorrhage into the plaque, thrombosis and aneurysmal dilatation of the vessels.

Q. What is the main pathology in syphilitic aortitis?

Ans. Endarteritis obliterans of the vasa vasora of aortic wall results in tree bark appearance of the intima of aorta.

Q. What is the commonest cause of righ sided heart failure?

Ans. Chronic obstructive pulmonary disease is the commonest cause of congestive cardiac failure.

Q. Differentiate between vegetations in different endocarditis?

Ans.
- Rheumatic fever - Small, warty vegetations along lines of closure, sterile
- Nonbacterial thrombotic endocarditis - small, warty, sterile, along lines of closure.
- Libman Sack's endocarditis - medium sized, flat, verrucous, on both surfaces of valves, sterile
- Infective endocarditis - large, bulky vegatations on valve ausps, non-sterile, high risk of embolisation

Q. Name some risk factors for atherosclerosis?

Ans. Age, hyperhomocystienemia, hypertension, diabetes, hyperlipidemia, obesity, smoking.

Q. What are the ways in which Ischaemic heart disease may present.

Ans. IHD can present as angina, myocardial infarction or sudden cardiac death.

Q. What ar the major criteria for clinical diagnosis of rheumatic fever.

Ans. The Jones major criteria are:
- Migratory polyarthritis of large joints
- Subcutaneous nodules
- Sydenham chorea
- Carditis
- Erythema marginatum

Q. Name important predisposing factors to infective endocarditis.

Ans.
- Damaged endocardium/valves
- Immunocompromised individuals
- I/V drug abuse

Q. Which organism is responsible for Rheumatic fever.

Ans. Rheumatic fever is an immunologically mediated disease due to Group A (hemolytic) streptococci.

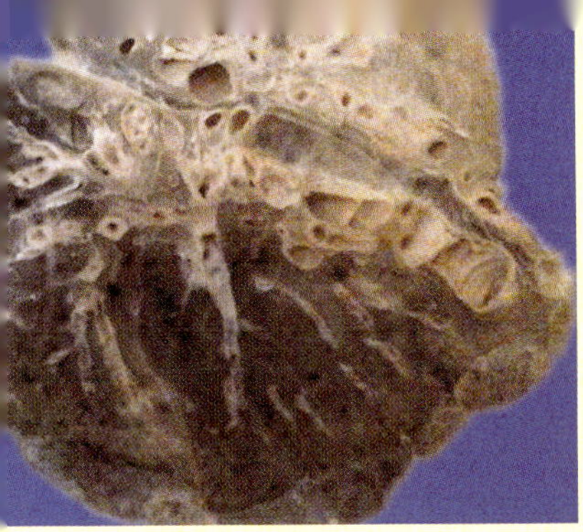

22

Respiratory System

ORGAN IDENTIFICATION

Lungs are identified by the spongy texture, the bronchial tree which branches out from the hilum, the narrow apex superiorly, the concave diaphragmatic (inferior) surface and the curved pleural surface. Anthracotic pigment is prominent in most adult lung specimens, imparting a black-grey speckled appearance. Right lung has 3 lobes while the left has 2 lobes and lingula.

Microscopically the alveoli with characteristic polygonal angular shape and the bronchioles with columnar ciliated lining are seen. If bronchi are included in the section, cartilage is seen in their wall. Black anthracotic pigment is seen inside macrophages and around bronchioles.

Emphysema

Emphysema is permanent dilatation of alveoli with destruction of alveolar walls. Grossly the lung is enlarged and spongy (much more in panacinar than in centriacinar emphysema). Blebs or bullae filled with air may be present, especilly at apex or along margins (Fig. 22.1).

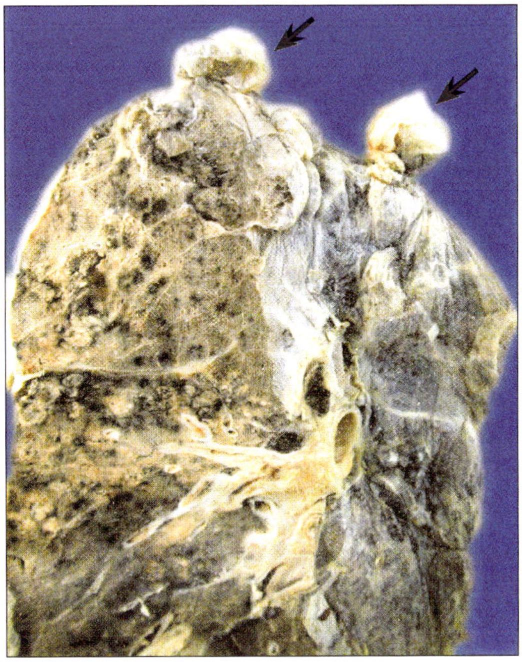

Fig. 22.1: Emphysematous lung. Spongy parenchyma and a few bullae (↙↙) are seen at upper lobe.

Microscopically it showed septal destruction and alveolar dilatation without inflammation. Dilatation manifests as large alveolar spaces with rounded contour instead of polygonal shape, with thin septae (Fig. 22.2). Destruction is seen as free tags of septae projecting into these large bullous spaces.

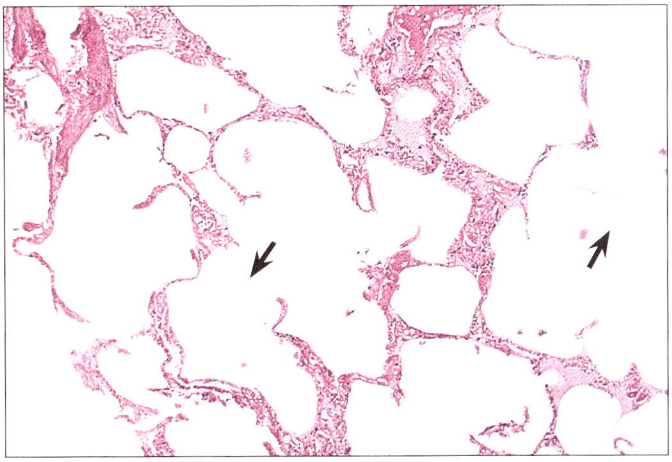

Fig. 22.2: Emphysema – dilated alveoli and large irregular spaces with disrupted alveolar septae (↑).

Bronchiectasis

Bronchiectasis is characterised by irreversible dilatation of bronchi with infection and destruction of bronchial wall. If severe, it is easily recognised by the markedly dilated bronchi (Fig. 22.3). If milder, it is diagnosed by the bronchi being easily visible and traceable till less than 2-3 mm. from pleural surface (normally not traceable till so close to pleura). It is a disease of remissions (when the dilated bronchi have a smooth lining) and exacerbations (when they are lined by purulent exudates).

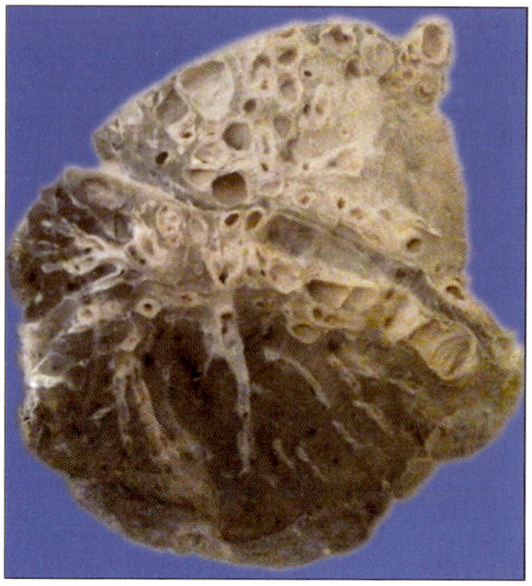

Fig. 22.3: Slice of lung showing bronchiectasis. Bronchi are thick walled and dilated.

Lung abscess

Lung abscess is a focus of suppurative necrosis (cavity containing pus and necrotic material). It may be single or multiple and measure upto a few centimeters in size. If acute and pyogenic, it is surrounded by a zone of hyperaemia. If chronic, it may be walled off by fibrosis in its wall (Fig. 22.4).

Lobar Pneumonia

Lobar pneumonia is infective consolidation of a whole lobe or lobes, most often due to pneumococci. It classically goes through 4 stages:

(a) **Congestion**, when lungs are red, heavy and boggy, oozing blood stained fluid on cutting;

(b) **Red hepatisation**, when the lobe is reddish brown and firm to feel instead of spongy;

(c) **Grey hepatisation**, when it is firm and greyish (Fig. 22.5 A), and

(d) **Resolution**, when it is partially airy with frothy exudate or cut surface.

Pleura may show fibrinous thickening. Gross appearance is most characteristic in the grey hepatisation stage.

Microscopically, *congestion stage* shows filling of alveoli with fluid with few polymorphs and RBCs, with marked congestion of septal vessels. In the *red hepatisation stage*, alveoli cannot be distinctly made out because the entire lumen is filled with fibrin, RBCs and polymorphs. In *grey hepatisation stage*, RBCs have been mostly lysed. The predominantly fibrinous exudate shrinks from the alveolar walls resulting in a narrow peripheral clear zone so that the alveoli can be clearly delineated from their contents (Fig. 22.5B and C). In lobar pneumonia, all the alveoli show uniform appearance, whatever the stage.

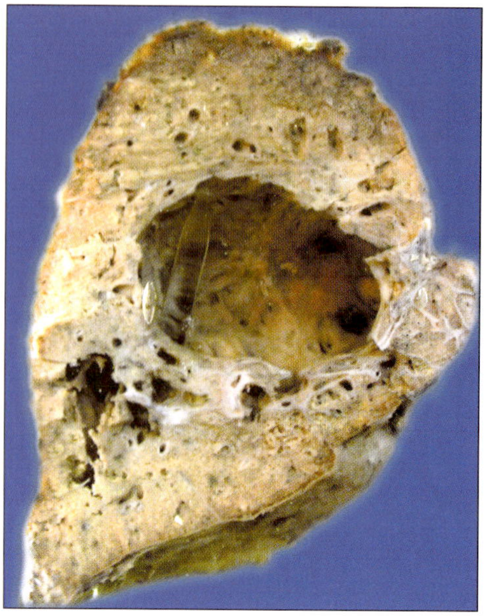

Fig. 22.4: Chronic lung abscess cavity. Surrounding lung shows bronchopneumonic changes (consolidation).

Bronchopneumonia

Lung shows patchy and focal consolidation and suppuration in relation to bronchi. These are seen as small necrotic yellow areas. They are common in the base of lungs.

In contrast to lobar pneumonia, lesion in broncho pneumonia is patchy. Involved areas show a bronchus with acute inflammation in its wall and in the surrounding alveoli. Necrosis (suppurative) may be seen. More peripherally, alveoli may be normal or show edema.

Tuberculosis

Pulmonary tuberculosis may manifest in any of the following morphological forms:

(a) ***Ghon focus***. This is seen in primary tuberculosis, as a 1-2 cm lesion which is caseous to calcified, present subpleurally near the interlobar fissure (i.e. upper part of lower lobe or lower part of upper lobe) (Fig. 22.6). Hilar nodes also show caseation/calcification (Ghon complex).

(b) ***Apical lesion***, seen in secondary tuberculosis, may be a fibrocaseous lesion, i.e. an area of caseous necrosis surrounded by variable fibrosis. This may heal on its own leaving a fibrocalcific scar or progress to an apical cavitary lesion. Overlying pleura often shows thickening.

(c) ***Tubercular bronchopneumonia***, when it spreads through the bronchial tree. Patches of caseation are seen distributed in the rest of the lobe/lung. Lesions may be extensive and confluent to involve nearly the whole lobe.

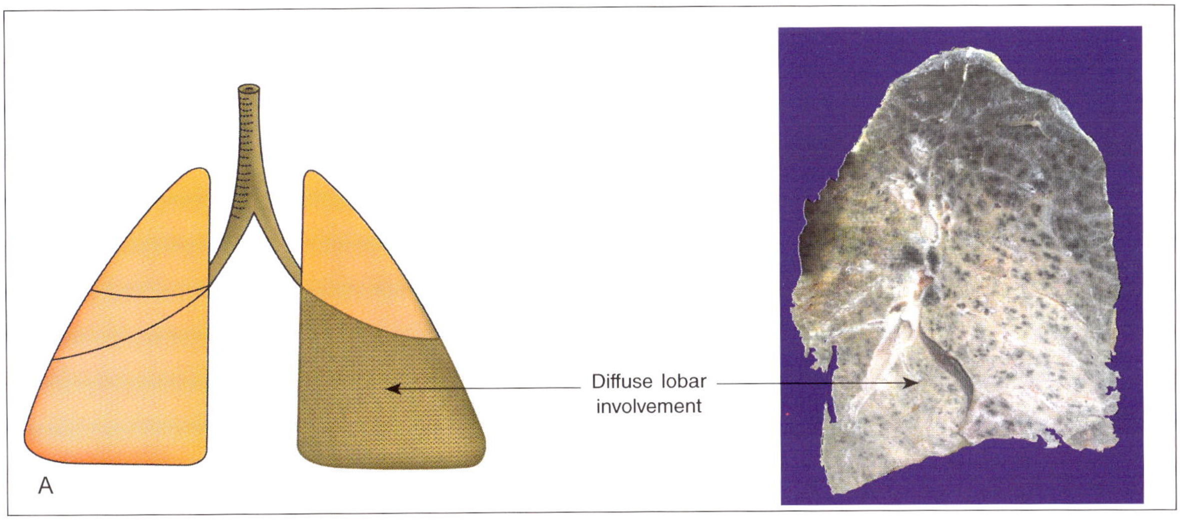

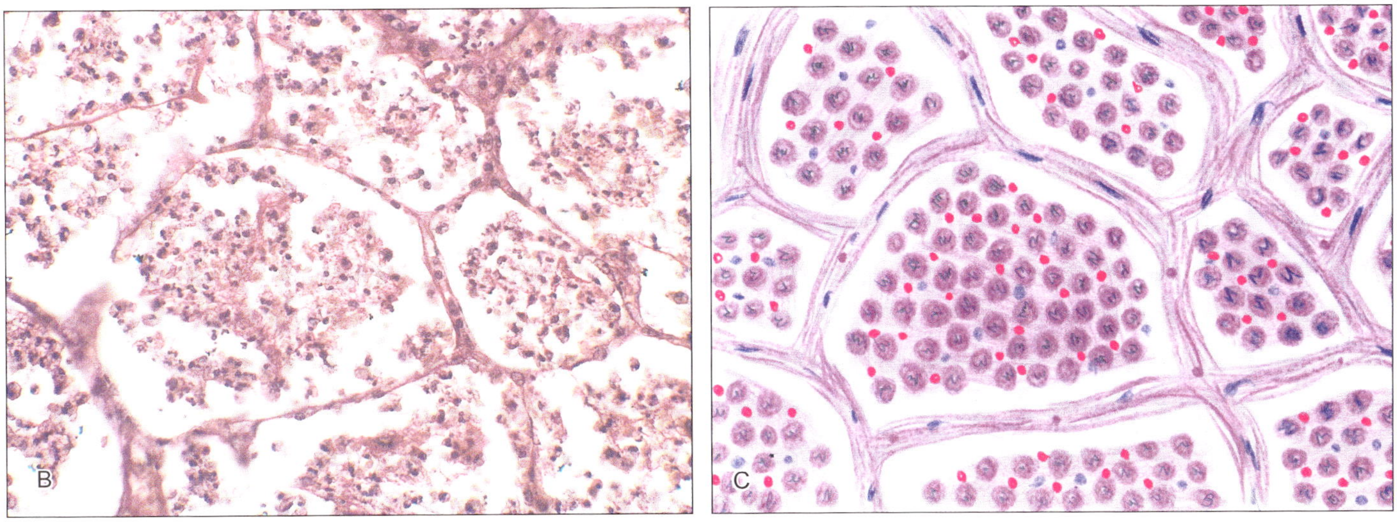

Fig. 22.5: A. Gross appearance of lobar pneumonia B. and C. Lobar pneumonia – alveoli with intact septae and lumen filled with fibrin and exudate.

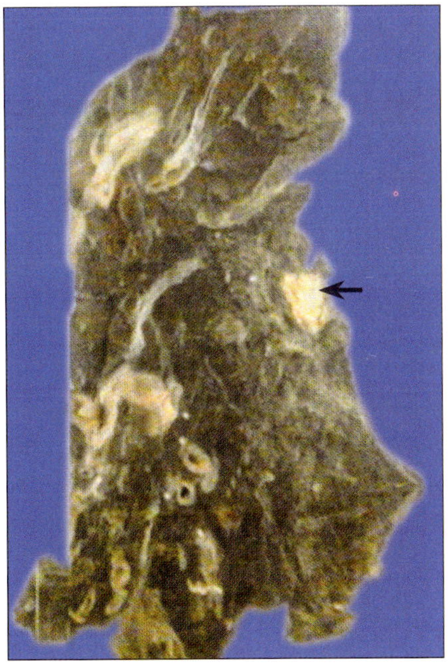

Fig. 22.6: Calcified Ghon focus seen subpleurally (↑).

(d) ***Miliary tuberculosis*** is due to haematogenous spread to rest of the lung (or to other organs). It is seen as small millet sized (1-2 mm) caseous lesions scattered all over the lobe/lung.

Microscopically examination. Whatever the gross morphological picture, the histological hall mark is the caseating epitheloid cell granuloma with Langhan's giant cells (Fig. 22.7).

Bronchogenic carcinoma

Most bronchogenic carcinomas arise in major bronchial branches, i.e. close to hilum of lung. It starts as an irregular elevated or ulcerated lesion. It grows as a fungating intraluminal mass or fans out into lung parenchyma as a greyish white, firm to hard lesion with irregular margins (Fig. 22.8). Large lesions may show foci of haemorrhage and necrosis.

Microscopically, the most common type is squamous cell carcinoma which may be poorly to well differentiated

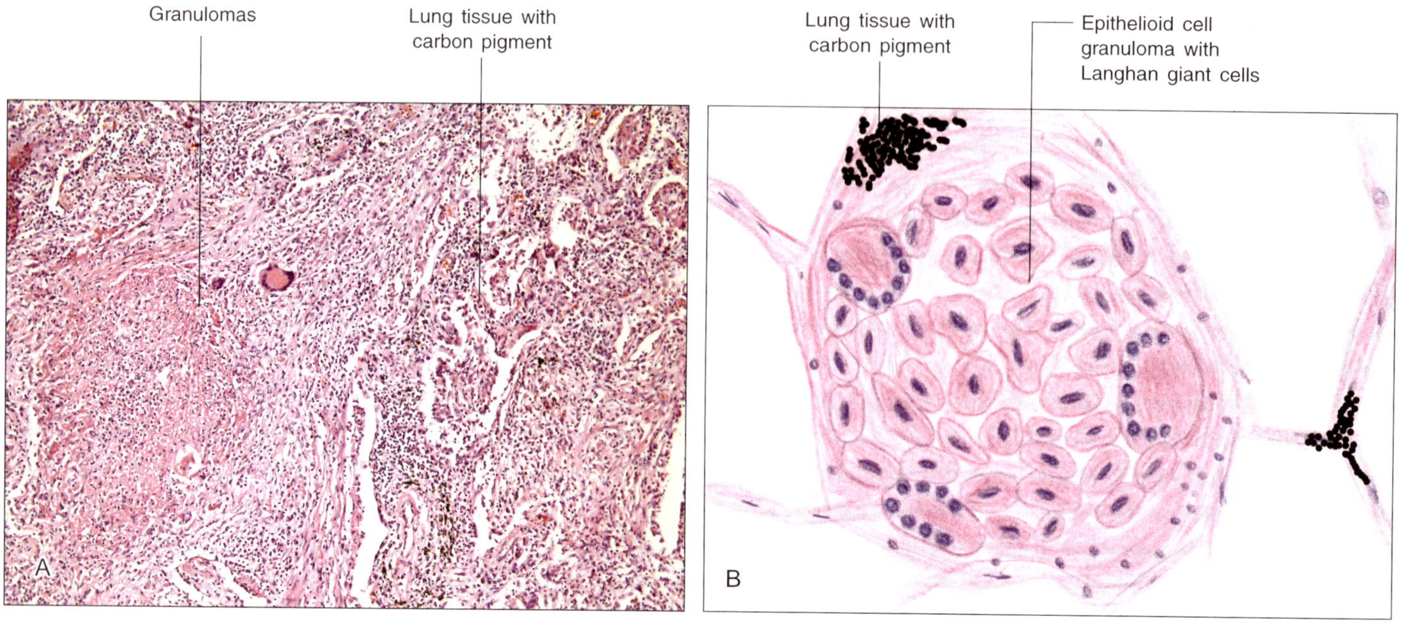

Fig. 22.7: A. and B. Tuberculosis – The typical lesion of epithelioid cell granuloma with Langhan giant cells and caseous necrosis.

(Fig. 6.8). Surrounding bronchial mucosa (non-carcinomatous area) usually shows squamous metaplasia and dysplasia.

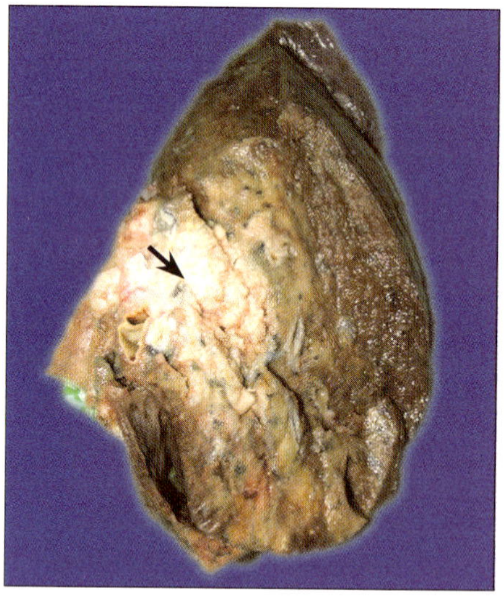

Fig. 22.8: Bronchogenic carcinoma – bronchial origin (↘) and parenchymal infiltration seen.

Metastatic deposit lung

Metastatic deposits in the lung, in contrast, presents as multiple, rounded lesions scattered in the peripheral lung parenchyma (Fig. 22.9).

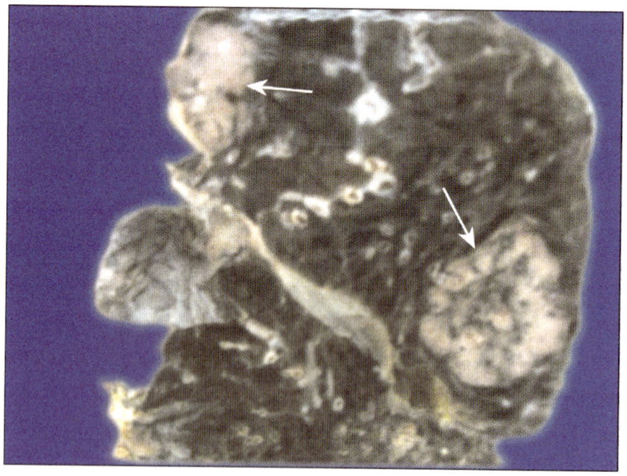

Fig. 22.9: Well circumscribed metastatic deposit in slice of lung.

VIVA-VOCE

Q. Name the granulomatous diseases of the lung?
Ans. Tuberculosis, sarcoidosis and berylliosis.

Q. Which lung tumour is associated with paraneoplastic syndrome?
Ans. Small cell carcinoma lung which secretes calcitonin, ACTH and vasopressin.

Q. Which enzyme deficiency results in panacinar emphysema.
Ans. Alpha-1-antitrypsin deficiency.

Q. Why secondary tuberculosis involves the apical region of the lung?
Ans. In apical area of the lung, O_2 tension is high and that promotes mycobacterial proliferation.

Q. Which bronchopulmonary diseases may lead to secondary amyloidosis.
Ans. Long standing bronchiectasis, lung abscess and pulmonary tuberculosis may lead to secondary amyloidosis of AA type.

Q. Which disease may progress to lung carcinoma/mesothelioma?
Ans. Asbestosis of lung

Q. What is Cor pulmonale?
Ans. Right sided heart failure due to chronic obstructive lung disease.

Q. What are the causes of hemoptysis?
Ans. Causes of hemoptysis are tuberculosis, bronchogenic carcinoma, bronchiectasis, lung abscess, pulmonary infarction and left ventricular heart failure.

Q. Describe different types of emphysema?
Ans.
- Centriacinar: involve central acini with sparing of peripheral alveoli, seen in smokers in the upper lobe
- Panacinar: involve entire acinus, base of lung, seen in α1-antitrypsin deficiency
- Distal acinar/paraseptal: distal acinus involved, smokers, associated with pneumothorax
- Irregular: Irregular acinar involvement associated with fibrosis and/or scarring.

Q. Name risk factors for bronchogenic carcinoma?
Ans.
- Smoking, air pollution, occupational exposure (Asbestosis, Radiation, Uranium)
- Genetic mutations affecting p53, Rb, K-vas, L-myc.

Q. What are the microscopic types of Bronchogenic carcinoma?
Ans.
- Squamous cell carcinoma
- Adenocarcinoma
- Small cell carcinoma
- Bronchoalveolar carcinoma
- Carcinoid lung

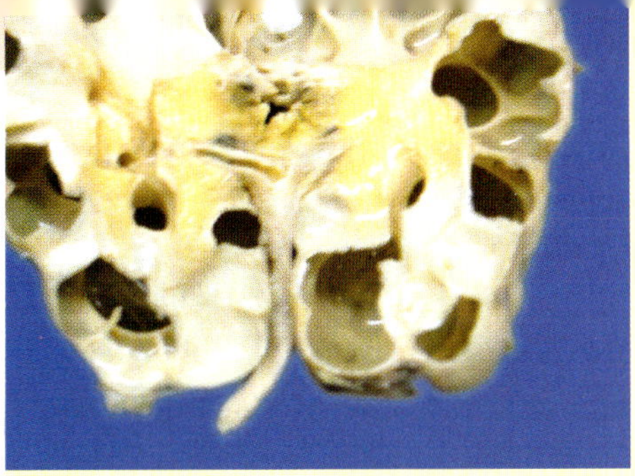

23

Urinary System

ORGAN IDENTIFICATION

Kidney is identified by its bean shape and the ureter arising from the pelvis at the hilum. Normally, the external surface has a smooth thin transluscent capsule. If capsule is stripped off, the renal surface is smooth (occasionally fetal lobulation markings may persist normally). Cut surface shows the darker triangular pyramids distinct from the paler cortex. The apices of the pyramids open into calyces which open into the renal pelvis. Pelvicalyceal system has a smooth glistening lining. A small amount of fat is present in the peripelvic area.

Urinary bladder is a muscular organ in the shape of an inverted pyramid. Mucosa is smooth but may show trabeculations due to contraction of muscle coat.

Microscopically, kidney is identified by the glomeruli and the tubules with cuboidal lining. Normally these structures are closely packed with interspersed blood vessels, without any visible amount of interstitial stroma. Bladder is identified by the transitional lining, lamina propria and muscle coat.

GLOMERULONEPHRITIS

Glomerulonephritis (GN) is characterised by glomerular changes with secondary or minor changes in the tubules and interstitium. Changes are diffuse and bilateral.

Acute Proliferative GN (APGN)

Glomeruli are hypercellular due to proliferation of epithelial cells of the tuft as well as polymorphs infiltration. The enlargement of the tuft obliterates the Bowman's space (Fig. 23.1). Interstitium may show edema and congestion but no significant inflammation is seen.

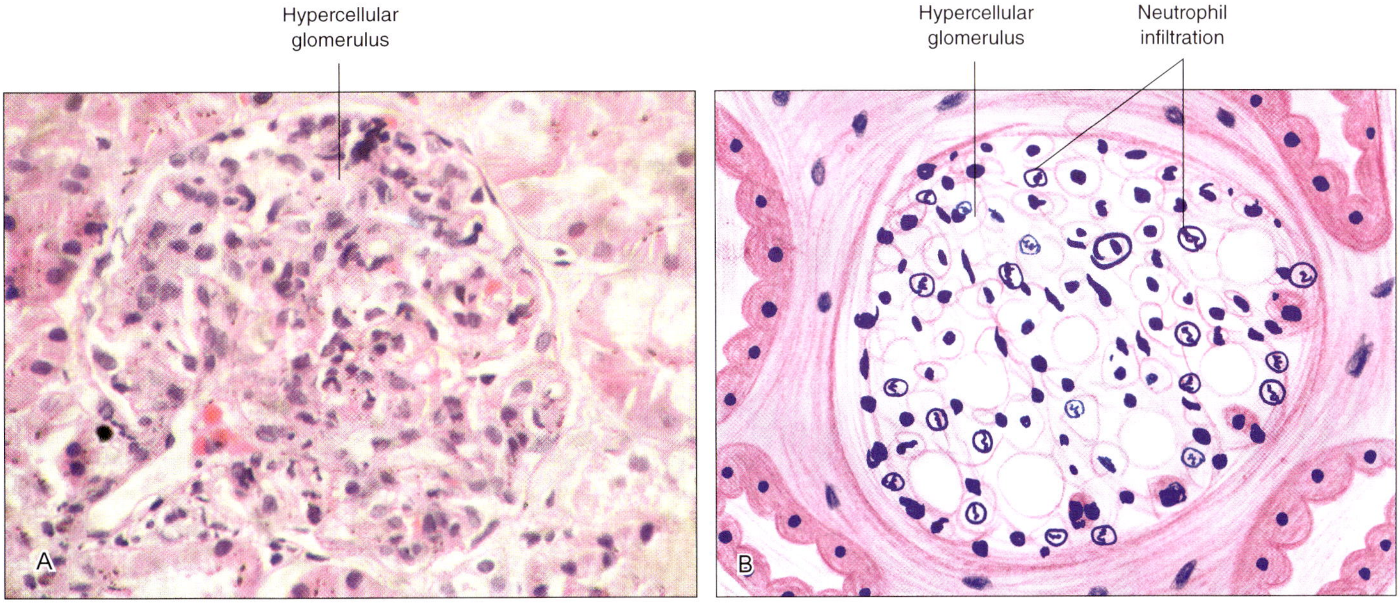

Fig. 23.1: A. and B. Hypercellular glomerulus of APGN. Epithelial cells proliferation and neutrophilic infiltration seen with obliteration of Bowmans space.

URINARY BLADDER

Calculi may be present in the urinary bladder and cause obstruction as well as cystitis.

Carcinoma bladder

Carcinoma bladder is usually a papillary carcinoma. It is an exophytic growth attached to bladder wall by a broad base. Its surface is covered by thin, delicate papillary fronds (Fig. 23.17).

The commonest type is transitional cell carcinoma. Tumour is papillary with thin fibrovascular core covered by epithelium (Fig. 23.18A). The epithelium is of transitional type with varying degrees of increase in number of layers, atypia, lack of polarity and presence of mitotic figures (Fig. 23.18B). Tumour cells may infiltrate the lamina propria and muscularis.

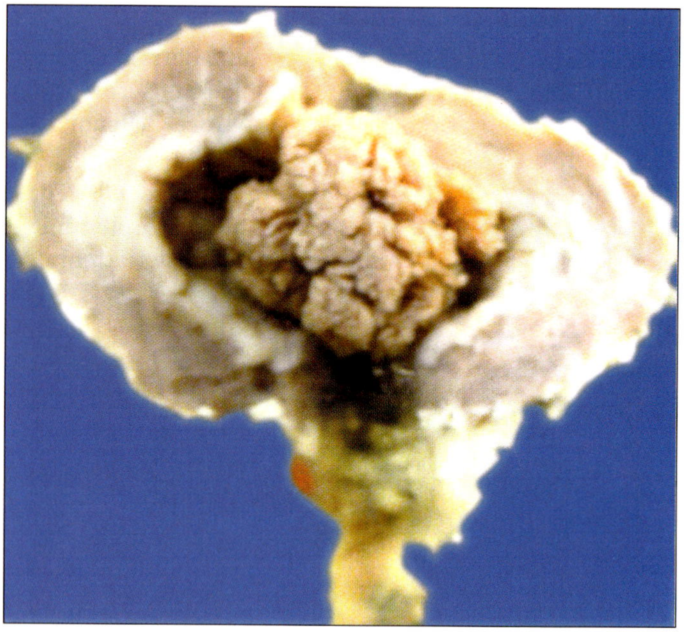

Fig. 23.17: Papillary carcinoma occupying whole lumen of urinary bladder. Bladder wall is hypertrophic and thick.

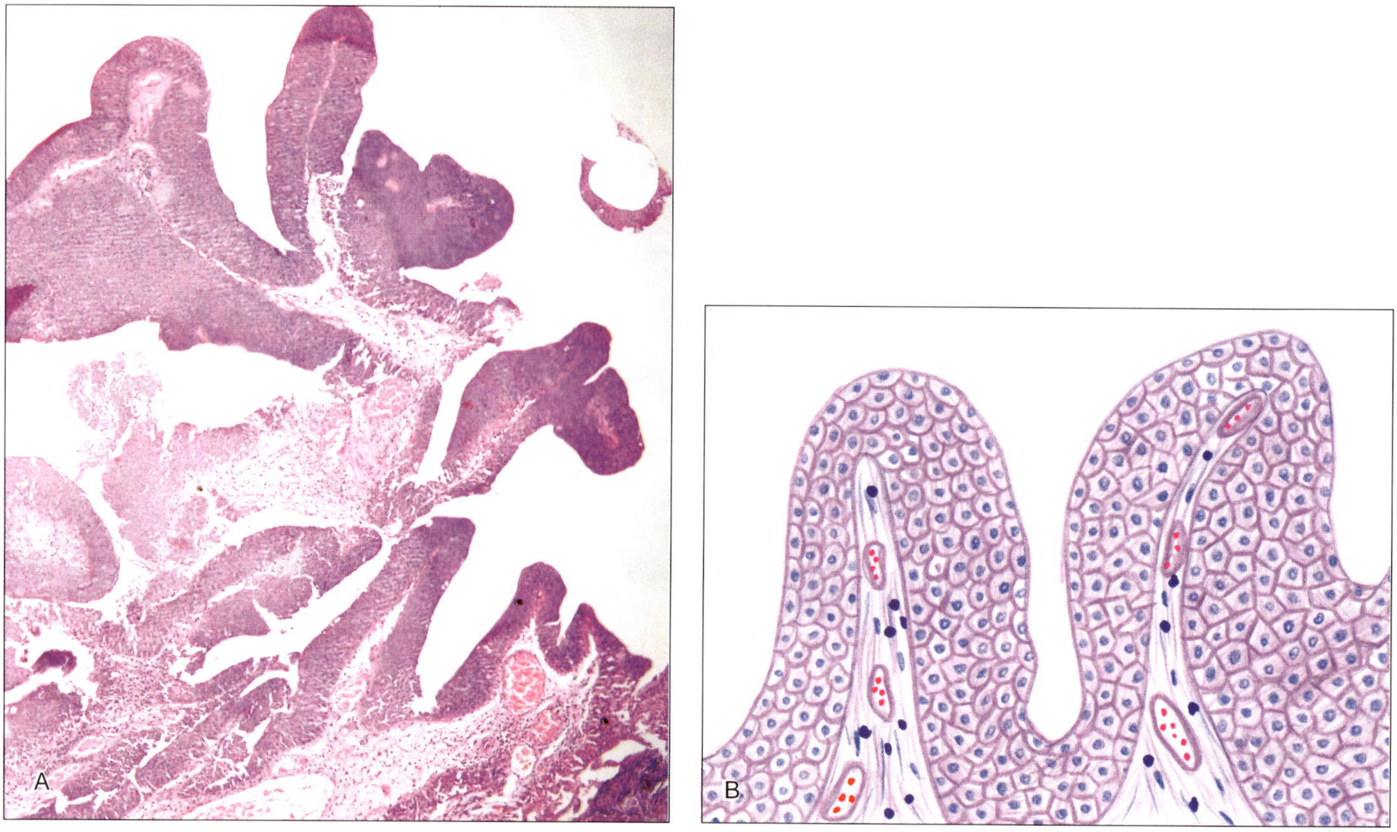

Fig. 23.18: A. and B. Transitional cell carcinoma urinary bladder shows papillary structures with thin fibrovascular core covered by transitional epithelium

VIVA-VOCE

Q. What is nephrotic syndrome?

Ans. Nephrotic syndrome is a clinical syndrome characterized by albuminuria (> 3.5 g in 24 hours), hypoproteinemia, hyperlipidemia, lipiduria and generalized anasarca

Q. What are the causes of "large pale kidney"?

Ans. Large pale kidney is seen in membranous glomerulonephritis, diabetic glomerulosclerosis, membronoproliferative glomerulonephritis and amyloidosis kidney.

Q. Epithelial crescents in glomeruli are seen in?

Ans. Rapidly progressive glomeru-lonephritis, Good Pasture syndrome and Henoch-Schonlein purpura.

Q. What are the causes of "flea bitten kidney"?

Ans. Flea bitten kidney is seen in malignant hypertension, infective endocarditis, rapidly glomerulonephritis, focal glomerulonephritis of SLE, Henoch-Schonlein purpura and Good-Pasture syndrome.

Q. What are the causes of "granular contracted kidney"?

Ans. It is the end stage kidney seen in chronic glomerulonephritis, chronic pyelonephritis and benign nephrosclerosis.

Q. In which diseases, oval fat bodies are seen in the urine?

Ans. Oval fat bodies in the urine (lipiduria) are seen in nephrotic syndrome.

Q. In which disease is the kidney waxy on cut section?

Ans. Amyloidosis.

Q. What is the clinical presentation of polycystic kidney?

Ans. Polycystic kidney, an autosomal dominant congenital disease may present with hematuria, hypertension, flank pain and urinary tract infection.

Q. What are the causes of hematuria?

Ans. Some of the causes of hematuria are

– Acute glomerulonephritis
– IgA nephropathy
– Renal cell carcinoma
– Bladder carcinoma
– Malignant hypertension
– Renal infarct
– Renal stones
– Bladder stones
– Severe trombocytopenia
– Renal tuberculosis

Q. Which is the commonest type of renal stone?

Ans. Calcium oxalate stones are the commonest.

Q. Which parasitic disease involves bladder?

Ans. Schistosoma hematobium affects urinary bladder, may lead to squamous metaplasia of bladder epithelium and finally squamous cell carcinoma bladder.

Q. What is the pathology of minimal change disease?

Ans. Glomeruli are normal on light microscopy. Diffuse flattening of foot processes of glomerular visceral epithelial cells occurs, which can be seen on electron microscopy.

Q. What is the pathogenetic mechanism of Good-Pasture syndrome?

Ans. Antibodies are formed against glomerular basement membrane and basement membrane lung which may result in haemorrhage in lung and kidney (Anti basement membrane disease) resulting in hemoptysis and hematuria.

Q. In renal cell carcinoma, why do the tumour cells demonstrate a clear cytoplasm?

Ans. Cells are clear because of the presence of glycogen and lipids-phospholipids and cholestrol ester.

Q. Which chemical carcinogen is associated with bladder cancer?

Ans. Aniline blue dye

Q. Describe various types of renal stones?

Ans.

- Calcium oxalate - most common, radioopaque in acidic urine
- Uric acid - hyperuricemia, radiolucent in acidic urine
- Magnesium ammonium phosphate - struvite/triple stone, staghorn calculus, proteus infection in alkaline urine
- Cystine - Genetic defect in cystine absorption
  - in acidic urine

Q. Classify microscopic types of renal cell carcinoma?

Ans.
- Clear cell carcinoma - most common, deletion of 3p (VHL gene), arise from proximal tubular cells.
- Papillary carcinoma - Papillary growth, psammoma bodies, arise from distal tubules
- Chromophobe carcinoma - cells with pale, eosinophilic cytoplasm with perinuclear halo, arise from intercalated cells of collecting ducts.
- Collecting duct carcinoma arise from collecting duct cells in the medulla.

Q. Risk factors for Renal cell carcionoma?

Ans.
- Nongenetic - Tobacco, hypertension, obesity, estrogen therapy, asbestos exposure, acquired cystic disease, VonHippel Lindau syndrome
- Genetic factors - Trisomy 7, 16, 17
  - Loss of y
  - t (x; 1)

Q. What factors predispose to pyelonephritis?

Ans. Urinary obstruction, instrumentation, vesico-ureteral reflux, diabetes mellitus, immunosuppression and septic emboli.

Q. Name some causes of silent hematuria.

Ans. Renal cell carcinoma, urothelial tumours, renal tuberculosis.

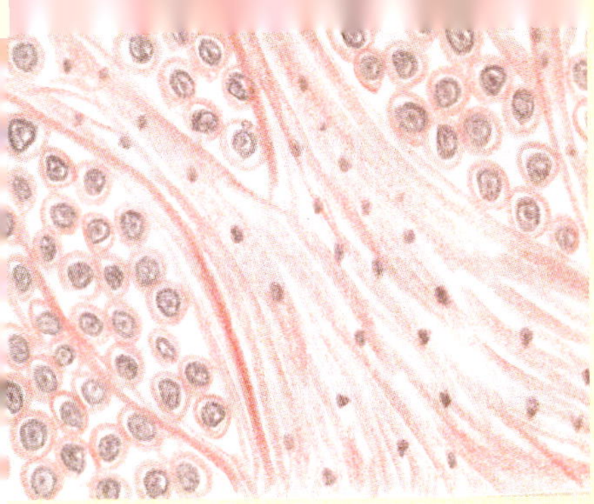

24

Male Genital System

CARCINOMA PENIS

Grossly, organ is identified by the shape and the skin covered proximal part of the shaft, as the carcinoma most commonly affects the distal part (glans and prepuce). It is usually a varrucous exophytic (cauliflower like) growth destroying the tip of penis and variable extent of the shaft (Fig. 24.1). Microscopically, it is usually a well differentiated squamous cell carcinoma (Fig. 6.8).

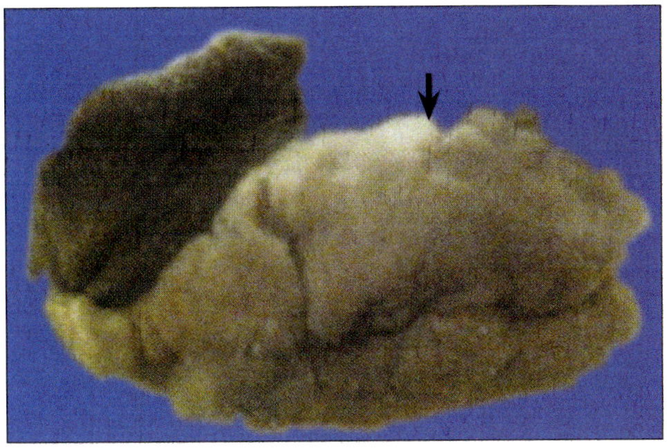

Fig. 24.1: Amputated penis. Distal part is replaced by fungating growth (↓).

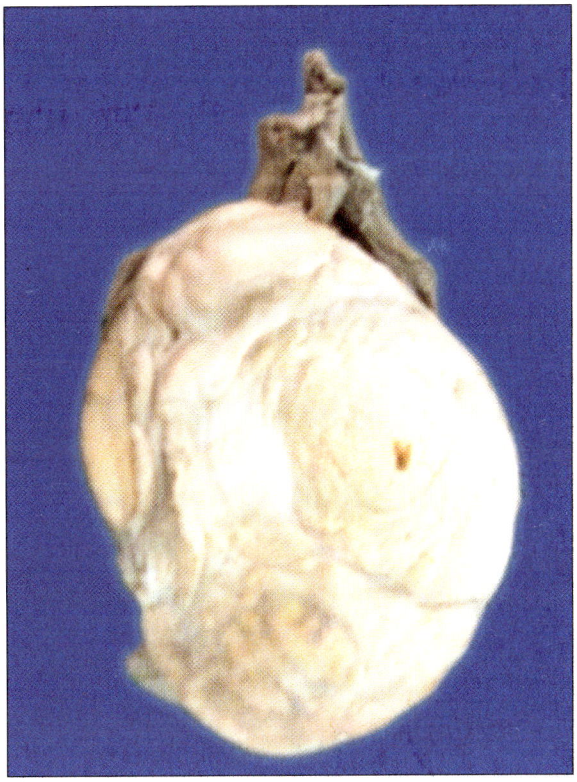

Fig. 24.2: Seminoma testis. Homogenous cut surface.

TESTICULAR TUMOURS

Testis is usually replaced by tumour, but is identified, by its ovoid shape which is maintained and by the spermatic cord attached at its upper pole. The external surface is covered by the glistening tunica. Grossly, testicular tumours can be differentiated into seminomas and nonseminomatous.

Seminoma

Seminomas which on cut surface are homogenous and greyish white, usually without haemorrhage or necrosis (Fig. 24.2).

Microscopically, the tumour is made up of monomorphic large polygonal cells with clear cytoplasm and central vesicular nucleus with prominent nucleolus. These cells are in sheets interspersed by thin fibrous septae infiltrated by lymphocytes (Fig. 24.3).

Nonseminomatous germ cell tumours

Nonseminomatous germ cell tumours (teratoma (Fig. 24.4), embryonal carcinoma, choriocarcinoma) which may be smaller and show variegated appearance, haemorrhage and necrosis (Fig. 24.4).

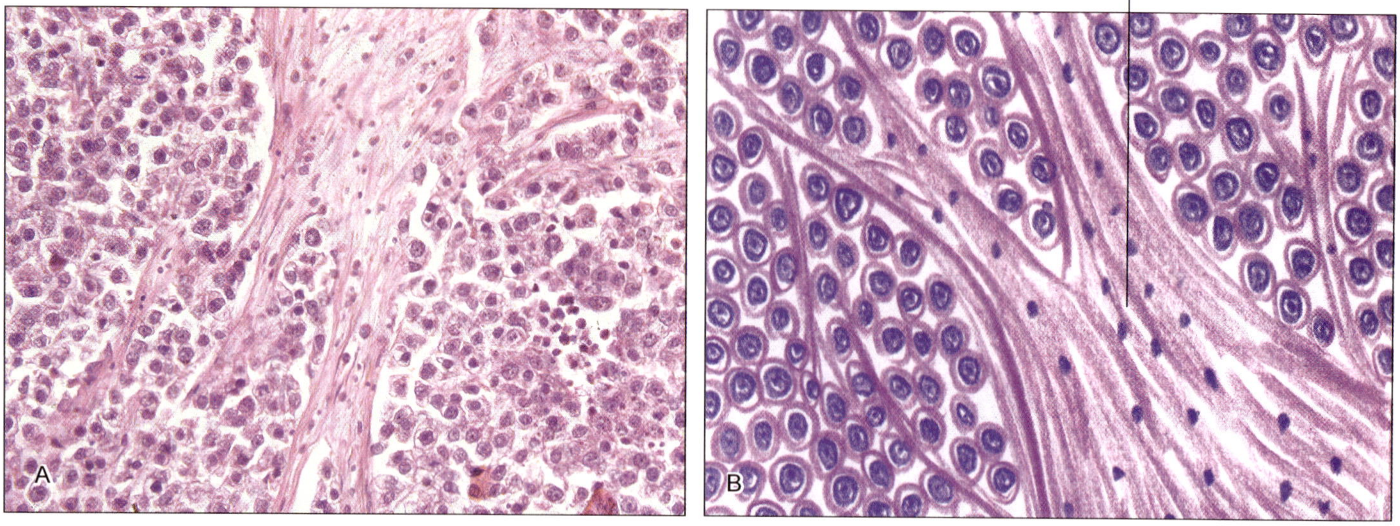

Fig. 24.3: A. and B. Seminoma testis showing large germ cells and septae with lymphocytes; Seminoma cells are large with clear cytoplasm.

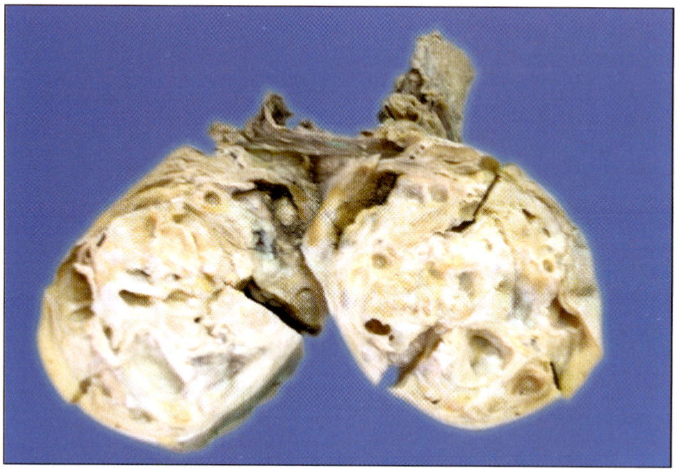

Fig. 24.4: Teratoma testis. Note variegated cut surface.

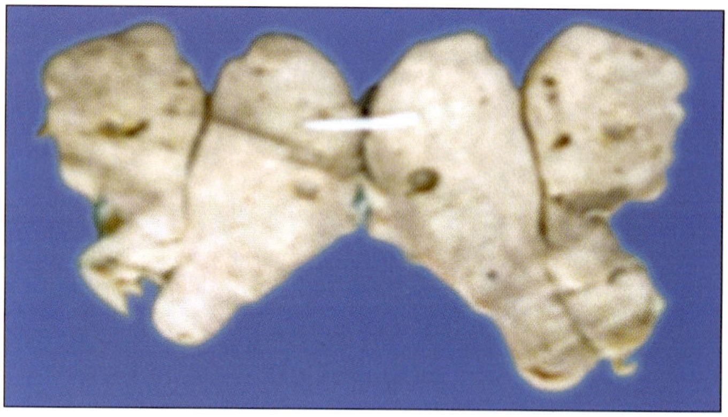

Fig. 24.5: Bisected specimen of nodular hyperplasia of prostate. Note nodularity and cribriform appearance.

Nodular hyperplasia of prostate

Prostate gland is identified by the 2 major lateral lobes. The lobes are enlarged and nodular on external and cut surface. Nodules vary from firm, greyish white fasciculated (when predominantly fibromuscular) to soft pink with cribriform to microcystic areas (when predominantly glandular) (Fig. 24.5).

Microscopically tissue is identified by close admixture of the fibro muscular component and the columnar mucus secreting glandular component. Nodules may have varying proportions of the 2 components – some nodules being totally fibromyomatous and others having predominantly glandular proliferation. Aggregates of small and large glands are seen, some dilated and containing corpora amylacea (eosinophilic inspissated secretions) and others thrown into papillary infoldings of the epithelium (Fig. 24.6). Lining columnar cells have small basal nuclei without nucleoli and are surrounded by a layer of flat cuboidal basal epithelium (features that help in differentiating it from carcinoma where the basal layer is absent and the lining cells, though monomorphic, show prominent nucleoli).

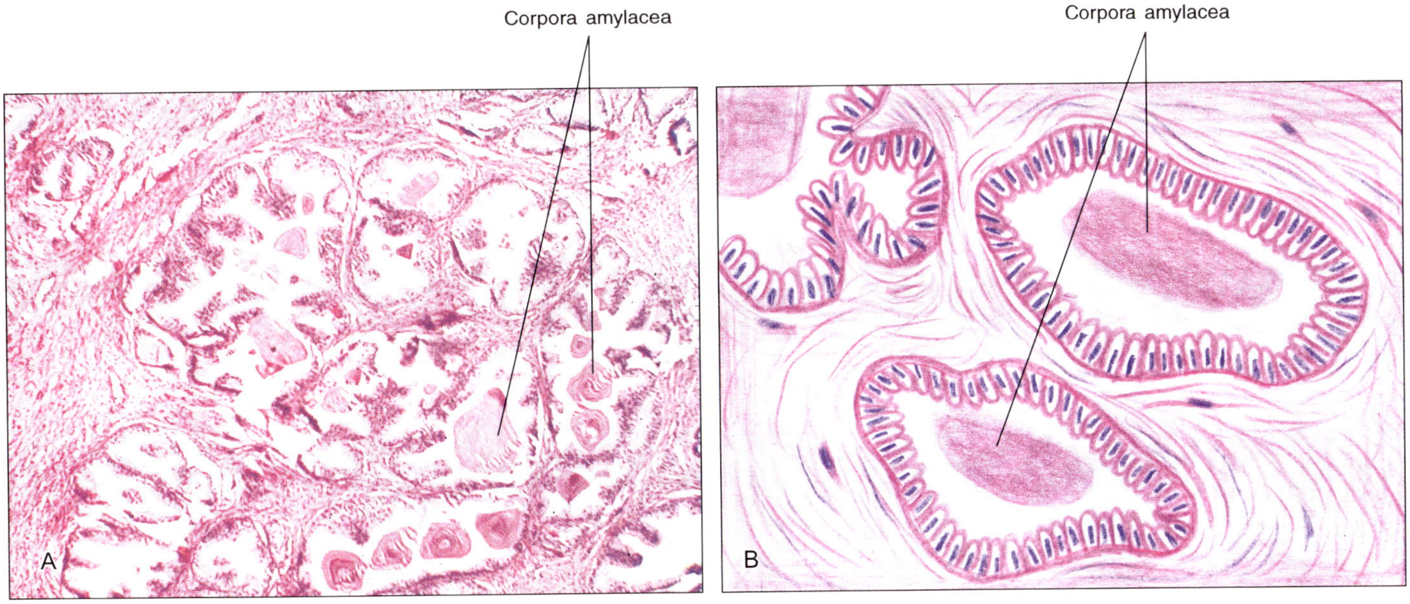

Fig. 24.6: A. and B. Nodular hyperplasia prostate showing nodules, hyperplastic glands and corpora amylacea inside gland lumina.

VIVA-VOCE

Q. Name the germ cell tumours of testis?
Ans. Seminoma, teratocarcinoma, choriocarcinoma and embryonal carcinoma.

Q. In seminoma testis, which lymphnodes are the site of metastasis?
Ans. Paraaortic lymph nodes are the sites of metastasis since lymphatics accompany the right and left testicular veins which open in inferior vena cava and left renal vein respectively.

Q. In carcinoma prostate, name the serum marker, which is helpful in diagnosis and assessing response to therapy?
Ans. Prostate specific antigen.

Q. What is the type of cancer of penis?
Ans. The commonest type is squamous cell carcinoma penis.

Q. Are testicular teratomas benign or malignant?
Ans. Testicular teratomas, by and large are malignant and most ovarian teratomas are benign.

Q. Name various tumor markers used in testicular tumors?
Ans. LDH levels indicate tumor load, AFP levels are increased in yolk sac tumor and HCG levels are increased in choriocarcinoma.

Q. What is the difference between seminomatous and nonseminomatous tumors of testis?
Ans. Seminoma is radiosensitive, remains localised, has good prognosis. Non-seminomatous tumors are aggressive require aggressive chemotherpy.

Q. What are the complications of undescended testis
Ans. Infertility and testicular malignancy

Q. Which tumour is commonest in testis of males over 60 years of age?
Ans. At this age, lymphoma is the commonest tumour.

Phyllodes tumour. This, on gross examination, is a nodular tumour, well circumscribed like a fibroadenoma, but much larger in size (around 10 cms or more) (Fig. 26.3). It is differentiated from a large fibroadenoma only on microscopic features.

Carcinoma breast

Tumour is usually seen on cut surface of the specimen as a greyish white hard to gritty lesion with irregular margins and greyish white streaks extending into surrounding tissue (Fig. 26.4). Some tumours may be mucoid. Larger tumours may show haemorrhage, necrosis, ulceration and fungation on skin etc. Nipple and areola may be ulcerated or retracted (Fig. 26.5).

Microscopic examination shows an infiltrating duct carcinoma, with cords and nests of malignant epithelial cells infiltrating the breast tissue. Cells are seen in sheets or clusters, with hyperchromatic nuclei, mitotic figures etc. (Fig. 26.6). Duct differentiation may or may not be seen. Areas of haemorrhage and necrosis may be seen. Foci of intraductal carcinoma (ducts filled with the malignant cells in cribriform, solid or comedo pattern – central necrosis) may be seen in the surrounding tissue. There may be fibrosis of the stroma (Fig. 26.6).

Fig. 26.4: Cut surface of carcinoma breast. Infiltrative growth seen involving most of the breast tissue. Cut section of nipple seen for identification

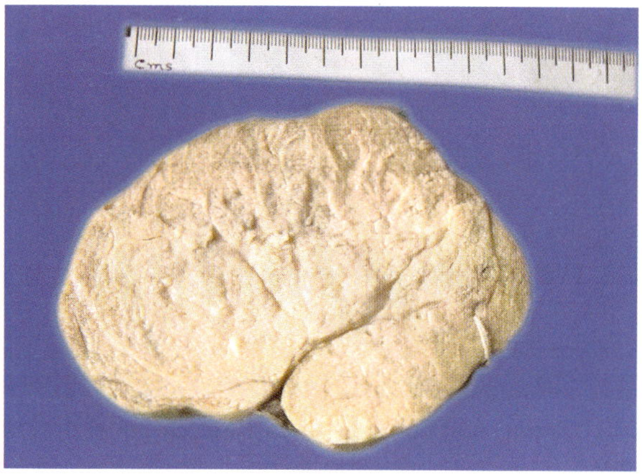

Fig. 26.3: Phyllodes tumour. It is much larger than fibroadenoma.

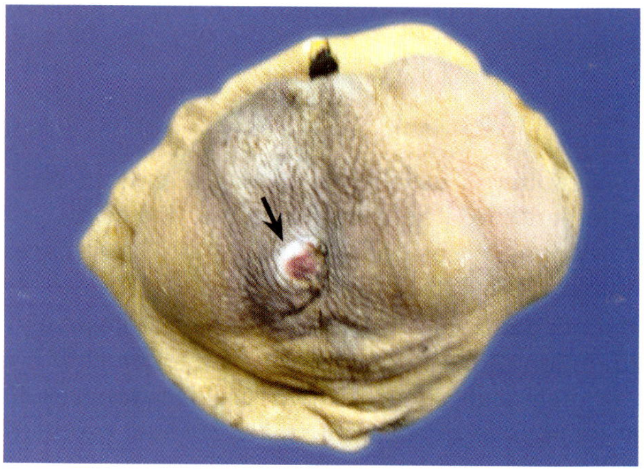

Fig. 26.5: Carcinoma breast ulcerating the skin and nipple (↑).

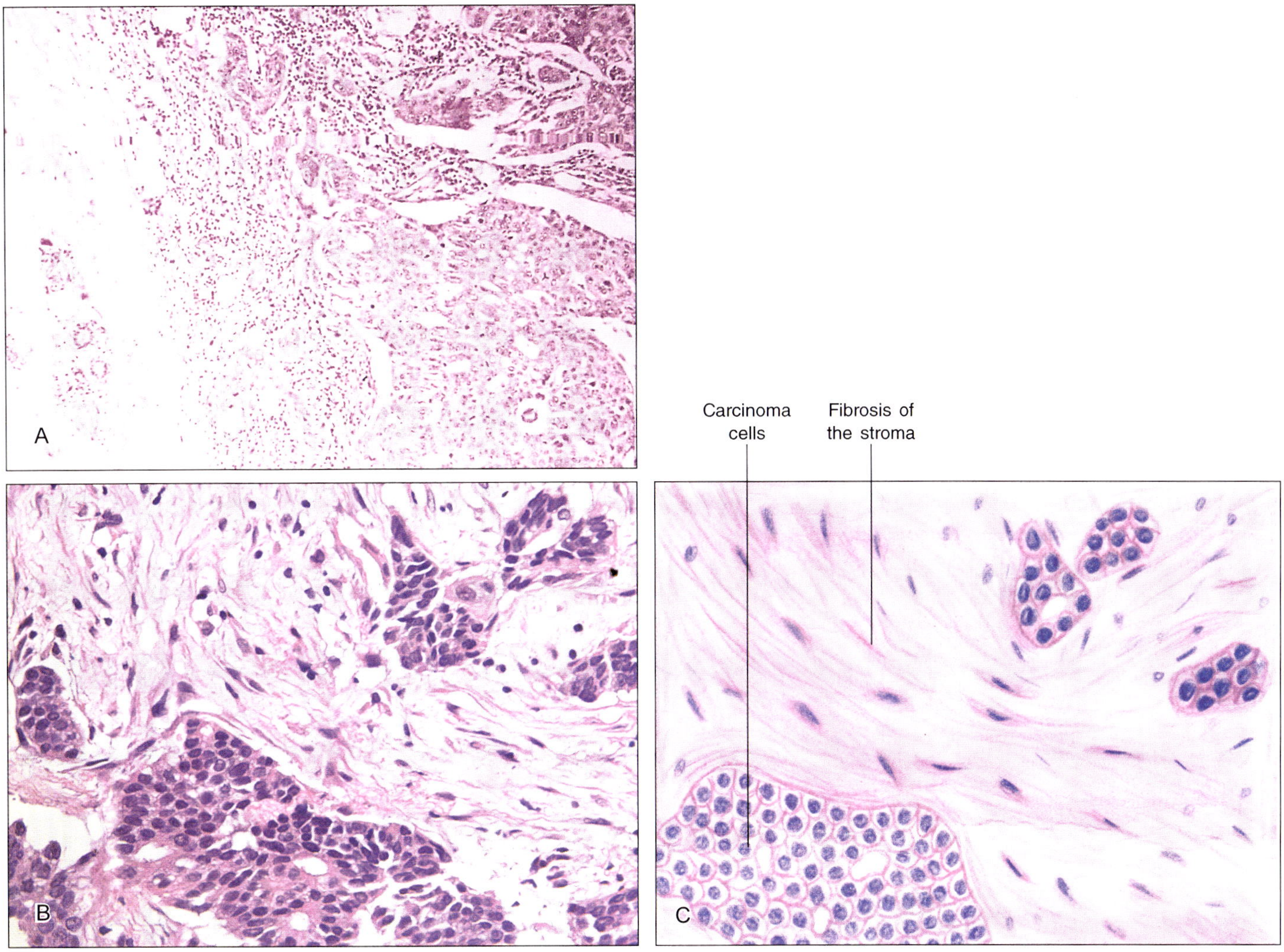

Fig. 26.6: (A) Infiltrating duct carcinoma breast. Note normal lobule on left and the carcinoma on right. (B) Infiltrating duct carcinoma breast shows cords of carcinoma cells with hyperchromatic nuclei and fibrosis of the stroma.

Infarct spleen

Splenic infarcts are pale infarcts which are roughly wedge shaped and pale, with a broad base on capsular surface and apex in the splenic pulp. Infarct may be bordered by a narrow hyperaemic dark zone separating it from the surrounding pulp (see Fig. 4.10). Infarcted area shows coagulative necrosis separated from normal area by a hyperaemic zone.

Amyloidosis spleen

Spleen is moderately to markedly enlarged. Amyloid may be deposited in the follicles giving a white speckled appearance ⟶ Sago spleen. Or it may deposit as irregular patches in the red pulp ⟶ Lardaceous spleen.

LYMPH NODES

Normal lymph node on microscopy shows a capsule, subcapsular sinuses, cortical lymphoid follicles (with pale germinal centres and peripheral mature cells), paracortical area (with T-lymphocytes) and the medulla (plasma cells, lymphocytes and sinuses) closer to the hilar region.

Tubercular lymphadenitis

The lymph node is enlarged. Several nodes may be matted together. Cut surface shows foci of caseous necrosis ⟶ cheesy (creamy white) colour and texture (Fig. 27.2). If the specimen is of hilar or tracheobronchial group, black deposits of anthracotic pigment may also be associated.

This is recognised microscopically by the presence of caseating epithelioid cell granulomas in identifiable lymph node tissue (Fig. 27.3).

Reactive hyperplasia

Lymph node shows varying degrees of 3 components:

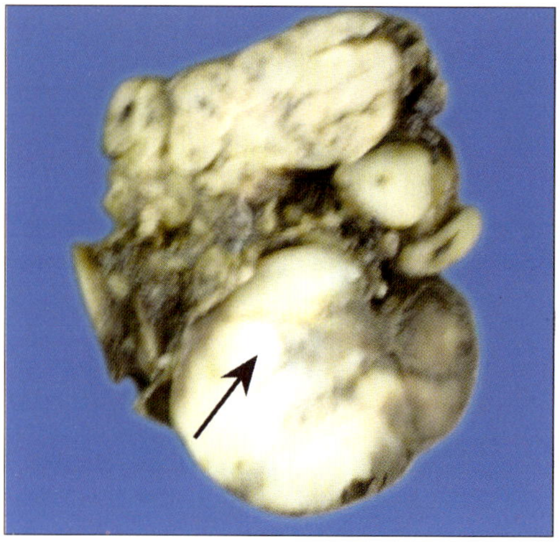

Fig. 27.2: Tubercular lymphadenitis – caseation (↗) seen on cut surface.

(a) activation of B cell response causing enlarged cortical lymphoid follicles with prominent germinal centres (Fig. 27.4);

(b) T cell response resulting in widening of paracortical area, and

(c) histiocytic response seen as widened lymphatic sinuses filled with reactive histiocytes. The important features to distinguish this from lymphoma are preservation of architecture of lymph node and a mixed population of the reactive cells (Fig. 27.4).

Lymphoma

Lymph nodes are enlarged and greyish white to fleshy in colour and texture. The whole group of nodes may be enlarged, seen as discrete nodes or as an adherent mass (Fig. 27.5).

The type of lymphoma can be identified only on microscopy, aided by Immunohistochemical markers.

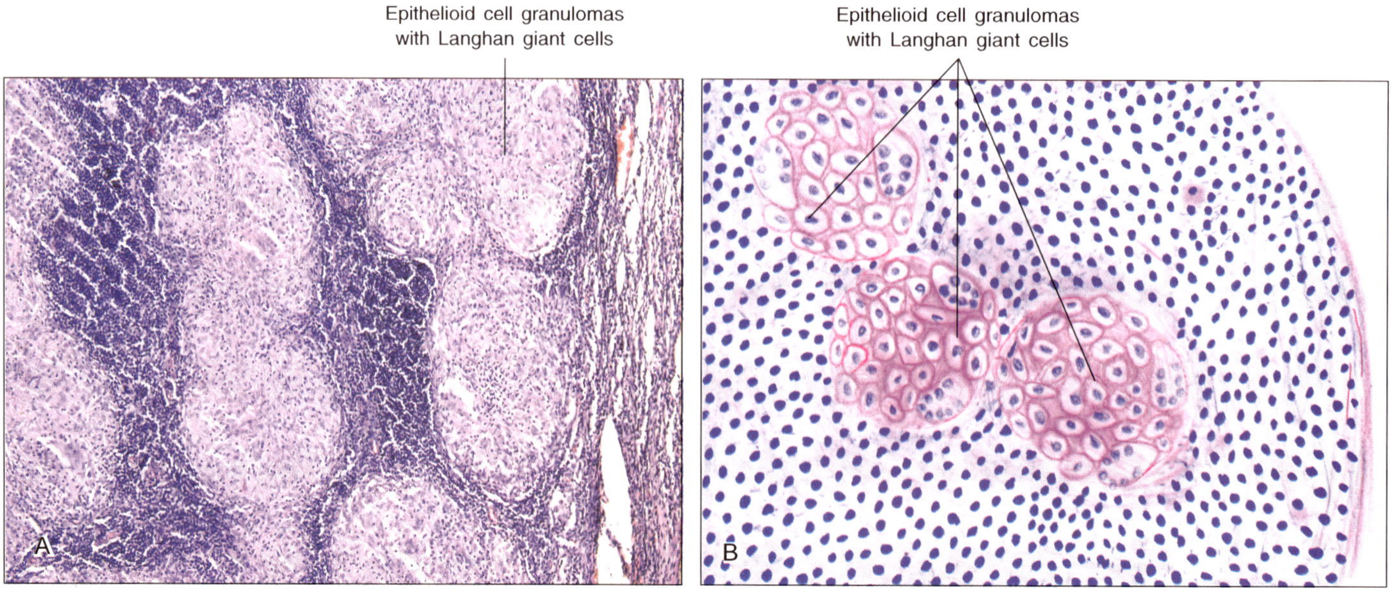

Fig. 27.3: A and B. Section from the lymphnode shows multiple epithelioid cell granulomas.

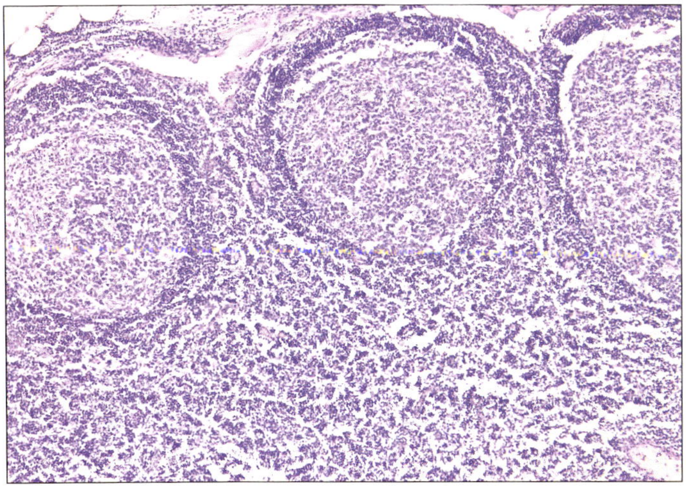

Fig. 27.4: Reactive lymphnode with prominent lymphoid follicles with pale germinal centres.

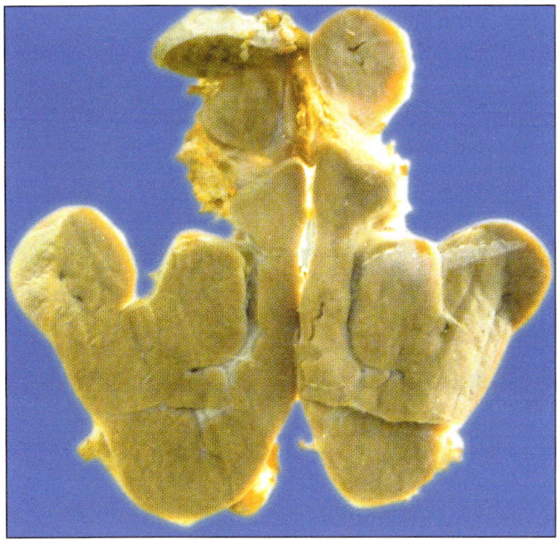

Fig. 27.5: Group of nodes showing lymphoma – fleshy cut surface.

Hodgkin lymphoma

The mixed cellularity type is most characteristic. Lymph node architecture is lost and is replaced by a mixed population of cells comprising of lymphocytes, histiocytes, plasma cells and eosinophils (Fig. 27.6). The diagnosis is based on identifying the Reed-Sternberg cells. R.S. cell is classically large with abundant amphophilic cytoplasm (Fig. 27.6). It has 2 large, vesicular nuclei which are mirror images of each other, with a large amphophilic nucleolus in each (owl eye appearance) (Fig. 27.6). Variations of R.S. cells, like bilobed, mononuclear variant, or having more than 2 nuclei can also be seen.

NonHodgkin lymphoma.

The normal architecture is lost and is replaced by a monomorphic population of cells, which may be uniformly small, resembling more mature lymphoid cells or large (Large cell lymphoma) representing stages in activation and maturation (Fig. 27.7).

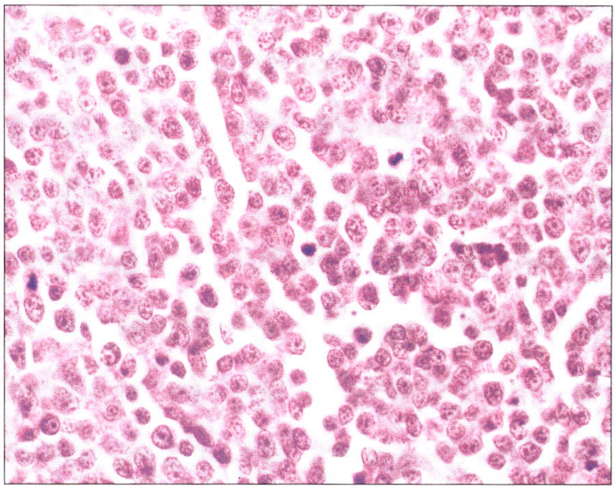

Fig. 27.7: Non-Hodgkin Lymphoma – architecture effaced by monomorphic cells.

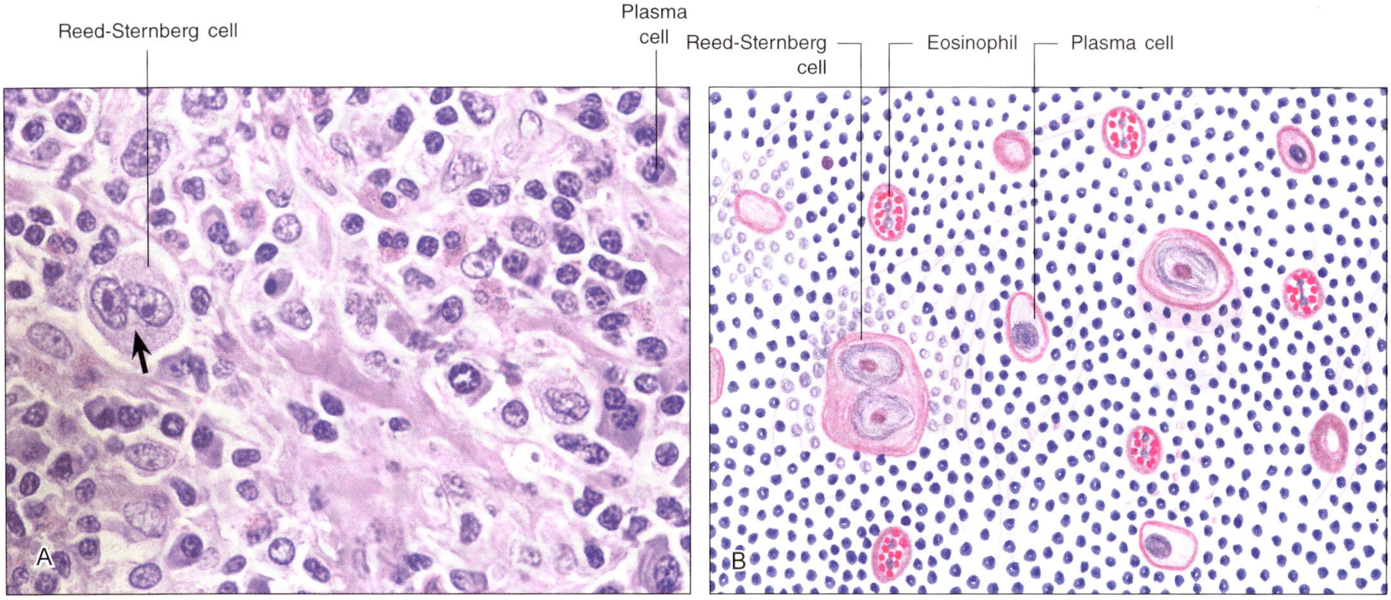

Fig. 27.6: A. and B. Hodgkin Lymphoma – R.S. cell ↙, in a background of lymphocytes, plasma cells, eosinophils and mononuclear variants.

VIVA-VOCE

Q. What is the commonest type of Hodgkin disease in India?
Ans. Mixed cellular type of Hodgkin is the commonest in India.

Q. Which is the commoner type of Non-Hodgkin lymphoma (NHL)?
Ans. B cell-NHLs are commoner than T-NHLs

Q. What is the genetic abnormality in follicular lymphomas?
Ans. t(14; 18) translocation is the common abnormality in follicular NHLs.

Q. In which disease, Gamna-Gandy bodies are seen in the spleen?
Ans. Gamna-Gandy nodules are seen in chronic venous congestion spleen.

Q. What are the causes of massive splenomegaly?
Ans. Chronic myeloid leukemia
Kala-azar
Malaria
Gaucher's disease
Myelofibrosis

Q. What are Lacunar cells?
Ans. Lacunar cells are variants of Reed-Sternberg cells seen in "nodular sclerosis" type of Hodgkin disease.

Q. In which Non-Hodgkin lymphoma is a starry sky appearance seen?
Ans. Burkitt lymphoma.

Q. Name lymphomas associated with HIV infection?
Ans.
- Hodgkin lymphoma
- Burkitt lymphoma
- Diffuse large B cell lymphoma
- Primary effusion lymphoma
- Body cavity large cell lymphoma

Q. Which Hodgkin lymphoma has the best prognosis?
Ans. Nodular sclerosis type

Q. Which Hodgkin lymphoma has the worst prognosis?
Ans. Mixed cellularity type, lymphocyte depletion type.

Q. What is the genetic abnormality in Burkitt hymphoma?
Ans. t (8; 14) t (2; 8) and t (8; 22) are common abnormalities in Burkitt's lymphoma.

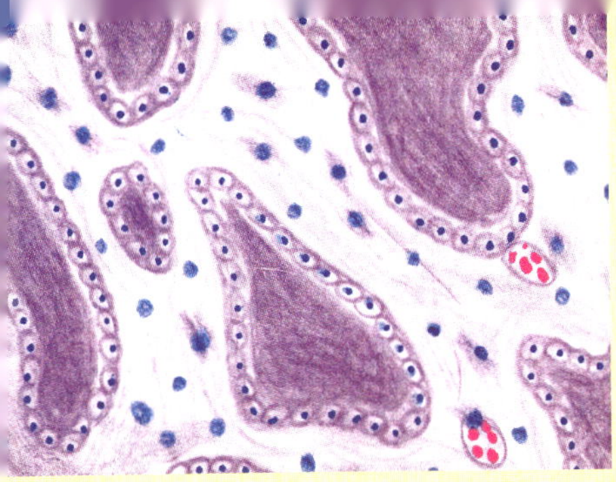

28

Thyroid

ORGAN IDENTIFICATION

Thyroid is a bilobed organ with the lobes connected by isthmus. It has a smooth external surface covered by a thin transparent capsule. Cut surface is uniformly glistening and tan coloured.

Microscopically, the gland is made up of acini lined by cuboidal cells and containing pale eosinophilic staining thyroglobulin. In the normal state, the acini vary little in morphology and the interstitium is minimal.

Nodular Goitre

Both lobes of thyroid are enlarged with nodular external surface, often asymetrically. Cut surface shows nodules of varying sizes and textures. Some are glistening and dark tan while others may be more solid and paler. Fibrosis and calcification may be seen (Fig. 28.1).

Microscopy shows the effects of repeated cycles of hyperplasia and involution. Nodules may show large dilated acini with flat cuboidal epithelium and thick colloid as well as acini with low columnar lining and thin colloid with peripheral scalloping. The acini vary greatly in size (Fig. 28.2). Interstitium shows fibrosis. Organising haemorrhage with cholesterol clefts and hemosiderin laden macrophages as well as foci of calcification may be seen.

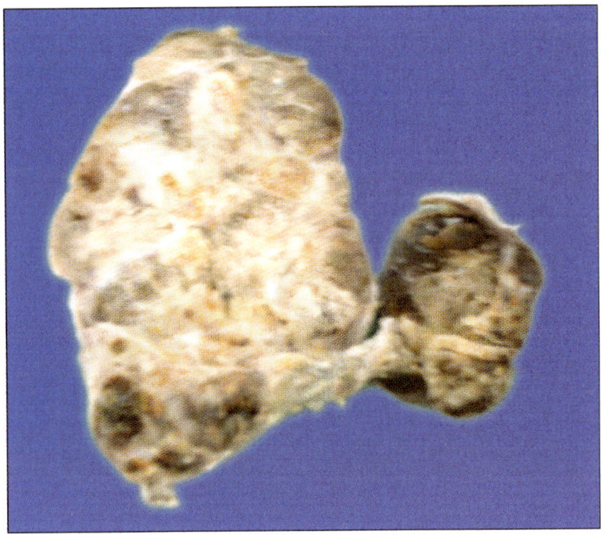

Fig. 28.1: Multinodular goitre. Note nodularity, asymmetrical enlargement and colloid filled cysts.

Solitary thyroid nodule

Though occasionally a goitre with a dominant hyperplastic nodule may present as a solitary nodule, majority of solitary nodules are neoplastic. On cut surface they are well circumscribed greyish white (or grayish tan if colloid is present), and well delineated from the surrounding normal thyroid (Fig. 28.3). It is not always possible to differentiate adenoma from carcinoma unless frank infiltrative edges are seen.

Papillary carcinoma

Tumour nodule shows acini with complex papillae. Cells are columnar with water clear to ground glass nuclei with nuclear grooves (infoldings). Small round foci of calcification (psammoma bodies) may be seen in the papillae. At the margins, tumour is seen to infiltrate between surrounding acini (Fig. 28.4).

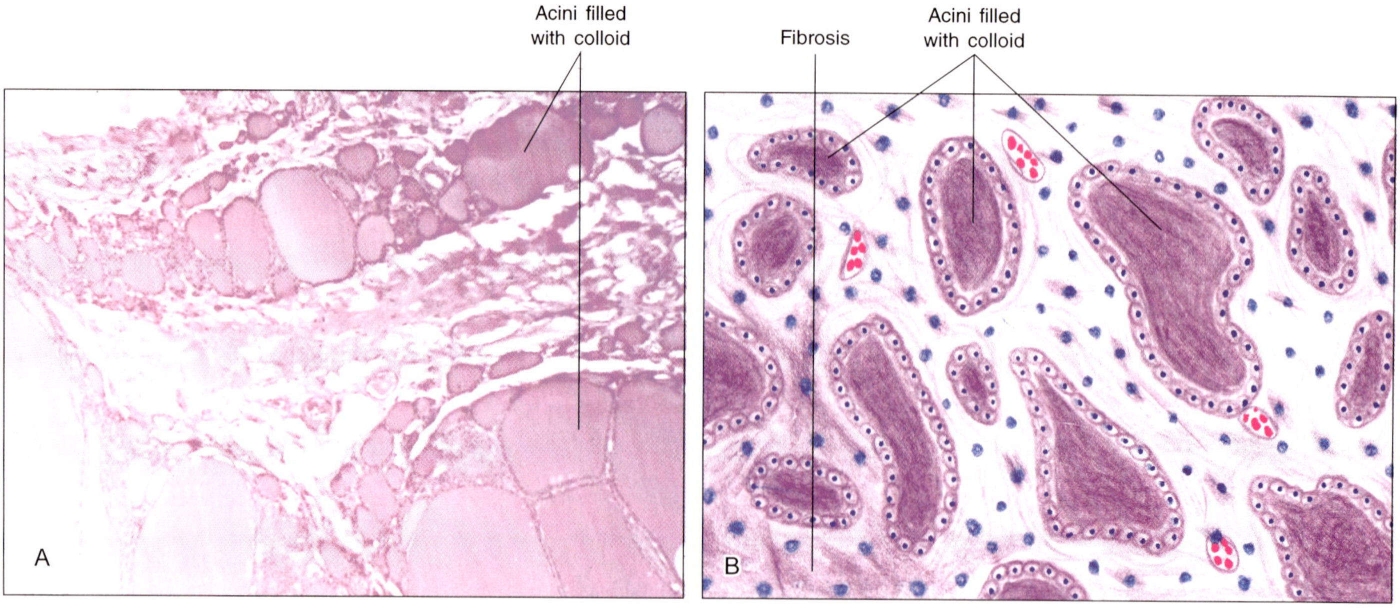

Fig. 28.2: A. and B. Nodular goitre with marked variation in size of acini and intervening fibrosis.

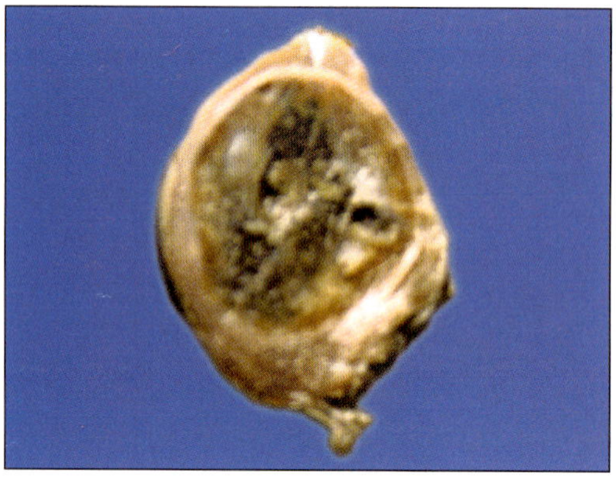

Fig. 28.3: Solitary thyroid nodule.

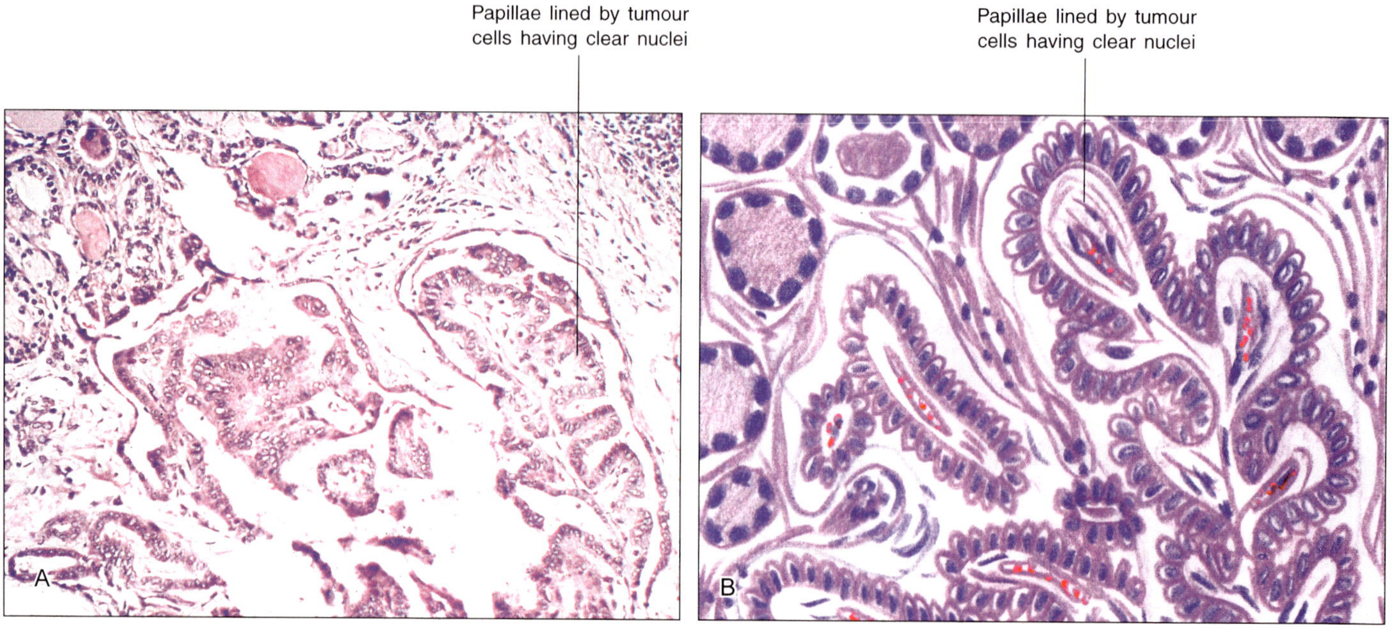

Fig. 28.4: Papillary carcinoma thyroid infiltrating surrounding acini. Note papillae and clear nuclei.

Hashimoto thyroiditis

The characteristic feature is extensive lymphoid infiltration with lymphoid follicle formation and destruction of acini, which are fewer and smaller (Fig. 28.5). The acinar cells show Hurthle cell change – cellular enlargement with abundant dense pink cytoplasm and vesicular nucleus (Fig. 28.5).

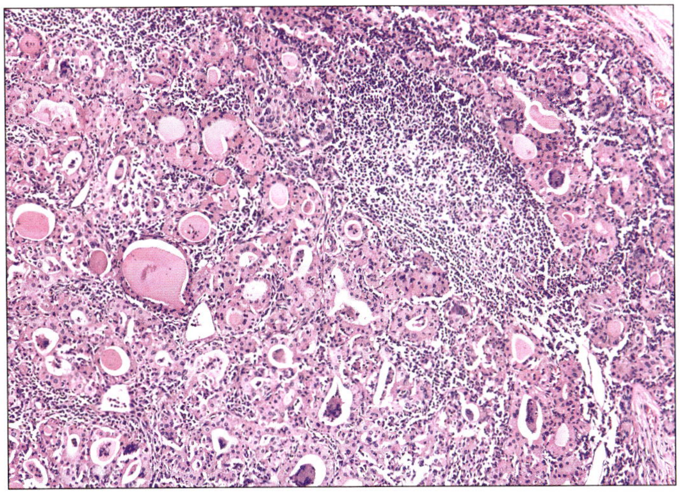

Fig. 28.5: Hashimoto thyroiditis. Section shows lymphoid infiltration with formation of lymphoid follicles. Acini are fewer and smaller. Acinar cells are large with pink cytoplasm-Hurthle cell change.

VIVA-VOCE

Q. What is the commonest malignant tumour of thyroid?
Ans. The commonest malignant tumour is Papillary carcinoma thyroid which has good prognosis.

Q. Which thyroid tumour demonstrates amyloid deposition in the tumour?
Ans. Medullary carcinoma thyroid, originating from C-cells of thyroid demonstrates amyloid secreted by tumour cells.

Q. Name the tumours in which Psammoma bodies are seen?
Ans. Psammoma bodies are seen in
(a) Papillary carcinoma thyroid and
(b) Papillary adenocarcinoma ovary (serous type)
(c) Meningioma - psammomatous type

Q. How do papillary carcinoma thyroid and follicular carcinoma thyroid spread?
Ans. Papillary carcinoma thyroid - lymphatic route
Follicular carcinoma thyroid - vascular route

Q. How can diagnosis of Hashimoto thyroiditis be made?
Ans. (a) By FNAC
(d) High levels of thyroid microsomal antibodies
(c) Presence of anti-TSH receptor antibodies
(b) Presence of antibodies to thyroid peroxidase (TPO).

Q. What are the microscopic features of Hashimoto thyroiditis?
Ans. Lymphoid aggregates with acinar destruction and Hurthle cell change.

Q. What nuclear features are seen in Papillary Carcinoma Thyroid?
Ans. Nuclei have finely dispersed nuclear chromatin, with optically clear appearance (Orphan Annie eye nuclei); intranuclear pseudoinclusions and nuclear grooves.

Q. What is Graves disease?
Ans. It is an organ specific auto immune disorder due to autoantibodies to TSH receptor.

Scanned

Marksheet
photo
Id card
Signature

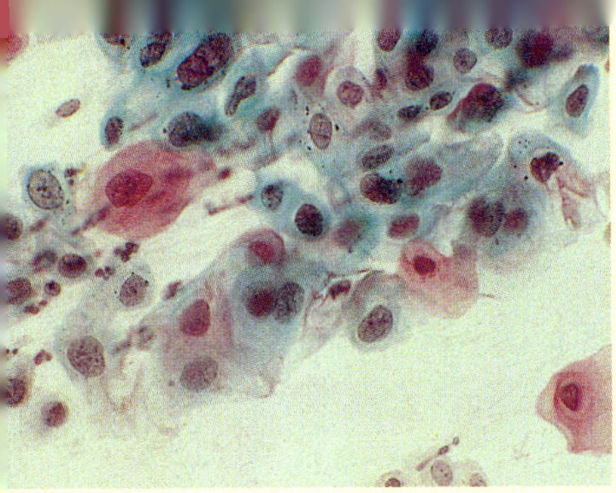

30

Cytopathology

Cytology is the study of shed off cells which are obtained from various body cavities, mucosal surfaces and cells obtained from various organs/masses by needle aspiration (FNAC). Therefore it involves:

(a) Exfoliative cytology
(b) Aspiration cytology.

EXFOLIATIVE CYTOLOGY

Cells lining the pleural, peritoneal and other cavities and surface epithelia are being shed off and more so in cases of malignancy where there is loss of cohesion of cells. Study of these cells helps in diagnosing various disease states, dysplasia and malignancy.

Sites where exfoliated cells are studied:

- Body fluids – pleural, peritoneal, peri-cardial and synovial fluids.
- Surface epithelia:
  - cervix
  - vagina
  - oral cavity
  - respiratory tract
  - urinary tract
  - gastrointestinal tract
- Buccal smear (and peripheral blood smear) for sex chromatin.

PLEURAL FLUID EXAMINATION

Pleural effusion is observed in many pulmonary parenchymal diseases like tuberculosis, lung carcinoma, metastatic lung deposits, pneumonias, lung abscess, and pulmonary ameobiasis. Pleural fluid in inflammatory and neoplastic diseases is an exudate while in non-inflammatory conditions like congestive heart failure, the fluid is a transudate.

Collection of pleural fluid

Patient is made to sit and the dull area on percussion is made out; the area is cleaned with alcohol and iodine and under aseptic conditions, pleural fluid is collected using a 19G needle with a syringe after injecting xylocaine into the skin. About 10 ml of fluid is collected in an anticoagulant like heparin - 30 units for 10 ml fluid for diagnostic purposes. 4 ml is sent for biochemical analysis like proteins, specific gravity etc., 1 ml of fluid is taken for cell count i.e. 0.04 ml of fluid is added to 0.4 ml of WBC (Turk's) fluid and cell count is carried out. Remaining 5 ml is used for cytological examination.

Cytology of pleural fluid

5 ml of fluid is centrifuged at 2500 rpm for 30 minutes. Supernatant can be kept for any other test, if required. Deposit after centrifugation is collected, placed on a slide and spread over it.

Fixation

The slide is dipped in a mixture of ethanol-ether for 30 minutes to fix the deposit for Pap staining and in methanol (after air-drying) for Giemsa staining.

Staining

Fixed slide is stained with Papanicolaou's stain – the stain of choice. Hematoxylin and eosin and Giemsa stain can also be carried out.

Papanicolaou (Pap) staining

Procedure

(a) Take the fixed smears and hydrate them through 80%, 70%, 50% alcohol to distilled water.
(b) Place the smears in Harris' Hematoxylin solution for 4 minutes.

(c) Wash in running tap water.
(d) Dehydrate upto 95% ethyl alcohol.
(e) Stain the slides with OG-6 (Orange-G) solution for 1-4 minutes.
(f) Rinse the slide 10 times in 95% alcohol.
(g) Stain in EA-36 (Eosin-A) solution for 2-4 minutes.
(h) Rinse the slide in 3 jars containing 95% alcohol.
(i) Dehydrate, clear and mount the slide.

Malignant cells, if present, are characterized by anisonucleosis, hyperchromatic nuclei with 1-2 prominent nucleoli. Some of the cells are pleomorphic. Cells show squamoid characters, malignant squamous pearls, anucleated squamous cells and tadpole cells in squamous cell carcinoma. Adenoid pattern is seen in adenocarcinoma. Investigate the patient further to confirm whether the patient has primary/metastatic cancer in the lung.

Ascitic fluid: Ascitic fluid is processed as the pleural fluid and can be examined for malignant cells.

LATERAL VAGINAL WALL SMEAR

These smears are suitable for cytohormonal assessment. The material is obtained from the lateral vaginal wall (using Ayre's spatula) (Fig. 30.1) and are preferable to posterior fornix pool smears.

Fixation

Smears are fixed when they are wet. Any of the following fixatives may be used:

- 95% alcohol in a coplin jar;
- a mixture of 95% alcohol + ether (equal parts); or
- spray fixative.

Staining

Papanicolaou stain.

Fig. 30.1: Ayre's spatula to take material from lateral vaginal wall/cervix.

Results

Superficial cells – mature, polygonal, eosinophilic cytoplasm with pyknotic nuclei.

Intermediate cells – polygonal squamous cells with eosinophilic/cyanophilic cytoplasm with vesicular nucleus as differentiated from superficial cells.

Basal-parabasal cells – Small, oval, squamous cells, cyanophilic cytoplasm with large vesicular nuclei.

Study of lateral vaginal wall smears and the respective ratio of basal-parabasal cells/intermediate cells/superficial cells (K.P. index) is useful in assessing ovulatory/anovulatory cycles.

CERVICAL SMEAR

Cervical smears are made from cervical os using an Ayre's spatula (wooden/plastic) (Fig. 30.1) which is rotated through 360° to get the material from exocervix and squamocolumnar junction (Fig. 30.2). The material obtained on the Ayre's spatula is smeared on glass slides. Smears are fixed and stained by Pap stain.

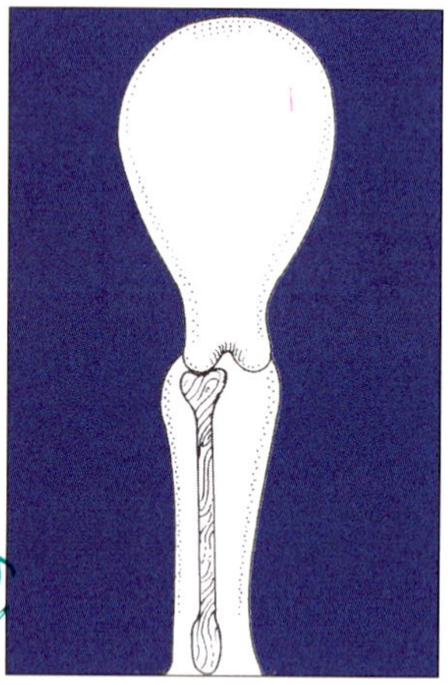

Fig. 30.2: Method of taking cervical smear.

Dysplastic cells

These cells are seen singly and have clear-cut cell borders. Cell size is almost similar to normal cell. Nuclear morphology is the hallmark – nuclear enlargement with irregular outline and chromatin condensation.

Malignant cells in squamous cell cercinoma cervix

Cells are discrete and smaller than the normal ones. Cells with rounded border are predominant. Nucleus is enlarged with coarsely irregular nuclear chromatin (Fig. 30.3).

Cytoplasm is eosinophilic in tadpole shaped cells and sometimes keratin pearl is present. Elongated and bizarre shaped malignant cells are often seen.

OTHER BODY FLUIDS AND SPECIMENS

- **Peritoneal fluid** is obtained by tapping of ascites.
- **Sputum** may be collected after deep morning cough and solid particles/blood specked areas are smeared over slides. Useful in cases of primary and metastatic malignancies of lung.

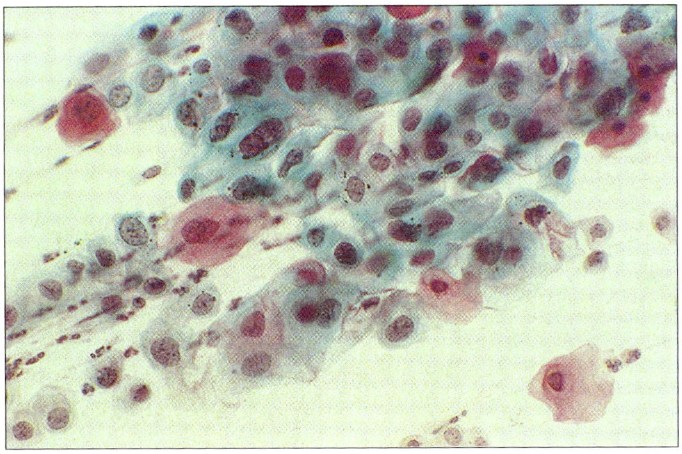

Fig. 30.3: Cervical smear showing malignant squamous cells in a case of carcinoma cervix.

- **CSF** is obtained by lumbar puncture, and *cytospin* preparation is made.
- **Endoscopic brushings** from bronchi/stomach are subjected to cytospin for deposit.
- **Urine centrifugation** in suspected bladder, and kidney malignancies. The deposit is stained and examined.

BUCCAL SMEAR FOR BARR BODY

Method

- Patient is made to have a mouthwash.
- With a thin wooden spatula, inner surface of the cheek is scraped and the material over the spatula is smeared on glass slides.
- Smears are fixed in ether-alcohol mixture.
- Papanicolaou's staining is carried out.

Result

Examine under oil immersion objective lens for a Barr body which is seen as a solitary condensation on nuclear membrane in the intermediate buccal cells (Fig. 30.4). There is one Barr body per nucleus in 20-80% of the cells in a normal female. In XXX female, 2 Barr bodies are observed while in *Turner Syndrome*-XO – Barr body is not visualised. In *Klinefelter syndrome*, XXY, Barr body is present in males.

Peripheral smear neutrophils can also be examined for drumsticks in the neutrophils (Fig. 30.4).

LEUCOCYTES - NUCLEAR SEXING

Anomalies of sex chromosomes can be diagnosed by nuclear sexing. Cells of the buccal mucosa demonstrate a Barr body. In the neutrophils, one X-chromosome is visualised as a *drumstick* in a normal (XX) female, but not in males. Absence of drumstick is encountered in *Turner Syndrome* (XO), while one drumstick is discerned in *Klinefelter Syndrome* in males (XXY).

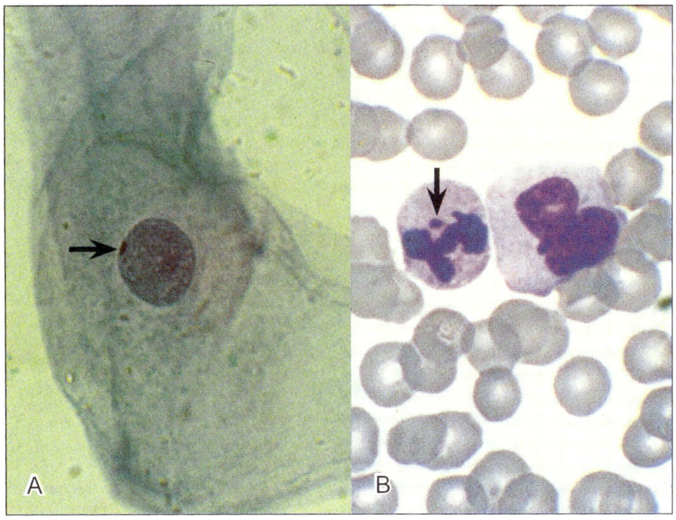

Fig. 30.4: (A) Buccal smear showing Barr body. (B) Neutrophil showing "drumstick".

Method

1. Make 2 peripheral blood smears, and air dry.
2. Fix them in methanol and stain with Giemsa stain.
3. Scan the smear with an oil immersion objective.
4. "Drumstick" is seen as 1.5 micron round to oval nuclear material attached to nucleus by a thin thread like stalk as shown in Fig. 30.4.
5. Examine at least 100 neutrophils. In a normal female at least 5-7 drumsticks are visualised.

FINE NEEDLE ASPIRATION CYTOLOGY (FNAC)

In FNAC, a thin bore needle (22G/23G) is introduced into an organ and small amount of tissue/cells is aspirated. Aspirated material is spread on the slide using a coverslip and smears are stained with Giemsa/Pap stain.

FNAC of thyroid nodule (Fig. 30.5)

Steps

- Examine the patient.
- Localize the thyroid nodule to be aspirated.

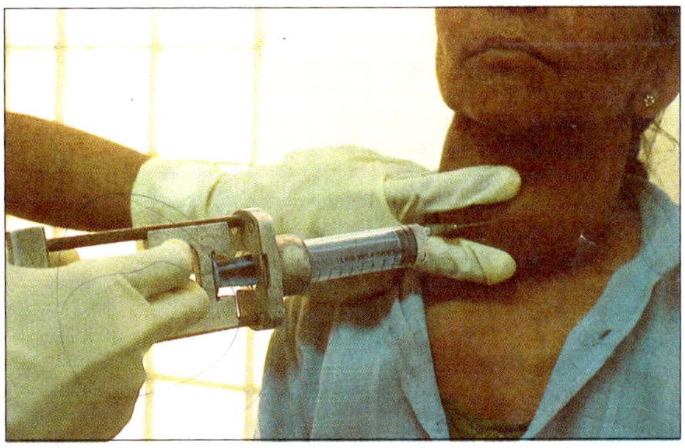

Fig. 30.5: Technique of FNAC of thyroid using a Franzen's syringe holder.

- Clean the overlying skin with alcohol.
- Fix the thyroid nodule with fingers of one hand.
- Introduce the needle of the 20 ml syringe preferably fixed in Franzen's syringe holder.
- Move the needle back and forth 1-3 mm to soften the tissue.
- Apply suction and minimal aspirate may be visible in the hub of the needle. Release suction.
- Withdraw the syringe with needle.
- Seal the puncture site.
- Disconnect the needle from the syringe and fill syringe with air, reconnect the needle and blow out the material in the needle onto a slide.
- Make smears of the material using a coverslip.
- Fix the smears in methanol for 10 minutes and stain with Giemsa stain.
- (If blood is aspirated, stop the procedure. Another site in the mass may be tried with a new needle and syringe.)

Common sites for FNAC

- lymph nodes
- breast
- salivary glands
- thyroid
- soft tissue masses
- kidney, liver, intraabdominal masses under ultrasound/ CT guidance.

FNAC of Tuberculous lymphadenitis

Smears are cellular with multiple epithelioid cell granulomas – showing epithelioid cells with oblong nuclei and abundant pale cytoplasm (Fig. 30.6) and Langhan's type of giant cells. Background demonstrates lymphocytes and acellular necrotic – (caseous) material. At times, reactive lymphocytes are present in the backround.

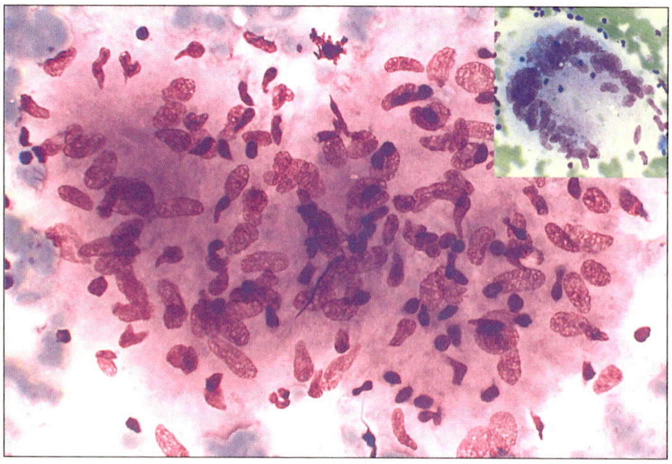

Fig. 30.6: FNAC lymphnode showing epithelioid cell granuloma with Langhan's type of giant cell (inset) in a case of tuberculous lymphadenitis.

FNAC of Fibroadenoma breast

Smears are cellular with clusters of benign ductal cells arranged as finger like projections, bipolar naked nuclei and stromal fragments showing loose connective tissue (Fig. 30.7).

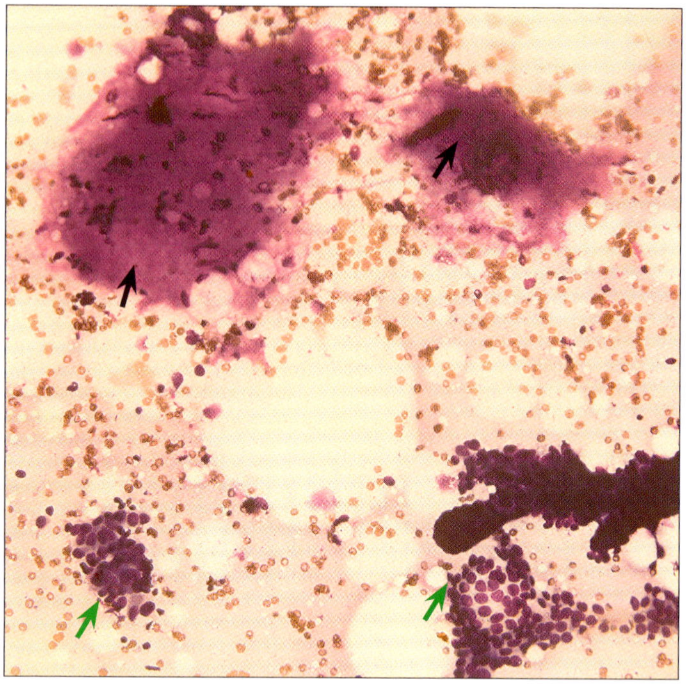

Fig. 30.7: FNAC from fibrodenoma breast showing metachromatically stained stromal fragment (↑) and scattered ductal cells (↑).

Infiltrating duct carcinoma breast

FNAC smears are very cellular and clusters of loosely cohesive malignant cells of variable size and shape are present. Cells are larger than ductal cells and demonstrate high nuclear: cytoplasmic ratio, coarse nuclear chromatin with prominent nucleoli. The background may be haemorrhagic, or clear or show necrotic material (Fig. 30.8).

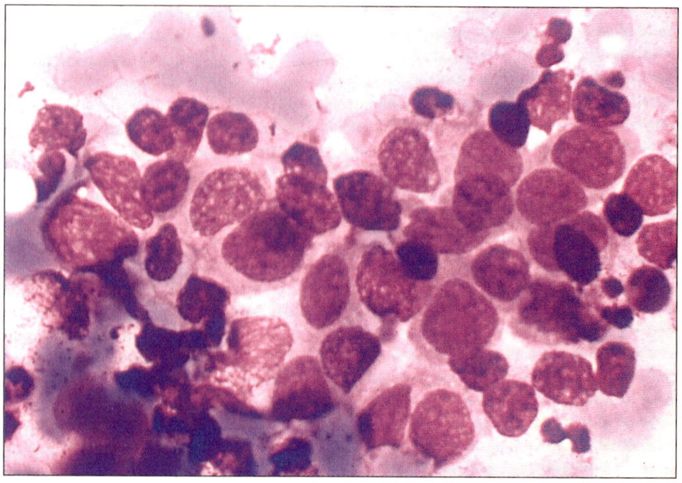

Fig. 30.8: FNAC of breast carcinoma demonstrating loosely cohesive malignant cells with high N/C ratio and coarse nuclear chromatin.

VIVA VOCE

Q. What are the indications for buccal smear?

Ans. In suspected cases of Klinefelter syndrome (XXY), Turner syndrome (XO) and superfemales (XXX). It is also used for sex defining in children with ambiguous external genitalia.

Q. What is the use of Pap smear?

Ans.
- Smears made from posterior vaginal pool are used for hormonal assessment in which superficial, intermediate and basal-parabasal cells are counted and their ratio to one another assessed.
- Cervical scrape smears are useful for diagnosis and screening of women for cervical dysplasia and early cervical cancer.

Q. What stains are carried out on the FNAC smears?

Ans. Giemsa stain, Pap stain and Hematoxylin and eosin are the usual stains carried out.

Q. How is the Pap smear taken from cervix? What are the indications?

Ans. Smear is taken from squamocolumnar junction of cervix, using an Ayre's spatula. It is indicated in suspected cases of carcinoma cervix and non-healing ulcer cervix (to look for dysplasia) and as a screening test for CIN in women over 40 years.

Q. How are dysplastic cells made out in a Pap smear?

Ans. Dysplastic cells have a much higher N:C ratio which steadily increases as dysplasia progresses from mild to severe. Also, nuclear irregularity and chromatin clumping are present.

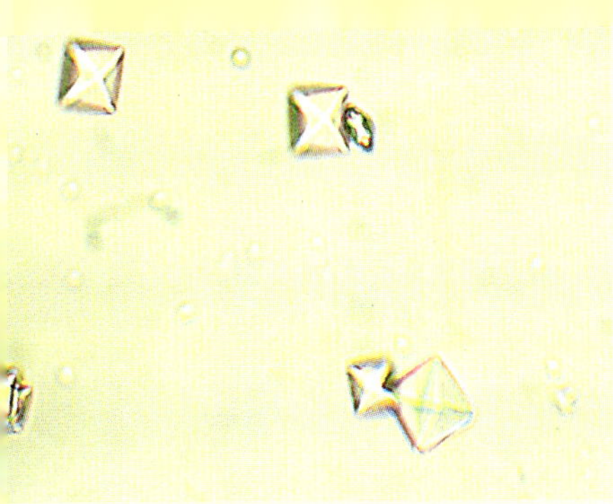

31

Urine Examination

Kidneys play an important role in elimination of excess body water, waste products of metabolism like urea, creatinine uric acid, and regulation of electrolyte balance and osmotic pressure of body fluids. Nephron is the functional unit of the kidney and there are more than one million nephrons in each kidney. Blood, while passing through the glomerulus, filters off many substances into the Bowman's space. In the tubules, there is reabsorption of substances and water and also secretion of certain substances resulting in formation of urine which passes from tubules into the pelvis of kidney and thence into the urinary bladder.

Analysis of urine reflects the state of the function of kidneys and also of the urinary tract. Urine examination should precede all other invasive/non-invasive diagnostic investigations for renal function.

Collection of Urine Specimen

Urine should be collected in a clean, dry and, preferably, sterilized container. The female patient is instructed to separate labia with one hand and urethral opening is cleaned with a moist cotton swab. She is asked to void urine and the first 10-25 ml of urine is not collected (discarded) and the remaining urine is collected in a clean container. In males, glans and meatal opening is cleaned with a cotton swab and urine is collected in the same way as in females. The first few mls of urine is discarded since it contains urethral and prostatic secretions which may be required if investigating urethra and prostate. *First morning samples* are preferred since these are the concentrated samples and casts, crystals etc. if present, are easily demonstrable.

Preservation of Urine

Urine sample should be examined within 2 hours. If delay is likely to occur, then sample needs preservation.

(a) Keep the sample in the **refrigerator** without any preservative.

(b) **Toluene** – Add a few drops till it forms a thin layer on the surface of urine.

(c) **Conc. HCl** – 1 ml of conc. HCl for 125-150 ml of urine.

(d) **Formaldehyde** – 1 drop for 15 ml of urine. Cells and casts are well preserved.

PHYSICAL EXAMINATION

Colour

Normal urine is amber coloured due to the presence of urochrome pigments i.e. urobilinogen. Urine may be **almost colourless** when it is very dilute, **smoky** because of red blood cells, **cola coloured** due to hemoglobin in PNH, PCH, **orange-brown** due to urobilin and **yellow** due to bilirubin. In alkaptonuria, urine becomes **dark coloured on standing** due to the presence of homogentistic acid. Concentrated urine sample may be **deep orange** in colour. Urine may be **milky** due to pus or chyle (chyluria).

Volume

In normal adults, 24-hour urinary collection is 600-2400 ml. In infants, the volume is 300-600 ml/day. Volume is measured by collecting 24-hour urine samples in a measuring cylinder.

Polyuria (increased volume, more than 2.5 litres in 24 hours) is observed in cases of excessive fluid intake, diuretic therapy, chronic kidney disease, diabetes insipidus, mental disorders, diabetes mellitus and primary aldosteronism.

Oliguria (decreased volume, less than 500 ml in 24 hours) indicates reduced renal secretory activity as in dehydration due to diminished intake, excessive loss, renal insufficiency, shock, burns, crush syndrome and lower nephron nephrosis.

Anuria is the term used when the quantity is markedly diminished, usually less than 125 ml in 24 hours.

Odour

Typical urine smell may be modified by the presence of acetone (in ketonuria) imparting a fruity odour. Ammoniacal odour is due to bacterial decomposition. "Mousey" odour is present in cases of phenylketonuria. In severe U.T.I. the smell is putrid.

Reaction

Urine is normally acidic with pH varying from 4.6 to 8. Urinary pH is measured using

(i) **litmus paper**
- acidic urine turns blue litmus paper red
- alkaline urine turns red litmus paper blue.

(ii) **pH indicator paper strips** which are impregnated with methyl red and bromothymol blue which can measure a pH range of 5.0 to 9.0.

(iii) **Strip multistix method**.

Alkaline urine results from metabolic and respiratory alkalosis, phosphaturia, ammonia producing urea splitting bacteria like proteus, potassium deficiency and hyperaldosteronism. Intake of fruits of the orange (citrus) family results in alkaline urine.

Specific gravity

Normal specific gravity of a 24-hour urine sample is 1.008 to 1.030, average being 1.016.

Methods of measuring SG

(i) Urinometer (Fig. 31.1)
(ii) Refractometer
(iii) Dipstick method (Fig. 31.2)

Urinometer and refractometer methods are more accurate as compared to dipstick method.

(i) ***Urinometer***. SG can be measured by a urinometer which is calibrated for a temperature correction also. For every 3°C rise in room temperature beyond the calibration temperature (usually 20°C), .001 is added to the recorded reading; and .001 subtracted for every 3°C fall in temperature.

Precaution – Urinometer should not touch the walls of container.

(ii) ***Refractometer***. When urine quantity is less than 100 ml. It is based on the principle that refractive index of a solution varies with the amount of dissolved substances which determine SG.

Procedure
- Place a drop of urine on glass surface of a refractometer.
- Look through the meter towards light source.
- Record SG of urine.

Precaution – Urine should be clear (not turbid).

Fig. 31.1: Urinometer

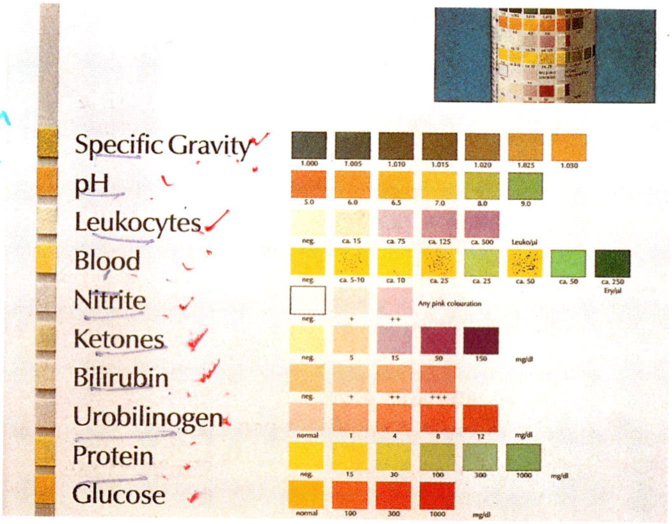

Fig. 31.2: Multistix (uristix) for 10 parameters.

(iii) ***SG by Dipstick Method***. SG is recorded by change of colour on the strip and compared with the colour chart on the multistix bottle.

Principle – The strip area contains polyelectrolyte and an indicator (bromothymol blue). Its colour changes as H^+ in urine is displaced by Na^+/K^+ in the patient's urine. Na^+/K^+ ion concentration is higher in concentrated urine with a high SG.

SG of urine is dependent on the nature and amount of the dissolved constituents. Urine concentration and dilution is modulated by the tubular absorptive and secretory functions thereby affecting the SG and osmolality of urine.

and mortality. Monitori
effect of anti-hyperten
damage. It is now ack
predictor of myocardi

Methods of Assay

(a) **Immunometric assay**
used is solid phase, sa
assay using a gold-
antibody complexes a
(b) **Nephelometric** ass
based on measuring
sensitivity.

REDUCING SUB

Reducing substances are t
the cupric hydroxide of
oxide. Such substances a

Sugars – glucose, fruct
Non-sugars – ascor
glucuronides, salicylates
Glycosuria – presence

- diabets mellitus
- renal glycosuria
- pregnancy
- alimentary glycosuri
- I.V. infusion of gluco
- increased intracrania

Fructosuria – occurs
grapes and oranges.

(i) Benedict's qualita quantitative)

This test detects the pres
urine and is not specific

Procedure

- Take 5 ml of Benedict tube.
- Boil to exclude prese reagent.
- Add 8 drops of urine.
- Boil the mixture for 5 m colour of the precipitate due to reduction of cupri

$Cu(OH)_2$ + Reducing su
(coloured ppt.)
Blue colour of solution
No ppt. – *Negative.*
Greenish solution – *Tr*
Green ppt. – +: *0.5-1%.*

Specific gravity is increased in dehydration, restricted fluid intake, diarrhoea, vomiting, fever, excessive sweating, diabetes mellitus, albuminuria and acute glomerulo nephritis.

Specific gravity is decreased in excessive fluid intake, diabetes insipidus and *end stage kidney* – chronic glomerulonephritis and other renal diseases like bilateral polycystic kidneys, chronic pyelonephritis and hypertension when concentration power of kidney is severally affected resulting in a *low and fixed* specific gravity of 1.008-1.010.

Urine Concentration Test

This test assesses the ability of kidneys to concentrate urine.

Procedure

- the patient has an early dinner at 6 p.m. and **no food/water** after 7 p.m.
- discard the urine samples voided during the night
- the first morning sample at 7 a.m. is discarded and bladder emptied completely
- a second specimen is collected at 8 a.m. i.e. 14 hours of deprivation of water
- check the S.G. of this sample; it should be >1.022.
- if the S.G. is less than 1.022, take another sample at 9 a.m.
- S.G. of this sample should be >1.022.

Interpretation

- If S.G. is <1.022, concentrating ability of kidney is impaired.
- Normal value: 1.022-1.034.
- If S.G. is low and fixed at 1.010, it indicates total loss of concentrating power of kidney, as in chronic glomerulonephritis.

EXAMINATION OF URINE FOR ABNORMAL CONSTITUENTS

Centrifuge urine in 2 test tubes at 2000 r.p.m. for 5 minutes and perform the following tests on supernatant. Sediment can be used for microscopic examination.

PROTEINURIA

It indicates injury to glomerulus resulting in albumin crossing the basement membrane. The tests employed actually test for the presence of albumin.

Before testing for proteinuria, pH of the urine is checked. If alkaline, urine should be acidified with a few drops of glacial acetic acid.

Sulfosalicylic acid test

Take 2.5 ml of urine in a small test tube. Slowly pour 2.5 ml of sulfosalicylic acid over urine. Wait for 5 minutes. Presence of a cloudy precipitate indicates the presence of proteins in urine. However, it also precipitates mucus and Bence Jones proteins.

Composition of sulfosalicylic acid solution

Sulphosalicyclic acid	20 gm
Magnesium sulphate	50 gm
Sodium sulphate	10 gm
Add water to	100 ml

Heat method

If pH of the urine is alkaline, add a few drops of glacial acetic acid to make it acidic. Otherwise, proteins may not precipitate on heating, while phosphates may precipitate.

Fill three-fourth of a test tube with urine and heat the upper part of the urine on a Bunsen burner. Proteins, if present, coagulate (do not boil the urine, as it causes mixing of the upper and lower parts of urine and traces of proteins cannot be appreciated). Lower part of the urine acts as a control for checking turbidity in the heated upper part. Add a few drops of 10% glacial acetic acid. Phosphates, if present, dissolve, while proteins persist since denatured protein is less soluble and is precipitated.

Interpretation. Protein in urine is reported as negative, trace, +, ++ and +++.

White cloudiness	+	(<0.10%)
Granular white ppt.	++	(0.1-0.25%)
Floccular ppt.	+++	(0.25-0.50%)
Thick opaque ppt.	++++	(>0.5%)

Heller's method

Take 5 ml of urine in a test tube and add a few drops of conc. nitric acid. Presence of proteins is indicated by a white ring at the junction of urine and acid.

Dipstick method

Strip is dipped in urine. Change in the colour is compared with the colour chart for proteins provided on the container (Fig. 31.2).

Principle

The dipstick is impregnated with citrate buffer at pH 3.0 and bromophenol blue indicator which is yellow at pH 3.0 and greenish blue at pH 4.2. B. blue at pH 3.0 has a major unionised component and a minor ionised component.

If urine contains proteins, protein + minor ionised component of B. Blue ⟶ combine; combination (of

protein + B. blu
balance between
is reached.

↑ ions of B. blue

Strips are sensit
of albumin in the

Fig. 31.3 Esbach's

Quantitative es
(albumin) in ur

Protein excretion
suspected cases of
and orthostatic/pos
out using Esbach'

Esbach's reag
picric acid – 1 gm i
and make up the v

Method. Check
a few drops of gla
filter the urine.

- Dilute the urir
sp. gr. to 1.008
- Fill the Esbac
with urine.
- Pour the Esba
two thorough

(i) Rothera's test

Take 4 ml of urine in a test tube. Add a few crystals of sodium nitro-prusside and saturate the urine with ammonium sulphate by mixing vigorously. Add a few drops of liquor ammonia along the wall of the tube. Development of a purple ring indicates the presence of acetone/acetoacetic acid or both.

(ii) Gerhardt's test

Take 8 ml of urine in a test tube.

- Add 10% Ferric chloride solution drop by drop; a precipitate forms.
- Add more $FeCl_3$ solution and the ppt. disappears.
- Filter it and add excess of $FeCl_3$ to the filtrate.
- A red colour indicates positive test.

The test is positive whenever acetoacetic acid and β-hydroxybutyric acid are present in urine. The test should be carried out on fresh urine, since acetoacetic acid in urine decomposes to acetone on keeping.

(iii) Heat test

This test detects the presence of β-hydroxy-butyric acid. Presence of β-hydroxybutyric acid is usually accompanied by acetoacetic acid which can be demonstrated by Rothera's test. Urine is acidified, equal volume of water is added and boiled to half the volume. This removes acetone and acetocetic acid. Add 1 ml of hydrogen peroxide which converts b-hydroxybutyric acid into acetone which reacts with sodium nitroprusside and liquid ammonia to give purple red colour.

(iv) Dipstick method

The reagent strip for ketones is based on Rothera's test, in which alkaline nitroprusside becomes purple with acetone/acetoacetic acid. The colour is compared with that of the chart (Fig. 31.2). The test is sensitive and it should be performed on fresh urine before acetoacetic acid decomposes to acetone.

UROBILINOGEN

Urobilinogen is normally present in urine in an amount of 2-4 mg in a 24-hour urinary sample.

Causes of increased urobilinogen in urine

- various hemolyte anemias like:
  - thalassemia
  - sickle cell anemia
  - hereditary spherocytosis
- pre-icteric phase of infective hepatitis.

Decresed/absent urobilinogen in urine

- obstructive jaundice – bilirubin does not reach the intestine and so is not converted into urobilinogen.

Principle

Ehrlich's reagent in conc. HCl reacts with urobilinogen/porphobilinogen and forms an aldehyde, giving vermilion red colour.

Procedure

Take 2.5 ml urine in a test tube and add 2.5 ml of Ehrlich's aldehyde reagent (para-dimethyaminolbenzaldehyde). Mix the two. Presence of urobilinogen is indicated by development of vermilion red colour. Add 10 ml of saturated sodium acetate solution to the mixture. Vermilion red colour changes to pink colour. Development of a deep pink colour indicates increased urobilinogen excretion. The test can be carried out by 1 in 10, 1 in 20, 1 in 40 or 1 in 100 dilution of the urine sample. In a normal person no pink colour is produced at 1:20 dilution, so positivity at this dilution or more indicates increased urobilinogen.

Precaution. This test should be carried out on a freshly voided urine, since urobilinogen gets oxidised to urobilin; the conversion can be prevented by adding a few crystals of anhydrous sodium carbonate to urine.

Dipstick method

This method is based on the Ehrlich's aldehyde reagent. The strip is coated with p-dimethyl-aminobenzaldehyde which reacts with urobilinogen with the formation of red coloured compound and is matched with the colour given in the colour chart on the container of the dipsticks (Fig. 31.2).

BILIRUBIN

Bilirubin is normally not present in urine.

It is excreted in urine whenever there is increased serum level of direct acting bilirubin as in

- obstructive jaundice
- hepatocellular jaundice.

Fouchet's test

Principle

Fouchet's reagent contains Trichloroacetic acid and Ferric Chloride which oxidise bilirubin to biliverdin which gives a dark green colour.

Method

- Take 10 ml of urine in a test tube and add 3 ml of 10% barium chloride solution.
- Mix the two.
- Filter the mixture through a filter paper (Whatman No. 1).
- Bilirubin along with barium salt remains on filter paper.
- Spread the filter paper onto another filter paper.
- Add a few drops of Fouchet's reagent onto the filter paper.

- Greenish blue waves of colour indicate bilirubin. Darkness of the colour indicates amount of bilirubinuria.

Interpretation

A positive test indicates the presence of bilirubin in cases of hepatocellular jaundice and obstructive jaundice, while it is absent in hemolytic jaundice.

(ii) Dipstick method

The test is based on a coupling reaction between bilirubin and diazonium salt. The test area is impregnated with stabilised diazotized 2,4 dichloraniline which forms a brown compound with bilirubin and the colour is compared with the colour-chart (Fig. 31.2).

BILE SALTS

Sodium and potassium salts of glycocholates and taurocholates – bile salts – reduce the surface tension of urine. Normally, bile salts are not present in urine.

Hay's Sulphur Test

Take 10 ml urine in a test tube and sprinkle sulphur powder over its surface, watch for 5 minutes. Sulphur powder sinks to the bottom of test tube in the presence of bile salts in urine. The test is *positive* in hepatocellular and obstructive jaundice.

TEST FOR Hb/BLOOD IN URINE

Hematuria denotes presence of red cells in urine and urine is smoky. Some of the RBCs may lyse in urine resulting in hemoglobinuria (Table 31.1). Hb in urine is present in PNH and PCH.

Hematuria

Urine is red/cola coloured in hemo-globinuria and severe hematuria and smoky in mild hematuria. RBCs are demonstrable in urinary sediment in the latter (Table 31.1).

Table 31.1: Hematuria and hemoglobinuria

Hematuria	Hemoglobinuria
• Urine is smoky.	Urine is red/cola coloured due to conversion of Hb to acid hematin.
• On centrifugation, deposit demonstrates RBCs.	No RBCs in the deposit.
• Caused by kidney and bladder pathology.	Caused by intravascular hemolysis.
• Benzidine test and Dipstick test positive.	Both tests positive.

Causes of hematuria

See table 31.2.

Causes of hemoglobinuria

- paroxysmal nocturnal hemoglobinuria – PNH
- paroxysmal cold hemoglobinuria – PCH
- incompatible blood transfusion
- severe burns
- autoimmune hemolytic anemia – AIHA
- march hemoglobinuria
- snake bite
- blackwater fever (Falciparum malaria)

Benzidine test

Principle

Gl. acetic acid ⟶ lysis of red cells.

Lysed red cells release ⟶ Hb.

H_2O_2 + Peroxidase ⟶ H_2O + O
(from Hb)

O + Benzidine ⟶ Blue colour.
(chromogen)

Hb contains peroxidase activity while in cases of hematuria, Hb is released by lysis of red cells.

Method

- Take 2 ml of urine in a test tube.
- Add 2 ml of Benzidine reagent and mix. Benzidine reagent is a mixture of an equal volume of saturated solution of benzidine in glacial acetic acid and 6% H_2O_2.
- Blue colour indicates the presence of Hb/blood in urine.

Dipstick test

Very small amount of Hb/RBCs are detected.

Principle

The reagent area is impregnated with organic peroxide and the chromogen is orthotoluidine.

- Organic peroxide (reagent) ⟶ H_2O + O
  peroxidase (from Hb)
- O + Chromogen (orthotoluidine) ⟶ Oxidised chromogen (colour)

Method

- Urine sample is mixed thoroughly so that sedimented RBCs are mixed.
- Dipstick is dipped in urine for the time given.
- Colour is matched.

Amorphous urates

These appear as light red amorphous sediment and dissolve on heating. These are usually excreted in patients of gout.

Crystalline urates

Sodium urate crystals are needle-shaped and pigmented and occur in acid urine. These dissolve on heating and reappear on cooling.

Cystine

These crystals are colourless, refractile hexagonal plates, with unequal sides. These are soluble in alkali and are diagnostic of cystinuria – an inborn error of metabolism.

Phosphates

Triple phosphates of calcium, magnesium and ammonium appear as prism-shaped crystals (Fig. 31.9) and are associated with an alkaline pH of urine due to urea splitting bacteria.

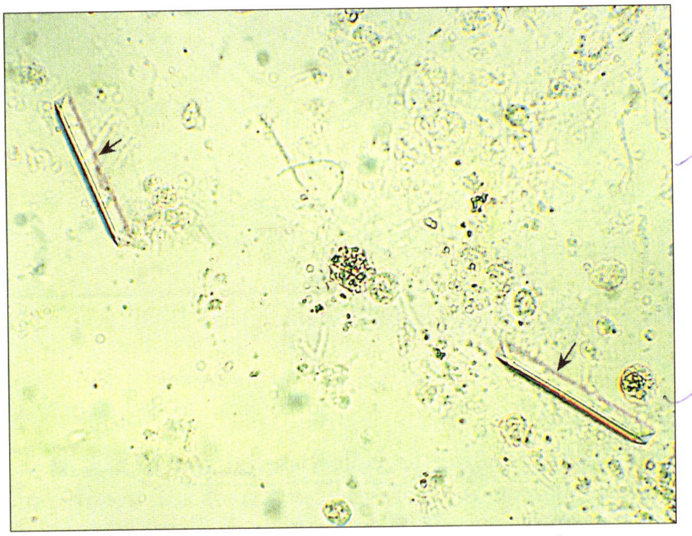

Fig. 31.9 Prism shaped triple phosphate crystals (↑).

Amorphous phosphates

These are seen as colourless amorphous sediment in an alkaline urine and are dissolved in dil. acetic acid.

Calcium carbonate

These crystals are in the form of granules/spheres and dissolve on acidifying the urine.

CASTS

Casts are formed by solidification of mucoproteins – **Tam Horsfall proteins** in the distal convoluted tubules and collecting tubules. These casts may be proteins (hyaline casts) or have trapped granular debris (granular casts), epithelial cells (epithelial casts), leukocytes (leukocyte casts), fatty casts or waxy casts. Presence of cast indicates a renal disease.

To visualise the casts, it is essential to examine the urinary sediment in minimum light. Casts are cylindric structures with parallel sides and rounded ends.

Hyaline casts

These are transparent, cylindrical bodies (Fig. 31.10), found in cases of fever, congestive heart failure, acute proliferative glomerulonephritis chronic glomerulonephritis and after exercise.

Granular casts

These casts are cylindrical bodies with granules (Fig. 31.10), found in cases of chronic glomerulonephritis, and indicate renal damage. Granules are formed from degenerating epithelial cells. In renal failure, broad granular casts are observed.

Cylindroids

Cylindroids have one tapering end while the other end is round and the sides are not parallel. These probably represent the abortive casts.

Fatty casts

They contain fat (cholestrol/triglyceride) and are demonstrable in cases of nephrotic syndrome. Sometimes it is made up of epithelial cells with intracellular fat deposited on the hyaline cast.

Leucocyte cell cast

These contain white cells in the cast. These are present in the urine in acute pyelonephritis, interstitial nephritis and acute glomerulonephritis.

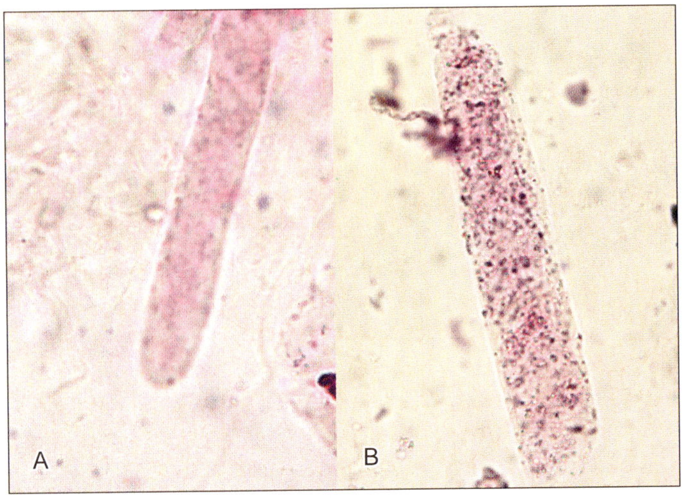

Fig. 31.10: (A) Hyaline casts (B) Granular casts in the urinary deposit

Red cell casts

These are formed by conglutination of red cells in the tubular lumen. These are present in cases of acute glomerulonephritis, malignant hypertension, Henoch-Schonlein purpura and other glomerular lesions like SLE and Good Pasture syndrome.

Waxy casts

These are more opaque as compared to hyaline casts, and are found in amyloidosis, end stage kidney and CRF.

Epithelial casts

These are formed when epithelial cells form the predominant part of the cast as in cases of toxemia of pregnancy and toxic nephrosis.

PARASITES

Commonly encountered parasites in urine are:

- Trichomonas
- Ova of Schistosoma hematobium
- Microfilaria

(i) Trichomonas

It is occasionally seen in fresh urine specimens in cases of Trichomonas urethritis/vaginitis. This is recognised by being globular in shape, 14-17µ in size, flagellate and motile in fresh urine.

(ii) Ova of S.hematobium

These are demonstrable in endemic areas in the middle east. It is not common in India.

(iii) Microfilaria

Microfilaria of W.bancrofti is a rare finding.

MALIGNANT CELLS

Malignant cells may be demonstrable in renal/bladder malignancies.

Procedure

(a) Take urine in four test tubes and centrifuge at 2500 r.p.m. for 15 minutes. Discard the supernatant. Take the deposit and spread on the glass slides. Fix the slides in methanol for Giemsa stain; in alcohol-ether mixture for Pap stain. Stain with Giemsa and Pap stains and look for malignant cells.

(b) Cytospin preparation yields a greater number of cells and, therefore, is a better method to look for malignant cells. Stain with Pap stain. If cellular material is more, it may be fixed in formalin and **cell block** may be made and sections provide enough cells to look for malignancy.

OTHER CELLS

Spermatozoa

Sometimes sperms may be present in urine, and are easily recognised by their structure and mobility (Fig. 31.11).

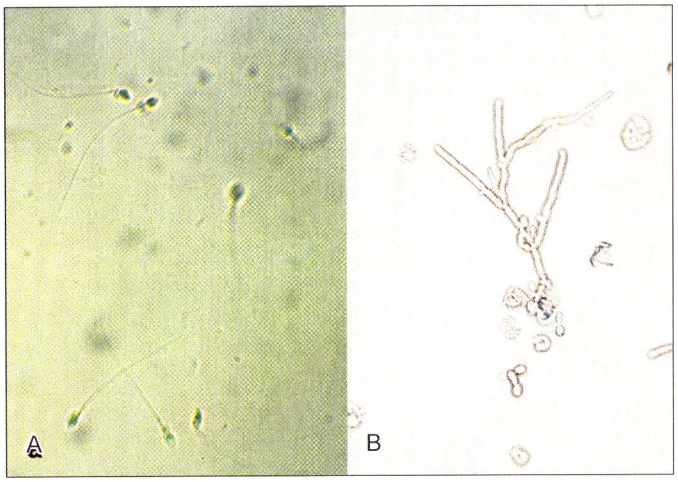

Fig. 31.11: (A) Spermatozoa (B) Yeast cells in urinary deposit

Yeast cells

Budding yeast cells (Fig. 31.11) are seen in patients with U.T.I. in immunosuppressed patients, like diabetics and patients on cytotoxic drugs. Collection in a clean container is very important so as to differentiate it from contaminants.

REAGENT STRIPS FOR URINE TESTING – MULTISTIX

Thin strips of plastic 5-8 mm wide and about 10 cm long with single/multiple discrete cellulose squares are available. These squares are impregnated with reagents for testing glucose, protein, pH, S.G., hemoglobin, ketone bodies, bilirubin and urobilinogen. There are single test strips e.g. diastix for glucose and multistix for multiple tests (Fig. 31.2).

The basis of various tests is described under demonstration of respective substance in urine.

AUTOMATED URINE ANALYZER

Now automated analyzers are available in which urine sample loaded tubes are placed. The equipment analyses the various cells by fluorescent flow cytometry and results are available in a few minutes. In many of them centrifuged urine is analyzed thus reducing the inherent errors of urine sediment analysis. The equipment gives pH, specific gravity, color, clarity, glucose, ketones, urobilinogen bilaubin, protein, occult blood and the formed elements like RBCs, WBCs, epithelial cells, casts, bacteria, crystals, sperms and yeast.

35

Instruments for Viva Voce

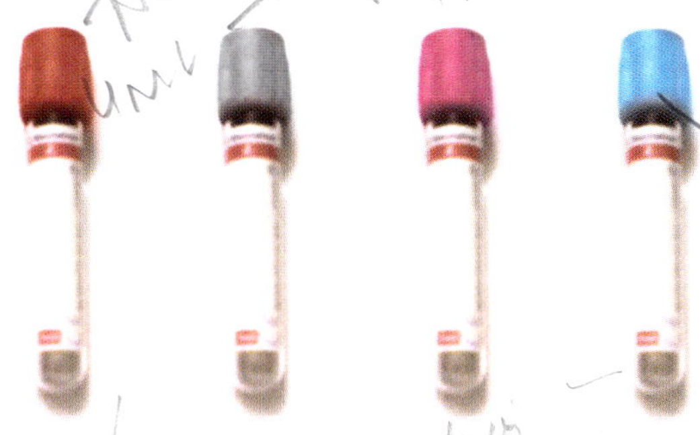

Fig. 35.1: Vacutainers

Fig. 35.2: Hb pipette

Fig. 35.3: Sahli's comparator - square

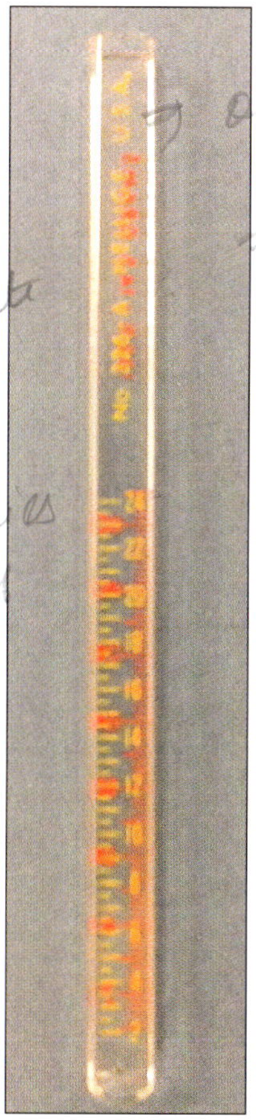

Fig. 35.4: Sahli's hemoglobin tube - square

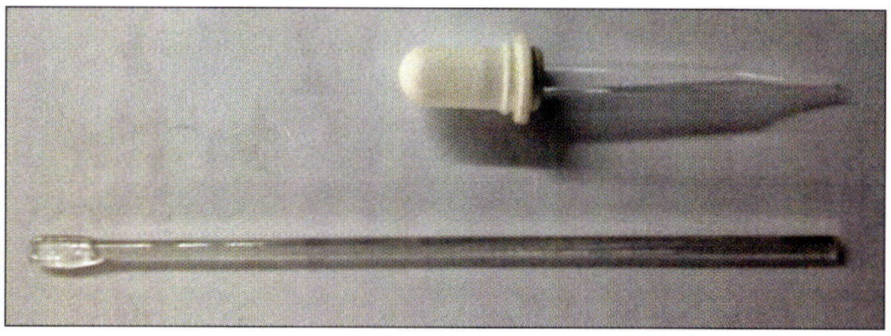

Fig. 35.5: Glass rod as stirrer and dropper

Fig. 35.6: WBC pipette

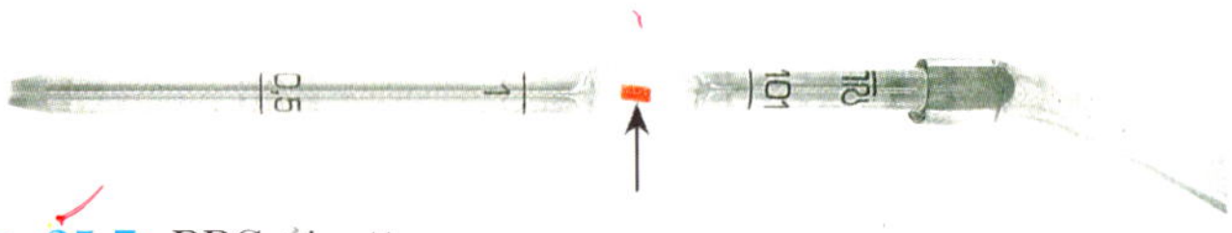

Fig. 35.7: RBC pipette

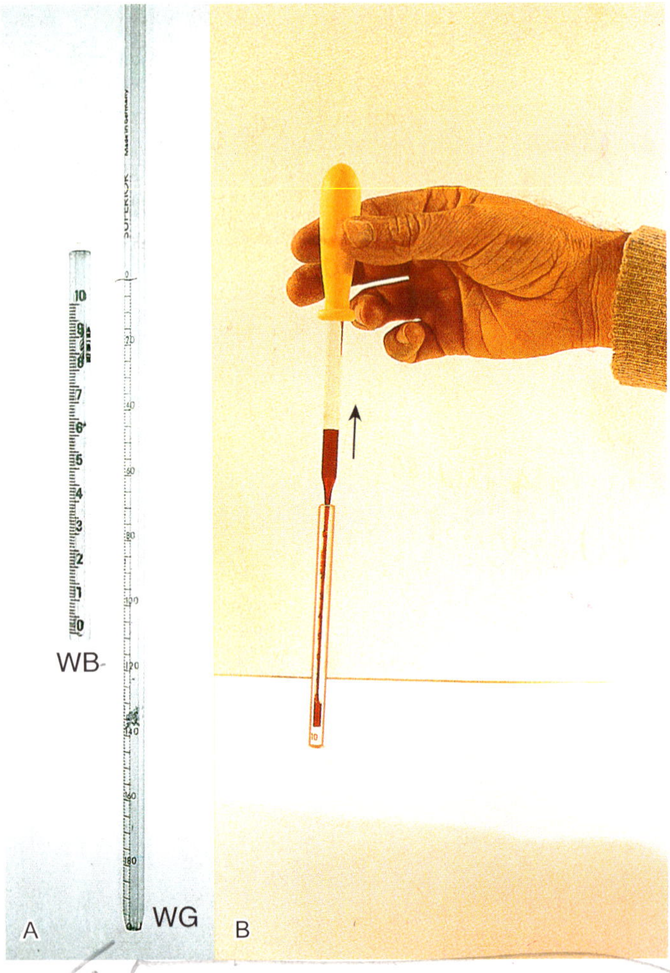

Fig. 35.8: Wintrobe tube (WB) and Westergren pipette (WG)

Fig. 35.9: Salah needle

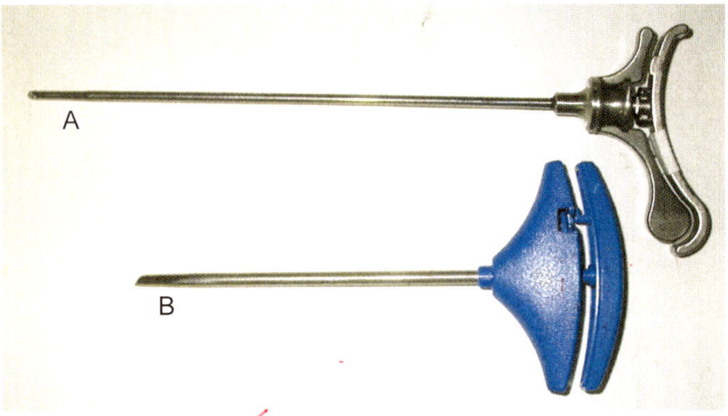

Fig. 35.10: A. Jamshidi Needle - all steel B. Jamshidi Needle disposable

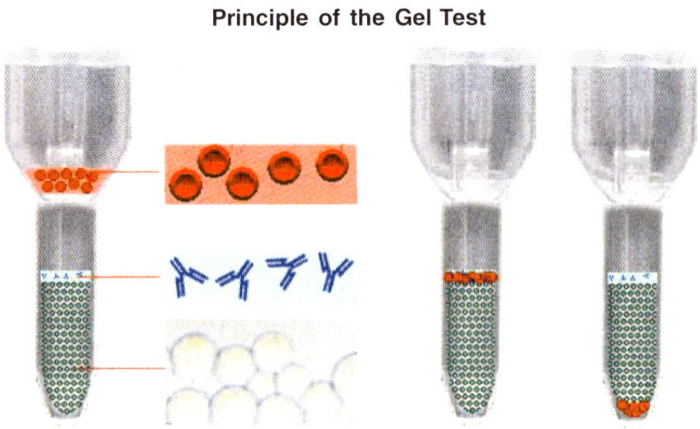

Fig. 35.11: Microtyping gelcard for blood grouping

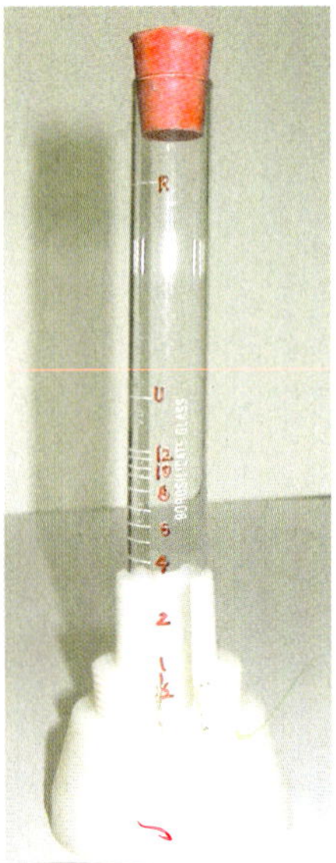

Fig. 35.12: Esbach's albuminometer

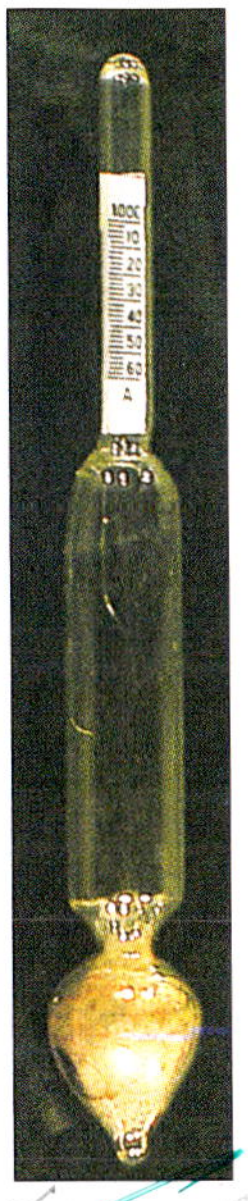

Fig. 35.13: Urinometer

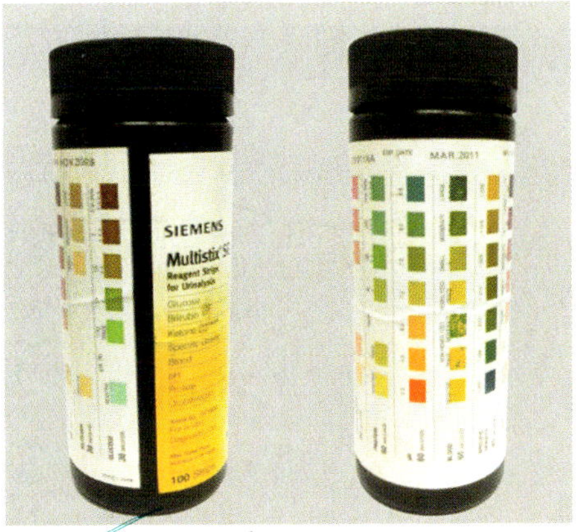

Fig. 35.14: Multistix. The bottle shows the various tests that can be carried out on the urine sample

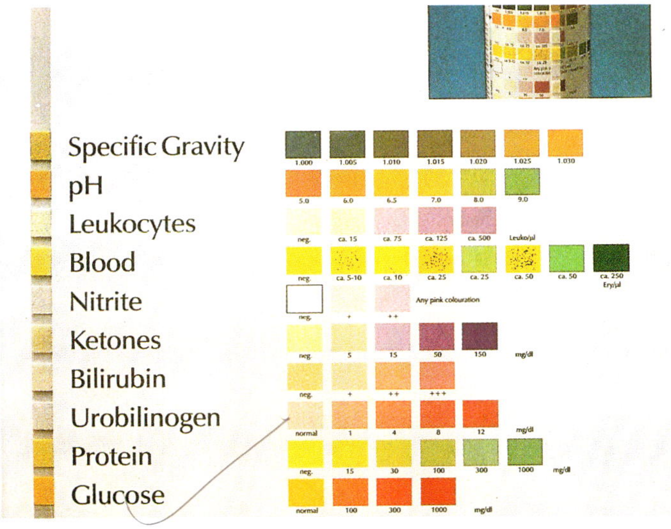

Fig. 35.15: Multistix. Colours given indicate +, ++, +++ positivity of various abnormal findings in urine

Fig. 35.16: Lumbar pucture needle

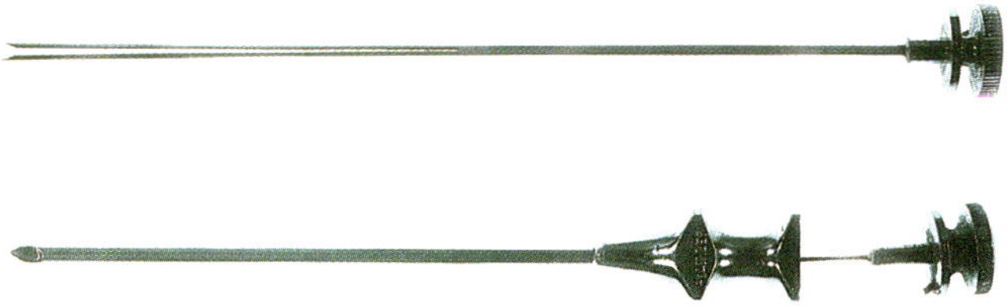

Fig. 35.17: Vim Silverman's needle for liver biopsy

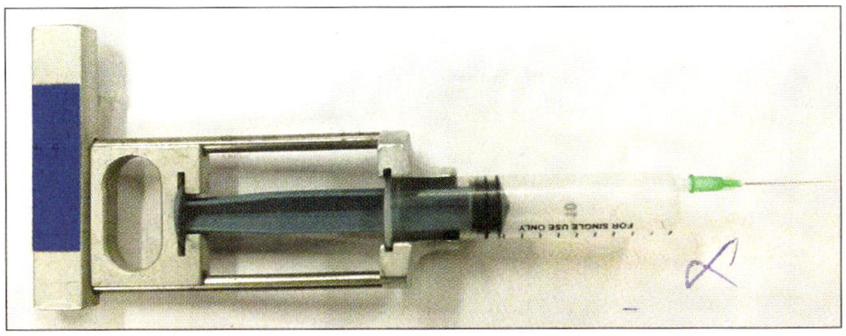

Fig. 35.18: Franzen's handle for FNAC

Fig. 35.19: Ayre's stapula to take the cervical smear.

Normal reference values in chemical pathology

Investigation		Reference Value	Units
S. Alanine aminotransferase	ALAT, SGPT	5–35	U/L
S. Amylase		60–180	U/L
S. Aspartate aminotransferase	ASAT, SGOT	0–35	U/L
S. Bilirubin	total	0.3–1.3	mg/dl
S. Bilirubin	Conjugated	0.1–0.4	mg/dl
S. C-Reactive protein - CRP		< 10	mg/L
S. Calcium	total	8.7–10.2	mg/dl
S. Chloride		102–109	meq/L
S. Cholestrol Desirable - < 200 mg/dl Boderline - 200–239 mg/dl High - ≥ 240 mg/dl		150–230	mg/dl
S. Creatinine		0.6–1.2	mg/dl
Creatinine clearance		70–120	ml/min
B. Glucose fasting		75–100	mg/dl
B. Glucose PP (Post prandial 2 hours)		<200	mg/dl
S. Gamma glutamyt transpeptidase (γ-GT)		9–58	50–150
S. Lactate dehydrogenase	LDH	115–221	units/L
S. Lipids	total	400–800	mg/dl
S. Lipoprotein – low density	LDL as cholesterol	< 100	mg/dl
S. Lipoprotein – high density	HDL as cholesterol	40–60	mg/dl
S. Phosphatase Acid		1–5 2–10	KA units/dl Units/L
	Prostatic fraction	Upto 4	Units/L
S. Phosphatase Alkaline		33–96 4–12 0.56–1.63	units/L KA units/dl
S. Phosphate as phosphorus		2.5–4.3	mg/dl
S. Proteins	total	5.5–8	gm/dl
	Albumin	3.5–6.0	gm/dl
	Globulin	2.0–3.5	gm/dl
	A/G ratio	1.5 : 1– 3 : 1	–
S. Potassium		3.5–5	meq/L
S. Sodium		135–145	meq/L
B. Urea		20–40	mg/dl
S. Uric acid		2–6	mg/dl
Urea nitrogen (BUN)		7–20	mg/dl
B - Blood			
S - Serum			

VIVA-VOCE

Q. How can gestational diabetes be diagnosed?

Ans. Gestational diabetes is screened by glucose challenge test in which 50 gm of glucose is given. After 1 hour, blood sample is collected. If blood sugar is > 140 mg/dl, it is suggestive of gestational diabetes and 3 hour glucose tolerance test is required.

Q. What enzyme is used as a marker of alcohol abuse?

Ans. γ-glutamyl transferase.

Q. What is the utility of estimating glycosylated hemoglobin (HbA1C)?

Ans. HbA1C is of utility in evaluating glycemic control. It indicates the blood sugar level over the previous 3 months.

Q. What is the reliable parameter to evaluate iron stores?

Ans. Serum ferritin level

Q. Non-protein nitrogen (NPN) includes?

Ans. NPN includes urea, creatinine and creatine.

Q. What is the pH of blood?

Ans. pH of blood is 7.35–7.45

Q. What is the site of synthesis of glucagon?

Ans. Glucagon is synthesized in α cells of pancreas.

Index